Library Collection Development Policies

A Reference and Writers' Handbook

by
Richard J. Wood
Frank Hoffmann

The Scarecrow Press, Inc.
Lanham, Md., & London

SCARECROW PRESS, INC.

Published in the United States of America
by Scarecrow Press, Inc.
4720 Boston Way
Lanham, Maryland 20706

4 Pleydell Gardens, Folkestone
Kent CT20 2DN, England

British Cataloguing-in-Publication Information Available

Library of Congress Cataloging-in-Publication Data

Wood, Richard J. (Richard John)
Library collection development policies : a reference and writers' handbook /
by Richard J. Wood and Frank Hoffmann.
p. cm.
Includes bibliographical references and index.
1. Collection development (Libraries)—United States. 2. Collection development
(Libraries)—United States—Policy statements. I. Hoffmann, Frank W., 1949–
II. Title.
Z687.2U6W66   1995   025.2'1'0973—dc20   95-15474   CIP

ISBN 0-8108-3039-6 (cloth : alk. paper)

Printed in the United States of America

⊖™ The paper used in this publication meets the minimum requirements of
American National Standard for Information Sciences—Permanence of
Paper for Printed Library Materials, ANSI Z39.48–1984.

To

Lynne Wood

and

Lee Ann Hoffmann

whose understanding of the time

devoted to this book

is greatly appreciated

TABLE OF CONTENTS

ACKNOWLEDGEMENTS

The authors wish to express their appreciation to the library directors, collection development librarians, and others across the United States who sent us their policies with permission to reproduce them in whole, or in part, for this book. They have made a valuable contribution not only to this book but to the librarians or others who may adopt or modify these policies for their use.

For those libraries whose policies are included in Part Two of this book, the names and locations of the libraries, along with the names of the contributors, are listed (unless they asked not to be named) under Libraries Whose Policies Are Represented. Contributors are included whether their policies were included in whole or in part.

We would also like to thank those individuals and libraries who sent us policies, but were not included. Space limitations were the primary reason for exclusion.

We would also like to thank several individuals who are employed by Newton Gresham Library, Sam Houston State University, Huntsville, Texas, for their help in electronically scanning and formatting the policies included in this book: Dan Konopnicki, Systems Coordinator; Frieda LeFlore, Secretary to the Director of Library Services; and Stephanie Rivers, her student assistant.

PREFACE

This book arose from several shared expectations of the coauthors. First, librarians in all types of libraries who are attempting to write or revise their respective institution's collection development policies should benefit from a reference resource containing representative policies from all types of libraries across the United States. The book also attempts to provide librarians with models of collection development statements in the formulation or assessment of their own respective policies. Students of library science, as well as practitioners, should benefit from seeing policies already being utilized effectively in school, public, academic and special libraries of all sizes.

Second, as a manual or reference tool, this book should serve as a good starting point for librarians, library managers, library volunteers, library users, governing board members, or students of library science who need to study, develop, rewrite, or evaluate collection development policies. They should find valuable rationales, reminders, additional selection criteria, new policies, and useful sections or passages of other libraries' statements that they might adapt for inclusion in their library's policy.

Third, by including representative polices used successfully as a guide to collecting practices in libraries of all types, the time and energy of librarians and others who are developing, assessing, or rewriting their own respective collection development policies should be saved. This book should override at least some of the need--and common practice--of calling or writing other library directors or collection development librarians for their libraries' policies. Because the authors recognize that not all of the policies included herein may be recognized as exemplary, librarians are advised to request policies from similar libraries they know to have well written, and effective collection development policies.

Knowing that no work of this nature can provide all of the information or policies required to accomplish these stated objectives, however, the authors have cited many works, themselves frequently cited in the literature, that readers should consult for more in-depth information. Writers such as Futas, Gorman, Van Orden, Evans, and Broadus are some of the prominent or recognized authors who are referred to in the text. By including as many selections from their works as relevant and feasible to the topic at hand, the authors hope to inspire readers, particularly students of library science, to consult these important works as needed.

It is impossible to say how many libraries in the United States have collection development policies because libraries are not surveyed by any professional association for this information. It is evident that most of the writers cited in this book believe that the majority of libraries do not have one. In the authors' experience, they are more common among academic, research and public libraries. For this reason, we include as many non-academic and non-public library policies as we thought reasonable. Readers should find Futas' (1984) work very valuable because it still contains many worthwhile examples of academic and public library collection development policies. Boyarski and Hickey's recent (1994) collection development manual for community colleges contains eleven complete policies and seven partial documents. Interestingly, they included a small portion of Hillsborough Community College's and St. Petersburg Junior College's policies--while we included most of their policies--without any prior knowledge.

The value of these policies rests on a basic and primary role of librarians and libraries both currently and traditionally in the United States--collection management. It has remained their raison d'etre. Librarians make collections of books, journals, and other materials available and accessible to users by selecting, acquiring, organizing, maintaining, and preserving the material that they believe their users will use or need. The availability of materials and information in electronic format has not changed this role fundamentally. Indeed, libraries are often evaluated by students, faculty, researchers, and the general public by what is on the shelves, or otherwise available through electronic means.

This book is organized into two parts. The first part contains the background information that should be studied before considering whether or not to write or revise the library's collection development policy. To make such a decision, readers will need answers to a number of questions. What is a collection development statement? Why is such a policy important for a library? The answers to these questions are found in Chapter One. It explores what has become known as a collection development policy and defines these terms.

This chapter also delineates the key part that a collection development policy can play in providing useful, needed, and core library material.

Users who become frustrated by not finding what they want in a library collection are likely to seek other sources, especially electronic. Worse, frustrated library users may vote against library bond issues in their communities because the library generally did not acquire the material wanted by the residents. When library directors and governing boards fail to get the political and budgetary support they need to develop collections responsive to the needs of their clientele, it is often because the library failed to implement the policy properly. Chapter Two covers policy implementation. It focuses on how to study and analyze the informational and recreational reading needs of the citizens the library is supposed to serve. Environmental scanning, data gathering, and community analysis are very important bases of implementing a successful collection development policy. Chapter Two discusses what steps should be taken preliminarily, as well as after the policy has been approved and implemented. They will also learn the importance of gathering, organizing, and assessing data and information about the community, users, library circulation, library policies and procedures, etc. Readers shall learn how to achieve involvement and consensus in the development of the collection development statement. Other political and public relations factors that can be the difference between success and failure are explored here as well.

Chapter Three is concerned with delineating the essential elements of a collection development policy, including the library's mission statement, selection criteria, collecting responsibilities, intellectual freedom policies, preservation, and budget allocation considerations. A list of special criteria for selecting sound recordings has been included to illustrate the complexity of selection criteria.

Part Two contains the collection development policies, in part or in whole, of a number of academic, public, governmental, special or other libraries. A closer look reveals a great diversity among the policies. The diversity of policies underlines the importance of knowing the library's mission and clientele.

Librarians consulting this book for examples, however, should not limit themselves to examining policies of only public, or only academic libraries. Rather, it is advisable to review the statements of different types of libraries because, for instance, school and academic libraries often function as the public library for their students, staff and faculty. Public library policies relating to recreational reading, genealogical materials, video tapes, etc., may be useful to non-public librarians as well. The Library of Congress' policies covering manuscript, motion picture, sound recordings, photographs, and fine arts are included because libraries of all types might collect in one or more of these formats. Libraries with subject oriented or departmental libraries may find the Marine Science example very useful. The New Mexico State University's policy for electronic materials is included because many libraries are now collecting CD-ROMs, computer software and other electronic media. Likewise, many libraries, particularly large academic and public institutions, have small to large law collections and will find Tarlton's Law Library policy very useful as a guide. A variety of policies were included because the authors regarded them as exemplary, specialized, and/or representative of what may be found in libraries. Finally, we suggest that it is not advisable to "cut and paste" pieces of other libraries' policies to create a policy that should be custom fit. The cut and paste technique, however, can prove useful and time-saving if it is employed to "get the ball rolling," encourage discussion, etc.

In conclusion, readers should find practical advice here, as well as policies that may assist them in developing a comprehensive and useful collection development policy. This, in effect, is the primary purpose behind the work.

REFERENCES

Boyarski, Jennie S. and Kate Hickey, eds. *Collection Management in the Electronic Age: A Manual for Creating Community College Collection Development Policy Statements.* CJCLS Guide #1. Chicago, IL: American Library Association, 1994.

Futas, Elizabeth, ed. *Library Acquisition Policies and Procedures.* Second Edition. Phoenix, AZ: Oryx, 1984.

LIBRARIES WHOSE POLICIES
ARE REPRESENTED

For policies included in this book, whether whole or in part, the names of libraries and their addresses appear below. The names of the library administrators or others who sent the policies are also included, unless not known or requested not to be included, in case readers want to contact the particular library for further information.

Brazosport Independent School District; P. O. Box 2; Freeport, Texas 77541.

California State University Library; 2000 Jed Smith Drive; Sacramento, California 95819-6039; Charles Martell, Dean and University Librarian.

Cypress-Fairbanks Independent School District; District Professional Library; Steeplepoint South; 10300 Jones Road; Houston, Texas 77065; Susan A. Kelley, Coordinator of Library/Media Services.

Fairbanks North Star Borough Public Library; 1215 Cowles Street; Fairbanks, Alaska 99701; June Pinnell-Stephens, Collection Development Librarian.

First Baptist Church; 1229 Avenue J; Huntsville, Texas 77340; Dr. Bonnie Thorne is the contact person.

Haltom City Public Library; P. O. Box 14246; Haltom City, Texas 76117-0246; Dr. Deborah J. Karpuk, Director of Personnel and Information Services.

Hillsborough Community College; District Administration Offices; P. O. Box 31127; Tampa, Florida 33631-3127; Derrie Roark, Associate Vice-President of Learning Resources Services.

Hirsch Library; Museum of Fine Arts; P. O. Box 6826; Houston, Texas 77265-6826; Jeannette Dixon, Librarian.

Houston Public Library; 500 McKinney Avenue; Houston, Texas 77002; Brenda Tirrell, Coordinator of Materials Selection.

Huntsman Chemical Corporation Library; 5100 Bainbridge Blvd.; Chesapeake, Virginia 23320; Janet Mitchell, Librarian.

Illinois State Library; 300 South Second Street; Springfield, Illinois 62701. Thomas J. Dorst, Associate Director for Library Services.

Jennings County Schools; Jennings, Indiana; 800 West Walnut Street; North Vernon, Indiana 47265; Jim Neff, High School Librarian.

The Library of Congress; Washington, D. C. 20540-1030; Prints and Photographs Division; Bernard F. Reilly, Head, Curatorial Section; Peter H. Bridge, Collections Policy Coordinator.

Mickey Reily Public Library; 604 South Matters; Corrigan, Texas 77939; Debra Jewell, Director.

National Library of Medicine; 8600 Rockville Pike, Bethesda, Maryland 20894; Duane Arenales, Chief, Technical Services Division.

New Mexico State Library; 325 Don Gaspar; Santa Fe, New Mexico 87503; Karen J. Watkins, State Librarian.

New Mexico State University Library; P. O. Box 3475; Las Cruces, New Mexico 88003-3475; Charles Townley, Dean.

Ohio State University; Human Ecology Library; 1787 Neil Avenue; Columbus, Ohio 43210-1295; Leta Hendricks, Head Librarian.

Petersburg Public Library; P. O. Box 549; Petersburg, Alaska 99833; Joyce Jenkins, City Librarian.

St. Petersburg Junior College; Bennett Library; P. O. Box 13489; St. Petersburg, Florida 33733; Dr. Susan Anderson, Director of Libraries, and the Collection Development Committee.

Shell Oil Company; 1281 Two Shell Plaza; P. O. Box 587; Houston, Texas 77001; Habiba Alimohammad, Information Analyst, Information and Library Services.

University of Texas, General Libraries; Austin, Texas 78713; Policies of the Marine Science Institute Library; P. O. Box 1267; Port Aransas, Texas 78373; Ruth Grundy, Librarian; and the Tarlton Law Library; 727 E. 26th Street, Austin, Texas 78705; Roy Mersky, Director of Research.

PART ONE

RATIONALE,
IMPLEMENTING A POLICY
AND
POLICY COMPONENTS
OF
COLLECTION DEVELOPMENT
POLICIES

1

POLICY RATIONALE

Collection development policies are found in many school, public, academic, and special libraries of all sizes throughout the United States. Professional associations, representing these libraries, endorse the development and use of these policy statements by libraries. Few librarians seem to question their importance, although there are a number of barriers to their implementation, as we shall see shortly. In this chapter, the authors lay the foundation for the development of collection development policies by defining collection development, and by outlining reasons why such policies are advantageous to libraries, as well as why it is worth overcoming the barriers to doing so.

Definitions

Collection development, a common practice for libraries and information agencies of all types, is concerned with "making certain the information needs of the people using the collection are met in a timely and economical manner, using information resources produced both inside and outside of the organization" (Evans, 1987, p. 13). For academic libraries, collection development is defined by Breivik and Gee (1989, p. 109) as "the planned purchase of materials in all formats to match instructional and research needs of the campus within the current fiscal restraints and resource sharing opportunities."

Cassell and Futas (1991, p. 2) have indicated that the process of collection development comprises a number of distinct processes which, to paraphrase them, are as follows:

- Learning about the goals, objectives, and priorities of the institution;
- Learning about the collection that currently exists and the relationship it bears to the community it serves;

- Developing policies to select, acquire, discard, maintain, and evaluate collections from this time forward;
- Learning how and what to select and acquire for the clientele you now have;
- Learning to recognize what needs to be looked at and how frequently, to make sure that your client base has not changed in the years since you last looked at it;
- Developing procedures to handle the policies; and
- Developing procedures to evaluate, revise, and pass on these policies to future patrons, board members, staff, and librarians who join after the process has been completed.

A collection development policy represents a written compilation of the library's plans geared to correcting collection weaknesses as well as maintaining inherent strengths (Evans 1987, pp. 65-66). In addition to providing a plan of action, Evans says, the policy should guide the library staff's thinking and decision making.

Finally, while many librarians may regard them as aspects of collection management, libraries' collection development policies more often than not include statements regarding the selection, deselection, acquisition, organization, assessment and preservation of materials for libraries' collections. Thus, there may be selection, preservation, and acquisition policies that are part of collection development policies, or independent of them.

The authors prefer to leave debates regarding these definitions to other writers and continue the common practice of calling the documents in Part Two of this book, "collection development policies." Likewise, readers can locate variant definitions of "selection" which, in this work, is seen as just one of the aspects of developing a collection. Readers desiring more information about preservation or maintenance of collections should consult Evans' work and some of the other texts cited in this chapter.

Importance of the policies

Testimonials in the library literature as to the importance of utilizing collection development policies proliferate or, as Merritt (1979, p. 67) says, "abound in the literature of the profession and in the official pronouncements of national, state, and local public and school library associations. The articulate members of the profession are unanimous in their support of the need for preparing a formal selection policy for every library, no matter how large or how small it may be."

As early as the mid-1950s, the American Library Association, in *Public Library Service* (1987, Standard No. 87, p. 32), advocated that every public library should have a written policy covering materials selection and collection maintenance. For school libraries, the American Association of School Librarians' Board of Directors also issued a similar statement (1961, p. 3) asking school boards to formally adopt such policies "as a basis for consistent excellence in choice of materials and as a document that can be presented to parents and other citizens for their further understanding of the purposes and standards of selection of school library materials."

A number of authors provide very specific advantages applicable to most libraries. Gardner (1981, pp. 222-224), for instance, provides us with a broad range of reasons which we paraphrase as follows:

- It forces staff to think through library goals, commit themselves to these goals, identify long- and short-range needs of users, and establish priorities for allocating funds to meet these needs;
- It helps assure that the library will commit itself to serving all parts of the community, both present and future;
- It helps set quality standards for the selection and weeding ;
- It informs users, administrators, governing bodies and other libraries of the collection's scope and nature to facilitate coordination of collection development among the institutions;
- It helps minimize personal bias by selectors;
- It serves as a good in-service training tool for new staff;
- It helps assure continuity in collections of any size, and spare staff from unwarranted criticism;
- It provides a means of staff self-evaluation, or for evaluation by library staff, governing board members, or outsiders;
- It helps demonstrate that the library is running a business-like operation;

- It provides information to assist in budget allocations;
- It contributes to operational efficiency in terms of routine decisions, which helps junior staff; and
- It serves as a tool of complaint-handling with regard to selections or deselections.

Evans (1987, p. 67) provides an even more lengthy list of functions which a written collection development policy, if properly applied, can perform:

- It informs everyone about the nature and scope of the collection;
- It informs everyone of collecting priorities;
- It forces thinking about organizational goals to be met by the collection;
- It generates some degree of commitment to meeting organizational goals;
- It sets standards for inclusion and exclusion;
- It reduces the influence of a single selector and personal biases;
- It provides a training/orientation tool for new staff;
- It helps ensure a degree of consistency over time and despite staff turnover;
- It guides staff in handling complaints;
- It aids in weeding and evaluating the collection;
- It aids in rationalizing budget allocations;
- It provides a public relations document;
- It provides a means of assessing overall performance of the collection development program; and
- It provides outsiders with information about the purpose of collection development (an accountability tool).

In addition, Evans stresses usefulness of the policy as a means of communication with users.

It should be noted also that the policy can help focus communication during collection management and staff assessment processes. For example, evaluators of order librarians or bibliographers who, contrary to policy, order second copies or titles outside of the users' subject needs or the curriculum, can show them the policy section that addresses these concerns. Staff assessment, as well as collection assessment efforts, therefore, should together help to assure uniformity and fairness of collecting practices. Combined with staff development and training efforts, moreover, all such efforts are directed toward building the specified collecting objectives stated in the policy. This is the reason we, as well as the authors cited in this book, nearly unanimously stress the importance of involving so many in the data gathering, community analysis, needs assessment, writing or revising the mission statement and collecting objectives.

David Farrell (1991, pp. 55-56) contributes perhaps the most precisely focused set of policy functions in the literature. These include the following:

- It establishes priorities for collection development;
- It describes collection strengths and weaknesses for the library's staff, administration, and constituencies, and supports grant proposals, funding requests, and accreditation surveys;
- It provides information for determining library-wide collection management policies . . . ;
- It educates librarians responsible for collections and assists in establishing staffing needs and priorities; and
- It communicates between libraries for purposes of developing and maintaining cooperative collection building and resource sharing programs.

In short, collection development policies that are readily available to everyone in the community and on the library staff are very valuable, multi-purpose tools. They can improve communication, public relations, staff development, training, and assessment. On the other hand, they should reduce miscommunication, misunderstanding, stress, and time spent in handling complaints and training by clarifying procedures (how does . . . , or what happens when . . .) and roles (who does what). The opposites are likely to occur when decisions are based on personal considerations. Thus, by concentrating the positive attention of library staff, library administrators, and others on a specified plan and specific collection policies and procedures, chances are greatly improved of everyone's moving in a positive way to build a balanced collection in a deliberative and careful manner. In the long run, the policies not only save everyone's time and energy on collection responsibilities, but also help defend and protect library staff and governing board members from unwelcome pressures within the community or governing boards themselves. Finally, when everyone who should be or wants to be involved has approved the policy, the statement gains a sense of formal authority quite unlike any unwritten or informal approach to collection management.

Policy variance by type of library

Mission, collecting objectives, selection criteria, community analysis and concern about censorship or intellectual freedom are some of the ways that policies differ significantly by type of library. Readers can see the differences by examining the policies included in Part Two. The academic and school library policy statements reflect the importance of the curriculum and break down collection objectives by far narrower subjects, or classification ranges (although only one or two subject policies are included due to space limitations). The policies of public libraries tend to stress meeting the recreational and more general subject needs of the clientele they serve. The policies of special libraries and departmental libraries are, of course, the most focused.

The emphasis placed on factors relating to intellectual freedom, labeling, or censorship varies by type of library, as well as from library to library. Public libraries, for example, often focus on intellectual freedom concerns because of population character- istics or demographic variables. The complexities of melding together the widely differing backgrounds and perceptions of a heterogenous population characterizing most medium- and large- sized communities is often reflected in collection development policies of public libraries. In communities across Texas and other areas, for example, where "conservative" minded individuals and groups are notorious for wanting to dictate library and school textbook selections, it behooves library managers to include statements and procedures that better prepare them and their staff

for censors. A prime example of this approach can be found in
Appendix A, containing the Montgomery County (Conroe, Texas)
Library System's policy, titled "Materials Selection and Accessibility
Policy." It aims at preventing problems arising from pressures it
perceived might have come from the conservative elements in the
community. Either this approach worked, or the library management's fear was unfounded, because censorship efforts did not
materialize to any notable degree.

We chose not to discuss intellectual freedom or censorship
issues further than this because scores of books and articles have
been written on this subject; space limitations prevent further
coverage. The reader will find these issues addressed by the
policies reproduced in this book, including the American Library
Association's statements on intellectual freedom, and the Library
Bill of Rights (see Appendix B).

On the other hand, academic librarians have been less preoc-
cupied with censorship than public librarians due to the tradition of
academic freedom which allows instructors to profess and assign
readings to students as they wish. Other concerns of academic
librarians are summarized in an essay by Farrell (1991, p. 52):

> Written policies first appeared in the early post-war decades;
> they proliferated between 1960 and 1980 when, first, collection
> budgets expanded rapidly, then, later, severe budgetary re-
> trenchment forced a reexamination of collection development
> goals in most research libraries. Most recently, the force of
> extraordinary factors external to scholarship and knowledge
> per se--among them a rapidly escalating increase in
> published information, the "floating" dollar coupled with
> dramatic foreign currency fluctuations, and the application of
> computer technology to the production, transmission, storage,
> and retrieval of information--accelerated the pace of change
> and the cost and methods of maintaining a research library
> collection.

> The combination of these factors has caused collection
> development librarians to think in new ways about their work,
> to redefine goals and pay closer attention to their planning
> and policy-making functions.

One of those new ways of thinking about collection development that appeared about 1980 was the RLG (Research Libraries Group) Conspectus which, as will become evident in Part Two, is reflected in many policy statements. Collection development librarians and directors of research level libraries helped to focus much attention on collection development activities. Smaller academic and public libraries, as well as school and school district libraries, library consortia of all sizes, and the American Library Association, have embraced the Conspectus as discussed by Wood (1992).

Very good examples of how the Conspectus is incorporated into collection development policies are found in Part Two of this book. Readers can find how libraries of all types have done so by examining the policies of California State University, the Illinois State Library, Tarlton Law Library, and St. Petersburg Junior College. Illinois State Library's policy provides definitions readers need to be familiar with to understand the Conspectus. The Tarlton Law Library's policy shows how the Conspectus can be modified to meet a library's specialized needs.

Barriers to policy development

Despite the numerous, aforementioned advantages of developing collection development statements, library managers need to be prepared to overcome objections. This assumes that library management is first a proponent of developing a collection development policy.

Gorman and Howes (1989, p. 4) note that few of the great librarians in the history of libraries ever compiled such documents. Rather, they:

> . . . simply relied on their genuine passion for literature and inbred instinct for what was "right" when collecting . . . . And no one would deny that the British Library, the Library of Congress, the Bibliothèque Nationale, the university libraries of Cambridge and Oxford, Harvard and Yale are among the world's great repositories . . . and without benefit of a written collection development policy.

Adams (1984, p. 93) provides a rationale for this state of affairs in his study of nineteenth-century Australian libraries: " . . . To some extent this is understandable when we examine the management structure of the libraries of the period, where the role of librarian was usually shown to be little more than caretaker or curator of the collections." Merritt (1979, p. 67) explains the lack of development in a substantial number of libraries as the result of "natural human procrastination rather than to disagreement or opposition, though some disagreement may indeed exist."

Evans (1987, p. 66) feels many libraries have chosen to make do without a written policy in view of the fact that an effective document of this type requires accumulating (as an ongoing process) a significant amount of data relating to:

- The strengths and weaknesses of the collection at hand;
- The community being served and where it is going;
- Other resources available locally (to patrons) and those accessible through interlibrary loan.

Thus, the preliminary steps required before writing the policy do take considerable time for planning what data and information to collect, and how. Since these data sets change, policies need to be revised from time to time. Evans goes on to explain that the need for continuous revision is another reason why policies are lacking. He also notes that the library's policy "needs to change to reflect a changing community and, therefore, the librarian's thinking and data collecting are never finished. Some librarians say it is not worth the trouble: as soon as the plan is on paper, the situation has changed so much that the plan is out-of-date--so why bother?"

Gardner (1981, p. 229) lays much of the blame on library management, noting,

> . . . they may not realize the importance of such a document. There are still library administrators in positions of authority today who came into the library profession before such a document was thought important. Since some librarians also think of collection development policies as public relations gimmicks rather than as day-to-day working tools, they do not

see the necessity of writing such a document. Often the impetus for getting a collection development policy on paper comes from the lower ranks of a library staff, from individuals frustrated at attempts to carry out their jobs when no written guidelines are available.

The latter situation, Gardner stresses, leaves staff at the whim of the chief administrator.

Finally, the paucity of published material offering guidance to librarians might also explain this situation. Farrell (1991, p. 58) notes that the library literature offers little coverage devoted to policies after they have been issued. He suggests that this surprising state of affairs might exist because the use of the policy after its development was not given enough thought. Farrell's comments should prompt library directors or others to determine why the library's policy is not used when this happens. It should be suggested that library directors make certain that the policy is widely distributed and, if possible, available through the institution's local area network or computer system for both display and downloading..

Gorman and Howes (1989, p. 4) explain that "the nature of modern documentation may be characterized as unspeakably complex, diverse and amoeba-like. In terms of geographical, chronological and linguistic breadth, the material in which any library has an interest spans a broad spectrum of countries, periods and languages. This recorded knowledge encompasses all aspects of human experience; it is truly multi-, inter- and cross-disciplinary. Furthermore, disciplines are constantly changing their nature and focus as new trends rise and fall." They also cite area studies, new literatures, and bio-ethics that "become established with frightening regularity" and "exert significant impact on the nature, quality and quantity of recorded knowledge; and all of this becomes reflected in what libraries collect." Gorman and Howes (1989, pp. 4-5) also discuss the problem that the volume of publishing causes by noting the number of titles listed by subjects in standard bibliographical reference tools for books and serials.

In conclusion, rationales against utilizing a collection development policy notwithstanding, libraries committed to a progressive, proactive problem-solving approach to issues such as collection management are likely to insist on the presence of a collection development policy. As Gorman and Kennedy say (1992, p. xii) after examining the reasons against having policies: "We have explored the basis of these opinions and make a firm recommendation that flexible and well constructed policy statements are not a luxury, or even simply useful, but are in fact essential parts of the administrative and professional armoury." Libraries choosing otherwise run the risk of exacerbating the inevitable problems which arise during the process.

REFERENCES

Adams, John. "More Than 'librarie keepers'," In: *Books, Libraries and Readers in Colonial Australia: Papers from the Forum on Australian Colonial Library History Held at Monash University,* 1-2 June 1984, edited by Elizabeth Morrison and Michael Talbot. Clayton, Vic.: Graduate School of Librarianship, Monash University, 1985, pp. 93-101.

American Association of School Librarians. *Policies and Procedures for Selection of School Library Materials.* Chicago: American Library Association, 1961.

American Library Association. *Public Library Service.* Chicago: American Library Association, 1956.

Breivik, Patricia and E. Gordon Gee. *Information Literacy; Revolution in the Library.* Washington, DC: American Council on Education, 1989.

Cassell, Kay Ann and Elizabeth Futas. *Developing Public Library Collections, Policies, and Procedures.* Series Editor: Bill Katz. New York: Neal-Schuman, 1991.

Evans, G. Edward. *Developing Library and Information Center Collections.* Second Edition. Littleton, CO: Libraries Unlimited, 1987.

Farrell, David. "Policy and Planning," In: *Collection Management: A New Treatise*, edited by Charles B. Osburn and Ross Atkinson. Greenwich, CT: JAI, 1991.

Gardner, Richard K. *Library Collections: Their Origin, Selection and Development*. New York: McGraw-Hill, 1981.

Gorman, G.E. and B.R. Howes. *Collection Development for Libraries*. London: Bowker-Saur, 1989.

Gorman, G. E. and J. Kennedy. *Collection Development for Australian Libraries*. Second Edition. Wagga Wagga, NSW: Centre for Information Studies, 1992.

Merritt, LeRoy Charles. "Writing a Selection Policy," In: *Background Readings in Building Library Collections*, Second Edition, edited by Phyllis Van Orden and Edith B. Phillips. Metuchen, NJ: Scarecrow, 1979, p. 67.

Wood, Richard J. "A Conspectus of the Conspectus," In: *Collection Assessment: A Look At the RLG Conspectus*, edited by Richard J. Wood and Katina B. Strauch. New York: Haworth, 1992, pp. 5 - 23.

2

IMPLEMENTING A POLICY

Once the decision to develop or revise a library's collection
development policy has been made, the hard work of implementing
such a document begins. This chapter outlines the preliminary and
basic steps to writing and establishing a collection development
policy.

Preliminary steps

There are a number of advisable preliminary steps that should be
considered by library management and library governing bodies
prior to writing a collection development policy as follows:

- Surveying user groups;
- Reviewing the goals and objectives of the institution of which
  the library is a part;
- Determining the environmental characteristics likely to have an
  impact on the library collection;
- Compiling specifications for the development of the library
  collection; and
- Determining current selection requirements.

These preliminary steps are aimed at learning the needs of the
library's clientele, scanning the environment, and setting collection
parameters.

Environmental scanning, community analysis, needs assessment, data gathering, survey methodology--these are some of the
terms used by authors to describe some of the preliminary steps or
processes used prior to writing the policy. We cannot take the time
here to explain how these various processes differ from one
another; readers may consult any number of excellent books on
each topic by writers in various fields. Some of the authors cited in
this work offer more details as well.

In order to assure that the library will be adequately meeting
the needs of its constituency, however, information must be

compiled relating to the various user groups. This data can be obtained largely by gathering and analyzing existing, and as up-to-date as possible, institutional and community records about the population being served. Relevant factors include size and characteristics of the population both general and specific: age, education, employment, unemployment, etc., of the population in general and by sex, race, ethnicity, and religion. It is important to gather feedback from library staff, current library users, as well as non-users. Surveys and questionnaires are prime devices for acquiring user input.

In addition, *The Intellectual Freedom Manual* by the American Library Association (1983, p. 159), hereinafter called the ALA manual, says that these tools should touch upon the following areas:

- Population characteristics: age, education, employment level, and others;
- Size of each user group;
- Primary purpose of each group in using the library;
- Kinds of material used in accomplishing these purposes; and
- Kinds of activities engaged in during the accomplishment of these purposes.

While the characteristics of the population and community in which the library is found are most important, the mission and objectives of the library and parent institution, if any, are the cornerstone on which a collection development policy is constructed. This is because many types of libraries (school, public, academic and special) can all be found within the same community and, therefore, differ in collecting practices widely due to institutional missions and objectives.

In looking at how various factors impact the collection development in public libraries, the ALA manual (1983, p.159) has identified the most notable environmental sources and how they can affect a library collection:

- Statements of objectives available in a public document designed to inform all concerned persons:
  a) General needs the library is designed to fulfill;
  b) Activities or standards most valued; and

    c) Distinction in some field of endeavor.
- Public records outlining the institution's objectives in a less
  direct manner:
      a) Annual reports of the institution;
      b) Charter of the institution;
      c) Published history of the institution;
      d) Records of the governing body; and
      e) Budget.

Environmental factors--and their impact on a library's collection--
should also be considered in the preparation of a policy. The ALA
manual (1983, p. 159) cites a number of these characteristics as
well as their implications:

ENVIRONMENTAL FACTORS	PROVISIONS AFFECTED
Relative geographical isolation	Materials related to the cultural and recreational needs of users
Economic structure	Materials related to specific educational needs
Presence/absence of library resources external to the institution	Degree of self-sufficiency; completeness of resources
Presence/absence of postsecondary learning institutions	Scholarly/technical works
Relationship to local industries	Technical reports and business materials
Relationship to local professional/cultural groups	Specialized subcollections

While these factors are stated more in terms of public libraries, all
libraries will want to consider them to the extent that they are
relevant. Academic librarians, for example, often serve as the
campus' public library. After data relating to the above factors has

been compiled, the collection should be reviewed so as to ascertain the types (and depth) of materials required in the various areas of concern. According to the ALA manual (1983, p. 160), the following information is needed for each area:

- Number of library materials currently held;
- Total number of relevant materials available;
- Percent of total materials held; and
- Distribution of current holdings by publication date.

At this point in time, the ALA manual (1983, p. 160) says these collection areas should be evaluated according to specific user purposes such as recreation, self-help, continuing education, and business. While these purposes relate more, of course, to public libraries, many school and academic libraries must often meet the same criteria to some degree while meeting their primary collecting objectives relative to the curriculum. Some company and special libraries might maintain a small collection of paperbacks acquired as gifts. In any case, the collection specifications should be compared to the existing collection. The effectiveness of any policy depends on how accurately each of these factors is documented.

Policy development and approval

Much of the effort involved with the development of a policy may be directed toward the ultimate acceptance by the library's governing entity. This may be a school board, board of trustees, county commissioners, university administration, or the like.

Evans (1987, pp. 78-79) outlines below a developmental process calculated to achieve passage, and then, guarantee community, staff, and administrative consensus before a problem arises:

- The head librarian appoints a staff committee to draft a basic policy statement, which is to be submitted to the head librarian.
- The head librarian reviews and comments on the draft and distributes it to the staff for their comments and suggestions.
- The original committee then incorporates the comments and suggestions into a revised, final statement. Perhaps a general meeting will be needed to discuss the interim draft before the final version is prepared.

- The final draft statement is presented to the governing board for review, possible revision, and eventually, approval.
- Another valuable step can be taken between board review and final approval. That step is to hold an open meeting for patrons to hear about and comment upon the proposed policy. Members of the drafting committee, the head librarian, and representatives of the governing board should be present to explain, describe, and if necessary, defend and modify the statement.
- The final step is to prepare multiple copies of the final statement for the library staff and those patrons desiring a copy. A good public relations device is to prepare a brief condensed version for distribution to each new user of the library.

Copies should, of course, go as well to members of the library's governing board, significant donors, librarians and others who select library materials, etc. All of these steps are designed to achieve consensus, as well as acceptance and support.

Cassell and Futas (1991, pp. 108-113) provide a more detailed, ten step, practice-based model as follows:

- Begin
- Involve people
- Meet
- Organize
- Lead the group
- Gather information
- Analyze and synthesize
- Evaluate
- Develop a policy
- Reiterate.

In describing the first step, they say:

> begin . . . . Do not be daunted by the preplanning and other financial, time, energy commitments that must be made . . . . Once the initial decision has been made, everything will follow from that point . . . . Remember, the process that results in the product is just as important as the product itself, some even believe more important.

In describing the second step, involving people, Cassell and Futas stress that success requires involving those people who both need and want to be involved from the beginning. The third step, meeting with everyone involved to discuss the process and final product, they say, might be the most important step because:

> ... it is the one at which people jockey for positions within the group, take on their eventual group roles, and begin building true consensus. It is important that the facilitator at this meeting be good, since the process and product that finally evolve are probably due more to the dynamics of this meeting than any other. These first meetings, in which the agendas are not filled with reports from subcommittees, can be difficult because they are not easily controllable .... Yet it is just these differences of opinions, preferences, needs, and outlooks that are so important to the process. Arguments should be encouraged, and constructive criticism should be helped along.

The third through sixth steps that Cassell and Futas outline involve the librarian deciding how to structure committees with specific assignments and responsibilities, call meetings frequently, provide committee members with necessary information about library policies, library budgets, library hours, users and non-users, etc. Presentations of facts are made to the smaller groups on an informal but frequent basis. Providing necessary information, they stress, also may mean giving leaders information about how to handle committee members and processes. Since gathering information about the community might necessitate surveys or questionnaires, this step may be the longest as such instruments may need to be tested. Cassell and Futas believe that the larger group should meet every month or so to keep everyone working in conjunction with one another and to bring about a melding of functions (p. 109). They describe, for example, the fifth step as leading the group so that members "begin to feel the importance of what they are doing so that each will try to achieve the goals of the group and begin to have a sense of common goals." The seventh step, they say (p. 110) is to:

analyze and synthesize . . . . Making decisions about selection, maintenance, evaluation, and weeding are the end
products of the gathering of all the information and its
analysis and synthesis . . . .Your job at this step is to see that
the information collected has a purpose . . . .The best information will get you nowhere if the correct interpretation of it is
not made. There are many methods of analysis, and having
a good statistician around to look at the data collected, at
least in the census and questionnaire parts of the information
gathering, would be a good idea. It is valuable now to go
over some of the statements that are part of the library's
traditional philosophy, goals, and mission, if they exist. If they
do not exist currently, by the data-analysis stage they should
be in draft form. Be sure to have them considered by the
widest number of people involved in the process.

The eighth step described by Cassell and Futas is to use analysis
tools to evaluate how well the library collection meets the needs of
its clientele. Specifically, they stress (p. 110):

the criteria by which to judge the collection must be discussed
along with the interests of the community. In the case of the
collection development process, make decisions on: the value
of the collection; how to select and weed the collection; what
kind of materials, subjects, and formats the library should
supply; and any kind of services the library might provide but
does not currently.

Only after all of this work has been done, the ninth step, developing
the policy statement, begins. More will be said about this later in
this chapter. The tenth step Cassell and Futas outline is the
repeating of the others. They say (p. 113):

. . . do it over again! This time, correct any mistakes that were
made. . . . Now that the product exists in a state that has
passed the governing body, and the process has been
completed, the library may decide to use the process, the
product, and the individuals who participated in them to do
library promotion with the community that the library serves.
A good way to do that is to have the policy ready for distribu-

tion to the people who come into the library, to send it out to
the voters, to go to country fairs, street fairs, or other "shows"
to have a table set up for just the library and staffed by
professionals and other individuals connected with the library
to "talk up" the library to the entire community. If there are
well-attended town meetings, this might be an appropriate
time to bring forth this public relations document. If you can
get the community to talk about the library, it may give you
more visibility . . . .

In summary, Cassell and Futas advocate initiating the process by
involving those who need and want to be involved, gathering and
analyzing the data needed to assess the collection and user needs,
and then writing the statement.

The consensus approach to policy writing appears to be widely
accepted--and practiced--within the library field. Futas (1984, p. xii)
notes, and wholeheartedly supports, this state of affairs in her most
recent compilation of academic and public library policies:

> More people have had a hand in their production, and this
> shows in the documents themselves. Many policies are not as
> easily read since they have been produced by committee, but
> if one reads the justification for the document, one will see that
> committee involvement is deliberate--the more who partici-
> pate in the process, the stronger the document will be.

In addition, LeRoy Merritt (1979, pp. 68-69) provides one of the more
detailed accounts of the interpersonal dynamics inherent in the
committee approach to policy development:

> The actual writing of the policy statement should start with a
> meeting of the professional staff to discuss the need for
> writing a statement, the benefits to be gained from the
> process, and the anticipated usefulness of the statement once
> it has been written. The meeting should continue with some
> discussion of the technique to be used in the writing and
> particularly the need for making positive statements about the
> kinds of materials which are to be selected for the library,
> avoiding insofar as possible all statements negative or
> restrictive in character. It must be kept in mind that the

concern is with a selection policy, not a rejection policy. Instructions on technique should include the concept of depth as well as breadth, so that the library staff would concern itself with the relative superficiality or exhaustiveness of selection in each literary form and subject area.

A division of the various subject areas among the professional staff would follow. The smaller the staff, the larger the areas would have to be; in very large libraries there might even be committees of the staff to work in each area. If possible these allocations, as well as the responsibility for selection itself, should take into account the subject background and interests of the staff . . . .

After some weeks, there might be a series of staff meetings to discuss and to edit the whole developing statement so that it meets with the approval and assent of the entire staff. A good deal of give-and-take discussion might occur during these meetings . . . .

Merritt (1979, p. 69) goes on to delineate how to secure public support:

When there is general staff agreement that the best book selection policy possible for the time has been created, the librarian might well present a draft to the library board, the city manager, the city council, or other supervisory authority. Again the object would be to promote discussion, suggestions, possible revisions, additions, or better phrasing. These suggestions, all of which should be cordially and sincerely received, would then go back to another series of staff meetings for more discussion until the staff and supervisory authority are in substantial agreement.

Merritt adds that the librarians or other qualified staff should, at the same time, begin talking to civic, educational, and social groups about the policy, showing them a draft copy, and inviting input. While Merritt's remarks are addressed to public librarians, his points should be well taken by school, academic and special librarians. Faculty and administrators in schools or academic institutions, for example, should be involved in the policy development process in the same way. Merritt (1979, pp.70-71) concludes,

the policy statement should incorporate all usable suggestions from individuals and community organizations. After it
has been completed to the satisfaction of the library staff and
approved by the supervisory authority, it should be published
as a separate document for internal use by the library staff,
for use by patrons as the occasion arises, and for general
distribution to interested individuals and organizations within
the community. It would be desirable also to publish the
whole document or substantial portions of it in the local press
along with a complete list of the organizations which have
participated in preparing the document. Before the use of the
completed policy is discussed, it should be noted that the job,
done once, is not likely to have been done for all time. Communities and their reading interests and needs change with
the passage of time, as does the pattern of book production.
Revisions of the basic policy statement will have to be made
as conditions change, and the whole document ought to be
reviewed at regular intervals, probably every five years.

In school and academic institutions, copies should, of course,
go to department heads, and key administrators and library
supporters. Likewise, in special libraries, copies should be given
to company or agency executives. In all cases, newsletters and
other publicity should announce its availability in the library and
other offices. For very lengthy statements that make it unfeasible to
reprint the entire statement, publicity should provide readers with
a summary of key elements to the extent possible. An ongoing
column may be preferable (one section at a time in each
issue, for instance).

In order to ensure the long-term vitality of the policy, Farrell
(1991, p. 58) has recommended consideration of five points during
the compilation process as follows:

- Who will use the policy statement?
- Will the statement be a resource for training and evaluating
  collection specialists, for developing collection assessment
  projects and funding proposals, for preparing accreditation
  reports, and so forth?
- Can the policy be easily updated, uploaded and downloaded,
  manipulated?

- Will the policy be accessible in a machine-readable format?
- Will the policy be coordinated with (and accessible to) librarians in institutions with which cooperative agreements exist?

Farrell (1991, pp.58-59) adds that after the policy has been in place for a reasonable time span, its utility should be assessed by a number of evaluative criteria as follows:

- Has the policy been incorporated into processes for training and evaluating collection specialists; are new collection specialists introduced to the policy?
- Does the policy offer specific guidance for budget allocations, for grant and other funding proposals, and for collection evaluation projects?
- Is the policy reviewed and revised on a scheduled basis and, in any case, when programs, personnel, and budget changes are scheduled?
- Are collection specialists reminded of policy and routinely involved in reviewing and revising it?
- Is the policy statement referred to specifically by working groups inside and outside the library, and in appropriate documents such as strategic plans?
- Does the policy reflect collection budget, cataloging, preservation, retrospective conversion and other priorities?
- Do members of the faculty know the existence of the policy; do they refer to it in relevant written documents and in oral communications?

Gardner (1981, p. 229) cites a couple of additional points to be kept in mind throughout the implementation process:

. . . a collection development policy, since it deals with controversial and touchy issues, needs to be formulated in calm and quiet, not in a moment of crisis. A policy statement adopted hastily in the midst of a crisis will never stand the test of time. It will remain an ad hoc solution to one particular issue. Furthermore complaints can be dealt with much more effectively when an agreed-upon policy exists than they can when decisions have to be made in the heat of battle ... in coordination with other libraries in the area

. . . either in a hierarchical system or through a division of responsibility among equals . . . . Any good, detailed collection development policy should assist neighboring libraries in their collection building plans as well, since it will inform them of the goals of their neighbor. Greater coordination of collection building should therefore be possible.

Futas (1984, p. xiii) also advises going slowly and carefully in the preparation of the document. She cites part of a letter she received from one practitioner to illustrate the way *not* to write a policy:

> When I became director . . . last year, it [the library] had never had a written selection policy. So I bought yours and proceeded to piece together a rough draft, using excerpts from your examples, with a minimum of modifications. I presented this draft to the student-faculty committee with the expectation that it would be demolished and reassembled, but, to my chagrin (because I would have taken greater pains to achieve a coherent philosophy and literary style had I anticipated their reaction), they accepted it to the letter, chapter and verse.

Although that director's approach may be far too commonplace, a thoroughgoing process that involves in some way everyone who needs to be involved ought to ensure that each library governing board approves the best, most appropriate, and most widely accepted policy possible.

A final word of caution regarding the policy implementation process: just as the library expects administrators, patrons, and others outside the institution proper to honor the conditions outlined in the policy, so librarians must be prepared to both enforce and apply them in practice. These provisions represent mere paperwork without a concerted, ongoing effort to render them a vital planning tool.

REFERENCES

American Library Association, *The Intellectual Freedom Manual*, Second Edition, compiled by the Office for Intellectual Freedom,

American Library Association. Chicago: American Library Association, 1983.

Cassell, Kay Ann and Elizabeth Futas. *Developing Public Library Collections, Policies, and Procedures.* Series Editor: Bill Katz. New York: Neal-Schuman, 1991.

Evans, G. Edward. *Developing Library and Information Center Collections.* Second Edition. Littleton, CO: Libraries Unlimited, 1987.

Farrell, David. "Policy and Planning," In: *Collection Management: A New Treatise,* edited by Charles B. Osburn and Ross Atkinson. Greenwich, CT: JAI, 1991.

Futas, Elizabeth, ed. *Library Acquisition Policies and Procedures.* Second Edition. Phoenix, AZ: Oryx, 1984.

Gardner, Richard K. *Library Collections: Their Origin, Selection, and Development.* New York: McGraw-Hill, 1981.

Merritt, LeRoy Charles. "Writing a Selection Policy," In: *Background Readings in Building Library Collections,* Second Edition, edited by Phyllis Van Orden and Edith B. Phillips. Metuchen, NJ: Scarecrow, 1979.

3

POLICY COMPONENTS

Given the diversity of libraries by size and type, it follows that the character of libraries' collection development policies should vary a great deal from one institution to another. This is demonstrated by examining the policies of academic, public, school, and special libraries in Part Two of this book, as well as Hoffmann's analysis of the public and academic collection development policies included in Futas' work (1984, Appendix C).

Library functions impacting policy

The collection management objectives of each library--as well as its overall service philosophy--will also significantly influence the structure of the policy. Farrell (1991, pp. 60-61) notes that many library functions having an impact on collection development in research level libraries are often described in terms of written policy as summarized below:

- **Acquisition Policy:** Describes principles and procedures for acquiring materials selected for collections, guidelines for searching the library's bibliographic databases, bibliographic verification, programs for managing gift/exchange/approval plan/blanket orders, handling replacement and duplicate orders, and for selecting and assigning vendors.
- **Budget Allocation Policy:** Describes principles, objectives, and methodology for allocating the materials budget and how budget allocation data is collected, analyzed and used.
- **Cataloging Policy:** Describes priorities for providing bibliographic access to collections, including current receipts, backlogs, and retrospective conversion of records.
- **Collection Management Policy:** Addresses a library's selection, collection development, collection assessment, preservation, acquisitions, cataloging, networking, and interlibrary lending policies. A collection development policy more narrowly describes a library's collection, as well as its clientele, its

strengths and weaknesses, and its subject, geographical, linguistic, and other parameters.

- Conspectus (also RLG Conspectus): A consortial collection development policy, incorporating descriptive analysis of collections in more than one research library. The RLG Conspectus, developed by members of the Research Libraries Group, is an apparatus consisting of "worksheets" (an analytical framework based upon the Library of Congress classification scheme and subject headings) and associated documentation.
- Cooperative Collection Development Policy: Defines collection development and service agreements between cooperating libraries within a system or consortium. It may address issues including division of selection responsibility, resource sharing and document delivery, preservation, and technical processing priorities.
- Gifts Policy: Defines procedures for accessioning, evaluating, acknowledging and processing gifts. It may include policy and procedure for donor relations including gift appraisals for use with tax returns, and other considerations in accepting (or declining) gifts.
- Interlibrary Lending and Resource Sharing Policy: Defines policy and procedures governing interlibrary lending, resource sharing, and document delivery resources and programs.
- Machine-Readable Data Files Policy: Defines collections policy for digitized information, including software, datatapes, and CD-ROM, and access to extramural databases. It may include policy relating the responsibilities of the library, the computing center and campus network in acquiring and providing access to digitized information, and policy governing use of the library's budgets for materials, equipment, and software in support of machine-readable files.
- Preservation Policy: Defines principles and procedures for maintaining the physical condition of the collections (including conservation, reformatting, and binding). It may include priorities for allocating preservation resources and criteria and methods for selecting and treating materials.
- Restricted Funds Policy: Defines purposes, distribution and use of endowments and other special purpose funds.
- Review and Deselection Policy: Defines policy for review of materials appropriate for transfer between, and/or withdrawal

from, the collections. It may include guidelines for the cancellation of subscriptions and disposal of unneeded materials.

■ Selection Policy: Defines policy for selection of materials according to format, subject, language, geographic area or date of imprint, etc. Selection policy is closely aligned with acquisition policy, and is a key element of a collection development or collection management policy.

Basic policy components

Calvin Boyer (1979, pp. 81-82) recommends an outline of components for collection development policy policies as follows:

I.   Community Description and Analysis

II.   Responsibility for Selection, Legal and Delegated

III. Intellectual Freedom and Procedures for Complaints

IV.   Policies by Clientele Served
      A. Adult
      B. Young adult
      C. Children
      D. Readers of limited skill
      E. Students
      F. Blind, physically handicapped, shut-ins

V.   Policies by Format of Material
      A. Books
         1. Hardback books
         2. Paperbacks
         3. Textbooks and lab manuals
         4. Synopses and outlines
      B. Slides
      C. Films and filmstrips
      D. Newspapers
      E. Recorded sound--Records, tapes, cassettes
      F. Printed music
      G. Pictures

      H. Maps
      I. Pamphlets
      J. Periodicals
      K. Government documents
      L. Manuscripts and rare books
      M. Microfilms

VI.   Policies by Subject of Material
      A. Fiction
      B. Non-fiction
      C. Reference materials
      D. Foreign language materials
      E. Medicine
      F. Law
      G. Sex
      H. Drugs and drug usage
      I. Semi- and pseudo-scientific materials
      J. Religion
      K. Genealogy and heraldry
      L. Guns, explosives, jujitsu, etc.

VII. Gifts Policy

VIII. Weeding, Discarding, Replacement, Duplication Policies

IX.   Relationships to Other Libraries and Library Systems in Collection Development

The above outline, however, fails to provide a broad-based perspective necessary in order to reflect the realities facing contemporary libraries. Bartle and Brown (1983, pp. 5-13) have assembled considerably more topics that need to be included, such as:

- Objectives of the library
- Community and its needs identified
- Purpose of the selection process
- Functions of the library
- Context of selection
- Authority for selection policy

- Responsibility for implementation
- Priorities (types of use and categories of material)
- Controversial issues
- Censorship
- Categories of exclusions
- Statement on Freedom to Read
- Selection criteria
- Collection standards: quantity
- Collection development targets
- Selection methods: organization
- Acquisitions categories and coverage
- Ordering methods

Cassell and Futas (1991, p. 111) have also compiled a comprehensive inventory of essential policy components. While allowing for the fact that variations exist regarding the inclusions of a particular library, their list of typical policy features is far less confusing than that provided by Bartle and Brown.

- A needs assessment statement that marks out the boundaries of the community to be served.
- A description of the clientele that discusses who is to be served by the collection that is developed.
- A statement of the philosophy of service that includes the goals, objectives, mission, and priorities of the library in regard to its community and its patrons.
- A selection statement that includes criteria, principles, formats, subjects, and responsibilities.
- A collection evaluation procedure including the criteria for determining whether the collection is of value to patrons and the community. . . .
- A statement regarding maintenance of the collection that includes replacement, mending, binding, duplication of titles or volumes, plus the weeding of the collection, and the procedures to be followed in doing so.
- An intellectual freedom statement concerning the overarching principle against censorship and how it is dealt with in this particular library. It is not enough to append statements such as the Library Bill of Rights or the Freedom to Read Statement to an already existing policy, which contains everything else.

It is important to write your own statement about the library and what its librarians think about censorship. In some instances, usually where there have been censorship problems, a procedures manual is enclosed in, or appended to, the written collection development policy.

- A review statement concerning how long it will be before the process is repeated.
- A formal passage of the policy statement through the governing body of the library [and written documentation to that effect] is the final step. Without this step the foregoing policy and the process that led up to it are just interesting exercises for the people who participated in them.

Gorman and Howes (1989, p. 28) say that the confusion with respect to definitions of selection policies, acquisition policies, and collection development policies is related to:

. . . the inconsistent use of descriptors for collection development statements. A collection development policy is not a selection policy, nor is it an acquisitions policy; and no effective policy statement will try to encompass all of these areas in a single document for one very simple reason: they are fundamentally different in intention and content. Both selection and acquisitions policies are basically procedural statements indicating in some detail how policies are to be implemented and by whom. Underpinning and preceding these statements are the actual collection development policies, which provide a rationale for the existence of collections and indicate what they will contain for the foreseeable future. These policies, then, deal with "why" and "what" issues, while selection and acquisitions address the practicalities of "how" and "who." Perhaps the clearest way to highlight the distinctions is to think in terms of a hierarchy. The highest level in this hierarchy is the planning function, policy formulation; from this flows selection, which involves decisions about what to include or exclude. Selection, in other words, is a direct function of collection development in that it applies the principles stated in the collection development policy document . . . .While the criteria and methodology for selection are separate from collection development planning, they are certainly not independent of planning as embodied in a policy document. Acquisitions, the third level in the hierarchy and the one that actually gets material into the library, is the process that implements selection decisions which have arisen from the collection development plan.

The hierarchical relationship between these collection building policy and procedural statements is illustrated by Gorman and Howes (1989, p. 29) as follows:

Collection Development Policy
- Statement of general principles;
- Why the collection exists;
- What it shall contain; and
- Internal and external audiences.

Procedure 1: Selection Procedures Statement
- Statement of specific practices;
- How to implement the collection development policy;
- Who does selecting;
- Criteria for selecting materials; and
- Primary internal audience of selectors.

Procedure 2: Acquisitions Procedures Statement
- Statement of specific practices;
- How to implement selection decisions;
- Who does acquisitions work;
- Statement of specific acquisitions procedures;
- Internal audience of acquisitions personnel.

In view of their hierarchy, a thorough document would include components organized under headings which approximate those cited below:

- Title/Cover Page
- Signature Page
- Table of Contents
- Background Information for Community/Organization
- Responsibility for Collection Management
- Objectives of the Library Collection

- Evaluation Criteria
    General Criteria (Objectives)
    Specific Evaluative Criteria
- Format Guidelines
    Inventory of Formats
    Proportional Designations
- Selection Aids
- Acquisition Policies and Procedures
- Intellectual Freedom
    Philosophy Statement
    Procedures for Handling Complaints
- Collection Maintenance/Weeding
    Policy and Procedures
    Evaluative Criteria
- Special Considerations
    Special Collections
    Networking Agreements
    Levels of Selection
    Input by Non-Librarians
    Gifts
    Replacements
    Duplicates
    Evaluation and Inventory (e.g., Collection Mapping)
- Glossary
- Appendices
    Forms (e.g., Evaluation of Materials, Complaint, Gift)
    Policy Documents (e.g., Freedom to Read Statement)
- Index

Description of the components

1. Title/Cover Page
This page serves to identify both the type of document and particular library collection being addressed.

2. Signature Page
Sometimes included on the title page, this section confers legitimacy on the overall policy through the signatures of all relevant administrative personnel.   Ideally, supervisory and advisory board members, principals, library district coordinators,

corporate middle managers, vice presidents/deans for academic affairs, commissioners, and county judges are included as applicable to the type of library. As has already been shown, all of these individuals should be provided ample time prior to this stage to become acquainted with the contents of the document.

It is important to bear in mind that administrative personnel are far more likely to be supportive of a collection development policy that has been compiled at a time other than in direct response to an outside challenge such as attempted censorship.

3. Table of Contents

The policy functions as a reference source (i.e., usage involving isolating specific bits of needed information) for most librarians, patrons, and others who consult it. Accordingly, it is imperative that a blueprint of its contents be available in order to expedite accurate, efficient searching techniques. The following features are likely to enhance the utility of the Table of Contents:

- Headings should correspond, word-for-word, with those contained in the text.
- Subheadings should be included, if possible, with a uniform cutoff point (regarding what is to be included) established throughout the text.
- Page numbers should be included in the text and cited for each Contents heading.
- Appendices, tables, and other sidebar-type information should be noted at their proper sequence within the text.

4. Background Information for Community/Organization

This section functions as a prelude to setting library collection goals and objectives and should note the attitudes and behavioral characteristics of potential users as well as users of the library. A significant amount of demographic information can be obtained from organization files (e.g., student data in schools and other academic institutions), city/county records, and state (e.g., licensing) and federal (e.g., census figures) sources.

Ready information such as this does not reveal valuable information regarding a library's users and non-users. For information concerning how users or non-users regard the library's resources and services, the library may decide to conduct its own

use and user studies. If so, Gorman and Howes (1989, p. 148) say planners should start out by considering the following questions:

- What is the goal of the study?
- What are the parameters of the study? Which segments of the collection are to be studied?
- What kinds of samples are to be taken of the population?
- Which specific aspects of collection development are to be analyzed?
- Which aspects of collection use are to be analyzed?
- Can the necessary information or significant data be gathered?
- Is the method appropriate for the purpose?
- What is the possible range of findings that might result from the surveys?
- What are the practical benefits that might result from any findings?
- What are the implications of the process itself in terms of likely impact on services, operations and the political environment in which the library operates?

Such studies should utilize the key stages identified with most examples of scientific research:

- Establishment of purpose and objectives;
- Review of previous research;
- Selection of data to be collected and methodology to be followed;
- Selection of population sample;
- Determination of data analysis methodology;
- Determination of the methods of presentation and utilization of results;
- Provision of the information needed to encourage replication of the study.

5. Responsibility for Collection Management

Two points should be emphasized in this statement. First, the administrators to whom the librarian answers within an organization (e.g., dean of academic affairs, principal, school district superintendent, supervisory board) possess the ultimate responsibility for all decisions relating to library operations. All decision making on a daily basis concerned with collection management should, however, be delegated to the professional librarians or to the library staff. The latter represent the only personnel appropriately qualified to carry out such a mission. Every effort should be taken to communicate to administrators that outside interference would be detrimental to executing a coherent collection development plan. In practice, however, many libraries-- even those possessing written collection management policies-- have cited a particular administrator as the person responsible for selecting materials.

Callison's 1975 study (1990, p. 29) noted that only 27 percent of school library policies had a statement to the effect that this responsibility should be "delegated from the board to the librarian," while a 1985 study revealed that 42 percent of the library policies surveyed still lacked such a clause. The 1975 study also indicated that both the district superintendent and school principal were cited more frequently than the librarian as the first person to contact if library materials were formally challenged.

6. Objectives of the Library Collection

Once the library has studied its constituency in the light of its prime institutional imperatives, general evaluation criteria can be formulated. These objectives should be applied to the collection as a whole, thereby serving as a balance to specific evaluative criteria (which are employed in the consideration of individual titles). Examples include:

- Proportional representation of all constituent interests and needs within the collection;
- Achievement of a balance between differing viewpoints, philosophical perspectives, etc.; and
- A particularized interpretation of the broader goals of the parent institution (if one exists). In other words, a school library should be primarily concerned with providing support for curriculum imperatives.

Evans' (1987, pp. 82-107) analysis of the coverage of selection principles in eleven notable textbooks spanning the years 1925-1981 identifies the "quality versus demand" issue as being at the core of responsible and responsive selection. Gorman and Howes (1989, p. 185) have synthesized the five basic arguments favoring user wants from exponents within the library literature:

- A librarian does not have the right to impose his/her views about what is best for his/her users;
- People should be provided with what they will use, not with materials that will sit on shelves unread;
- Collecting what people want does not automatically mean that only one level of quality will be the result, because users are different enough that their wants will result in a broad range of qualities;
- If users financially support the library, they have a right to determine exactly what goes into the collection; and
- Giving people exactly what they want ensures that they will read, and this helps to build an important habit.

As advocates of user needs, Gorman and Howes (1989, p. 186) tend to focus on the following points:

- The library has an obligation to meet user needs by supplying high quality materials;
- The library has a positive obligation to educate its users, and it does this by exerting constructive influence on thought and attitudes;
- The library is not in competition with the mass media retailers, most of whom supply what consumers want very effectively;
- The library ought to be improving the tastes of its users, and it can do this by providing information which otherwise might not be available or not be chosen; and
- Without motivation, public tastes on the whole are remarkably mundane and disinclined toward "the best" in any field.

The literature has generally argued for a perspective which takes the middle ground in this controversy. In short, the collection objectives should make every effort to be all-inclusive rather than exclusionary in concept.

7. Evaluation Criteria

It could be argued that evaluation criteria constitutes the heart of a library's collection development policy. Both general and specific types of collection assessment criteria should be included; in fact, the two tend to counter-balance each other. Specific evaluation criteria are applied to each item which may be considered for the collection. General criteria--or collection objectives--are applied to the character of the overall collection. If one is emphasized to the exclusion of the other, the collection will generally lose whatever semblance of balance and proportion it may have had.

The criteria employed can vary widely by type of library, collection goals and objectives, and formats included. Robert Broadus (1981) includes the criteria in his work *Selecting Materials for Libraries* as follows:

A. General Considerations:
   - User needs and wants;
   - Holdings of other libraries; and
   - Lacunae (gaps in the collection).

B. Specific Criteria for Books:
   - Content:
     1) Recency;
     2) Truth (e.g., authoritativeness, whether it meets the present consensus of expert opinion);
     3) Freedom from bias.
   - Reputation of author or publisher;
   - Presentation (style of writing, readability, etc.);
   - Special features (e.g., detailed, logical, accurate index; bibliography; footnotes; pictorial formats--diagrams, maps, drawings);
   - Paper, typography, and design;
   - Physical size;
   - Binding;
   - Paperbacks as a factor.

C. Specific Criteria for Nonprint Media Instruction Value:
   - Entertainment value;
   - Preservation of facts and ideas.

D. Guidelines Regarding the Characteristics of Various Media Formats:
- Choice of media formats:
  1) Effectiveness of communication;
  2) Purposes and uses;
  3) Convenience of use;
  4) Equipment required;
  5) Durability;
  6) Price.
- Choice of specific materials:
  1) Basic criteria for acquisitions: novelty, truth, recency, accuracy, reputation of the sponsor;
  2) Arrangement of the material;
  3) Content;
  4) Technical quality;
  5) Distracting elements (e.g., commercial huckstering) eliminated or at least kept under control;
  6) Timeliness; and
  7) Applicability to patron needs.

Gorman and Howes (1989, p. 237) have noted that the process of utilizing evaluative criteria to select materials for libraries poses various challenges for collection developers. Perhaps the most notable challenge is how to apply the written statements to decision making in the selection process because selection is specific while policy is general, discursive, and incomplete. It is not easy, then, to apply general policy statements to the complexities of everyday selection decisions.

Many texts on the subject--including Arthur Curley and Dorothy Broderick's *Building Library Collections* (1985), William Katz's *Collection Development: The Selection of Materials for Libraries* (1980), and the aforementioned Broadus work (1981)--treat specific selection criteria independently (i.e., they do not relate the various criteria to each other). In short, these sources do not indicate which criteria are the most important and when they should be applied.

Other weaknesses include inadequate, extraneous, cumbersome, and poorly developed criteria or formulas. The need to utilize well-defined criteria in the title-by-title evaluation of library materials cannot be emphasized enough. The failure of many libraries to follow through in this regard can be attributed to a number of factors, including: (a) a lack of motivation; (b) a shortage of time; and (c) little understanding of the medium under scrutiny. As a result, selection decisions are typically determined by either consulting the review literature (which is spotty and uneven in its coverage of most formats) or relying upon one's own subjective (and oftentimes superficial) judgment.

Reviews of CD-ROM reference databases can be found in the professional literature, but many of the questions and concerns raised by this relatively new format in most libraries are problematic and unique to this format. The difficulty in applying general policy statements arises not only because of computer hardware, telecommunications, networking, and software consider-ations, but also differences between print and electronic formats themselves. The fact that the same indexes, abstracts, encyclo-pedias, etc., are now not only available in both print, CD-ROM and other electronic formats, but also from different sources, illustrates the complexity of the situation.

The CD-ROM format poses new and different questions in terms of collection development, library use, library management, database maintenance, and public relations: How do the same or similar CD-ROM indexes offered by subscription agencies, automation vendors, and other suppliers differ in their search engines? Does one search engine work equally well for scientific, medical, and general periodical databases? Should the library switch to a new, but superior search engine for a medical or specialized database although it poses user training problems for reference librarians? If the materials budget does not increase enough to pay for the new electronic formats, can the printed reference subscription be canceled? If the CD-ROM database is the preferred format of reference librarians and users alike, but does not index more than five years of the periodicals indexed, must the library continue the paper subscription? If not, will users be offered free online searches? Is a CD-ROM database's additional flexibility gained by keyword and Boolean searching cost-justified? Is the product user friendly? Does it require the need for staff and user training? Does the product have good documentation? Does the database license agreement require restrictions in terms of downloading, access, and duplication of documentation? Does the institution's legal counsel have to review the license? The policies of New Mexico State University, Tarlton Law Library (University of

Texas), and California State University in Part Two address some of these questions. Tarlton Law Library's policy on electronic formats may be of special interest to law librarians, or directors of libraries with large collections of legal materials and online database search services such as LEXIS.

Example: Evaluative criteria applicable to the selection of sound recordings.

It may be instructive to study those criteria which are applicable to sound recordings. The problems of everyday selection decisions are illustrated by the criteria below for the selection of sound recordings. This medium—which encompasses cylinders (2-minute brown and black wax, 4-minute wax, blue amberol vinyl), records (78s, 45s, longplaying discs, 12-inch singles, 16-inch radio transcriptions, etc.), wire recordings, open reel tapes, 8-track tapes, audiocassettes, compact discs, digital audio tapes, digital compact cassettes, mini-discs, etc.--represents perhaps one of the least understood areas of library collection development. The following outline will serve to provide a model of the details to consider in the evaluation of a given format (or family of formats).

Performance Factors

(a) Artistry and/or musicianship:
- Technical proficiency displayed by the performers involved; e.g., timing, characterization, creativity, improvisational skills (if applicable);
- Nature of the performance; i.e., whether the recording was produced in the studio, live in concert, or informally in "the field," a living room, etc.;
- Message or intent of the composer, artist(s), etc.; and
- Its value as a social document.

(b) Quality of the recording's production values:
- Environment in which the recording took place; e.g., the echo achieved by 1950s rockabilly songs through the utilization of small studios without acoustical padding;
- Mix of the instruments; e.g., muddy, hot (most notable in disco material), dampened beneath vocals (often found in

live recordings where the bass frequencies, in particular, lack sufficient delineation);

- Breadth of frequency range present; e.g., acoustic recordings (pre-1925) lack audio information at both the high and low ends of the sound spectrum;
- Type of fidelity employed; e.g., stereophonic, monaural, electronically reprocessed stereo, quadraphonic, surround-sound;
- Nature of channel separation; e.g., echo effect, presence of crossover (Jimi Hendrix simulating a spaceship take-off, the "Ping-Pong" sonics of Enoch Light, etc.);
- The appearance of extraneous noise connected with the recording process; e.g., distortion, sounds not intended to be picked up by microphones; and
- Special characteristics of note; e.g., electronic feedback, phasing, the editing of an original take, overdubbing additional vocal and/or instrumental lines (600 voices in 10cc's 1975 hit, "I'm Not In Love").

(c) Physical quality of the disc/tape medium:
- Amount of pops, ticks and other surface noise;
- Degree of warpage (regarding records and compact discs, precipitating factors include shrink wrap, exposure to heat/sunlight, poor pressing technique);
- Quality of vinyl with respect to potential for wear (generally, the greater the amount of polyvinyl chloride present in records and tapes, the greater the likelihood of optimum durability combined with sound quality);
- The presence of scratches or other marks caused by the production process;
- Whether or not a record has been repackaged (i.e., returned in the past due to some imperfection);
- Quality of the pressing; poorly produced discs may be characterized by distortion, off-center stamping, jagged or nicked edges, etc.;
- The presence of foreign matter embedded in the grooves of a record; e.g., paper or steel wire resulting from the process of scraping labels off of discs which are to be recycled; and
- The presence of pin-hole gaps in the aluminum matrix containing digital information in compact discs.

Reputation of the Author/Composer, Artists and/or Musicians, Record Company, etc.

(a) Regarding the composer:
- Quality of overall output;
- Styles employed; and
- Relevance in relation to a given event, person, trend, school of thought (e.g., Wagner and Gluck's influence on musical drama; Crosby, Stills, Nash and Young's "Ohio," which immortalized the Kent State massacre; Bob Dylan's commentary on a boxer's murder trial, "Hurricane").

(b) Regarding the record company:
- Stylistic inclinations previously exhibited (e.g., Buddah, a "bubblegum" label, suddenly going "progressive"; Motown, a black soul label, acquiring white pop singers);
- Quality of artists within its stable;
- Money and effort expended by company in helping an artist realize his/her goals (reflected in studio time provided, producers employed, degree of creative autonomy allowed);
- Degree of promotion provided;
- Types of companies:
  1) major mainstream labels; e.g., Sony/CBS, BMG/RCA, MCA, EMI/Capitol, WEA (Warner/Elektra/Asylum);
  2) minor mainstream labels ("independents"); e.g., Motown, Island, Alligator, Rhino;
  3) specialty branch operations; e.g., Library of Congress' Archive, Smithsonian, Walt Disney's Buena Vista;
  4) mail order; e.g., Candlelight, Cindy Lou, Lakeshore; and
  5) specialty distributors; e.g., K-tel (department stores and supermarkets), Hit Records (drug stores).

Complementary Print Material

(a) Includes liner notes, libretti, photo albums, song lyrics, etc., on covers or separate inserts;

(b) Can be judged as to:
- Authenticity (particularly regarding biographical and discographical data);

- Objectivity;
- Amount of information present;
- Authenticity (e.g., Leonard Feather assessing the legacy of a jazz musician);
- Who wrote them (e.g., Johnny Cash on Bob Dylan in *Nashville Skyline*);
- The striking nature of the text (e.g., Andrew Loog Oldham's hard sell rap on the early Rolling Stones albums).

(c) Rarely the prime determining factor in the selection of sound recordings; however, it may be the ultimate consideration when all other criteria balance out with respect to two or more recordings. Complementary materials are most applicable to the classical genre where competitive versions (in some cases approaching one hundred in number) of a given work exist.

Packaging of the Recording

(a) Facets to be evaluated:
- Sturdiness of jacket/cover construction;
- Attractiveness of the cover art;
- Composition of the inside sleeve; e.g., plastic, paper of varying levels of quality; and
- Utility of housing employed:
  1) most frequently used types of record album casings: regular slip covers, boxes, unipaks, twin packs;
  2) problems associated with record boxes: the paper used to secure the two halves of the box is frequently torn apart, and the records are highly susceptible to warpage due to a lack of support.

Extra Features
(a)   Includes the design of the record label, vinyl/shellac color, special covers (e.g., pop-up gatefolds (Jethro Tull's *Stand Up*), various gimmicks such as a "three-sided record" (Johnny Winter's *Second Winter*) and heart-shaped discs (Motown's "We Love You Pops");
(b)   Should exercise little influence on the development of library collections concerned with everyday usage; and

(c)   May be of value, however, to archives as objects of research and/or intellectual curiosity.

Comparison of Available Formats

(a) Superiority of records over analog tape formats:
- Relative ease in locating individual selections;
- Absence of hiss due to poor recording techniques;
- More attractive packaging;
- Ease of storage (upright as with books);
- Widest range of titles available prior to the late 1980s;
- Software less expensive;
- Greater automatic capabilities;
- Longer playback time possible via a changer; and
- Discographical data and other inserts more likely to be available (and in larger dimensions).

(b) Superiority of analog tape formats over records:
- Greater variety of hardware to choose from;
- Needles must be continually replaced on record players-- records are subject to wear (i.e., sonic degradation) with each playback;
- Sound quality of records more readily affected by care and handling;
- Recording capacity;
- Digital playback capability;
- Playback equipment more portable; and
- Adaptable to everyday use in vehicles.

(c) Superiority of compact discs over records and analog tapeformats with respect to:

- Digital sound reproduction;
- Greater durability;
- Players rarely require maintenance (e.g., replacing playback heads or needles);
- Greater breadth of reissued material available;
- Random access of any point in recording possible;
- Source easier to tape with higher quality results; and
- No wear resulting from playback.

(d) Problems with compact discs compared with analog formats:
- Relatively new, unproven medium; nobody knows what will ultimately happen to source material over time;
- Not as portable as the cassette; bumps, jolts, etc., can disrupt tracking of the laser beam which reads software;
- List price of mainstream material more expensive;
- Less playing time than with most analog tape configurations;
- Reveals flaw in original masters not readily discernable in the analog formats; and
- Production process more expensive and complicated.

Availability of Recordings

(a) Most dependent on a title's popularity, social, musical significance, etc.;

(b) Sources, including:
- For in-print recordings:
  1) Retail outlets;
  2) Library jobbers;
  3) Record companies;
  4) Record clubs;
  5) Special television offers.
- For out-of-print recordings:
  1) Retail outlets--remaining stock, cut-outs;
  2) Peripheral transactions--flea markets and yard sales, auctions, and private offer to/from an individual;
  3) Specialists including dealer lists/ads and agents, record hunters.

Potential Popularity

Gorman and Howes (1989, p. 235) have attempted to rectify the void in the literature regarding a "practical" and "holistic" model for microselection (i.e., the evaluation and acquisition of materials on a per-title basis). Their text delineates a model developed by the collection development librarians at the University of North Carolina, Chapel Hill. While meant for academic libraries, their model possesses a high level of applicability to all selection decisions by:

- Identifying and defining the appropriate criteria;
- Displaying them visually to exhibit the relationship of the criteria to each other; and
- Incorporating a numerical rating system enabling the librarian to rank each title and, accordingly, align selection to available funds.

The model, which is adaptable (with minimal modifications) to any library type and material format, should provide greater precision and consistency to the selection process. It is comprised of two tables: Selection Criteria, and Selection Values. The latter is a numerical rating scheme to counter-balance the subjective aspect of selection and evaluation. The weighting of the criteria, which can be changed to reflect local emphases or truncated to indicate an intention of limiting certain types of materials, is based on perceived importance and permits stopping before completing the entire process. Instead of reproducing their model here in columnar format, the authors have summarized and interpreted it (below); readers may want to see their original table (Gorman and Howes' Table 1, p. 243). It shows six "Selection Criteria," listed in priority importance. The number of potential points for each selection criterion is also included in our summary as follows:

1) Subject--30 points
2) Intellectual content--25 points
3) Potential use--variable points
4) Relation to collection--variable points
5) Bibliographic considerations--variable points
6) Language (variable points)

The total number of points should be no more than 100 for each title. Titles receiving 67 to 100 points would merit a first priority, 34 to 66 points a second priority, and the rest a third priority.

The reader may notice in the discussion below that cost is not a selection criterion. Rather, Gorman and Howes point out (p. 241) that cost is a purchase criterion that can result in greater consideration for the selected title. Also, the criteria can be used to prioritize expensive titles. Within each criterion, their table shows criteria for first, second and third priorities as follows:

Subject: First-priority material directly supports programs or institutional emphasis, major field of scholarship or inquiry. Second priorities are "ancillary to programs, specialized topics, or minor fields." Third priorities are tangential to them.

Intellectual content: This criterion is concerned with how the selector relates the value of the acquisition to the literature. First-priority material includes key or seminal works, titles by key authors, major critical studies, substantial new contributions, etc. Second priorities include general essays, narrowly focused titles offering narrow intellectual perspectives, and popular treatments. Third-priority material includes raw or unedited material, marginal or polemical works, and trivial literature or propaganda.

Potential use: First-priority material includes works related to known research or program interests and patron requests. Second-priority works include general interest titles and those recommended by patrons without specific or immediate need. Third-priority choices may present problems of accessibility and infrequent use.

Relation to collection: This criterion is like the first (subject) but concerns the title's specific "fit" in the particular collection, not the entire universe of literature. First-priority items are central or closely related to the existing collections, provide specialized information about a central strength, or are necessary to the intellectual strength of the collection. These titles might fill in gaps, establish balance, etc., in the collection. Second-priority items develop the collection in these respects, while third priorities may complete serial holdings, sets, specialized material, or cooperative agreements.

Bibliographic considerations: These relate more to the reputation of the publisher and type, or format of publication.

First-priority selections are by distinguished, major trade or specialized publishers, significant sponsoring bodies, etc., while second-priority choices include popular and less significant publishers, and published dissertations. Third-priority materials include research reports, unpublished dissertations, working papers, or pamphlets.

Language: First-priority selections are in the major and working languages. Secondary choices offer treatment of local and national issues. Tertiary choices are peripheral to the topic and accessible to a small number of users.

The three levels of priority, according to Gorman and Howes (p. 242), are conditioned by the relationship of the title to the collection as follows:

- The title is essential and the first to be reviewed against available funding;
- The title is an important addition to the collection, and users would expect to find it; and
- The title is appropriate, albeit peripheral, in value to the collection and there is a possibility of use.

8. Format Guidelines
It would be virtually impossible to note every format included in a library somewhere. The following list, however, includes the more notable examples likely to be found in library collections:

- Books (hardcover, paperback, monographs, textbooks);
- Manuscripts and related archival material;
- Newspapers;
- Periodicals, conference proceedings;
- Government publications (local, state, federal, international, multinational);
- Pamphlets, broadsides, etc.;
- Printed music;
- Maps;
- Vertical file materials;
- Pictures, photographs, posters, framed art, postcards, etc.;
- Microforms;

- Slides;
- Audio recordings (cylinders, phonorecords, wire recordings, open-reel tapes, 8-track tapes, cassettes, compact discs, flexi-discs);
- Video recordings (3/4-inch U-Matic, VHS, Beta, 8mm, laserdiscs, VHS discs, CEDs);
- Films (8mm, 16mm, 35mm, 70mm);
- Filmstrips;
- Media kits (slides/filmstrips and audio format);
- Computer software;
- CD-ROM software;
- Realia (3-dimensional learning materials; e.g., games, specimens); and
- Collectibles, museum objects (e.g., matchbook covers, clothing fashions, political campaign buttons and stickers).

There are a number of criteria to consider in determining which formats to include in a collection:

- Space availability;
- Size of the materials budget ;
- Client needs; and
- The presence of high quality donor collections.

Some institutions prefer to concentrate on information require-ments, adding those formats that best fulfill these needs. In cases where the acquisition (and maintenance) of equipment is necessary for playback poses a problem, libraries may have to either pass on a given format or have the contents transferred to a more usable format (e.g., 78 r.p.m. discs to audiocassettes).

9. Selection Aids
Given the immense variety of materials available to library collection developers as well as the comparatively limited amount of time in which to carry out this operation, it is of paramount importance to utilize tools which identify and evaluate potential holdings. Gorman and Howes (1989, p. 248) delineate the major classes of selection resources as follows:

BIBLIOGRAPHIES

    (1) Evaluative:
        (a) Subject bibliographies: total or selective coverage;
        (b) Standard lists: current, retrospective, out-of-print;
        (c) Guides to the literature; and
        (d) Library catalogs.

    (2) Alerting:
        (a) National bibliographies;
        (b) Trade bibliographies.

REVIEWS

    (1) Guides: digests and indexes;
    (2) Journals:
        (a) General;
        (b) Subject specialist journals;
        (c) Library journals: official or commercial;
        (d) Specialist book selection journals;
        (e) Newspapers: tabloid or quality.

ADVERTISING

    (1) Display advertisements;
    (2) Direct mail; and
    (3) Advance notices.

To the above list could be added useful sources such as fanzines, publisher and jobber representatives, and mass media tie-ins. The latter category would include both treatments of a particular subject in more than one format (e.g., a book which adapted to film) and promotional appearances by authors, recording artists, film actors, etc., on radio and television talk shows.

    A wealth of selection aids can be found for any type and size of library. For example, Van Orden's text (1988) provides an inventory of commercially published sources nearly thirty pages in length geared largely to K-12 settings. The following list includes some of the classic titles which would be of value to virtually any library collection:

AUDIOVISUAL GUIDES

Media Review Digest. Annual. Ann Arbor, MI: Pierian, 1973/
1974 - . Provides approximately 60,000 citations from more
than 150 journals devoted to films, video tapes, and other
audiovisual formats.

Schwann-1: Record and Tape Guide. Monthly. Boston: Schwann,
1949 - . Includes "in-print" information for compact discs and
audiocassettes distributed in the U.S.

BOOK REVIEWS AND BIBLIOGRAPHIES--CURRENT

American Book Publishing Record. Monthly, with annual
cumulations. New York: Bowker, 1960-. Based upon U.S.
publication listings appearing first in the *Weekly Record.*

Book Review Digest. 10/year, with annual cumulations. New York:
Wilson, 1905 - . Includes excerpts of reviews to approximately
6,000 titles per annum.

Book Review Index. Bimonthly, with annual cumulations. Detroit,
MI: Gale, 1965 - . Each annual volume includes over 100,000
review citations to 60,000 titles; culled from some 460
journals (almost 400 more than those employed in *Book
Review Digest*).

Books in Print. Annual. New York: Bowker, 1948 - . Available
on microfiche, CD-ROM, and online as well as the print
format, the overall family of titles includes *The Publishers'
Trade List Annual* (a collection of publishers' catalogs,
available since 1873), *BIP--Author Index*, *BIP--Title Index*, the
Subject Guide to Books in Print (1957 -), one volume listing
publishers, and a mid-year supplement (some twenty
volumes in all). Includes all books distributed in the United
States

Cumulative Book Index. Monthly, annual cumulations. New York:
Wilson, 1898 - . Lists all English language books published in
the U.S. and Canada and selective others.

Fiction Catalog, edited by Juliette Yaakov. Irregular, with annual supplements. New York: Wilson, 1908 - . Lists fiction works recommended for public libraries, and features analytical annotations, sometimes including excerpts from reviews.

National Union Catalog. This series of publications includes pre-1956 imprints (London: Mansell, 1968 - 1980, 685 volumes; supplement, 1980 - 1981, 68 volumes); a 1956 - 1967 cumulation (Totowa, NJ: Rowman and Littlefield, 1970 - 1972, 125 volumes); and Library of Congress cumulations (Government Printing Office) covering 1968 - 1972, 1973 - 1977, 1978, 1979, 1980, 1981, 1982. LC covers 1983 to present in microfiche format. The various compilations cover the books issued within the designated time frame. The reported accessions of over 1,000 North American libraries are included. Formats other than books (e.g., 16mm films, filmstrips, phonorecords) have also been covered for varying periods of time. For more complete coverage of the various media formats, particularly during the past decade, librarians would be better served to consult either commercial bibliographies or the larger bibliographic utilities which document the reported holdings of participating institutions (e.g., OCLC, RLIN).

BOOK REVIEWS AND BIBLIOGRAPHIES--RETROSPECTIVE

American Reference Books Annual. Littleton, CO: Libraries Unlimited, 1970 - . Reviews of some 1,500 notable reference sources published during the past year.

Books for College Libraries. Irregular. Chicago: American Library Association, 1967 - . The compilation of over 50,000 titles is geared to support a basic undergraduate curriculum.

Children's Catalog. Irregular, with annual supplements. New York: Wilson, 1909 - . Lists some 5,500 titles deemed useful to school libraries and the children's departments of public libraries.

Elementary School Library Collection. Irregular. New Brunswick, NJ: Bro-Dart Foundation, 1965 - . A core collection of some 10,000 books, periodicals, audiovisual titles, etc.

Guide to Reference Books; Covering Materials from 1985 - 1990. Supplement to the Tenth Edition. Edited by Robert Balay. Chicago, IL: American Library Association, 1992. Annotated listing of notable reference tools; international in scope.

Junior High School Library Catalog. Irregular, with annual cumulations. New York: Wilson, 1965 - . A listing of about 4,000 volumes of value to students in grades 7 - 9.

Public Library Catalog. Irregular. New York: Wilson, 1934 - . A selective, classified listing of over 8,500 non-fiction titles.

Reader's Adviser. Irregular. New York: Bowker. Includes annotated bibliographies regarding the best books of the major subject fields.

Senior High School Library Catalog. Irregular, with annual cumulations. New York: Wilson, 1926 - . Includes over 5,000 titles appropriate for students in grades 10 - 12.

GOVERNMENT PUBLICATIONS

Monthly Catalog of U.S. Government Publications. Monthly. Washington, D.C.: Government Printing Office, v. 1 - , 1895 - . Index to federal documents processed through the G.P.O.

GPO Sales Publications Reference File. Bimonthly. Washington, D.C.: Government Printing Office. 1978 - . Microfiche index to federal documents and subscription services sold by the G.P.O.

GUIDES TO MICROFORMS

Dissertation Abstracts International. Monthly. Ann Arbor, MI: University Microfilms International, 1938 - . Cites doctoral dissertations deposited for microfilming with UMI by over 400 institutions (largely in North America). Also available in CD-ROM format.

Guide to Microforms in Print. Annual. Westport, CT: Microform Review, 1961 - . A listing of titles available for retail.

Microform Review. Bimonthly. Westport, CT: Microform Review, 1972-. Reviews of new microform releases.

National Register of Microform Masters. Annual. Washington, D.C.: Library of Congress, 1965 - . Covers foreign and U.S. books, pamphlets, serials, and foreign doctoral dissertations.

GUIDES TO SERIALS

IMS Ayer Directory of Publications. Annual. Fort Washington, PA: IMS Press, v. 1-, 1869 - . Current North American newspapers.

International Directory of Little Magazines and Small Presses. Annual. Paradise, CA: L.V. Fulton, v. 1-, 1965 - .

Irregular Serials and Annuals. Annual. New York: Bowker, v. 1- , 1967 - . Updated between editions by *Ulrich's Quarterly.* Covers non-periodical serials and international documents.

Katz, William A. and Linda Sternberg, eds. *Magazines for Libraries.* Irregular. New York: Bowker, 1969 - .

MLA Directory of Periodicals: A Guide to Journals and Series in Languages and Literatures. Biennial. New York: Modern Language Association of America, 1978/79 - . International language and literature serials.

Serials Review. Quarterly. Ann Arbor, MI: Pierian, v. 1-, 1975 - . Old and new serials.

Standard Periodical Directory. Biennial. New York: Oxbridge, v. 1-, 1963-. Includes North American periodicals and annuals.

Ulrich's International Periodicals Directory. Annual. New York: Bowker, v. 1-, 1932 - . Also updated by *Ulrich's Quarterly.* Current journals.

PAMPHLETS, LEAFLETS, ETC.

Vertical File Index. Monthly. New York: Wilson, 1923/34 - . Includes titles likely to be of value to libraries.

PERIODICAL REVIEW SOURCES

Booklist. Semimonthly. Chicago: American Library Association, 1905 - . Reviews books, audiovisuals, and selected documents.

Choice. Monthly. Chicago, IL: American Library Association, Association of College and Research Libraries, 1964 - . Focuses on scholarly or academic books likely to be considered by an undergraduate college library.

Kirkus Reviews. Semimonthly. New York: Kirkus Service, 1933 - . Coverage emphasizes fiction titles.

Library Journal. Bimonthly. New York: Bowker, 1876 - . Broad coverage of media (primarily books) relevant to all types of libraries.

School Library Journal. Monthly. New York: Bowker, 1947 - . Wide-ranging coverage of juvenile media titles.

Gorman and Howes (1989, pp. 249-250) advise subjecting those selection tools being considered for active use to the following tests:

- Why does it exist at all? What can it do that is not already done elsewhere?
- How well does it perform in its coverage of current publishing?
- What types of material are intentionally included and excluded?
- What types of material are likely to be excluded because of their very nature, not because of deliberate choice?
- What subject areas are included and excluded?
- What kind of information is offered about the works mentioned, and how much of it is offered?
- For whom is the tool itself intended--librarians, general readers, subject specialists?

- What is the physical format of the tool itself, in particular its availability in different formats, and the frequency of appearance? The format of the selection tool may bear no relationship at all to the formats of the works it covers.
- What is the pattern of the cumulations? Does each cumulation supersede the earlier cumulations, or must some be kept for specified periods, for instance, pending the arrival of an annual cumulation?
- How current is it?
- What is the form of the classification scheme used? If it differs from the customary Dewey Decimal Classification or Library of Congress system, what are the details of the differences?
- What are the rules for filing, and which subject headings are used?
- What special methodology should be employed in order to make best use of it?
- Which questions to emphasize will depend upon the particular characteristics of a given library collection?

Selection aids are employed at two stages in the collection building process:

- On a current, ongoing basis to identify and assess newly released titles; and
- Retrospectively, to determine those previously overlooked items which merit inclusion in the collection. Retrospective sources-- which consist largely of selective bibliographies either in book form or appended to survey periodical articles--not only act as a safety net in cases where the spotty coverage characterizing the review literature leads to the omission of worthy materials, but enable a library to make up ground after collection building objectives have been modified (e.g., the implementation of new courses/disciplines within a school curriculum).

10. Acquisitions Policies and Procedures

Evans (1987, p. 213) indicates that a library's acquisitions department, or unit, should have both library-wide and departmental or unit goals. The former include the following areas:

(a) Developing a knowledge of the book and media trade;
(b) Assisting in selection and collection development processes;
(c) Processing requests for items to be added to the collection;
(d) Monitoring the expenditure of allotted funds; and
(e) Maintaining all required records and producing reports regarding expenditures.

Internal goals, to paraphrase Evans (1987, p.214), typically include the following:

(a) Acquiring material as quickly as possible;
(b) Maintaining a high level of accuracy in all work procedures;
(c) Keeping work processes simple (thereby achieving the lowest possible unit cost; and
(d) Facilitating close working relationships with other library units as well as suppliers.

Both types of goals should be reflected in the acquisition procedures outlined within the collection development policy. The focus and breadth of such procedures may vary from one institution to another; however, most will touch on the following issues:

- Staff responsibilities (e.g., due to the structure and routine characterizing acquisition work, many tasks can be delegated to either technical assistants or clerks);
- Selection of an order source;
- Selection of an order method (e.g., firm order, standing order, blanket order, approval plan, gift, exchange);
- Use of a competitive bidding system;
- Physical preparation of an order; and
- Order routines, including the processing of requests, pre-ordering, order placement and receiving.

The "Technical Services" section of the Elkhart Public Library policy represents a written example of acquisitions procedures (Futas, 1984, pp. 363-364):

Preliminary order forms will be sent by Subject Specialists and Department Heads to Technical Services where the information will be typed on order forms. Orders will be compiled and sent to vendors. Technical Services will be responsible for filing order slips in the order the Selection Area immediately after the order is prepared in order to prevent duplication in ordering. Technical Services will clear invoices, process, and return leased books. Approval plan books and donated books will be placed in the Selection Area for consideration by selectors and will be either processed or disposed of by Technical Services after a specified period of time. Provisions may be made to hold books until reviews are available. Cancellations will be reported by Technical Services to the appropriate Subject Specialist who will initiate a reorder if desired. Books subject to withdrawal will be reported to the appropriate Subject Specialist so that orders ay be initiated before catalog cards are withdrawn. Time limits for these procedures will be set by Technical Services. Technical Services will maintain the Superintendent of Documents deposit account by keeping department ledgers, requesting transfer of funds, and placing orders received from Subject Specialists and Department Heads. Processing priorities will be as follows:

1) Patron requests;
2) Pre-publication orders (high demand books ordered through purchase plans such as Booking Ahead and the McNaughton lease plan);
3) Immediate needs (books for programs, booklists, media tie-ins, dated or seasonal materials);
4) Reference;
5) Standing orders;
6) Regular orders; and
7) Approval plans and donations.

11. Intellectual Freedom

This concept is, in actuality, reflected in many components of a policy; e.g., library collection and service objectives, responsibility for collection management, evaluative criteria, format guidelines, and acquisition procedures. The importance of intellectual freedom within a democratic society, however, renders it imperative that a portion of the policy be dedicated to:

- delineating the philosophy of the library regarding controversial material; and
- outlining procedures for handling complaints.

While some libraries have chosen to develop their own outlook on dealing with cases of censorship, documentation suggests that a greater number have opted for basing their stance on an endorsement of one or more policy statements developed by the American Library Association for this purpose.   ALA's core document is the Library Bill of Rights--in essence, an adaptation of the First Amendment to the U.S. Constitution to a library context-- first adopted by its governing council in 1940. Most of ALA's other policy statements represent further elaboration of concerns covered in a more general fashion by the Library Bill of Rights. "Standard" documents adopted by the American Library Association intended to express the particular concerns of a given institution are as follows:

- Free Access to Libraries for Minors;
- Administrative Policies and Procedures Affecting Access to Library Resources and Services;
- Statement on Labeling;
- Expurgation of Library Materials;
- Diversity in Collection Development;
- Evaluating Library Collections;
- Challenged Materials;
- Restricted Access to Library Materials;
- Exhibit Spaces and Meeting Rooms;
- Library-Initiated Programs as a Resource;
- The Freedom to Read;
- Intellectual Freedom;
- Policy on Confidentiality of Library Records;
- Resolution on Governmental Intimidation;
- Freedom to View (originally drafted by the Educational and Film Library Association's Freedom to View Committee).

A number of these are reproduced in Appendix B and, therefore, not also reproduced in Part Two of this book. ALA's *Intellectual Freedom Manual* (1983, p. 165) cites the advantages of having a previously agreed upon complaint procedure available:

... knowing that a response is ready and that there is a procedure to be followed, the librarian will be relieved of much of the initial panic which inevitably strikes when confronted by an outspoken and perhaps irate library patron. Also important, the complaint form asks complainants to state their objections in logical, unemotional terms, thereby allowing the librarian to evaluate the merits of the objections. In addition, the form benefits the complainant. When citizens with complaints are asked to follow an established procedure for lodging their objections, they feel assured they are being properly heard and that their objections will be considered.

The presence of a complaint form can play a key role in the re-evaluation of the materials process. Accordingly, ALA has adopted a complaint form which it encourages libraries and librarians to utilize.

Futas' book contains Thornton Community College's well delineated policy for handling complaints about controversial materials which bears citing (1984, p. 501); it reads:

Controversial Materials--Opinions may differ regarding the appropriateness of materials for any library. Resolution of conflicts between freedom of expression and information and the community's right to restrict certain materials' use is often a difficult task. In an attempt to ensure the rights of all parties, the LRC staff has established procedures for dealing with complaints against materials housed in the LRC for the use of its patrons. These procedures are in the *Intellectual Freedom Manual* (1983, pp. 501-502) as follows:

1) Any citizen of Thornton Community College District or any authorized representative of any organization whose main office is located within the political boundaries of the District may initiate a complaint challenging LRC materials considered objectionable, provided that the complainant has read, viewed, or audited the entire work being challenged. No complaint against passages taken out of context or based on partial examination of a work will be considered.

2) The complainant will be referred to the Director of Learning Resources as the first step in the challenge process. In the Director's absence, this step will be either postponed or referred to the Dean of Career Programs.

3) If the complaint is not resolved at this point, the Director will convene an ad hoc committee to review the work in question. The committee will consist of 1) LRC staff member(s), 2) faculty member(s) representing the subject area most closely related to the work in question, 3) the LRC Director (ex officio), and 4) student representative(s) selected through the Student Government Association.

4) The committee will review the complaint in an open meeting, making its decision by simple majority. The LRC Director will vote in case of a tie.

5) When the committee reaches a decision, a formal report will be given to the complainant, the President of the College, the Vice-President for Educational Services, and other interested parties. A copy will be filed in the LRC Director's office.

6) If the complainant disputes the decision of the committee, he/she may appeal to the Vice-President for Educational Services and/or the President. Final responsibility for resolving the matter rests with the Board of Trustees. No complaint form is required in the policy of the institution (Thornton Community College).

12. Weeding and Collection Maintenance

Weeding--defined by McGraw (1956, p. 270) as "the practice of discarding or transferring to storage excess copies, rarely used books, and materials no longer of use" --constitutes an important, albeit frequently underestimated and underemployed, aspect of the collection development process. Evans (1987, p. 292) recommends the approach to weeding, or "deselection," as it is often called, as follows:

Before a weeding program is implemented, an evaluation of library policies and goals must take place. This evaluation should also include analysis of the present situation, consideration of possible alternatives, feasibility of a weeding program in terms of all library operations, faculty cooperation, types of libraries involved, types of materials collected, and (a very important factor) cost. Some of the data for the weeding program should have come from the collection evaluation activities that the selection officers and others have undertaken on a regular basis. An active (i.e., ongoing) weeding policy should be part of the library's collection development policy. Selection and weeding are similar activities: first, they are both necessary parts in an effective collection development program, and second, both require the same type of decision-making rules. The same factors that lead to the decision to add an item can also lead to a decision to remove the item sometime later. Book selection policy will determine weeding policy.

The centerpiece of the written collection maintenance program should be a listing of weeding criteria. An excellent example of such a list has been compiled by the University of Wisconsin-Stout Library (Futas, 1984, p.74):

1) How important is this publication?
   a. Is it included in a general guide to reference works . . . ? [See *Guide to Reference Books*, p. 54.]
   b. Is it listed in a subject bibliography, produced either here or elsewhere?
   c. How is it rated by faculty members and subject specialists?
2) How comprehensive is this publication? Are its scope and depth such that it belongs in the reference collection?
3) Is the discipline one which requires a large group of reference works? If not, is this work truly essential, or is it a marginal one which could be sent to the general collection or be discarded?
4) What is the language of the publication? If it is not English, will its use be very light?
5) How frequently is this publication likely to be used in the future?
6) Is there a later edition which supersedes this publication? If so, what is the appropriate disposition for this and older editions?
7) How old is the publication? If it is an older work, is the subject matter such that current information is required by the vast majority of patrons?
8) Is the work a continuation? If so, should some or all of the older volumes be sent to the stacks?

9) Is the material in this work largely or entirely duplicated in other reference works? If so, does demand justify the duplication?

10) Are there multiple copies of this title in the reference area? If so are they justified by heavy demand on the publication?

11) Is the book badly worn, defaced, or otherwise in poor condition? If so, can it (or should it) be replaced?

12) Is the work principally a bibliography? If so, is its scope so narrow that it should go into the main collection (e.g., single-author bibliographies; highly specialized, technical or scientific lists)? Is it inappropriate for any collection?

13) Is the work (entry) complete? If not, should (can) the gaps be filled?

14) Do existing reference works cover current reference needs? Are there gaps in the information available that should be filled if possible?

The weeding section of a collection development policy will also often include an outline of procedures for the process. The Missouri Western State College Library (Futas, 1984, pp. 552-553) has assembled an extremely workable set of steps for carrying out this operation:

1) Go to the shelves with a book truck, a pencil and scrap paper.

2) Examine the items on the shelf to determine whether they fall into any one of several categories as follows:

   a. Out of date: Information is no longer accurate. Be sure to examine for special indices or other special materials perhaps unavailable elsewhere.

   b. Inappropriate: Material is either far too juvenile or too advanced for our student population.

   c. Later editions: There are later editions on the shelf which supersede the material in the earlier editions. Watch for classics in the field.

   d. Multiple copies: No more than three copies should be on the shelves except in the most unusual circumstances. For example, it may be wise for the library to have five copies of a particular critical work on Shakespeare because of its authority, but there is no need for five copies of a text in microbiology. A factor determining how many copies of a title should remain on the shelf would be the number of usages shown on the book card.

   e. Condition: A title may be pulled by you for either deletion or for repair or binding. Be sure you clearly mark which process you are suggesting for that title.

3) Return the books to be withdrawn to the office of the technical processes librarian. There they will be checked against standard bibliographies to determine whether they should be retained or deleted.

4) A two year period (from July to June) is available for completion of the task. At the end of that period the task is assigned to the library staff for completion.

13. Special Considerations

Each library will have a number of unique features which distinguish it from otherwise similar institutions. If these features have a notable impact upon the library's collection development process, they probably should be included within the policy. Consortial and cooperative agreements, special collections, and gift policies appear frequently now in collection development policies. Some examples are included below from Futas' (1984) work.

Special Collections. Alabama Public Library System (Futas, 1984, p. 455):

Alabamiana will be purchased regardless of merit. Old and out-of-print Alabamiana will be acquired when available and practical. Two copies of Alabamiana will be purchased: one for the Alabama Room and one for the circulating collection. The criteria to determine that a book is Alabamiana are that the author be born in Alabama, reside in the state at least five years or write the work(s) as a consequence of residency in Alabama; or that the book be set in Alabama or has at least one-third of the subject-matter dealing with Alabama. However, only one copy of a dissertation on an Alabama subject will be acquired.

Networking Agreements. The Tri-College Library's Acquisition Policy (Futas, 1984, pp. 491-492):

PURPOSE: The Tri-College University is a consortium consisting of Concordia College, Moorhead State University, and North Dakota State University. Its purpose is to provide a broader range of programs, more extensive facilities and a greater depth of resources for the students and faculties of the three institutions than would otherwise be available. The purpose of this policy is to serve as a guide to cooperation in collection development for the three institution libraries.

PHILOSOPHY: TCU Librarians recognize that cooperation in collection development will tend to result in an interdependence of the individual collections. However, in response to the dual economic realities of increasing materials costs and tightening budgets; in accord with accrediting agencies' recognition of "accessibility" as a factor in collection building; and in accord with assessment of the long range viability of the Tri-College University Consortium, the libraries agree to implement this program under the following provisions:

A. This collection shall not substitute for development of adequate individual collections based on the obligation to support curricular and user needs.

B. Cooperation shall be implemented through the TCUL Acquisitions Task Force, who are delegated the primary responsibility for collection development.

C. Task Force decisions shall be guided by the following considerations:
   1. The curriculum and user needs of the individual libraries.
   2. The selection and acquisition policies of the individual libraries.
   3. The existing identified strengths of the individual library collections.
   4. The cost, demand for, and accessibility to an individual item.

D. Within these guidelines, TCU Libraries may:
   1. Compare selections to be purchased for the purpose of reducing unnecessary duplication.
   2. Combine existing holdings of items (such as incomplete sets).

3. Contribute to purchasing for the completion of sets.
4. Jointly purchase specific items.

For academic institutions at least, providing materials for the students, faculty and other primary clientele of the parent institution is the foundation on which cooperative agreements rest. If all of the library's materials budget must be spent on "core" material, little or none of the library's budget will support consortial agreements. However, where two or more libraries in the same community have the same subject collecting objectives such as history or business, cooperative agreements can create more in-depth subject coverage to the benefit of the members. This is particularly true with respect to periodical subscriptions, expensive sets, microform collections, and materials that are expected to have less use even though they may be regarded as essential to own. Librarians intent on establishing cooperative agreements are advised to concentrate on subject collecting interests they hold in common with others.

Gift Policy. The donation of materials or money (earmarked for the collection) represents a potentially valuable means of augmenting the library's holdings. As with all good things, however, the library's acceptance of gifts assumes a number of possible pitfalls:

- The inherent temptation to lower selection standards because the donated materials haven't entailed the expenditure of funds;
- The care required in dealing with a benefactor who is likely to have an emotional attachment to the donated materials, an inflated idea of its value, and a desire to impose certain restrictions on the transaction; and
- The time and energy spent sifting through mountains of materials, many of which wouldn't meet the library's evaluative criteria.

If a library decides on a program of encouraging donations, then a gift section should be included within the policy. The above mentioned problems are likely to be diffused by including a set of policy guidelines governing both the conditions for accepting and disposing of gifts. Buis (1991, p. 10ff.) argues that the policy should include:

- Consideration of the library's present and future needs;
- Acceptability and disposition of gifts without restrictions;
- Appraisal responsibility;
- Tax implications;
- Information concerning gifts other than library materials; and
- Methods of acknowledging donations.

The gift release form ought to be central to such a program. An essential element of such forms is a statement such as the following:

I/We hereby give, transfer, and deliver all of my/our rights, title and interest in and to the property described below to the AnyName Library as an unrestricted gift, along with whatever literary rights I/we may possess to this property.

Dated this _____ day of _____, 19_____

_____
Signature

_____
Address

The library can include a statement saying that it "hereby accepts and acknowledges as an unrestricted gift the collection or item(s) described below and agrees to administer it/them in accordance with its established policies." There should be lines for the date and signature of the library director underneath this statement. The form should have space for a general description of the collection. If the patron includes a list of items, it should be attached and kept on file with the form for documentation.

The following gift statement (Buis, 1991, p. 11) covers the majority of points needed within a policy:

Kent Library welcomes the donation of books and other material for its collections provided the donated resources remain consistent with the policies and mission set forth in the library collection development plan. Although donated material is appreciated, it must be clearly understood that donated items will be carefully reviewed for their overall contribution to the library's mission.

It must be understood that donations are not necessarily "free." Processing costs in terms of material, computer time, and personnel, must all be weighed before placing a possible gift in the appropriate library collection. From the outset, if a gift is obviously not suited for the collection, the Collection Development Librarian will assist the prospective donor by discussing other possible alternatives for the material.

All accepted gifts will be acknowledged by the Library Director and become property of the library. In receiving such gifts, Kent Library accepts no responsibility for appraisal valuation. If, after careful review, the material does not complement the selection criteria for collection development or the mission of Kent Library, the library staff will deal with the gift in an appropriate manner. In the case of gifts which are added to the library collection, the material will be processed and treated as any item acquired through purchase. Examples of gift material which are likely to be cataloged and placed in the appropriate collection are the following:

- Material which naturally enhances the library's mission in support of the university curriculum;
- Local or state historical material;
- Material with research potential;
- High-use items; and
- Special Collection material.

Donated items which receive low priority for inclusion into the library collection are:

- Foreign language material which does not support the foreign language curriculum or substantially benefit individuals involved in the university's international studies program;
- Religious or spiritual literature with limited curricular or research potential;
- Older editions of monographs already in the stacks;
- Material considered duplicate copies of rarely used items;

- Genealogical material (usually referred to the local public library);
- Materials in poor physical condition;
- Literary materials by authors who are not identified in Kent Library's "Literary Author's List";
- Mass market paperbacks;
- Generally, critical material on particular authors whose works are not listed in the library collection;
- Material which is considered only "part of the whole" and there is little likelihood of receiving or purchasing the remainder of the series or set.

In the case of inappropriate material, once a gift becomes the property of Kent Library, the general procedure for handling the unwanted item is as follows:

1) Donate the gift to a Southeast Missouri public library, through the means of a newsletter to such libraries.
2) Donate the gift directly to the local library or other area public libraries as either an addition to their collection or for book sale material, e.g., genealogical material.
3) Gifts of periodicals and books may go into the library's duplicate exchange program: a cooperative enterprise between Kent Library, the Universal Serials and Book Exchange, and other libraries.
4) If the gift material is not accepted by either a Southeast Missouri library, the local public libraries, or duplicate exchange, then the item is discarded.

The library will not appraise gift items, and any appraisal information used by the donor for tax purposes is the responsibility of the donor. The library accepts no responsibility for the valuation of any gift resources and its actions will remain consistent with all laws and regulations involving library donations. At this writing, the Tax Reform Act of 1984 clearly dictates the responsibilities of the acquiring library and donor in all such transactions. Financial donations are accepted by Kent Library, subject to the policies and guidelines set forth by the university administration. For the majority of monetary donations, the library reserves the right to use the funds for planned purchases in collection areas of need.

Evaluation and Inventory. Any cooperative collection development agreements should be noted in a library's collection development policy. Readers will find several examples of libraries' policies that do so in Part Two: Fairbanks North Star Public Library, Hillsborough Community College, the Illinois State Library, and the National Library of Medicine.

In examining the policies of these libraries, readers should note that they use the RLG Conspectus, or an adaptation such as the Pacific Northwest libraries' (WLN's). The Conspectus was originally developed for and by the research libraries in the United States. Ferguson et al. (1988) should be consulted for definitions of the original codes and collecting levels. The codes generally are meant to describe the intent and intensity of the library's bibliographers, or order librarians, to acquire materials. A library's desired or existing collection level might range from no collection, or desire to collect (code 0), to exhaustiveness (code 5).

The Library of Congress Classification is used as the basic structure for coding a library's collection or collecting practices. Research libraries may assign values to as many as 7,000 call number classifications. Smaller libraries assign values to much broader call number ranges. A library using the Dewey Decimal Classification system, however, can use the same Conspectus codes.

An example of the latter is a research level university library supporting a strong doctoral program by buying every book, periodical, audiovisual, and CD-ROM, no matter what language, on a particular subject. In Part Two, the National Library of Medicine's policy comes closest to realizing this objective. As large as it is, the National Library of Medicine acknowledges its inability to assemble, on its own, a comprehensive, complete or exhaustive collection in just one broad subject. It presents strategies for identifying particular types of materials that it will collect and preserve and is worth reading for this aspect alone.

The Pacific Northwest Conspectus project, however, has modified the six original codes, 0 - 5, developed by the research libraries. The RLG's codes did not meet the needs of most of the Alaska and Pacific Northwest libraries which are mostly small to medium sized academic and public libraries. They developed additional codes (2a, 2b, 3a, 3b, and 3c), for instance, to adequately represent their collections in terms of "acquisitions commitment (AC)," "collecting goals (GL)," and "current level of collection strength (CL). Some libraries call these by different names, such as "Existing Collection Strength or ECS" and "Desired Collecting Intensity or DCI," as outlined by Wood (1992, pp. 6 - 7). These Conspectus codes and terms are defined in Illinois State Library's policy.

Readers should consult Forcier's (1988) article for more background information. Wood and Strauch's (1992) book and the article by Blake and Tjournas (1994) present advantages, disadvantages, and criticism that readers, librarians, library directors, and students should read before deciding whether to adopt the Conspectus as a collection development, collection assessment, or basis for cooperative collection development agreements.

Readers interested in cooperative agreements should also examine Illinois State Library's "Illinois Collections Analysis Matrix," or ICAM. The ICAM is an adaptation of the RLG Conspectus methodology for developing an online database. The policy of the National Library Medicine, a research and national library for biomedical literature, is included in Part Two, partly because it demonstrates how libraries cooperate in terms of building and preserving materials by subject (biomedical literature) at the comprehensive level.

14. Glossary

Collection development policies often employ terminology which is confusing to the reader, particularly non-library staff. Such terms vary from highly technical jargon and/or acronyms (e.g., AACR2, MARC, multimedia, technical services) to the vague application of words possessing a multitude of meanings (e.g., materials, resources, intellectual freedom, formats). If utilized within a collection development policy, these terms should be defined as to their specific application. In that digressions within the text would serve to undermine its effectiveness as a reference source, cross-references referring the user to a glossary might well represent the most effective means of supplying definitions as needed.

15. Appendices

Just as the clarification of terminology is perhaps best handled in a separate glossary, an appendices section containing key documents, forms, etc., might prove a useful addendum to a policy. The following items would represent typical inclusions within an appendices section:

- Applicable materials evaluation forms;
- A gifts policy handout for use by potential donors;
- A gifts disclaimer form;
- Any ALA documents adopted by the library as part of its intellectual freedom policy;
- A reconsideration of materials form;
- Any contracts concerned with cooperative acquisitions, resource sharing, etc.

16. Index

This option should only be considered in cases where a detailed table of contents is not present. Otherwise, the time and expertise required to both prepare and then maintain (as modifications to the policy are made) an index would appear to be prohibitive. It is important, however, to view the policy as a reference tool in that the majority of users will be consulting it in hopes of efficiently locating selected bits of information.

Policy layout and style

Attention to a number of physical layout features can greatly enhance both the attractiveness and utility of the policy. Points to consider should include:

- Utilization of a looseleaf notebook or similar flexible and easily expandable format will make replacing parts of policies easier. Such formats allow pages to be modified, added to, or deleted as necessary without affecting the integrity of the remaining text. When using this type of format, however, it is especially advisable to code each page with the page number, date, name of word processing file as to the most recent revision in order to better monitor ongoing updates.

- Liberal use of blank space in the margins as well as between paragraphs, sections, etc. The text should then look more appealing in addition to facilitating efficiency in efforts to locate and assimilate needed information.

REFERENCES

American Library Association. *The Intellectual Freedom Manual*, Second Edition, compiled by the Office for Intellectual Freedom, American Library Association. Chicago: American Library Association, 1983. p. 165.

Bartle, F.R. and W.L. Brown. "Book Selection Policies for Public Libraries," *Australian Library Journal*. 32:3 (1983) 5-13.

Blake, Virgil and R. Tjournas. "The Conspectus Approach to Collection Evaluation: Panacea or False Prophet?" *Collection Management*. 18 (3/4) (1994) 1-31.

Boyer, Calvin J. "Introduction to Selection Policies in American Libraries," In: *Background Readings in Building Library Collections*, Second Edition, edited by Phyllis Van Orden and Edith B. Phillips. Metuchen, NJ: Scarecrow, 1979. pp. 81-82.

Broadus, Robert N. *Selecting Materials for Libraries*. 2nd ed. New York: H.W. Wilson, 1981. Source material taken specifically from Chapters 3 ("Fundamental Principles of Selection"), 6 ("How to Judge a Book"), 14 ("Nonprint Materials: Nature and Use"), and 15 ("General Principles and Guides").

Buis, Ed. "Killing Us with Kindness or What to Do with Those Gifts," *Collection Building*. 11: 2 (1991) 10-12.

Callison, Daniel. "The Evolution of School Library Collection Development Policies, 1975-1995," *School Library Media Quarterly*. 19 (Fall 1990) 29.

Cassell, Kay Ann and Elizabeth Futas. *Developing Public Library Collections, Policies, and Procedures*. Series Editor: Bill Katz. New York: Neal-Schuman, 1991.

Curley, Arthur and Dorothy Broderick. *Building Library Collections.* 6th ed. Metuchen, NJ: Scarecrow, 1985.

Evans, G. Edward. *Developing Library and Information Center Collections.* 2nd ed. Littleton, CO: Libraries Unlimited, 1987.

Farrell, David. "Policy and Planning," In: *Collection Management: A New Treatise,* edited by Charles B. Osburn and Ross Atkinson. Greenwich, CT: JAI, 1991. pp. 60-61.

Feng, Y.T. "The Necessity for a Collection Development Policy Statement," *Library Resources and Technical Services.* 23:1 (1979) 39.

Ferguson, Anthony W., Joan Grant, and Joel S. Rutstein. "The RLG Conspectus: Its Uses and Benefits," *College and Research Libraries.* 49 (May 1988) 197-206.

Forcier, Peggy. "Building Collections Together: The Pacific Northwest Conspectus," *Library Journal,* 113 (April 15, 1988) 43-45.

Futas, Elizabeth, ed. *Library Acquisition Policies and Procedures.* Second Edition. Phoenix, AZ: Oryx, 1984. A survey of the contents of the complete policies of academic and public libraries included in this volume underscores this variance. The results of the survey are included in Appendix C.

Gorman, G.E. and B.R. Howes. *Collection Development for Libraries.* London: Bowker-Saur, 1989.

Katz, William. *Collection Development: The Selection of Materials for Libraries.* New York: Holt, Rinehart and Winston, 1980.

McGraw, H.F. "Policies and Practices in Discarding," *Library Trends.* 4 (January 1956) 270.

Oberg, Larry R. "Evaluating the Conspectus Approach for Smaller Library Collections," *College and Research Libraries.* 49 (May 1988) 187-196.

Van Orden, Phyllis J. *The Collection Program in Schools: Concepts, Practices and Information Sources.* Englewood, CO: Libraries Unlimited, 1988.

Wood, Richard J. "A Conspectus of the Conspectus," In: *Collection Assessment: A Look at the RLG Conspectus,* edited by Richard J. Wood and Katina B.Strauch. New York: Haworth, 1992.

PART TWO

COLLECTION DEVELOPMENT POLICIES
OF
ACADEMIC,
PUBLIC,
SCHOOL,
STATE,
SPECIAL
AND OTHER
LIBRARIES

CALIFORNIA STATE UNIVERSITY
Sacramento, California

CONTENTS

[Note: The Acknowledgments, Preface, Introduction, Library Selection/Deselection Policies, Appendices A-D, and Index have been omitted due to space limitations.]

Revised 1993,
Barbara Charlton, Editor

COMMUNITY PROFILE

California State University, Sacramento (CSUS), draws students primarily from California and other areas of the western United States. It is a multipurpose regional institution with a special responsibility to meet the educational needs of the people in north-central California. CSUS enrolls approximately 24,500 students which converts to a full-time equivalent (FTE) of 17,400. Eighty-five to ninety percent of enrolled students are California residents. Examination of other characteristics reveals the diversity of the student body. One-third of the students at CSUS attend part-time. Their average age is thirty years, while twenty-four years is the average age of full-time students. Over 2,000 international students from more than 100 countries attend CSUS with Vietnam, Mexico, and Iran especially well represented. Asian, African, and Hispanic American students are the three largest ethnic groups represented other than Caucasian. To address the educational needs of California's growing multicultural population, the University has developed a wide range of educational equity programs, including the College Assistance Migrant Program, the Minority Engineering Program, the Minority Enrichment Business Program, and the Faculty Mentor Program.

CSUS offers educational programs at the baccalaureate and master's levels. In addition to degree programs in the liberal arts, there are significant graduate professional degree programs in areas such as business, education, engineering, social work, and health and human services.

The Library's collections are developed primarily to support these academic programs and the special educational programs such as Extended Learning and the Open University which offer courses directed at special segments of the community. Library collection development is responsive to the academic, and to a lesser extent, the extracurricular needs of students, the teaching and research needs of faculty members, the work of university administrators, staff members, and governance bodies such as the Academic Senate, and members of the Sacramento community.

As the Capital Campus of the California State University system, CSUS has a special commitment to foster a strong, mutually beneficial relationship with the Sacramento community, including business, industry, government, and social and cultural institutions. Community users of the Library include members of the professions and the State Legislature, employees of public agencies and businesses, students enrolled in nearby institutions or in other postsecondary external degree programs offered in Sacramento, and students of local and regional secondary schools.

Access to both credit and non-credit courses without formal admission to the University is available to individuals of all ages, professions, and backgrounds through the University Office of Regional and Continuing Education (RCE). RCE administers a variety of programs, workshops, seminars, and conferences. These include special sessions, extension, certificate programs, and the Open University.

In addition to RCE, at the system-wide level the California State University is in the planning stages for Project DELTA (Direct Electronic Learning Teaching Alternative). This project is designed to meet projected enrollment demand for the 21st century through interactive electronic delivery of courses to remote users.

These [RCE] programs present a special challenge to the Library. Although books and other traditional library services are currently available only at the University Library, remote users with computer access and appropriate authorization are able to search EUREKA, the Library's computer catalog. At the present time there is not a mechanism providing document delivery service for books. Fee-based document delivery of periodical articles is available from CARL Uncover on EUREKA via FAX.

EUREKA is available on the Internet, an international computer network, thereby providing the potential for worldwide access to the California State University System Library collections.

RELATIONSHIP OF LIBRARY COLLECTION DEVELOPMENT
TO THE MISSION OF THE UNIVERSITY

(Indented text in this section excerpted from the University Mission Statement, CSUS Catalog 1992-94, pp. 9-10.)

California State University, Sacramento is a regional comprehensive public institution that is authorized to offer educational programs at the baccalaureate and master's levels, and, jointly with the University of California or approved private institutions, at the doctorate level. It fulfills related research and public service roles and maintains support services for students. The basic mission of the University is to preserve, communicate, and advance knowledge, to cultivate wisdom and encourage creativity, and to promote values ensuring the survival of humankind and improving the quality of life.

The University Library supports the mission and changing needs of the University through its programs and services. The Library selects, acquires, and manages its collection of books, serials, electronic information resources, and other library materials to support the broad educational mission of the University and to provide its large and diverse community of students, faculty, staff, and administrators with effective access to recorded information. Collection development directly supports the University instruction, research, and public service responsibilities which include curriculum-related instruction, extracurricular learning, research, and other campus and regional educational objectives.

The University offers undergraduate programs in the traditional liberal arts disciplines and in selected professional studies programs in business, education, engineering, and health and human services. Emphasis is placed on general education, which provides fundamental knowledge in areas of universal interest and applicability--natural sciences, social sciences, humanities and fine arts, as well as a solid foundation for a broad range of studies including pre-professional and professional programs.

At the graduate level, the University offers master's degrees and post-baccalaureate certificate programs. Major research centers based at the University inform its intellectual life and enrich its graduate programs. Our graduate programs prepare students to pursue doctoral studies, enter advanced professional training programs, and secure leadership positions in the workplace.

In building its collections, the Library acquires materials according to the priorities set forth in Presidential Memorandum 91-12, Instructional Program Priorities and Guidelines for Academic Planning, Resource Allocation, and Enrollment Management (July 1, 1991).

Library support for courses and programs that directly support and lead to the baccalaureate or master's degree in the liberal arts and sciences and professional fields, or the post-baccalaureate credential in fields of education, is a priority over courses and programs that are peripheral to these programs (e.g., minors, certificate programs, elective courses, centers and institutes, and intercollegiate athletics).

The range and depth of library materials required to support graduate programs are generally more extensive than for undergraduate programs. Primary rather than secondary source materials are typical. Library collections in support of professional school programs are developed to provide the strength necessary for the schools to meet all library related accreditation standards. In areas where certificate programs are offered, the Library's collections are tailored to support mandated requirements.

The University faculty's primary responsibility is teaching. They maintain direct and regular contact with students in all courses. Faculty enhance their teaching capabilities by maintaining currency in their fields and by engaging in independent scholarship and creative activity.

The University Library acquires materials in support of faculty and graduate student efforts to initiate and complete research for instruction and other purposes. The range and depth of the research collections are balanced in concert with other needs, especially undergraduate and graduate programmatic requirements. Through its other services, such as interlibrary borrowing, cooperative arrangements with other institutions, electronic access to information, and telefacsimile technology, the Library also facilitates access to research materials located at other institutions throughout the region, nation, and world. EUREKA, a computer catalog, replaced the card catalog in 1992. Qualified patrons can search EUREKA from their homes or offices.

The University is a regional resource that provides educational opportunities to a large geographic area through regional and continuing education and other off-campus offerings. We contribute to the cultural and economic development of the region.

The University Library supports all University external programs. Generally, this means facilitating access to on-campus library resources for participants in external programs. At times, the Library makes materials available directly to off-campus sites but can do so only under controlled and limited circumstances.

We encourage a vigorous exchange of ideas and resources with government, social and cultural agencies, and businesses and industries located within our region. University personnel promote the University's public service role through community service and the related tasks of an informed citizenry.

The importance of community support for the University and its Library has considerable bearing on the success with which the campus can carry out its mission and achieve its objectives. The Library continues to provide open access to materials in the collections. In building its collections, the Library attempts to acquire materials that serve the dual purpose of assisting our primary campus clientele and addressing the various interests of the regional community.

Our location in the State's capital makes us unique among California's public universities. We use this setting to advance the public good and to provide students and faculty with unequaled opportunities to be involved directly in public policy--

its formation, its implementation, its interaction with the private sector, and its linkages with public service.

LIBRARY SELECTION/DESELECTION POLICIES

RESPONSIBILITY FOR COLLECTION DEVELOPMENT

The primary responsibility for collection development and collection management rests with the subject-specialist reference librarians, although other librarians have collection development assignments within their areas of subject expertise. Subject-specialist librarians initiate orders for books, serials (including periodicals), and special-format materials. They are responsible for monitoring book approval plans, standing orders, and blanket orders linked to publishers and associations.

They also encourage the participation of teaching faculty in the development and management of collections. To facilitate consultation, academic departments are responsible for designating a faculty member to serve as a library coordinator. Faculty-library coordinators serve as liaisons to the Library, facilitating communication between the academic department and the appropriate subject-specialist librarian. Faculty-library coordinators serve as resource persons, alerting the subject-specialist librarians to curricular changes, faculty research interests, and new academic programs under consideration. They also channel departmental faculty requests for the purchase of materials to the subject-specialist librarian. Guidelines for faculty-library coordinators are reprinted in Appendix D, page 130.

The faculty-library coordinator's role is advisory. The responsibility for the balanced and coherent development of collections is that of the subject-specialist librarians, who work within the constraints of the library budget and under the general supervision of the Associate University Librarian for Public Services and Collections. [Librarian and departmental faculty-library coordinators are listed in Appendix D of CSU's policy.]

METHODS OF ACQUIRING MATERIALS

Library materials are either purchased or cost-free. Materials are purchased utilizing appropriate vendors and publishers. Purchased materials are acquired by firm orders to vendors or publishers, use of approval plans with vendors, blanket orders with publishers, and standing orders (including subscriptions) with vendors or publishers. Materials acquired at no cost are either gifts, free materials, or materials available from a depository program (government documents).

All materials are selected and/or reviewed for appropriateness by the subject-specialist librarians responsible for collection development. The Acquisitions Librarian determines which vendors to use and authorizes the placement of orders with vendors. Choice of vendor is determined by price discounts available, availability of materials, and timeliness of filling orders. In addition, all orders must be in compliance with state regulations; vendors and publishers must also comply with applicable legislative mandates. The Associate University Librarian for Public Services and Collections in conjunction with the Acquisitions Librarian and the subject-specialist librarians determine annual allocations for each subject area for the library materials budget, and monitor expenditures throughout the year.

COLLECTION LEVELS

Collection levels describe the relative size and nature of library holdings in specific subjects. The collection levels (below) are those recommended by the Collection Development Committee, Resources and Technical Services Division of the American Library Association in their *Guidelines for Collection Development*, Chicago, 1979, pp. 3-5. The levels are as follows: Comprehensive, Research, Advanced Study, Initial Study, Basic , and Minimal. These levels are used in the *Library of Congress Classed Profile* section. Present and desired collection levels are indicated. The full text defining each collection level is reprinted in the *Explanatory Notes*, preceding the Classed Profiles.

SELECTION CRITERIA

Intellectual Freedom
The CSUS Library collects a representative selection of materials on all subjects of interest to its users, including various opinions on controversial matters in the areas of politics, religion, and morals. No materials shall be excluded or withdrawn from the collection because of the race or nationality of the author(s) or because of the political, religious, or moral views expressed therein. The Library

will not allow any intrusion on this right by either majority or minority group interests. The Library subscribes to the policies set forth by the American Library Association in its Library Bill of Rights (1980), its statement on The Freedom to Read (Rev.1991), its Statement on Professional Ethics (1981), and the California Library Association's statement of policy on Intellectual Freedom in Libraries (1983). [These documents are reprinted in Appendix E [not included here]. The CSUS Library respects the intelligence and capability of its readers to distinguish persuasion from propaganda and proselytizing without library interference. (Adapted from CSU, Dominguez Hills *Collection Development Policy of the University Library*, 1980, Section II-D.)

Other Selection Criteria
  Support to the educational, research, and service programs of
    the University
  Strengths and weaknesses of the present collection
  Critical reviews/selection aids
  Demand by users
  Authority of author
  Accuracy
  Recency of data
  Adequate scope
  Depth of coverage
  Appropriateness
  Relevance to the community served
  Interest
  Organization
  Style
  Physical quality
  Special features
  Cost
  Inclusion in major indexes and abstracting services
  Inclusion in electronic information access services

CULTURAL DIVERSITY

The CSUS Library provides equal access to its collections, programs, and services. It is dedicated to serving the information needs of its diverse population and encouraging a multicultural understanding throughout the University community. Through its collections, resources, and liaisons with campus and community groups, and consistent with the basic mission of the University, the Library is committed to enhancing and strengthening the knowledge and appreciation of its users regarding the history, identity, contributions, and social conditions of diverse cultures. The preservation, collection, and dissemination of cultural materials, particularly as they relate to issues of race, ethnicity, national origin (with added emphasis on African American, Asian and Pacific American, Latinos, and Native Americans), gender, age, sexual orientation, human disability, and religion, have a high priority in the Library.

Goals of Collection Development
Through the acquisition of print and nonprint materials the Library endeavors to:

▸ Value the culture and language of its faculty, students, staff, and administration.

▸ Affirm the worth of diverse opinions, values, cultures, and people.

▸ Support the scholarly and research efforts in the areas of ethnicity, culture, race, pluralism, gender, age, sexual preference/orientation, human disability, and the history and origins of particular cultures.

▸ Help elucidate major concepts such as race, ethnicity, class, human disability, gender, age, sexual preference/orientation, and their influences upon the ways students think about themselves and approach issues and problems that confront their society.

▸ Support students taking courses on race and ethnic issues as part of their General Education Program requirements.

▸ Support the integration of the study of diversity into existing courses.

▸ Promote and support culturally diverse scholarship in higher education.

▸ Promote an understanding and collaboration among the different groups we serve where all individuals feel respected and where differences enrich the lives of all the members of the campus community.

CRITERIA FOR SELECTION OF MATERIALS
The criteria for selection of materials in areas of cultural diversity are similar to those used in other areas, for example, appropriate

audience level, language, effectiveness, currency, possible interdisciplinary application, equitable distribution of available budget, and filling of gaps in the collection. The Library strives to build a collection which reflects a diversity of materials, not an equality of numbers. Its policy reflects Article 2 of the Library Bill of Rights: "Libraries should provide materials and information presenting all points of view on current and historical issues. Materials should not be proscribed or removed because of partisan or doctrinal disapproval."

SELECTION AIDS FOR LIBRARY MATERIALS

Subject-specialist librarians routinely consult a variety of sources in order to select materials for the Library's collections. These may include standard library review sources such as *Choice* (for academic library audiences), *Library Journal* (for general and professional audiences), and *Science Books & Films* (for general and professional science audiences). Reviews for books, media, and software are also contained in subject-specific periodicals.

Publishers' brochures, promotional flyers, and other announcements are also used as selection aids. These sometimes serve as notification of the forthcoming release of a book and may include content and background information about the author. Small presses and out-of-print book dealers use this method of promoting their materials to libraries. Recommendations from faculty for titles within their area of expertise are encouraged.

A third category of selection aids includes bibliographies or subject-specific lists of materials which may be distributed by professional associations, libraries, or commercial publishers. These are particularly valuable in identifying well-known and reputable publications linked to specialized disciplines.

DESELECTION OF MATERIALS

In order to maintain a quality academic library collection, it is necessary to implement a process of deselection whereby irrelevant, outdated, duplicated, mutilated, or superseded materials are considered for removal. The goal of this process is to improve the quality of the collection as it relates to the support of the educational, research, and social mission of the University. Moreover, it frees shelf space which can be used for newly acquired materials.

Deselection is an essential responsibility of all librarians involved in collection development and is usually accomplished in consultation with teaching faculty. Ideally, deselection should not be done on a random, intermittent basis, but rather on a scheduled, graduated basis in conjunction with inventory control. However, given the broad scope librarians' responsibilities and the limited number of librarians, the current policy is to deselect on an intermittent basis.

As a rule, reference and special collections are given first priority for deselection, followed by other types of collections as time permits. A more desirable policy, and one that will be implemented as soon as adequate staff is available, is to pursue a regular, systematic deselection/inventory program in which criteria and procedures appropriate to each discipline are developed.

MATERIALS BUDGET ALLOCATION FOR SUBSCRIPTIONS

In recent years, significant price increases for subscription publications coupled with high inflation rates in the publishing industry have threatened to absorb an excessive portion of the Library Materials Budget. The Library Materials Budget is the amount of money allocated for books, periodicals (journals, magazines, newspapers), serials, subscriptions to online database services, maps, software, CD-ROMs and other electronic resources, media, and other library information materials. Expenses for these materials are carefully monitored and certain limits are established.

Periodical subscriptions are limited to a specific percent of the Library Materials Budget. The limit is adjusted each fiscal year to accommodate the recommendations of librarians and teaching faculty. Criteria for establishing the limit are: curricular relevance, faculty needs, and the assessment of current expenditures (inflation and price) for periodicals (including renewals and cancellations).

Suggestions for new periodical purchases are encouraged from teaching faculty and selected in conjunction with departmental faculty-library coordinators. Factors such as price, use, and curricular relevance are considered throughout the process.

The costs of other serial subscriptions, primarily loose-leaf services, annuals, and monographic series, are not limited in a formal way. However, titles are selected, retained, or canceled in an evaluation process similar to that for periodicals.

LIBRARY COLLECTION DEVELOPMENT POLICIES

PERIODICALS

The Library purchases periodicals (journals, magazines, newspapers) to support curricular and research needs. A select group of popular titles is purchased in order to provide for the general interests of the academic community.

Priority is given to those periodicals which are likely to be widely used and which are included in major indexes. When there is a well-documented need, the Library will attempt to acquire periodical backfiles.

The policy "Materials Budget Allocation for Subscriptions" establishes limits for periodical expenditures.

NEWSPAPERS

Newspapers are selected to include the major, nationally known newspapers of the United States, for example, *The New York Times*, *The Wall Street Journal*, and *The Christian Science Monitor*, as well as representative examples of regionally important titles. For California, the Library subscribes to local Sacramento newspapers such as *The Sacramento Bee* and newspapers from major metropolitan areas such as the *Los Angeles Times* and the *San Francisco Chronicle*. Because of budgetary constraints, and the availability of the extensive collections of the California State Library, lesser known California newspapers are generally not purchased. A high priority is given to the acquisition of indexes to newspapers held by the Library in order to facilitate their use.

Foreign and foreign-language newspapers are collected on a highly selective basis. Criteria considered are the extent of their reputation and influence, their usefulness to the academic community, and their relevance to the foreign-language programs.

Newspapers that are predominantly subject-oriented, such as literary, political, underground, or business newspapers, are acquired and processed as journals even though they are produced and distributed in newspaper format.

Microfiche or microfilm is the preferred format for backfiles of newspapers.

NEWSLETTERS AND CURRENT AWARENESS PUBLICATIONS

Newsletters and current awareness publications that specialize in summarizing timely information on specific topics, industries, legislation, grant monies, market conditions, and contents of journals are generally costly and/or ephemeral. Consequently they are carefully evaluated, and selection is limited to those that meet one or more of the following guidelines:

1) Are substantial publications with indexes or are indexed by commercial indexing or abstracting services.
2) Relate to the Sacramento area or California.
3) Serve a major industry or discipline.
4) Are internationally significant.

Newsletters that do not meet these criteria may be more appropriately purchased by academic departments and routed promptly to faculty members.

TEXTBOOKS

Because of frequent revisions, textbooks are acquired only if they are high quality materials which supplement the Library's permanent holdings and can be expected to remain significant over time. When needed in direct support of current teaching programs, they are requested primarily through reserve book lists. They are included in EUREKA, the computer catalog.

HOUSE ORGANS

Periodicals issued primarily for employees and customers by a business or other establishment presenting news of the firm and activities of the executives and employees--commonly known as house organs--are selected only if they represent major business enterprises located near or related to the Sacramento area.

THESES AND PROJECTS

The University Library obtains and provides access to all master's theses and projects completed and approved by the various departments and schools at California State University, Sacramento. CSUS theses and projects can be located via EUREKA, the computer catalog, by author, title, key word, and Library of Congress Subject Heading (theses completed through

1989), by author and department in the *Masters Theses & Projects 1950-1982* list, and from the Thesis Card Catalog located in the Humanities Reference Department. This catalog contains cards for most theses and projects through 1988 and for some in 1989. Supplemental booklets shelved nearby list theses completed after 1989 and are arranged by author and department.

CSUS theses and projects are shelved by author in the Humanities Reference Department.

Theses/dissertations from other universities will be acquired only on an exceptional basis. The reasons for this are (1) the authors are rarely established authorities, (2) the materials tend to be overly specialized, and (3) the quality is generally unpredictable. If a thesis/dissertation from another university fills a specific need unmet by other published materials, it may be considered for purchase.

DUPLICATE COPIES AND REPLACEMENTS

The purchase of duplicate copies of library materials is limited to those requested by faculty for use in the Reserve Book Room and those ordered by librarians because high use or replacement justifies more than one copy.

In recent years the high use of certain materials has resulted in unavailability, deterioration, and the increased theft and mutilation of library materials. In order to maintain basic library service, the acquisition of duplicate copies, both paper and microform, is necessary. In addition, for some periodicals, duplicate microform subscriptions save space and reduce the possibility of mutilation.

GIFTS

Books, Periodicals, and Other Library Information Materials, maps, computer software, media, etc., generally are accepted as gifts. Books donated in memory of specific individuals or purchased with gift book funds may be identified with gift bookplates. However, because library materials must be handled in a manner consistent with established library procedures, gifts with special conditions governing disposition are carefully reviewed. Materials not retained may be offered to other libraries, the general community, or sold in book sales such as those sponsored by the Friends of the CSUS Library. Retention is subject to the following criteria:

1) Relevance to the academic programs and mission of the University. 2) Relevance to the mission of the Library. 3) Appropriateness of content and format with regard to existing Library collections. 4) Potential usefulness. 5) Condition of material.

Gifts In-Kind

(Gifts not included in first paragraph.) The Library complies with the official California State University System Guidelines for Receiving and Crediting Gifts In-Kind (Presidential Memorandum #87-07). Gifts in-kind such as equipment, furniture, and paintings are desirable and acceptable. The Library retains the right to accept or decline gifts in-kind on an individual basis.

Value Appraisal

Appraisals for Tax Purposes. The Library is not in a position to assist individuals in estimating the value of a gift for tax purposes. Value appraisal for tax purposes is the responsibility of the donor.

Non-tax Related Appraisals. To ensure proper consideration of gifts that appear to have significant value, the Library may wish to establish value in advance.

ENDOWMENTS

The Library encourages and accepts endowments. A general endowment fund to which monetary gifts can be added has been established for the Library. Other endowments and gifts of money may include restrictions on expenditures, i. e., the purchase of specific materials, furniture, or equipment. Restrictions are acceptable providing they can be interpreted to be reasonably within the criteria noted above.

RARE BOOKS AND MANUSCRIPTS

The library will not actively seek rare books or manuscripts. However, if any are purchased to support the instructional programs or are accepted via gift or donation, the library will preserve the material through proper security and environment.

BOOKS WITH SOFTWARE

An increasing number of books acquired by the Library include accompanying software on floppy disk or CD-ROM disk. The floppy disks are in IBM-compatible, Macintosh, or Apple format.

At present most of the books which have accompanying software deal with topics in the sciences, technology, or the social sciences. The software complements and supplements the text with the following types of files: executable programs, programming languages, source code, tutorials, exercises, data, statistics, manuals, simulations, graphics, utilities, music, or macros.

The software may be freeware, shareware, or copyrighted. Users who check out books with accompanying software are responsible for compliance with stated license agreements and copyright laws. Users also assume all risks for any damage that might be caused by viruses which may be present on the disks. The Library does not scan such disks for viruses. The Library Systems Office archives the original copies of disks for replacement purposes in case of reported loss, theft, or damage.

The Library Software Collection computers in the Library Media Center (IBM clone, Macintosh SE, and Apple IIGS) are available upon request for the use of software which accompanies library books.

Whenever possible, records in EUREKA, the computer catalog, which describe books with accompanying software contain notes about hardware requirements.

ELECTRONIC INFORMATION SERVICES

The Library maintains an Electronic Information Service (EIS) to support the instructional and research needs of students, faculty, and staff. Through this service, mediated access is provided to hundreds of bibliographic, numeric, and full-text online databases. Direct access is provided to several bibliographic, numeric, and full-text databases available on CD-ROM and the Internet and to scores of library catalogs and campus-wide information systems on the Internet. These databases are produced by publishers, government agencies, and colleges and universities.

Hundreds of online databases covering all academic disciplines are available for mediated searching on a cost-recovery, appointment basis during regular business hours. Formats of publications indexed include periodicals, newspapers, government documents, microforms, books, dissertations, and nonprint media. Three systems (UnCover, LEXIS-NEXIS, and CitaDel) are available for free, direct access via the Internet whenever the Library is open. They provide coverage of periodicals and full-text sources in business, news, law, medicine, education, book reviews, and the academic disciplines in general. The Library contracts with various vendors to access online and Internet-accessible databases. Current contracts are with BRS, Dialog, DataTimes, STN International, Wilsonline, CARL/UnCover, Mead Data/LEXIS-NEXIS, and RLIN/CitaDel.

At present the Library offers free, direct access whenever the Library is open to a growing number of CD-ROM databases covering business, news, education, psychology, nursing, language and literature, government documents, and the academic disciplines in general. Current contracts are with UMI, Silver Platter, Information Access Company, Marcive, Bowker, NewsBank, and Behavioral Measurement Database Services. Scores of free databases produced by U.S. and international government agencies have been selected by the Government Documents Librarian. Providing additional access to these governmental databases is an on-going project.

An increasing number of library catalogs and campus-wide information systems are available for free, direct access via the Internet. These resources provide information on the holdings of academic and large public libraries around the world as well as many specialized, noncommercial databases. Local access is facilitated by a Gopher Information Client available on the campus network.

Contracts for commercial databases and systems are negotiated with vendors directly, via CLASS, or via the CSU Chancellor's Office. Electronic information services are selected in consultation with the Administrative Council, Public Service Unit Heads, and subject specialist librarians. Criteria used include the extent to which a new database or service enhances user access to information, improves the overall collection, or is relevant to the curriculum. In all cases it is the goal of EIS to ensure access to those electronic information services which are required to meet the educational mission of the University. Coordination of support, documentation, and training is provided by the Electronic Information Services Librarian.

A local area network and gateway via EUREKA, the computer catalog, have been implemented to enhance and maximize direct access in the Library to selected electronic information services. Direct access will be expanded to include network and dial-up users outside the Library and to hours when the Library is not open.

See the following document, Electronic Information Goals, for a statement of responsibilities the Library has identified that will provide access to a broad spectrum of information services and technologies.

ELECTRONIC INFORMATION GOALS

The CSUS Library's major responsibility is to provide access to the array of information services and technologies in support of the curriculum, independent learning, and research. The Library's Electronic Information Goals assume evolution towards a logical combination of traditional print resources, electronic formats, images, and sound. This emerging library will provide access to universal knowledge, without delay, at one's desk. To accomplish these goals, we must develop an intellectual understanding of the computer based environment as well as a hands-on, day-to-day effectiveness in applying this understanding to the information needs of the campus community.

- Offer an effective combination of electronic and print resources in the library.
- Integrate the use of electronic information resources into the curriculum in cooperation with the instructional faculty and the computer center.
- Network information from a variety of electronic formats, (including CD-ROM) to maximize both in-library and remote access.
- Evaluate redundancy among reference tools in all formats, including electronic, and modify collection practices as needed.
- Make library collections and services available to remote locations in order to support implementation of campus distance learning efforts.
- Offer mediated searches for the academic community. Target promotional efforts towards individuals doing research.

- Provide end-user electronic access to bibliographic, full-text, numeric, multimedia, and other types of information. Offer downloading and/or printing capabilities at all workstations.
- Use national and international networks such as the Internet. Provide library staff and users with those elements of the network that offer curriculum related information (e.g., databases, other Online Public Access Catalogs) as well as useful tools (e.g., e-mail, lists) in support of campus research and scholarly communication.
- Teach students to use electronic resources. Offer computer-assisted instructional methods to complement traditional approaches. Convert four library conference rooms into electronic multimedia classrooms to facilitate library instruction.
- Inform faculty about new sources of information by collaborating with faculty, holding workshops, and producing periodic news releases.
- Create an electronic information center that includes a staffed centralized location for end-user electronic services; library copying, faxing, scanning; software access; and an interactive classroom.
- Implement document delivery programs to various groups within the campus community.
- Analyze user needs with respect to types of information that fit well with HyperCard, expert system, and other similar technologies and implement such projects.
- Expand and promote the Software Collection.
- Pursue external support to supplement funding for electronic information access.

NETWORK-BASED MATERIALS

An increasing number of recently produced articles, serials, documents, and software are exclusively or initially available on the Internet. Announcements of the availability of network-based materials of interest to the Library and its clientele are frequently made via postings to electronic discussions groups (also known as electronic conferences or lists).

Much of this material is free and may be distributed without charge. Some material includes a statement of copyright or contains a request for proper acknowledgment. Some electronic serials require payment for subscription. Network access to commercial materials is increasing.

Usually this material is available on the Internet in either ASCII text file or binary file format. These files may be compressed and require decompression or "unzipping" to be used. They may also be coded for use with specific word processors, such as WordPerfect, or specific programs, such as HyperCard.

The most common method of acquiring such material for local access is via FTP (File Transfer Protocol), though electronic mail is also used. Local access may be either print-based or electronic-based. In the case of a document, the Library has the option to print it out and circulate it like a book or to provide electronic access via the local area network, electronic mail, or a public computer station. The Electronic Information Services Librarian is currently investigating access options for this type of material, as well as issues involved with its identification, selection, acquisition, cataloging, and archiving.

RECREATIONAL READING MATERIALS

In addition to purchasing materials directly related to the University's curriculum, the Library selectively acquires materials which provide users with a broad cultural background and which in some way may enhance their lives. The 1985 CS US *Student Life Study Report* stresses the University's commitment to all dimensions of student life.

These extracurricular materials are found throughout the Library's collections and include diverse subject areas, such as: popular fiction, popular biographies, sports and games, cookery, arts and crafts, and outdoor guides of local interest.

The Browsing Collection is a separate rotating collection of recent high-interest or popular titles. The subject-specialist librarians who select works which are popular, recreational, or leisure-oriented rely on standard reviewing sources as well as on user suggestions, local newspapers, and specialized bestseller lists such as "What They're Reading on College Campuses" in *The Chronicle of Higher Education*.

SHARING OF RESOURCES

The CSUS Library recognizes the fact that it cannot realistically hope to contain within its collection all the information necessary to satisfy the needs of all patrons. Therefore, the Library seeks to utilize the resources of other libraries and make our collection available to these libraries in return. Patrons may have access to other library collections through the following programs.

First, CSUS faculty and students can borrow directly from other CSUS campuses in California through the Mutual Library Use program. In addition, the CSUS Library has a reciprocal borrowing agreement with the University of California at Davis under which faculty and students have borrowing privileges at each library.

Second, the CSUS Library has a policy of encouraging patrons to use the resources of other libraries in the Sacramento area. They include the specialized libraries serving California state agencies (Resources Agency, Health Services, etc.); the California State Library which has strong documents, law, and California history collections; the Sacramento Public Libraries; and several medical libraries including the University of California at Davis Medical Center Library, the Paul H. Guttman Library of the Sacramento-Eldorado County Medical Society, Kaiser Permanente, and Roseville Hospital.

Third, through the interlibrary loan system, depending on availability, material will be requested from any library in the United States and, when feasible, other countries. Interlibrary loans are transactions in which library materials or copies of materials not owned by the CSUS Library are borrowed or faxed from other libraries for use by an individual. Limitations to this policy are:

1. The individual must be a CSUS student, faculty or staff member.
2. Requests per individual are limited.
3. Newspapers or manuscripts are available only in microform.
4. Periodicals, bound and unbound, are usually unavailable. Photocopies of single articles are available.
5. Audiovisual materials (sound recordings, slides, filmstrips, videotapes, photographs, film), software, expensive books with colored plates, fragile and/or oversized materials are usually not loaned.

6. Dissertations and master's theses are generally available by purchase only.
7. Although normally there is no charge for an interlibrary loan, some libraries impose a fee (for photocopies or loaning of books) which must be paid by the individual requesting the material.

The CSUS Library reciprocates by making its collection available to fill loan requests from other institutions.

CSUS is a member of the Mountain-Valley Library System. All members of this regional organization participate in reciprocal interlibrary loan and document delivery services.

Through its participation sharing of described above, the Library is able to provide access to a vast amount of to meet the information needs of the CSUS community.

SPECIAL AND FORM COLLECTION POLICIES
REFERENCE COLLECTIONS

Purpose

The purpose of this policy is to provide guidelines for the development and maintenance of the reference collections that support the library staff and users of our divisional reference departments.

Scope of Collection

The purpose of the reference collections is to make available resources, regardless of format, that provide information related to the curriculum, campus research, as well as other sources required for a university library. Reference sources are designed to be consulted or referred to for definite information rather than being read through. The contents are arranged to facilitate ready and accurate access. The CSUS reference collections contain the array of traditional reference tools such as encyclopedias, dictionaries, handbooks, almanacs, yearbooks, biographies, concordances, annuals, loose-leaf services, catalogs, bibliographies, directories, atlases, indices, etc. Also included are special files (e.g., pamphlets, annual reports), materials on microforms (e.g., telephone directories, college catalogs), and computerized sources (e.g., indices and information on CD-ROM format).

Responsibility

The responsibility for the selection and maintenance of the reference collections belongs to the heads of each department (Social Science and Business Administration, Education and Psychology, Humanities, Science and Technology) in coordination with the librarians responsible for selection in the various disciplines. Materials for the reference collections are selected on the basis of curricular need, reviews in library and discipline based sources, recommendations of California State University System faculty, and analysis by librarians. Selection criteria include consideration of the strengths and weaknesses of the existing collection relative to campus needs, author's reputation, topic currency, relative importance, date of publication, arrangement of the contents, relative cost of the publication, and language of the publication. Librarians study the typical library reviewing journals (*Choice, Library Journal, College and Research Libraries, Reference Services Review, RQ*, etc.) as well as publishers' leaflets and catalogs and the traditional reference book guides (e.g., Sheehy).

Language

For both general and subject reference works, priority is given to materials in English. Unique foreign language titles as well as foreign titles recommended by faculty to support the curriculum are also purchased.

Format

Hard bound editions are preferred over paperback editions except when a combination of use and cost dictates otherwise.

Duplication

Only the most important and frequently used sources are duplicated between reference departments, e. g., Library of

Congress Subject Headings, Ulrich's, encyclopedias, writing manuals, general indices of use to many disciplines, etc.

Weeding

The reference collections are constantly being evaluated as a routine part of collection development responsibilities. Periodically special weeding projects in specific areas are also performed. Old items that maintain permanent research value are kept in the reference collections. Other backfiles of annual publications are sent to the open stacks, some circulating and some noncirculating. General criteria considered in weeding include: the significance of the publication, its age and currency, the availability of later editions, its physical condition, and the duplication of the contents in more recent works.

ARCHIVES

The purpose of the University Archives is to provide the University with useful documentation of the people, policies, and events of its past. The primary patrons are officials of the University making use of the official records in their day-to-day work. Since the Archives is the repository not only for the official records of the University, but also for records generated by unofficial bodies affiliated with the University or its students, faculty or alumni, it also serves the persons involved in the work of these bodies. A growing use is made of the records in the Archives by persons other than officials of the University, mainly for historical and journalistic purposes.

It should be remembered that the University Archives does not collect in the same way as other parts of the University Library. It receives its materials entirely by deposit or gift. These materials are arranged in record groups--materials which are produced by a working office group or agency in the course of its normal operation, intended for its own use, and useful to others only incidentally. Since University Archives materials are normally used by these record groups, they are not arranged in a library classification system. In most cases, they are retained in the meaningful order in which they are deposited with some rearrangement as deemed necessary by the archivist. Monographs and periodicals that reflect the activity of the campus community are also retained. Records are by-products of activity, not the end product of the activity, and are consequently remarkable resources for discovery of the actual workings of an organization.

THE UNIVERSITY ARCHIVES COLLECTION CATEGORIES

Administrative Records
Includes minutes, reports, correspondence and other records of administrative offices, academic units, Academic Senate, and administrative and staff committees.

General Publications
Includes academic catalogs, class schedules, handbooks, announcements, directories, commencement and performance programs, research publications, University conference and symposium proceedings, newsletters, brochures, and ephemeral material.

Student Publications
Includes campus newspapers, yearbooks, miscellaneous periodicals, ephemeral materials, plus records of student administration and organizations.

Campus Publicity
Includes press releases, brochures, clippings, and other publications about the campus.

Support Group Records
Includes publications and records from support groups such as the Alumni Association, Hornet and Stinger Foundations, etc.

Master's Theses
One copy of all theses.

Pictorial and Visual Materials
Photographs and photographic negatives, slides, motion pictures, videocassettes, maps, microforms, art works, architectural plans and drawings.

Audio Materials
Speeches, events, oral interviews on audio- or videotapes.

Memorabilia
    Pennants, pins, block letters, etc.

SPECIAL COLLECTIONS—UNIVERSITY ARCHIVES

Special Collections are housed in the University Archives. Each individual collection has its own collection development guidelines which serve to define its collection boundaries and parameters. These guidelines are established in conjunction with the donor's deed of gift and the University Archivist or the Special Collections Librarian.

All materials in Special Collections are part of individual, named collections, which are housed as separate units. Each of these collections is valuable and important as a unit, giving added depth to or supplementing a curricular area of the University.

CSUS Special Collections currently include the following: Papers of former Congressman John E. Moss, former State Senator Albert Rodda, Sacramento Citizens Committee on Local Governmental Reorganization, Charles M. Goethe, Sacramento Peace Center, Women's Studies Collection, Port of Sacramento (Papers of Melvin Shore, 1st Port of Sacramento Director), the Papers of Assemblyman Phillip Isenberg (former mayor of Sacramento), and Randall Dickson's Folklore Archive.

The Oral History Special Collections include the Stanford Home, CSUS Oral History Project, California State Government Oral History Program, Social Welfare in California, Women Journalists, Japanese-American Florin Oral History Project, U. S. Department of Agriculture Forest Service, and the CSUS History Department Course 190 Oral Histories.

RESERVE BOOK ROOM MATERIALS

It is Library policy to place on reserve status all materials so designated by faculty members. If the material is not in our collection, it will be purchased or copied. The number of copies purchased is determined by the formula of one copy for every fifteen (15) students. There is no price limit. If a faculty member indicates that the material is available at the campus bookstore, it is purchased there, otherwise orders are processed on a "rush" basis by the Library Acquisitions Department.

In compliance with U. S. copyright laws, only one copy of copyrighted material will be duplicated for placement on reserve.

CALIFORNIA STATE AND LOCAL DOCUMENTS
Purpose

The Library collects, organizes, and catalogs in EUREKA, the computer catalog, all California state documents and provides brief permanent records in EUREKA for California local documents that support the educational, research, and service programs of the University. Provision is made for the needs of the community at large in accordance with our responsibilities as a selective California depository library as defined in the *California Government Code* sections 14,900-14,912. For example, the Library makes documents readily accessible and provides assistance in their use to qualified patrons without charge.

General Collection Guidelines

Language of Publication: California state documents are primarily in English, but a few Spanish materials are distributed by the California State Printer and are kept when deemed appropriate.

Chronologic Periods Covered: Emphasis is on current materials. The Library has been a selective California depository library since 1963. Retrospective materials are collected, whenever possible, to fill in the gaps in existing holdings or in response to specific requests.

Geographic Areas Covered: The California state and California local documents collections consist of California state, regional, and local documents. Regional documents emanate from regional government organizations, such as the Tahoe Regional Planning Agency and the California Manpower Coordinating Committee. Local documents come from city and county governments, and the emphasis of this collection is on documents from the city and county of Sacramento. When deemed appropriate, documents from other cities and counties are acquired.

Size
No restrictions are placed on size.

California State Library
The State Library Documents Section contains an extensive
California state documents collection. Its proximity to the
University provides a rich resource to California State
University System users who can either request state
documents through Interlibrary Loan or visit the library.
Since the California State Library does not collect local
county and city documents, the California State University
System Library relies on its own and surrounding library
resources, such as the Sacramento Public Library and the
County Law Library, for local Sacramento county and city
documents.

Types of Material
Treatment of Subject: The Library places no restrictions on the
subject of the collections. It receives all documents distributed
to selective depositories by the California State Printer and
acquires California nondepository documents from issuing
agencies. For Sacramento city and county documents, there is
an emphasis on collecting in the areas of business,
demography, energy, health, history, land use, and water
resources.

Forms of Materials: No restrictions are placed on the
format of material collected.

Reference Materials: Reference materials include materials
which provide information, such as statistical sources or
directories, and materials which facilitate access to the
collection, such as indexes and bibliographies. Both government and privately published compendia, handbooks,
directories, yearbooks, and indexes are examples of
reference materials.

Organization of the Collection
California state and local documents are classified in
Library of Congress and California state documents call

numbers. Both reference and circulating documents in the subject reference departments are arranged by Library of Congress call numbers. The California state documents stacks are arranged by California state call numbers. Regional and local documents are arranged by call numbers modified from the California state classification system. The Library also acquires local Sacramento city and county documents through a subscription to Greenwood Press' *Urban Documents Microfiche Collection*, which is located in Library Media Services.

Documents received from the California State Printer are processed for the documents collection. Exceptions to this policy are determined by the Documents Librarian and the subject reference librarians.

Selection of Materials

The Documents Librarian and the subject-specialist librarians are responsible for selecting material for the collections. Teaching faculty are encouraged to participate in selection.

Duplication

Duplication of material useful in the subject collections is appropriate, i.e., a statistical source such as the *California Statistical Abstracts* is duplicated in the subject reference departments.

Preservation

Government documents receive the same care as privately published material. Paper serials and monographic series are routinely bound as are nongovernment material.

Evaluation

Librarians regularly review, evaluate, and decide to or withdraw documents. The Library is required to retain material distributed by the State Printer for at least five years.

U.S. GOVERNMENT DOCUMENTS

Purpose

The Library collects, organizes, and catalogs in EUREKA, the computer catalog, publications of the federal government to support the educational, research, and service programs of the University. Publications of general interest, such as U.S. Congressional bills, Small Business Administration business guides, Social Security Administration handbooks, and the National Trade Data bank are also collected. The Library provides for the needs of the community at large in accordance with our responsibilities as a depository as defined in Title 44 of the *U.S. Code*. The public has free use of depository material and depository publications are retained for at least five years.

General Collection Guidelines

Language of Publication: Federal publications are primarily in English, but a few Spanish materials are distributed and may be selected where deemed appropriate.

Chronological Periods Covered: Emphasis is on current materials. We have been a designated selective depository library since 1963, and retrospective materials are collected as needed to fill in the gaps in existing holdings or in response to specific requests.

Geographic Areas Covered: No geographic restrictions are placed upon the collection. Special consideration is given to information relating to the western United States.

Regional Depository: As the regional depository for California, the California State Library receives a copy of each document that the Government Printing Office distributes and retains it permanently. The proximity of this collection allows the CSUS Library to tailor its collection to its own needs. CSUS documents users are able to obtain documents not at CSUS through Interlibrary Loan or by visiting the State Library.

Size

No restrictions are placed on size.

Types of Material

Treatment of Subject: The Library does not place restrictions upon the subject of the collection. In meeting the needs of the

University and the community, it collects approximately 33% of the publications which are available through the depository system. In selecting depository items, librarians select material from the sciences, social sciences, and humanities which meet the needs of the University curriculum. For nondepository material the Library subscribes to Readex publications in microfiche. Documents not in the depository or nondepository system are acquired individually as the need arises.

Forms of Materials: No restrictions are placed on the format of material collected. Formats include paper, microforms, maps, posters, and electronic or machine-readable.

Reference Materials: Reference materials include materials which provide information, such as statistical sources or directories, and materials which facilitate access to the collection, such as indexes and bibliographies. Both government and privately published compendia, handbooks, directories, yearbooks, and indexes (printed and automated) are examples of reference materials.

Organization of the Collection

Federal documents are classified in Library of Congress and Superintendent of Documents (SuDoc) call numbers. Both reference and circulating documents in the subject reference departments are arranged by Library of Congress call numbers. The federal documents stacks and microfiche are arranged by SuDoc numbers. Readex microprint cards are arranged by year and *Monthly Catalog* accession numbers.

Selected periodicals are not classed and are arranged in alphabetical order in the periodicals collection.

Documents received through the Depository Library Program are processed for the documents collection. Exceptions to this policy are determined by the Documents Librarian and the subject reference librarians.

Selection of Materials

The Documents Librarian and subject-specialist librarians select material for the collection. Teaching faculty are encouraged to participate in selection.

Duplication

Duplication of material useful in the subject collections is appropriate. For example, a statistical source such as the *Statistical Abstracts of the United States* is duplicated in the subject reference departments

Preservation

Government documents receive the same care as privately published material. Paper serials and monographic series documents are routinely bound as are nongovernment material. Microforms are kept in cabinets and segregated by type of microfiche, diazo or silver halide.

Evaluation

Librarians regularly review, evaluate, and decide to retain or withdraw documents. The Library is obligated by law to retain material distributed through the depository system for a period of five years.

INTERNATIONAL AND CANADIAN DOCUMENTS

Purpose

The Library collects, organizes, and catalogs in EUREKA, the computer catalog, international and Canadian documents to support the educational, research, and service programs of the University. The Library has been a selective depository for Canadian documents since December 1983.

General Collection Guidelines

Language of Publication: The Library primarily selects documents in English. International documents are also printed in other languages such as French and Spanish. Canadian documents are in English, French, or a bilingual format. Documents are selected in these languages as appropriate.

Chronologic Periods Covered: Emphasis is placed on current materials. Retrospective materials are collected as needed to fill in the gaps of existing holdings or in response to specific requests.

Geographic Areas Covered: No geographic restrictions are placed upon the collection.

Size

No restrictions on size. A Canadian selective depository library is required to retain all items.

Types of Material

Treatment of Subject: The Library acquires most non-copyrighted documents from main deliberative and subsidiary United Nations bodies on subscription from Readex. World Health Organization, Food and Agriculture Organization, UNESCO, copyrighted U.N. documents, and other intergovernmental publications are acquired through standing and individual orders.

International documents covering all subjects relevant to the curriculum are selected. These include, but are not limited to, the following: economics, geography, international business, international affairs, and sociology.

Canadian documents are selected to support academic programs on campus, including Canadian Studies. Subject areas emphasized are anthropology, business administration, economics, French, geography, politics, and sociology.

Forms of Material: No restriction is placed upon format.

Reference Materials: Reference materials include materials which provide information, such as statistical sources or directories, and materials which facilitate access to the collection, such as indexes and bibliographies. Both government and privately published compendia, handbooks, directories, yearbooks, and Indexes are examples of reference materials.

Organization of the Collection

International documents in paper are classified by Library of Congress call numbers and located in the appropriate reference departments. Readex United Nations microfiche are arranged alphabetically by U.N. agency, then by title. They are

shelved in microfiche cabinets located adjacent to the
Documents Department. Microcards are arranged like the
microfiche, except that they are stored in special boxes on
shelves next to the Documents Collection.

Canadian depository documents are classified and shelved
by the Canadian classification system in the Documents
Department stacks.

Selected periodicals are not classed and are arranged in
alphabetical order in the periodicals collection.

Selection of Materials

The Documents Librarian and subject-specialist reference
librarians are responsible for selecting material for the
collections. Teaching faculty are encouraged to participate.

Evaluation

Librarians regularly review, evaluate, and decide to retain or
withdraw documents. As a selective Canadian depository, the
Library is expected to permanently retain Canadian documents.
Exceptions to this policy are listed in the Canadian Government
Publishing Centre's *Depository Services Program*.

MEDIA (AUDIOVISUAL) MATERIALS

Responsibility for Selection of Materials

Media materials to support current academic programs are
selected in all subject areas by the Media Librarian, subject-
specialist librarians, and instructional faculty. For certain
selections, such as expensive items, it may be desirable to
consult with appropriate instructional faculty, and/or the
subject-specialist librarian, and/or University Media Service's
(UMS) personnel, and/or the Associate University Librarian for
Public Services and Collections.

Forms of Materials

1. Videocassette
2. Audiocassette
3. Compact disc
4. Videodisc (laser disc)
5. Slide/audio
6. Filmstrip/audio

7. 16mm film
8. CD-ROM

Technological advances may dictate expanding into other formats in the future.

General Collection Guidelines

The collection is developed on a selective rather than a comprehensive level. Emphasis is on selection of programs in videocassette format. The Library Media Center (LMC) will generally not duplicate those materials purchased for use in the Learning Skills Center on campus or the K-12 materials collected for the Curriculum Library in the Education/Psychology Reference Department.

Selection Criteria

Media selection criteria are similar to those used for book selection, for example, curriculum support, appropriate audience level, effectiveness, currency, possible interdisciplinary application, equitable distribution of available budget, and filling of gaps in the collection. Often, video titles are available for free preview. This aids decision-making since these titles are often costly. Additional considerations unique to this informational format are technical quality of the production (color quality, photography, graphics, etc.), sound quality, and compatibility with available hardware.

Videocassettes

Videocassette titles are obtained by: 1. Purchase from a commercial/educational distributor; 2. Licensing of programs copied off-air when such licensing is available; 3. In-house production, including Visiting Scholars; and 4. Gift.

In general, videocassette purchases require that the request be initiated by faculty and include names of colleagues who may also use the program and course numbers for which the program will be used. The Media Librarian may also select other well-reviewed titles to round out the collection, for example, in the area of cultural diversity. Some titles may be in a foreign language. All videocassette titles are requested to be furnished with closed-captioning, if available. The Media

Librarian may route advertisements to faculty and subject-specialist librarians seeking input to add newly released titles of which they might not be aware. Requests for purchase of current "feature film" titles in video format and best-selling fiction book titles on audiocassette are closely scrutinized. If a request for such items appears to have ample justification for instructional support, and if purchase will not cause an impact on the established use policies of the LMC, the Media Librarian may consider purchase. However, such purchases are the exception rather than the rule.

Telecourse Rights

Negotiations for, and funding of, the telecourse rights for any materials purchased for the permanent collection are not the responsibility of the LMC. Library-owned materials will not be released for such use unless a copy of the telecourse agreement accompanies the request. Materials in the LMC collection may not be used on campus as a fund-raiser or where any fee is collected from viewers and titles are not purchased for such intended purpose.

Other Media

Purchase of slide/audio, filmstrip/audio and 16mm film occurs infrequently and only at the request of faculty. Many of the titles in these formats have been re-released on videocassette or videodisc. When there is a choice, the preferred format is videocassette. The Media Librarian will ask the requestor if the preferred format is acceptable.

Audiocassettes and Compact Discs

Audiocassettes and compact discs are purchased not only by faculty request for instructional support, but also to provide some recreational listening materials for students, staff, and faculty. Programs may include classical music, popular music, and spoken-word. In addition, all presentations of the Visiting Scholars Program are recorded (with permission) by University Media Services, and an audiocassette recording is sent to the Library for inclusion in the permanent collection.

Gifts

Gifts in all formats are accepted with the understanding that the decision to include such material in the collection is the responsibility of the Media Librarian and, if necessary, the appropriate instructional faculty.

Replacements

A portion of the LMC materials (approximately is to replace damaged or worn out, high usage titles or to change formats (usually 16mm to videocassette).

Deselection

A deselection program for all formats is the responsibility of the Media Librarian in consultation with instructional faculty when necessary. The purpose of deselection is to maintain a collection which receives a high level of use, is not outdated in content, is still of good technical quality, and continues to support the current academic program. Deselected titles produced on campus are sent to University Archives. The Library Media Center strives to maintain a dynamic collection rather than an archival and historic collection.

MICROFORM MATERIALS

Microform is a generic term for any information storage medium containing images too small to read with the unaided eye. The selection of materials in microform rather than paper and/or the conversion of titles from paper to microform by academic libraries is increasing and is likely to continue to increase. Some of the reasons are:

1. To save storage space.
2. To reduce theft and mutilation.
3. To provide research materials that would otherwise be unavailable.
4. To increase availability, without waiting, of materials which otherwise might be in repair or at the bindery.
5. To reduce long-range costs.

This policy addresses: (1) formats, (2) types of materials suitable for selection in microform, (3) standards, (4) and bibliographic access. The of this policy is that it be used in conjunction with the appropriate selection criteria developed for each subject area. Selection of titles in microform is done by the subject specialists responsible for collection development. Selectors are encouraged to consult with the Acquisitions Librarian whenever a large collection, or a large number of titles, is being considered for purchase in order to coordinate planning for storage, equipment, and work load.

Forms of Materials
Microform collection formats include materials in microfilm, microfiche, microcard, and microprint. Selectors should consider only the purchase of microfilm and microfiche and of those, microfiche is preferred.

Types of Materials Suitable for Selection in Microform
Types of materials suitable for selection in microform are:

1. Materials available only in microform, e.g., back issues of newspapers, dissertations, out-of-print books and journals.
2. Materials which receive very heavy use in either hard copy or microform (e.g., college catalogs and telephone books) but which, if purchased in microform, provide more extensive coverage at less cost in a minimum of space.
3. Materials currently available in hard copy but which are subject to theft and mutilation, e.g., high use periodicals.
4. Scholarly journals which may be used infrequently, but have a high reference value; consider converting all but last 2-5 years to microform.
5. All new backfiles.
6. Duplicate copies of weekly news periodicals.
7. Duplicate sets of heavily used periodical titles.
8. Periodicals which present special problems in binding or handling, due to size or other format peculiarities.
9. Periodicals which lack special qualities of color, format, or printing.
10. Materials whose high cost would prohibit purchase in hard copy.

11. Periodicals which receive heavy usage because they are indexed in standard reference sources.
12. Materials whose chief function is to provide rapid, comprehensive and cumulative updating in a field (e.g., indexes and services), but which are available, manage-able, or affordable only in microform.

Standards

Nonarchival microforms (most of the Library collection) may be purchased as a diazo and/or vesicular product. Microform materials obtained for archival purposes should be a silver halide product. Microfilm should be purchased in 35mm only. Microfiche should not be larger than 4 x 6 inches in size nor of a higher reduction ratio than 48x, with 24x the preferred reduction ratio.

Bibliographic Access

Before purchasing large collections, it is recommended that subject-specialists determine whether or not bibliographic access tools are offered by the vendor as part of the collection. If commercial indexes are unavailable, purchase of the collection should not be considered.

SLIDE COLLECTION

The purpose of the Slide Collection is to make available 35mm slides for use by the faculty and students at CSUS. This collection is developed for and supports undergraduate and graduate instruction throughout the University, but primarily supports the School of Arts and Sciences.

General Collection Guidelines

Subject Matter: Subjects collected include, but are not limited to, art (historical and modern architecture, painting, sculpture, various decorative and minor arts), Western and Eastern civilization, history, sociology, anthropology, archaeology, ecology, costume, geography, theatre, dance, and world travel.

Language of Labels and Texts: Slides are mostly labeled in English. Foreign language textual material accompanying slides is not translated.

Chronologic Periods Covered: No restrictions.

Geographic Areas Covered: Subjects are worldwide in scope.

Forms of Materials
Slides--35mm color transparencies.
Printed--exhibition catalogs, scripts, printed material purchased or acquired with slides, and several basic art reference sources.

Selection Sources
There are no restrictions on sources. Slides are acquired from diverse publishers/organizations (including foreign), using the *Slide Buyer's Guide* (Visual Resources Association), and slide producers' and dealers' catalogs.

Selection Criteria
Relevance to University curriculum and programs.
Material in demand by faculty and students.
Material needed to strengthen the collection or to fill gaps.
Need to replace deteriorating slides.
Quality of slides. (See slide standards reprinted below.)

STATEMENT ON SLIDE QUALITY STANDARDS
Joint Art Librarians Society/Visual Resources Special Interest Group, College Art Association/Visual Resources Subcommittee on Slide Quality.

Color
The color should be as true as possible to the original work of art, neither over- nor underexposed, nor off-color due to the lighting or the film-type.

Film
The film should have fine-grained resolution, and color should be stable with a minimum shelf life of ten years. Duplicate slides should be newly printed as far as possible to maximize their shelf life. High contrast in duplicate slides should be controlled. The film should be clean with no dirt or scratches on the surface or duplicated onto the film from the master

transparency or negative. The size 24 x 36 mm is preferable; the supplier should indicate other sizes if used.

Photography

The slides must be in focus and full-frame as far as possible without being cropped. Lighting should be adequate and even throughout, and without glare or reflections. In photographing paintings and buildings, distortion should be avoided.

Information

Accurate and complete information is necessary: artist's full name, nationality and dates; title of the work; date and dimensions, if known; and location. Cropped slides should be identified as such, and details should be described. An indication of the orientation is important, especially on details and abstract works of art. It should be clear which is the front of the slide.

CURRICULUM COLLECTION

The purpose of the Curriculum Collection is to make available outstanding educational materials for preschool through grade twelve. This collection is developed and maintained specifically to support the undergraduate, graduate, and credential programs in the School of Education (See Supplement I appended to this policy), subject methods courses in other academic departments, and any other aspect of the University curriculum that may find the materials useful.

Materials selected for the Curriculum Collection represent a broad spectrum of viewpoints. Most clients are in the teaching credential program where the academic instruction prepares them to teach in a multitude of diverse circumstances. Being exposed to a wide variety of viewpoints is essential to enable them to form their own outlooks, while being aware of other valid beliefs. To this end, the fundamental principles advocated in the following documents (reproduced in full in Appendix E) are supported: The Library Bill of Rights (1980), The Freedom to Read (Revised 1991), and the Statement on Professional Ethics (1981) from the American Library Association; Intellectual Freedom in Libraries (1983) from the

California Library Association; and The Students' Right to Read (1982) from the National Council of Teachers of English.

Collection Guidelines

Curricular Levels and Subjects: The curriculum collection contains materials to support instruction from preschool through twelfth-grade levels; some materials may also be appropriate for adult basic education. Subjects covered include, but are not limited to: bilingual education, English as a second language, career education, handwriting, health, language arts, literature, mathematics, music, reading, science, social studies, spelling, and special education.

Language of Publication: The main language of the collection is English, although some materials useful for bilingual programs are available in selected other languages. Materials to teach foreign languages are also collected.

Chronologic Periods Covered: Materials are kept for approximately ten years, although special circumstances may require exceptions. A small collection of older California textbooks is maintained to provide opportunities to compare changing curricular styles and theories. Publications from local school districts and California state frameworks are retained forever.

Geographic Areas Covered: Emphasis is placed on materials published and/or used in the United States, with special interest in materials in use in California and the Sacramento region and materials about California.

Collection Formats

Textbooks: Textbooks are selected to represent all subjects taught in grades kindergarten through twelve. Textbooks in use locally are collected as comprehensively as possible (budget permitting), while California state-adopted textbooks (K-8) are collected selectively. A K-8 textbook not on the state adoption list or not in use locally is generally excluded unless purchase is requested by a faculty member or the item is unique and outstanding. Secondary textbooks are not adopted by the state, so selection decisions are based upon faculty request, local use, merit, and the need to cover a broad range of subject areas.

Curriculum Guides: The term curriculum guides is used loosely here to indicate courses of study, sample units, and teacher resource material not in textbook format. Curriculum guides for grades preschool through twelve are collected selectively except for local and California State Department of Education publications, which are collected comprehensively. Guides are in paper or microformat. In 1991 the Library negotiated with the Association for Supervision and Curriculum Development to be the depository for the curriculum materials displayed at their annual conference. Each year this outstanding collection consists of 400-600 recently published curriculum guides obtained from school districts throughout the United States.

Nonprint Media: Media materials for preschool through grade twelve instructional purposes are purchased very selectively. Formats include pictures, filmstrips, transparencies, slides, audiotapes, kits, simulation and other games, records, duplicating masters, and videotapes. At present, films are excluded (because of cost and equipment considerations). Equipment for previewing these materials is located in the Library Media Center. Media materials about instructional theory and methods or for teacher inservice are located in the Library Media Center.

Reference: Reference works covering curriculum materials are classified and located with the Education/Psychology Reference Collection, including *Textbooks in Print, and Audiovisual Marketplace*. Other reference works that support the Curriculum Collection are located in the Juvenile Reference Collection. Both reference collections are in close proximity to the Curriculum Collection.

Journals: Education and children's literature periodicals that discuss teaching strategies and review educational materials are collected, as are periodical indexes that provide subject access to this journal literature.

Computer Software: A representative collection of exemplary K-12 educational microcomputer software is collected as an integral part of the Curriculum Collection. This software collection is intended to provide opportunities for library users interested in the field of educational technology to familiarize themselves with the variety of educational microcomputer software programs available and to provide experiences in selecting and applying software for K-12 classroom use. In addition to the general collecting guidelines for subject and content discussed above, the following guidelines apply to software selection:

Software purchased must be compatible with computer hardware publicly available in the library. Operating systems necessary to run the software must also be available. Software purchased will fall within the following categories (in priority order):

Computer-assisted instruction (examples include drill-and-practice programs, tutorials, simulations).

Utility programs (such as newsletter and crossword generating programs).

Mini-authoring programs (menu-driven programs to enable teachers to create their own drill-and-practice programs).

Programming languages in common use at the K-12 level (such as Logo, Instant Pascal).

Entertainment programs, business/professional programs, or programming languages not relevant to K-12 teaching are excluded from this collection.

The Education Software Collection is housed in the Library Media Center in order to provide additional security and proximity to necessary equipment.

Collection Arrangement

Textbooks and media are classified in a modified version of the Dewey Decimal call number system. Grade levels appear as the last line of the call number. (In the case of high-interest, controlled vocabulary materials, interest levels are used instead of reading levels.) Media materials are indicated by use of the word "nonprint" preceding the call number. Curriculum guides are assigned accession numbers that begin with the subject area (e.g., Science 1732) and are shelved alphabetically by those subject areas, then numerically within each subject area.

Selection Criteria

Whenever possible, professional reviewing tools are consulted when making selection decisions. Selected titles are listed in Supplement III appended to this policy. The following criteria are considered when making Curriculum Collection decisions:

Strengths and Weaknesses of the Present Collection: This refers to subject, format, and learning style.

Demand by Users: This includes requests by subject as well as requests for specific items. Faculty requests receive special consideration and are purchased whenever possible. Requests by other users are also carefully considered.

Technical Quality: This refers to the quality of such features as binding, printing, sound, visuals, and arrangement.

Accuracy and Currency: Information presented should be as accurate and up-to-date as required by the subject matter.

Literary Values: Materials should foster appreciation of aesthetic and literary values.

Fairness: Whenever possible, information presenting all viewpoints on an issue should be provided, without bias. Controversial issues should be handled fairly.

Multicultural Awareness: The multicultural nature of today's society should be reflected in content and illustrations.

Educational Level: The collection should contain material for the advanced, average, and slow student. For individual items, the publisher's suggested grade level should seem appropriate to the content and approach of the material.

Overall Success in Meeting Educational Goals: Each item in the collection should function well as a whole to meet its expressed educational goals.

JUVENILE LITERATURE COLLECTION

The primary purpose of the Juvenile Literature Collection is to provide a collection of fiction and nonfiction written for children and young adults. It is developed and maintained to support courses and programs in the School of Education, the English Department, and other University courses in which juvenile literature is included in the curriculum. (See Supplement I appended to this policy.)

Unlike public library children's collections, this collection is intended primarily for adult use. Its purpose is to provide materials for student teachers learning to select appropriate reading materials for young people of different ages and abilities and to supplement textbooks at the elementary and secondary levels. It also serves researchers studying the development of children's books. (This collection is heavily used by the nonaffiliated segment of CSUS library borrowers. Although this has a significant impact on the collection, it is not one of its intended functions.) The wide variety of demands on this collection makes careful selection essential. A broad range of subjects and themes should be included at levels ranging from preschool through young adult. Also many viewpoints should be represented. To help accomplish this mission, the principles in the following documents (reproduced in full in Appendix E) are supported: Library Bill of Rights (1980), The Freedom to Read (Revised 1991), and the Statement on Professional Ethics (1981) from the American Library Association; Intellectual Freedom in Libraries (1983) from the California Library Association; and The Students' Right to Read (1982) from the National Council of Teachers of English.

Collection Guidelines

Age/Reading Levels and Subjects: The Juvenile Literature Collection includes materials for the age ranges of preschool through young adult. Depending on the level of difficulty, some materials of interest to young adults are not included in the Juvenile Collection, but are cataloged instead in the Library's main collection.

Subjects: All subject areas are represented in the nonfiction collection, especially those areas emphasized in the K-12 curriculum, such as the natural and applied sciences, history, and biography. Fiction titles include examples of a variety of genres and literary styles and represent a broad spectrum of themes and cultures.

Language of Publication: The main language of the collection is English, but examples of the literatures of foreign countries are represented, including material in French, Spanish, German, Chinese, and Vietnamese. This supplements the foreign language teaching materials in the Curriculum Collection. Unfortunately, in recent years funding has not permitted acquisition in this area.

Chronologic Periods Covered: Because the collection is used for research and for the teaching of literary criticism, it is important to provide materials from a broad time span. Selected reproductions of early works are purchased at faculty request and a few older materials are retained in order to facilitate comparisons.

Geographic Areas Covered: Although publications from the U.S. dominate the collection, works from foreign countries are included as examples of cultures throughout the world. Regional history materials are also sought.

Authors/Illustrators: Representation from a wide variety of authors and illustrators is emphasized.

Special Considerations: Current curricular needs require strengthening the Juvenile Collection in the following areas: high-interest/low vocabulary books, books about festivals and holidays, up-to-date material on foreign countries, science activity books, and examples of folk and ethnic literature.

Collection Formats
   Picture Books: Picture books are purchased as examples of the
   work of illustrators, for use in storytelling, and for use with young
   children.

   Fiction: Fiction titles are purchased for all levels, from picture
   books to young adult novels. An effort is made to collect stories
   that represent nontraditional role models and settings. Novels
   with more mature themes that could appeal to both young adult
   and adult readers may be placed in the Library's main
   collection at the discretion of the librarian responsible for
   collection development.

   Nonfiction: The scope of the nonfiction collection covers all
   subjects at all levels, but emphasis is placed on acquiring
   supplementary material for subjects taught in the K-12
   curriculum: the sciences, U.S. and California history,
   biography, other cultures and countries, drama, poetry, folklore.

   Reference Materials: The focus of the Juvenile Reference
   Collection is on materials used by students researching
   juvenile literature and developing thematic units which
   include fiction and nonfiction titles for young people.
       The majority of titles are bibliographies and guides to the
   literature. A few outstanding examples of reference materials
   for use by children are included (World Book, Childcraft), but
   these are exceptions.
       There is also a reference collection of all Newbery and
   Caldecott, and California Young Reader Medal award winners.
   Since the Juvenile Literature Collection is used by researchers
   and others studying children's books as a form, the reference
   collection is extensive.

   Nonprint Materials: The Juvenile Literature Collection is limited
   to printed sources.

Collection Arrangement
   Juvenile fiction, including picture books, is arranged
   alphabetically by author (via assignment of a Cutter number
   based on the author's name). The nonfiction and reference

collections are arranged by the Dewey Decimal Classification System. Books are not arranged by grade level and no indication of grade or reading level is made on the item. Oversize (q) books are interfiled with the rest of the collection.

Selection Criteria

The Juvenile Literature Collection is a teaching collection. In order to be effective for that purpose, it is important that a wide range of examples be included to illustrate the selection criteria that follow. The vast majority of the collection consists of the best in children's literature, but examples of controversial works and flawed or unsuccessful children's books have been included. Professional reviewing sources are consulted when making selection decisions. (A list of these titles appears in Supplement II later in this policy.)

General Criteria for Selection

1. Literary and aesthetic quality, including plot, style, setting, and characterization. Format and effectiveness of illustrations are also considered.
2. Strengths and weaknesses of the present collection.
3. Accuracy of content and presentation, including the presence of indices, glossaries and bibliographies.
4. Appropriateness of the topic and its treatment for the intended audience.
5. Quality of binding, printing, and layout.
6. Promotion of respect for the environment and for all living things.
7. Acknowledgment of the worth and contributions of all people and cultures.
8. Fairness and absence of bias when dealing with controversial topics.
9. User demand. Faculty and student requests will be honored when possible; other user requests will be carefully considered.

Additional Considerations

Local Authors: Works by faculty authors are purchased, and works by other local authors are carefully considered.

California History: Demand for this material is great; every effort is made to acquire all titles on this subject which meet the stated selection criteria.

Series Books: The usual practice is to select series titles on an individual basis unless all volumes are of outstanding merit or are dependent upon one another.

Controversial Works: Examples of controversial books are included so that students can obtain exposure to them.

Abridgments: Abridged versions of classics are purchased only at faculty request or if the book in question is judged to be outstanding in its own right.

Awards and Prizes: Funding limitations preclude automatic purchase of every award-winning children's book. Reference and circulating copies of all Newbery and Caldecott award winners are purchased, as are nominated and selected winners of the California Young Reader Medal titles. Other award-winning books are regularly reviewed for purchase and, depending upon collection needs and selection criteria, may be purchased.

SUPPLEMENT I

Courses/Programs Supported by the Juvenile Literature Collection

ED TE 103.0	Tutoring Children (typically 5 sections)
ED TE 120.1	Literature for Children
ED TE 146.1	Sex Role Stereotyping in American Education
ED TE 224.5	Children's Literature: Models and Teaching Strategies in the Elementary Classroom
ED TE 286.0	Literature for Adolescents
ED TE 321.2	Teaching of Reading
ED TE 321.4	Language Arts in the Elementary School
ED TE 383.1	Teaching Reading in the Secondary School
English 115A	Core Studies, I
English 115B	Core Studies, II

English 125   Studies in Applied Language, Literature, and
                   Composition

Other required courses for majors in the Education, English,
and Liberal Studies programs may require use of children's
books, as do methods courses for all the Single Subject
Credential Waiver Programs. The master's level Reading
Program also is supported by this collection.

SUPPLEMENT II

Especially Useful Review/Evaluation Sources

Children's Literature
Reference Books

Best Books for Young Adults. Annual. American Library
   Association. Young Adult Services Division. (Ref Juv A5127b)
The Best Science Books for Children. American Association for
   the Advancement of Science. (Ref Juv 028.5 W8557b)
Building a Children's Literature Collection. Association of
   College and Research Libraries, American Library
   Association. (Ref Juv 028.5 Q64b)
Children's Books. Annual. Library of Congress. (Ref Juv 028.5
   U585c)
Children's Books of the Year. Annual. Bank Street College.
   Child Study Children's Books Committee. (Ref Juv 028.5
   C5367s)
Science Books and Films. (Ref QZ 7401 S323 Index Area)

Periodicals

Booklist
   "Notable Children's Books"--March issue
   "Best Books for Young Adults"--March issue
   "High-Interest/Low Reading Level Booklist"--June issue
Center for Children's Books Bulletin
English Journal
Horn Book Magazine
Interracial Books for Children Bulletin

Language Arts
   "Teacher's Choices"--March or April issue
Library Journal
Reading Teacher
   "Children's Choices"--October issue
School Library Journal
   "Best Books"--December issue
Science and Children
   "Outstanding Science Trade Books for Children"--Spring issue
Social Education
   "Notable Children's Trade Books in the Field of Social Studies"--
   April or May issue
Wilson Library Bulletin

SUPPLEMENT III

Periodicals; Documents

Many review and information sources are useful when selecting instructional materials. Included are periodicals, books, and government documents. Below is a selected list of these publications.

Periodicals

American Biology Teacher
Arithmetic Teacher
Art Education
Arts and Activities
Childhood Education
Computing Teacher
Curriculum Review
Dramatics
Electronic Learning
English Journal
History Teacher
Journal of Home Economics
Journal of Reading
Language Arts
Mathematics Teacher

California State University

Media and Methods
Media Review Digest
Reading Teacher
Roeper Review
School Science and Mathematics
Science and Children
Science Teacher
Social Education
Social Studies
VocEd

Documents
California. Curriculum, Frameworks, and Instructional Materials
Unit. *Standards for Evaluation of Instructional Materials with Respect to Social Contents.* (Ref LB1584 C35 1986)
California. State Department of Education. *State Adoptions, Instructional Materials for Grades Kindergarten through 8th.* (Curriculum Text 372 cal K-8)

MAP COLLECTION
The purpose of the Map Collection is to make available awide assortment of individual maps for use by the faculty and students at CSUS. This collection is developed for and supports undergraduate and graduate instruction throughout the University.

General Collection Guidelines
Subject Matter: About half of the collection is devoted to U.S. topographic maps with complete collections for California, Oregon, Washington, Nevada, Arizona, and Hawaii. They show natural features and certain land developments, such as roads and cities, according to a set of conventional symbols, mainly contour lines. The remainder of the Map Collection consists of a broad variety of thematic maps such as geologic, physical, navigational, political, economic, social, and historical.

Language of Publication: The primary language featured on the maps is English, although many foreign languages are represented throughout the collection. In some cases, certain maps are only available in a foreign language, usually German.

Chronologic Periods Covered: Maps cover most historical time periods although no attempt is made to maintain a historical collection of maps for a specific geographic area.

Geographic Areas Covered: No restrictions. Special areas featured include Sacramento, the San Francisco Bay area, and California.

Forms of Materials: Maps vary by size and scale. While the vast majority are printed on paper, some maps are represented as relief maps on plastic. There are also a few globes. Usually maps printed on single sheets are acquired, but occasionally sets in booklet or folder form will be selected. The majority of the maps are stored flat in map cases. Folded maps, generally road maps, and those in envelopes, such as physical maps, are stored in file cabinets. Large-size maps (generally 3 x 3 or larger) are mounted on wooden dowels and hung from the ceiling as hook maps. A few maps are permanently hung in the map room and used for reference purposes (for example, Sacramento, San Francisco, California, and the United States).

Related Collections: The atlas collections within the Social Science and Business Administration Reference Department and the Science and Technology Reference Department are a necessary complement to the Map Collection. Gazetteers, cartobibliographies, directories, dictionaries, and other geographical references also form a useful complement to the Map Collection. The Collection Development Policies for these sources are covered in the specific subject areas.

Selection Sources

There are no restrictions on sources. The Library receives some series of maps from the U.S. Geological Survey, the Central Intelligence Agency, and other agencies through the Government Printing Office Document Depository Program. A similar arrangement exists for California state agencies. Maps appearing in *National Geographic* as well as those published as parts or supplements to monographs or series are kept in the Map Collection. Maps are also acquired from diverse publishers and organizations (including foreign) and map producers' and dealers' catalogs.

Selection Criteria
- Relevance to University curriculum and programs.
- Maps in demand by faculty and students.
- Maps needed to strengthen the collection or to fill gaps.
- New maps needed to replace those that have deteriorated.
- Quality and cost of particular maps.
- Time and cost of processing maps into the collection.

SOFTWARE COLLECTION

The Library maintains a software collection which provides on-site access to a variety of educational software of potential use in classrooms, elementary through university level.

Most of the software titles and all of the documentation do not circulate outside the Library and may not be copied. Access is provided via an IBM-XT compatible, a Macintosh SE, and an Apple IIGS located in the Library Media Center.

The types of software in the collection include: tutorials, simulations, educational games, datasets, bibliographic file managers, paint programs, and public domain software (which does circulate). The majority of the titles are Apple format and intended for use by elementary students and teachers.

Selection of software is done by subject-specialist librarians in consultation with teaching faculty and the Electronic Information Services Librarian. EUREKA, the computer catalog, includes records which describe the titles in the collection.

PAMPHLET FILE

Maintenance and selection of materials for pamphlet files was ranked as a Priority III activity in the California State University System Library Educational Priorities document drawn up in the Spring of 1993. As a low priority activity the following guide-lines will dictate pamphlet files within the California State University System Library:

Guidelines
1. Pamphlet files, if maintained, will be placed only in the four library subject departments: Humanities, Science,

Education and Psychology, and Social Science and Business Administration.

2. The heads of the subject departments, in consultation with the departmental subject-specialist librarians, will decide whether or not to maintain a pamphlet file.

3. If a department decides to maintain a pamphlet file, a librarian or librarians will be designated to select, weed, and support a subject index to the pamphlet file. The department's library assistant(s) will provide support for this activity.

4. Maintenance of pamphlet files will not be systematic nor will any routine ordering of materials be done (from the *Vertical File Index*, *Public Affairs Inormation Service.*, etc.). Materials processed for pamphlet files will be ephemeral, peripheral, or marginal publications. Requests to be placed on mailing lists for free materials may be done at the discretion of the subject-specialist librarian or librarians, but no materials will be purchased for the pamphlet files.

Selection

Criteria for inclusion of ephemeral, but valuable, materials in a pamphlet file are the following:

1. Materials should support the curriculum and have no other restriction on subject matter as mandated by the California State University System Library's adherence to the intellectual freedom documents reprinted in Appendix E, pp.131-140 [not reproduced as part of this policy due to space limitations].

2. Printed materials should be relatively short in length and have soft-cover binding.

3. Types of materials included may range from newspaper clippings to printed scholarly reports.

Deselection

It is recommended that the designated California State University System librarian(s) weed the pamphlet collection when their time allows and they judge weeding to be necessary.

LIBRARY OF CONGRESS CLASSIFICATION PROFILES

Explanatory Notes for Library of Congress Classed Subject Profiles

The subject profiles are organized by the Library of Congress Classification as recommended in the *Guidelines for Collection Development* (Collection Development Committee, Resources and Technical Services Division of the American Library Association, 1979, p. 6). Classes inapplicable to CSUS Library collections are excluded, and classes are expanded where necessary to more clearly reflect collection development practices.

Degrees/Programs/Clientele

This section specifies degree, or degree specialization, programs (Appendix A lists CSUS degrees and programs) and other user needs supported by the Library (research, instructional, recreational, general information, reference, etc.). Special clientele are described.

Collection Levels--Present and Desired

The present and desired levels toward which collection development should be directed to reflect changing interests and courses are indicated in the appropriate boxes. One of the following levels has been selected: comprehensive, research, advanced study, initial study, basic, and minimal. These collection levels were adapted from those recommended by the *Guidelines* cited above (pages 3-5). The full text for each is reprinted below:

Comprehensive level. A collection in which a library endeavors, so far as is reasonably possible, to include all significant works of recorded knowledge (publications, manuscripts, other forms) for a necessarily defined field. This level of collecting intensity is that which maintains a "special collection"; the aim, if not the achievement, is exhaustiveness.

Research level. A collection which includes the major published source materials required for dissertations and independent research, including materials containing research reporting, new findings, scientific experimental results, and other information useful to researchers. It also includes all important reference works and a wide selection of specialized monographs, as well as an extensive collection of journals and major indexing and abstracting services in the field.

Advanced study level. A collection which is adequate to support the course work of advanced undergraduate and master's degree programs, or sustained independent study; that is, which is adequate to maintain knowledge of a subject required for limited or generalized purposes, of less than research intensity. It includes a wide range of basic monographs both current and retrospective, complete collections of the works of more important writers, selections from the works of secondary writers, a selection of representative journals, and the reference tools and fundamental bibliographical apparatus pertaining to the subject.

Initial study level. A collection which is adequate to support undergraduate courses. This level includes a judicious selection from currently published basic monographs (as are represented by *Choice* selections) supported by seminal retrospective monographs (as are represented by *Books for College Libraries*); a broad selection of works of more important writers; a selection of the most significant works of secondary writers; a selection of the major review journals; and current editions of the most significant reference tools and bibliographies per-taining to the subject.

Basic level. A highly selective collection which serves to introduce and define the subject and to indicate the varieties of information available elsewhere. It includes major dictionaries and encyclopedias, selected editions of important works, historical surveys, important bibliographies, and a few major periodicals in the field.

Minimal level. A subject area in which few selections are made beyond very basic works.

Language of Publication
The language of publication in which materials are collected is indicated with preferences and depths of collecting, conditions for exceptions, and any excluded languages noted.

Chronologic Periods Covered
Major periods are emphasized. Significant restrictions, limitations, and exceptions are noted.

Geographic Areas Covered
Locations or countries emphasized and significant exceptions and exclusions are noted.

Notes on Forms of Materials
If there are limitations in the various forms of materials collected, they are described here.

Comments
Includes notes regarding further refinements or limitations on collecting policy, such as unique aspects of a subject collected, period or area qualifications that are not expressed in other sections, and any other factors pertinent to the particular collection. If a subject is interdisciplinary, the other contributing disciplines plus joint purchase or special selection arrangements are described.

Librarian Subject-Specialists
The librarian subject-specialists responsible for collection development within the Library of Congress classes listed in the profiles are identified by their last names at the end of the Comments section. Consult Appendix D for a list of librarian and faculty-library coordinators.

GUIDELINES FOR FACULTY-LIBRARY COORDINATORS
Three key factors promote the successful growth of library collections and services to meet the instructional and research needs of this campus: funds, collection development and reference specialists, faculty input.

As the Faculty-Library Coordinator for your area, the advice you give and the action you take will affect both the usefulness of the collections and the development of services necessary to meet campus informational needs. In addition, the liaison role that you assume for your colleagues forms a vital communication link to the Library so that their needs are addressed and their advice heard. Traditionally, the Coordinators have focused on ordering books and periodicals. While helpful, this activity neglects the other valuable contributions that faculty can make to the more general aspects of collection building:

1. Identify new and significant scholarly trends.
2. Report important shifts in the curriculum.
3. Comment on the usefulness (e.g., essential, obsolete, of questionable value) of collections and formats.

Each semester your library counterpart will schedule a meeting to discuss these aspects of collection development with you. You will also be able to discuss other areas of interest. As librarians we offer a variety of services from electronic access to information to library instruction programs. These are geared toward the development of information problem-solving, use of the Library, and research skills.

Vast resources are at your fingertips. How we help you and your colleagues will be at least partially determined by the type and quality of input that you provide to your library counterpart. The time you take now will reap benefits in the future.

APPENDIX E

[The documents listed below comprise the appendix but are not included here due to space limitations. They are reprinted from the following publications: California Library Association. Intellectual Freedom Committee. *California Intellectual Freedom Handbook; A Manual for California Librarians*, Third Edition. Sacramento, CA: The Association, 1992.]

American Library Association:
    Library Bill of Rights (1980)
    The Freedom to Read (Revised January 16, 1991)
    Statement on Professional Ethics (1981)

California Library Association:
  Intellectual Freedom in Libraries (1983)
National Council of Teachers of English:
  The Students' Right to Read (1982)

A MISSION AND GOALS STATEMENT
FOR THE UNIVERSITY LIBRARY

The mission of the University Library is to develop, manage, and maintain the library collection; provide access to, and instruction in, the use of the collection and any other information resources needed to support the educational programs and public service role of the University.

Goals

Collection:

* support the curriculum based on the level and types of degrees and programs offered, and the size and character of the student body.

* be organized in such a way as to make access to all the materials manageable for users; maintained in usable physical condition; and ensure a secure environment for the collection.

* support faculty research and professional development.

Services:

* provide patron access into the building sufficient hours per week to accommodate the information and study needs of the users in convenient and attractive surroundings which provide adequate and safe reading, study, viewing, and listening space.

* provide reference services which are available in response to users' needs for assistance and accurate information.

* develop computer-based access to information and resources as part of the broadening of the Library's role as an information center.

*   make available, through cooperative relationships with other libraries and agencies, information resources which are not part of the Library collection.

*   provide faculty and students with orientation to the Library and its resources and services, as well as library instruction in the use of the collection, whether print, nonprint, or computer based.

*   promote and advocate the use of the Library to support curriculum assignments and to develop life-long skills in the use of information.

*   support the University curriculum by providing adequate access to resources and equipment at remote learning sites.

Administration:

*   encourage and support professional development and continuing education for library personnel.

*   encourage and support library personnel in active involvement in University community activities.

*   provide state-of-the-art technology for library personnel to assist them in meeting the goals of the Library.

*   secure funding sufficient to meet the staffing, materials, and equipment needs of the Library.

HILLSBOROUGH COMMUNITY COLLEGE
Learning Resources Program
Tampa, Florida

I. MISSION AND GOALS STATEMENT
[Library's statement is not duplicated here.]

A. **Programs Offered**

Hillsborough Community College offers an Associate in Arts Degree (university transfer) and an Associate in Science Degree (career training). College Credit Certificate Programs are offered which provide about a year of concentrated study in specific vocational areas.

A wide variety of non-credit classes, such as computer training, business, environmental, and arts and crafts, are offered at HCC campuses and at sites around the county.

B. **Subject Areas to Support Programs**

All students who are in the Associate Degree programs must complete general education requirements in Communications and Humanities, Mathematics and Natural Sciences, and the Social Sciences. These core courses are supplemented by other academic and technical training courses to fulfill the requirements of each discipline. All special programs and non-credit classes have their unique needs which are also supported by the College.

C. **Variety of Formats for Learning**

The Libraries/Learning Resources Centers (LRC) at Hillsborough Community College provide resources to complement all the programs. These resources are in many different formats such as books, videos, microform, compact discs, films, slides, and online systems. The Libraries strive to keep as current as possible with the most up-to-date informational resources.

II. COLLECTION DEVELOPMENT POLICY

A. Intellectual Freedom Statement

1. The Library Bill of Rights—[not duplicated here, see Appendix B.]
The Library Bill of Rights adopted by the American Library

Association is the foundation upon which library collection development is based. The main thrust of this statement is that "libraries should provide materials and information presenting all points of view" and that libraries should challenge censorship.

2. Freedom to Read Statement--[see Appendix B of this book.] The Freedom to Read is a joint statement by the American Library Association and the Association of American Publishers. It is a basic statement on free expression and censorship as they pertain to libraries. The statement has seven points used by libraries to provide materials that "make available the widest diversity of views and expressions" and to provide materials that "enrich the quality and diversity of thought and expression."

3. Intellectual Freedom Statement--[not duplicated here] This statement uses as its basis the First Amendment to the United States Constitution, freedom of expression, to reaffirm the American Library Association's The Freedom to Read statement. The Intellectual Freedom Statement fosters support for the academic community through all legitimate means in defense of intellectual freedom.

B. Professional Library Standards
1. Southern Association of Colleges and Schools (SACS) Criteria for Accreditation--[not included in this book.] Hillsborough Community College is fully accredited by the Southern Association of Colleges and Schools (SACS). These Criteria state that the institution must have sufficient materials to support the institution; that materials must be well organized; that librarians, teaching faculty, and researchers must share in collection development; and that the institution must have a collection development policy.

2. American Library Association (ALA)/American College and Research Libraries(ACRL)/The Association for Educational Communications and Technology (AECT) Standards--[not included in this book.] These standards from the American Library Association and approved by ACRL and AECT apply specifically to two-year or three-year academic institutions

awarding an associate degree or certificate. Standard Six applies to library collections and addresses collection development policy, selection, scope of collection, weeding, reference collection, institution publications, and organization.

C. **Statements on the Copyright Law**
Hillsborough Community College adheres to the provisions of the U. S. Copyright Law and related guidelines, and has established an Administrative Rule (6HX-10-3.010) Copyright Law Compliance [not included in this book] and Administrative Procedures (3.500-3.509) Copyright Compliance [not included in this book] regarding compliance by college employees and students.

D. **Interlibrary and Intralibrary Cooperation**
At the request of patrons, as defined by Section E. Library/LRC Clientele, HCC Libraries/LRCs borrow from other libraries those materials which they do not own. This occurs in two ways. The first is to obtain the material from another HCC Library/LRC (intralibrary circulation). The second is to obtain the material from another library outside of HCC (interlibrary loan). Interlibrary loan is accomplished through the co-operative agreements and procedures as outlined by the Florida Library Information Network (FLIN), and by the Tampa Bay Library Consortium (TBLC). Both intralibrary circulation and interlibrary loan activities consume labor and material resources.

The use of material resources through these activities affects collection development. For instance, if a Library/LRC finds that a particular item is borrowed frequently by patrons through intralibrary circulation, or interlibrary loan, a purchase may be indicated. Conversely, if a circulating item is rarely used, it may be more suitable to obtain future editions of this title through intralibrary or interlibrary loan.

E. **Library/LRC Clientele**
The Libraries/LRCs provide students, faculty, staff, and administration with organized collections of print and non-print materials. These resources support the institutional and instructional requirements of the college, as well as the

individual needs and interests of its students. As a service, the Libraries/LRCs of HCC provide the community access to HCC collections.

F. Selection
HCC Librarians use the professional literature and other appropriate sources to identify and requisition resources in support of current and anticipated patron needs. The literature and sources allow Librarians to systematically determine the quality, value, and usefulness of those items selected for the collection.

1. Legal Authority
Administrative Rule (6HX-10-3.018) Selection and Disposal of Learning Resources Materials [not included in this book] and HCC Administrative Procedure (3.302) Disposal of Learning Resources Materials [not included in this book].

2. Responsibility
Librarians have the task of determining what materials the patrons want or need and are responsible for the scope and content of the collections. Therefore, the responsibility for coordinating and recommending the selection and purchase of library/learning resources materials rests with the Librarians.

3. Recommendations
The Librarians' most valuable assistants in the selection of materials are members of the teaching faculty. Input should be encouraged with the understanding that all recommendations must be approved by the Librarians before purchase and that budget constraints may limit the number of items that can be purchased.

Consideration will also be given to recommendations from administrators, staff, students, and members of the community. If it is determined that the materials are appropriate for the collection and if the budget allows, the materials will be recommended for purchase.

4. Selection Guidelines
HCC Librarians subscribe to levels 1, 2 and 3 of a 6-tiered ranking system to guide them in considering the depth and scope of the HCC collections. These 6 levels are:

Level 0–Out of scope; no holdings in the collection and nothing bought.

Level 1–Minimal level; only a few items in the library collection.

Level 2–Basic information level; highly selective collection that introduces and defines the subject and indicates varieties of information in it.

Level 3–Instructional support level; collection supports undergraduate or graduate-level course work and sustained independent study. This level is further divided into initial and advanced study.

Level 4–Research level; the library's collection contains materials necessary for dissertations and independent research.

Level 5–Comprehensive level; collection is exhaustive in a few, limited areas.

a. General Criteria
The Libraries/LRCs of HCC use the following criteria in selecting materials for their collections:

(1) Materials shall support and be consistent with the mission and goals of the College.
(2) Materials shall support the curriculum and cultural interests of the College community.
(3) Materials shall meet high standards of quality in factual content and presentation.
(4) Materials shall be appropriate for the subject area and for the emotional development, ability level, and social development of the students for whom the materials are selected.
(5) Materials shall realistically represent and foster respect for our pluralistic society.
(6) Biased or slanted materials may be provided to meet specific curriculum objectives.
(7) Materials chosen on controversial issues will be selected representing various views in order to maintain a balanced collection.
(8) Physical format and appearance of materials shall be suitable for their intended use.

b. Special Collections
Several of the Libraries/LRCs at HCC may have collections
that are kept separate from the rest of the materials. These
Special Collections are usually determined by the librarians
and set aside because of format, circulation requirements,
subject matter, or for purposes of preservation.

c. Gifts
It is the prerogative of the HCC Librarians to accept or reject
any gift. The Librarians retain the right to examine gift
materials before deciding on acceptance. They also retain
the right to dispose of gift materials, including books,
magazines, or audiovisuals, in an appropriate manner in
accordance with Administrative Procedure (5.005),
Donations (Appendix K), LRC Operating Procedure (5.110),
and Gift Materials (Appendix L). [Neither Appendix included
in this book.]

d. Collection Evaluation
The collections of HCC Libraries/LRCs are evaluated
continually by the librarians to provide information about the
relative value of each item to the collection. Evaluation is
also necessary to determine whether the College's aims,
objectives, or goals have been achieved in building
collections that are responsive to the needs of students,
faculty, and staff.

G. Weeding Process
Weeding is the process of discarding or transferring to storage
materials of all formats which are obsolete, unnecessary
duplicates, rarely used, or worn-out. Regular weeding
maintains the purposes and quality of library resources.

1. Legal Authority
Administrative Rule (6HX-10-3.018) Selection and Disposal of
Learning Resources Materials (Appendix M) and HCC
Administrative Procedure (3.302) Disposal of Learning
Resources Materials (Appendix J). [Neither Appendix included
in this book.]

2. Responsibility
The Librarians have the main responsibility for weeding.
Teaching faculty should be encouraged to provide input;

however, the Librarians have final approval for the removal of any library/learning resources materials.

3. General Criteria to Weed/Remove Materials
   a. Materials in poor condition. If heavily used, they should be replaced or repaired, if possible.
   b. Duplicates no longer needed.
   c. Older editions which have been replaced by newer ones.
   d. Materials that have not circulated for three to five years and are not classics.
   e. Materials that contain outdated or inaccurate factual content.
   f. Materials which no longer support the curriculum.
   g. Periodicals which are not indexed.

H. Challenged Materials
   1. Legal Authority
      HCC Administrative Procedure (3.510) Challenged Learning Resources Materials (Appendix N). [Not included in this book.]
   2. Procedure
      On occasion, someone may question or challenge the suitability of certain materials found in the College collection. A Library/LRC patron who approaches a staff member in person with such a challenge or question will be referred to a Librarian. Such questions will be met appropriately by the Librarian with reference to these collection development policy guidelines, including the Library Bill of Rights and/or The Freedom to Read statement.

      If a patron wishes to challenge formally the library's inclusion of an item, he/she will be directed to fill out the official "Request for Review" form and submit it to the Library/LRC. Written challenges about any Library/LRC item, sent to any office in the College, will be referred to a Librarian on the campus where the item is housed.

      A challenge of any item will be discussed by a Library Committee composed of the Library Cluster and the Associate Vice President of Learning Resources Services. This Committee will respond to the challenger using the attached reply form.

In the interim, the challenged material will not be removed from its usual place in the collection.
3. Forms [not duplicated here.]
   a. Request for Review
   b. Response to Review

I. Annual Review of Collection Development Policy by Library Cluster
    The Hillsborough Community College Collection Development Policy is a joint effort of the Library Cluster and the Associate Vice President of Learning Resources Services.

    Each academic year, a committee of the Library Cluster shall review this policy. The Committee shall consist of at least one Librarian from each campus and center.

    The Associate Vice President of Learning Resources Services and/or any member of the Library Cluster may propose a change in this policy to the Collection Development Committee.

    The Committee will submit proposed revisions to the Cluster. The Cluster shall present its approved version to the Associate Vice President of Learning Resources Services.

    The official Hillsborough Community College Collection Development Policy will be approved by the President of the College and the Board of Trustees.

March 15, 1993

NEW MEXICO STATE UNIVERSITY LIBRARY
Policy for Electronic Information Resources
Las Cruces, New Mexico

April 26, 1994

I. Location and Dissemination of Policy

In order to ensure a wide knowledge of and adherence to this policy, a copy resides with each Information Technology Reference Librarian in Branson Hall Library and New Library. A copy is available for public view in the Collection Management Department. In addition, the policy will be distributed to all Selectors.

II. Definition

The New Mexico State University Library policy for electronic information resources provides guidelines for the selection, acquisition, access to and maintenance of electronic resources. Electronic information resources are defined as the category of material accessible through the library which requires the use of computers. Current examples are CD-ROM products, machine readable datafiles that are either bibliographic, textual or numeric, electronic journals or remote databases, graphic or multimedia files, and courseware or instructional files.

III. Selection
A. Selectors' Responsibility

The primary responsibility for identifying and proposing the purchase of electronic information resources for the library lies with the Selectors who have subject specialist responsibilities, as well as relevant administrative heads, such as the heads of Reference, Government Documents, Special Collections, or Archives. In general, Reference will have the primary responsibilities for identifying core level and interdisciplinary indexes; Government Documents will have responsibility for identifying electronic materials in support of the federal documents program, and subject Selectors will identify research indexes, bibliographies, and/or electronic journals that support research collections. The subject content and intellectual level of each electronic information resource will not differ from the library's established collection development policies for each department and selectors should recommend the format which best serves the instruction and research needs of the discipline. Decisions for purchase will be coordinated with the Head of Collection Management.

B. Selection Criteria
Electronic information resources require new ways of looking at library collection development because of their complexity, cost and equipment requirements. A checklist for purchasing or accepting electronic information resources is attached and addresses such issues as hardware and software requirements, user interface requirements, product requirements, etc. Other criteria are ease of use (compared to the print equivalent), the currency factor (these products tend to be more current), popularity, and enhanced access to information. Computer files also may be selected to support academic programs or departments with high enrollment.

General abstracts and indexes will have priority over individual specialized reference tools, although an optimal balance of general and specialized indexes will be sought. Electronic sources may be selected because they can be networked or because they are heavily used through mediated searches. Very expensive electronic resources of campus-wide utility, such as locally mounted databases will be reviewed by special working groups and the Library Administrative Council.

IV. Budget, Purchase Negotiations and Licensing
Electronic formats, with the exception of online search charges, are to be included in the library materials budget under both mono-graph purchases (one time), or serials (subscriptions). Whenever possible the INNOVACQ file shall include the academic department, reference or core designation for all electronic format materials.

In general it is the responsibility of the Head of Collection Management with consultation from the Technical Services, Order/Receipts staff to negotiate licensing agreements with the vendor or publisher. The University Purchasing Department signs licensing and copyright agreements.

The Order/Receipts unit will maintain files of all licensing agreements. The department or unit which houses or provides access to an electronic resource is responsible for day-to-day oversight of licensing requirements.

Final responsibility for compliance with licensing agreements rests with the Library Dean, the Head of Collection Management, in consultation with the University Purchasing Department and the University Attorney, as may be necessary.

V. Other Policy Considerations

Duplicate copies and copies in multiple formats will be purchased only in cases of clearly demonstrated need when networking or other alternatives are not available or practicable. Replacement criteria will not differ from those used when considering the replacement of books or other materials, including demonstrated demand for the resource, cost of replacement, and availability through other campus or remote sources.

The Library procedures for accepting, evaluating, and processing gifts of electronic resources will be consistent with the selection requirement for all library materials. All other issues regarding electronic materials received as gifts shall be handled in accordance with the University Library's general Gift Policy.

Electronic resources will be reviewed periodically by the Selectors to assess their continuing value. It is the responsibility of the Selectors to weed from the collection electronic materials which are determined to be no longer of value.

VI. Checklist for Electronic Information Resources

Selection Criteria

- General abstracts and indexes have priority over individual specialized reference subject areas although an optimal balance of general and specialized indexes will be sought. Frequently electronic access tools include undergraduate, graduate and research level materials.
- User need/demand.
- Could an existing print subscription be canceled if this source were acquired?
- Is the additional flexibility gained through automation significant for this particular resource? Examples are wider access through a LAN or greater flexibility in searching.

- Evaluation of electronic products will be an on-going process, as well as take place during the annual serials review.

Product Considerations

The public services support required to make a resource available should be given early consideration in the selection process. Aspects of public services support to be considered are:

- Is the product user-friendly?
- Is the user interface consistent with other interfaces currently in use?
- Does the user interface provide quality keyword searching, downloading, and reasonable response time?
- Can records be marked and searching and printing be interrupted?
- The need for staff and user training.
- The availability and usefulness of manuals, guides, and tutorials from the producer.
- The need for a new publication document for users.
- Accessibility through a campus-wide network, such as NMSU-NET, and/or the library's local area network.
- Number of disks per index.
- Does the product contain additional information over the traditional format?
- How frequently is the product updated?

Vendor Considerations

- Can the vendor's claims be verified?
- Vendor/contract considerations
- Is a demonstration disk or trial account available?
- Has the vendor demonstrated reliability, good performance, and production of high quality products?
- Does the product have good documentation?
- Are software enhancements included in the purchase or lease price?
- Is maintenance for hardware included in the subscription price?
- Does the contract require restrictions, such as:
  - an obligation to return superseded disks
  - guarantee of limited access
  - restrictions on downloading
  - definitions of users and/or uses of the information

- protection from liability from patron use of information
- restrictions on duplication of the documentation accompanying the product
- The University Library will negotiate and comply with vendor licensing agreements.

Technical Considerations

- Is the required hardware currently available in the library? Does the existing hardware have sufficient system capacity and storage?
- If the vendor supplies a turnkey system, does it provide significant enhancements to the product not available from the current system?
- Are there sufficient staff expertise and resources to maintain the system (i.e., upgrades, backups, hardware, software)?
- If appropriate, are funds available for hardware and/or software maintenance contracts?
- Where will the equipment reside? Is there electricity? Network connections? Security from theft?
- Does the system work on an existing network (TCP/IP, Novell)?
- Can the system support adequate workstations for anticipated use?
- What is the quality of system documentation?
- Is the system upgradable or expandable?

THE HUMAN ECOLOGY LIBRARY
The Ohio State University
Columbus, Ohio

A. Introduction

The Ohio State University Human Ecology Library was established as a department library in 1959. The primary purpose of the Library is to support the classroom and research needs of the division and four departments comprising the College of Human Ecology: Department of Consumer and Textile Science, Department of Family Relations and Human Development, Department of Human Nutrition and Food Management, and the Division of Home Economics Education.

The Library is located with the College of Human Ecology in Campbell Hall. It currently occupies four converted classrooms. Room 325 contains the circulation/closed reserve desk, office, staff desks, encyclopedia case, and reference collection (Library of Congress Classification A through TX). Room 329 houses the reference collection (TX through Z), atlas case, and circulating materials. The Glass Case Collection, current periodicals, indexes and abstracts, microforms, career information, and bound serials (Library of Congress Classification B through H) are in Room 305. Microform readers, television monitors/VCR, theses and dissertations, bound serials (QP through Z) are available in Room 309.

The Library has over 30,000 catalogued holdings, 350 serial titles and an average circulation of 60,000 items per year. There is a seating of 108 seats and a total area of 3,098 square footage. Access to the collection is available 65 hours a week during Fall, Winter, and Spring quarters, and 15 hours a week during Summer quarter.

1. Clientele

The primary patrons of the Library are the faculty, staff, and students associated with the College of Human Ecology. The average undergraduate enrollment for the College is 1,220 plus 350 declared Human Ecology majors from University College (UUC). The secondary patrons are those from agriculture, business, education, engineering, fine arts, health sciences, physical education, social work, and sociology. The Library is also an information resource for businesses, institutions, organizations, and professionals in the community. The Library does not collect extemporaneous materials. However, the Library is a strong proponent of the American Library Association's *Library Bill of Rights* and makes every effort to fulfill every patron's request.

2. Curriculum

The College of Human Ecology offers the degree of Bachelor of Science in Human Ecology in family relations and human development, home economics education, home economics journalism, family resource management, human nutrition and food management, and textiles and clothing. Specialized degrees include Bachelor of Science in Hospitality Management and Bachelor of Science in Nutrition. The College offers Master of Science and Doctor of Philosophy degrees in home economics education, family resource management, human nutrition and food management, and textiles and clothing.

The Library contains resource materials for courses taught in apparel studies, child development, consumerism, costume, day care, dietetics, education, family studies, family therapy, fashion merchandising, financial management, food, furnishings, home economics, hospitality management, housing, human development, human ecology, nutrition, parenting, preschool, textiles, and vocational education.

3. Research

The Library supports the research of its faculty: Social perception of dress, textile product performance, consumer behavior, spending patterns, archaeological and historic textiles, child development, educative process, family and social action, Appalachian families, international family issues, home economics education, multi-cultural education, recruitment and retention in education, housing, teenage parenthood, home technology, home business, infant development, development through the life cycle, family therapy, play, adolescents and family, family stress and coping, nutrition therapy, trace elements research, hospitality and institutional management, human metabolism, lipids, edible oils, maternal and child nutrition, nutrition education, nutritional studies of populations.

4. Special Topical Collections
    The Library recently received 250 comprehensive button book
    and serial titles from the estate of Mrs. Ann U. Rudolph. Mrs.
    Rudolph was an information specialist and expert button
    collector. Her Button Collection is a lasting legacy to costume
    researchers.
        Other significant holdings on microforms are the Queen
    Victoria and Prince Albert Museum Color Microform Collection;
    Fashion Advertising Collection; Food and Nutrition Information
    Center on Microfiche; Index of American Design; The Lake
    Placid Proceeding; and theses and dissertations in the field of
    human ecology.
        The Glass Case Collection houses rare books, audio-
    visual materials, unique serials and monographs in the
    areas of child development, costume, fashion, home economics
    and human nutrition.
        Other special collections include the College of Human
    Ecology theses and dissertations, the J.C. Penney motion
    picture loops, Hailes Advertisements Scrapbooks, and the
    History of Costume (slides).

5. Other
    Not applicable.

6. Participation of Faculty in Collection Development
    The College has recently undergone reorganization. To
    minimize committee activity, the Library committee of five
    members has been reduced to department liaisons. The
    Library actively solicits input from College faculty, staff, and
    students via mailings and a suggestion box.

B. Nature of Subject Literature
The Human Ecology Library collection consists of interdisciplinary materials from the social sciences, applied sciences
and the arts with only 30% duplication within Ohio State
University Libraries system as a whole. Emphasis is placed on
significant literature to support the College curriculum of home
economics and human ecology.
    Subject coverage includes apparel studies, child
development, consumerism, costume, day care, design,

dietetics, education, family studies, family therapy, fashion merchandising, financial management, food, furnishings, health care, home economics, hospitality management, housing, human development, human ecology, nutrition, parenting, play, pre-school, textiles, and vocational education.

C. Nature of the Collection

The collection consists of monographs, reference materials, audiovisuals, closed reserve, computer software, serials, Glass Case Collection, vertical files, career information, microforms, and professional office material.

1. Reference

   The reference collection is interdisciplinary covering the areas of study in the College. Sources include general and specialized materials, statistical data, almanacs, atlases, annuals, bibliographies, catalogs, dictionaries, directories, encyclopedias, evaluations (tests), government documents, sourcebooks, research methods, thesauri, yearbooks, etc.

2. Monographs

   The monographs or circulating materials in the Library are interdisciplinary and reflect the heterogeneous nature of the collection.

3. Serials

   The Library currently receives over 350 annuals, catalogs, newsletters, magazines, journals, microforms, proceedings, and other serial titles. The main access resources are *Abstracts in Social Gerontology; Applied Science and Technology Index; Child Development Abstracts and Bibliography; Clothing and Textile Arts Index; Consumer Health and Nutrition Index; Education Index; Inventory of Marriage and Family Literature; Lodging and Restaurant Index; Nutrition Abstracts, Reviews--Series A; Reader's Guide to Periodical Literature; Sage Family Abstracts; Social Science Index; Textile Arts Index;* and *World Textile Abstracts.*

   The Library's serial collection encompasses subjects in child care, child development, consumerism, family relations, family therapy, fashion, hospitality management, economics, home economics education, human nutrition, textiles and clothing.

4. Unclassified
The Vertical File contains information of general interest in human ecology, company annual reports, career inform ation, and graduate school catalogs.

The Career Information Collection contains materials provided by the College Alumni Office and Library. This collection includes company profiles, current job notebooks, University employment vacancies, and other resources.

The Office Collection contains resource materials on bibliographic instruction, librarianship, management, and catalogs for publishers, equipment, and supplies.

5. Special Non-Library of Congress Classification Materials
Not applicable.

6. Cataloging Backlog Collections
Not applicable.

7. Other Collections
The Library has an extensive collection of closed reserve materials for classroom and in-house use. These titles include audiovisual materials, class files, computer software, costume resources, current journals, curriculum guides, and other publications.

D. Scope of Historical and Current Collecting Activity
The historical and current collecting reflects overall growth of the College and the field of Human Ecology. In the past, emphasis was placed on acquiring titles in clothing science, culinary arts, domestic science, family hygiene, household finance, interior decorating, and personal appearance.

1. Subject Coverage
Family Relations and Development covers child care, family studies, development through the life cycle, and family therapy.

a. Collection level--Research level
   BF   Psychology
   E   America
   HM   Sociology
   HN   Social history. Social problems. Social reform
   HQ   The Family. Marriage. Woman
   HV   Social pathology. Social and public welfare
   KF   Law of the United States
   RC   Internal medicine. Practice of medicine
   RJ   Pediatrics
   TX   Home economics

b. Language level--English

Home Economics Education covers vocational education, child care service, clothing service, food service, and journalism.

a. Collection level--Research level
   E   America
   HC   Economic history and conditions
   HQ   The Family. Marriage. Woman
   HV   Social pathology. Social and public welfare
   KF   Law of the United States
   LB   Theory and practice of education
   LC   Special aspects of education
   RA   Public aspects of medicine
   RJ   Pediatrics
   S   Agriculture
   TX   Home economics

b. Language level--English

[Remaining subject policies cover Human Nutrition and Food Management, Consumer Science, and Textile Sciences are in the same format.]

2. Access to Collection
   Access to the collection is currently through OSCAR, The Ohio State University Libraries' (OSUL) online catalog system and OhioLINK, the State of Ohio's statewide information system.

3. Subjects Excluded
   Some elementary, juvenile, and extracurricular materials are excluded from the collection.

4. Overlaps, Underlaps, and Gaps
   The interdisciplinary nature of the Human Ecology Library collection overlaps with other areas in University Libraries including Agriculture, Business, Education and Psychology, English, Theatre and Communications, Fine Arts, Health Sciences, Pharmacy, Science and Engineering, Social Work, and Sociology.

Collection	Subject
Agriculture	Extension, Food Science, Food Technology, Textiles
Business	Apparel Industry, Consumer Affairs Health Care, Hospitality Management, Textile Industry, Tourism
Education/Psychology	Early Childhood Education, Education, Family Therapy, Home Economics Education, Human Development, Life Cycle, Play
English, Theatre & Communications	Costume, Journalism, Theatre Set Design
Fine Arts	Antiques, Crafts, Design, Fiber Arts, Furniture, Interior Design
Health Sciences	Dietetics, Health Care, Human Nutrition
Pharmacy	Consumer Products, Toiletries
Science and Engineering	Biochemistry, Design, Housing, Interior Design, Textile Science

Social Work   Adolescence, Aging, Child Care,
                                     Family Studies, Housing

Sociology   Marriage and Family

The Human Ecology Library has "gaps" in core serials and subject reference sources. These omissions are most noticeable in nutritional biochemistry, textile science, and ecological studies.

5. Language Coverage
   Language coverage is primarily English. However, materials published in French, Italian, and Japanese languages are sometimes purchased to support textiles and clothing research.

6. Chronological Period Covered
   The chronological period begins with "Lucy" and continues through the present.

7. Chronological Publication Period Covered
   Publication date of materials is primarily late twentieth century. However, older titles are solicited and purchased when funding is available.

8. Geographical Areas Covered
   The geographic scope is primarily the Western World. However, the Library is dedicated to providing culturally diverse materials.

9. Specific materials Solicited for Gifts
   Out-of-print and missing publications, especially serials, are actively solicited.

10. Other Materials
    Not applicable.

11. Uncollected Materials
    The Library often adds materials to the career information and vertical files for the use of patrons.

E. Related Sources Pertaining Specifically to Collection

1. Non-OSUL Campus Resources
    The Center for Instructional Resources, State of Ohio Co-
    operative Extension, The Edgar Dale Media Center, The
    History of Art Slide Library, and the Nisonger Toy Library
    collect materials related to human ecology.

2. Local Resources
    Other resource centers include Chemical Abstracts, Columbus
    Metropolitan Library, Columbus School for Art and Design,
    Columbus State College, State of Ohio Cooperative Extension,
    Franklin University, and the State Library of Ohio.

3. Cooperative Agreements
    Not applicable.

4. External Memberships
    Not applicable.

5. Online Access
    Not applicable.

F. General Future Collection Plans
The Library would like to expand its space and collection. Additional classroom space will some day be added to accommodate
library staff offices and shelving. This additional space will allow
the two photocopiers to be relocated within the Library. The
purchase of two state-of-the-art microform reader/printers will allow
patrons to make print copies of unique microforms.

Future Library users will require additional computer hard-
ware/software for access to local and off-site databases on apparel
studies, child development, costume, day care, development
through the life cycle, family studies, family therapy, merchandising,
financial management, food science, home economics, human
ecology, journalism, nutrition, play, pre-school, textile science, and
other subjects.

The Library shall continue to collect materials on costume.
Mindata currently publishes unique microforms on costume and
design. The acquisition of these materials will be a great asset.

The Human Ecology Library will continue to augment its research collection and coordinate its efforts with other OSUL collections. Family Relations and Historic Costume are the strongest subject areas. The Library will build on these strengths and expand the collection in the areas of Life-Cycle Studies and Textile Science. Holdings in Consumerism, Home Economics Education and Hospitality Management are also significant. However, collecting patterns in these three areas will change after restructuring.

Human Nutrition is the weakest subject area. The Library will petition for additional funding to purchase core serial and monographic materials, especially in the area of nutritional biochemistry.

[Detailed Subject, Collection Intensity, and Language Coverage portion and verification process not included here but may be available from the library's Collection Development Office.]

The following mission statement of the Human Ecology Library is Appendix A of the library's policy:

The Human Ecology Library's primary purpose is to support the College of Human Ecology's classroom and research needs.

The Human Ecology Library fully adheres to and practices the American Library Association's "Library Bill of Rights."

The Human Ecology Library recognizes its role in collecting and disseminating materials and information to a diverse population. This library further appreciates its responsibility in promoting cultural pluralism and accommodating a wide variety of opinions and cultures. The library encourages the Ohio State University and university libraries faculty, and students to respect each patron's right to information without regard to age, ancestry, color, creed, economic status, gender, national origin, physiological condition, political beliefs, race, and sexual orientation. The Human Ecology Library openly invites suggestions to improve its collection, facilities, and service.

By Leta Hendricks
June 21, 1991

ST. PETERSBURG JUNIOR COLLEGE
St. Petersburg, Florida

1. MISSION/SERVICE PHILOSOPHY

Collection development is the means by which the SPJC Library provides organized collections of print and non-print resources that will meet institutional, curricular research, and instructional requirements, as well as the cultural and recreational needs of the college community. Collection development is achieved by librarians, administrators, faculty, staff and students working together to select library materials which best fulfill these needs.

A Collection Development Committee, consisting of those librarians responsible for collection development at each library site, meets regularly to amplify further the policies and procedures set forth in this manual.

A Profile of the SPJC Community

To better comprehend the scope of the SPJC college community, some background facts should be established. SPJC has five library sites. The sites at St. Petersburg, Clearwater, and Tarpon Springs are responsible for the development of traditional transfer programs as well as various career programs. The Health Education Center supports the college's nursing and allied health sciences programs. The fifth library site is at the Allstate Center, where the Criminal Justice programs are housed.

A college-wide Open Campus division is responsible for the development of career enhancement programs and for non-credit and community service programs. The SPJC Library serves the Open Campus through its site libraries.

As SPJC's mission statement, included in the college catalog, states, as a "comprehensive, open door community college" its mission is "to provide high-quality educational experiences to help a diverse student body and a dynamic community meet a broad range of educational goals."

The Library's clientele is composed of the student body, the faculty, administrators and staff, and residents of Pinellas County and the greater Tampa Bay area. According to SPJC's Office of Institutional Research, the Fall 1990 opening head-count for credit courses approached 20,000.

The student body is a diverse group both in personal and educational goals. There are full-time students attending college transfer programs during the day and evening, students with full-time jobs attending evening classes on a part-time basis, students enrolled in technical and vocational programs, and dual enrollment programs, also those enrolled in non-credit, continuing education courses.

The average age of the student body in 1990 was 26.0. There are now more part-time students than full-time. The average age variation for the part-time student was 6 years (older) than the full-time student. The number of educationally disabled students is increasing. In the Fall 1990, the student body was 40.3% male, 59.7% female; 90.2% white, 4.7% black, 2.2% Hispanic, 1.7% Asian, 0.7% American Indian and 0.6% non-resident alien.

The SPJC Library operates within a local library community that is diverse as well. Pinellas County has a newly formed library cooperative that extends county-wide library privileges to residents of most county communities. Other academic libraries include Eckerd College in St. Petersburg, the University of South Florida in Tampa and its Bayboro campus in St. Petersburg, and the University of Tampa. Cooperative library efforts are also pursued through the Tampa Bay Library Consortium. Cooperation with these various library entities extends the availability of resources and services to SPJC's own library users, and will continue to have some impact on SPJC's collection development efforts

2. LEVELS OF COLLECTION DEVELOPMENT

There are many formulas available in the library community defining the level of development for particular areas of the library collection. The SPJC Library has adopted the following definitions of support and has applied them to the curriculum supported at SPJC:

1) <u>Comprehensive</u>. This is complete coverage, with all identifiable non-ephemeral resources acquired. Since SPJC is a community college rather than a university, there is no area supported that could be defined in this manner.

2) <u>Strong</u>. Broad coverage that would satisfy most user needs. This level of development applies to SPJC's required courses and involves the greater amount of the purchasing budget.

3) <u>Basic</u>. Standard works containing general information, answering day to day questions. This level of development applies to elective courses and CLAST support of materials. A smaller portion of the purchasing budget is allotted for this category.

4) <u>Minimal</u>. Categories not included in the above, but useful for responding to demands. This level of development includes recreational-type materials and funds are expanded in this area after those listed above. A list follows indicating subject areas belonging to the Strong, Basic and Minimal development levels.

STRONG

Accounting
American History
American Literature
Animal Science Technology
Architecture
Art
Aviation Technology
Banking
Biology
Clinical Psychology
Computer Science
Criminology & Crim. Justice
Dental Hygiene
Developmental Psychology
Economics
Education, Deaf
Education, Early Childhood
Education, General
Educational Psychology
Engineering, General
English Literature
Environmental Studies
Ethics

Fire Administration
Graphic Arts
Health Services Management
Interior Design
Mathematics
Medical Laboratory Technology
Medical Records
Music
Nursing
Office Systems Technology
Paralegal/Legal Assistant
Philosophy
Physical Therapy
Political Science
Psychology
Radiologic Technology
Real Estate
Religion
Respiratory Therapy
Social Psychology
Study Skills
World Literature
Zoology

BASIC

Anatomy
Applied Psychology

Anthropology
Oceanography

Astronomy
Botany
Business Law
Chemistry
Children's Literature
Classical Literature
Comparative Politics
Creative Writing
Dance
Earth Science
Foreign Language/Lit.
Library Science
Local History
Mass Media
Medicine
Military Science
Occult Sciences

Pet Care
Photography
Physical Education
Physical Science
Physics
Psychology of Personality
Reading
Social Psychology
Speech
Sports
Statistics
Substance Abuse
Theater Arts
Transportation
Vocational Information
Women's Studies
World History

MINIMAL

Agriculture
Arts and Crafts
Astrology
Cookery
Gardening
Genealogy
Hobbies

Household Maintenance
Leisure
Materials/Visually Handicapped
Recreational Reading
Self Help
Travel

FACULTY/STAFF RESEARCH NEEDS are served with a collection of selected, specialized materials. In addition, a professional collection of general education materials is maintained. For research needs that extend beyond these resources, faculty and staff may use alternative library services, such as interlibrary loan and database searches. The proximity of the University of South Florida with its major university library is recommended to serve more advanced faculty/staff research needs.

COMMUNITY MEMBER NEEDS are served by the library collection within the framework of its primary function of curriculum support.

3. SUPPORT OF CURRICULUM

SPJC Curriculum Manuals are housed in each site library. Librarians remain current with curricular changes by consulting the manuals, serving on the Curriculum and Instruction Committee, consulting with faculty members performing C & I development research, consulting with Open Campus representatives about new course offerings and appropriate off-campus support, and through faculty and administrative contacts.

PROCEDURE

1) One librarian at each site is designated as the Collection Development Librarian by the Librarian-in-Charge.
2) The other site librarians are assigned as liaisons to the academic departments and report departmental needs and make purchase recommendations to the Collection Development Librarian.
3) The Collection Development Librarians consult the college catalog and analyze the collection to make certain the curricular needs at the site are met.
4) Collection Development Librarians review the Curriculum and Instruction Committee Agenda and Minutes to see what courses are being added, modified, or deleted. These items are distributed to faculty and attached to the *Blue & White*. C & I representatives from the libraries forward copies of approved new course proposals to the collection development librarians at the sites, who share this information with the Collection Development Committee.
5) The Collection Development Committee sends a written request via the Director of Libraries to the Dean of Open Campus requesting notification of any additions or modifications to the Open Campus course offerings, especially as they apply to the dual enrollment program, offerings at the Carillon Center, and other programs.

4. PURCHASE LIMITATIONS AND BUDGET CONSTRAINTS

The first priority of the SPJC Library is to support the academic programs and needs on the individual college sites. When library funds are severely limited due to budgetary constraints, priority will be given to library materials that support "Gordon Rule" classes, general education requirements and CLAST materials. Under such budgetary conditions, as specialized libraries the Allstate and Health Education Centers will give priority to maintenance of their basic collections.

PROCEDURE

As a rule, one copy of a title will be purchased. Duplicates will be purchased at the discretion of the Collection Development Librarian at each site.

1) Since academic materials are very expensive, site librarians will provide strong coverage of only those academic topics that facilitate highly visible library use/interest among the students and faculty on *their site*. For example, nursing and allied health subject matter will have strong coverage at the Health Education Center Library, but the other sites will carry only basic or minimal collections in these areas.

2) The site libraries will provide strong or basic foreign language resources for the languages taught at their sites, in proportion to the size of their collections. Languages not listed in the current SPJC catalog will have minimal coverage.

3) In order to use limited financial resources in the most economical manner, librarians will encourage the use of interlibrary loan and other cooperative/shared library resources systems.

5. COOPERATIVE COLLECTION BUILDING—AREA LIBRARIES

The SPJC Library is committed to cooperative efforts with other area libraries, including those in the school systems, colleges, universities and the county library cooperative. In the area of collection building every effort will be made to acquaint these library entities with SPJC's collection development policy, and to coordinate development when feasible. The Director of Libraries will act as liaison with the other libraries in this effort.

Current cooperative efforts include the housing of medical government documents from St. Petersburg Public Library's Federal Depository at SPJC's Health Education Center, a reciprocal borrowing agreement with Eckerd College, borrowing privileges for SPJC faculty at the University of South Florida, and the coordination of the Drug Free Environments resource center.

6. SCOPE OF INVOLVEMENT

As the curriculum is the most important influence on the development of the SPJC Library Collection, it is very important that librarians obtain suggestions and advice about materials selection from the faculty as well as from the administration. Recommendations from students are also welcomed. The College-wide Collection Development Committee, which has representation from all these groups, helps to provide advice on collection development in cooperation with the Director of Libraries.

Faculty members participate in collection development and are consulted by librarians regularly concerning recommendations for purchase of needed materials. Selection and budget allocation responsibility is retained by the library. Faculty members also are surveyed regularly to measure how well the library serves the needs of the programs and courses of study.

While the campus administration does not participate in formulating collection development policies, administrators are consulted on a regular basis for selection advice. Additions to the collection also will be reported to the campus administration.

The Student Government Association at each site participates in collection development by appointing a member, or referring suggestions/recommendations to a specific librarian at each site. Career staff personnel are encouraged to suggest additions to the collection through the librarians at the sites.

PROCEDURE
1) All librarians at each site participate in selection and collection development, with one librarian being designated as Collection Development Librarian.
2) Each librarian is assigned a subject area(s) with the responsibility of maintaining liaison with the departmental faculty involved.
3) Each librarian reads the review journals and is responsible for the production of bibliographies in the area as needed.
4) The Collection Development Librarian reads review journals and receives the suggestions of the other librarians concerning their special areas.
5) The College-wide Collection Development Committee meets regularly to discuss course requirements, new courses, trends,

purchase of costly materials, resource sharing, and to review certain selections. Each member of this committee may be assigned a subject area, with the delegate(s) from each site taking responsibility for selection for programs special to that site.

6) Surveys of faculty members and other college groups are coordinated through the Director of Libraries Office and the findings reported to the Collection Development Committee for future considerations.

7. MATERIALS SELECTION

As is stated in the SPJC Faculty Manual, it is the policy of SPJC through its libraries to select, commensurate with budgetary and space allocations, books and related materials that support:

1) The aims and objectives of the college.
2) The content of courses offered in the curriculum of a given campus.
3) The teaching methods of faculty members of a site.
4) The special needs of the students of a site, including leisure interests.

The college also supports the tenet that academic integrity and responsibility to the college community include free access to materials representing divergent points of view concerning controversial problems and issues. The college further subscribes to the following statements in the Library Bill of Rights concerning selection of materials:

1) As a responsibility of library service, books and other library materials selected should be chosen for values of interest, information, and enlightenment of all the people of the community. In no case should library materials be excluded because of the race or nationality or the social, political, or religious views of the authors.
2) Libraries should provide books and other materials presenting all points of view concerning the problems and issues of our times: no library materials should be proscribed or removed from libraries because of partisan or doctrinal disapproval.
3) Censorship should be challenged by libraries in the maintenance of their responsibility to provide public information and enlightenment.

4) Libraries should cooperate with all persons and groups concerned with resisting abridgment of free expression and free access to ideas. This selection policy applies equally to all learning resources materials, whether acquired by purchase, gift, or exchange.

Initial responsibility for materials selection is shared jointly by all site librarians who solicit faculty, administrators, staff and students for suggestions. The Collection Development Librarian at the site is responsible for analyzing gaps or weaknesses in the site collection and for suggesting purchases to correct them. Extremely expensive or unusual items must be approved by the Librarian-in-Charge and may be subject to approval by the Collection Development Committee and the Director of Libraries.

PROCEDURE–GENERAL GUIDELINES

1) Unless specifically requested and justifiable for faculty research, avoid recommending upper division and graduate level materials.
2) Some materials at the high school level are appropriate for academically challenged students.
3) Bibliographies, unless established as frequently used reference sources, are rarely used and of limited value.
4) Avoid over-buying for popular subjects in rapidly changing areas, especially where periodical sources will meet most user needs.
5) Titles on commonly researched subjects of lasting value, such as literary criticism, should be selected even though many other titles of this nature are in the collection.
6) Expensive items must be evaluated carefully to justify their purchase.
7) Duplicate copies are not purchased unless high demand for a particular class or curriculum procedure justify their need.
8) Give careful consideration to items with unusual formats that could cause circulation and shelving problems.

BOOK SELECTION

1) Consult the selection tools (journals of reviews, subject journals, brochures, publishers' catalogs, (Books in Print). A review from a reputable source is preferred over a publisher's blurb for new or unfamiliar titles.

2) Mark the items to be purchased and, when appropriate, the program or discipline for which it would be recommended (i.e., COMM for Communications, FA for Fine Arts, BUS for Business, etc.).
3) Attach justification for expensive or unusual items.
4) Send the information to the Collection Development Librarian, who will send it on to the Acquisitions/Order Department for further processing.

AUDIOVISUAL MATERIALS

1) Consult the selection tools. As reviews of many AV programs are not readily available, greater reliance must be placed on publishers' catalogs, etc. The reputation of the publisher should be accounted for when considering purchase.
2) Mark the items to be purchased and, when appropriate, the program or discipline for which it is recommended.
3) Attach form IT 403, Request for Video Purchase, for all video cassettes.
4) 1/2" videocassettes are the preferred film format over 3/4" and 16mm films.
5) Attach justification for expensive or unusual items.
6) Send the information to the Collection Development Librarian, who will send it to the Acquisitions/Order Department for further processing.

PERIODICALS

1) Faculty liaison librarians will recommend to the periodicals librarian titles to be added or canceled. Recommendations are based on:
   a. Curricular needs.
   b. Interest of students and faculty.
   c. Professional reviews.
   d. Recommendations of faculty.
   e. Inclusion in periodical indexes.
   f. Cost of the subscription.
   g. Other titles received on the same subject.
2) Give recommendations to the periodicals librarian by April so that they may be included on the subscription agency periodicals order. The periodicals librarian will consult with the Collection Development Librarian about the purchases.

ARCHIVES

The Archives Collection is housed at the SP campus and includes items relating to the history and development of SPJC and memorabilia about its students. It does not contain minutes of meetings, other than District Board of Trustees minutes, or student organization records, student records, or division activity records. Items to be accepted for collection include:

DBT Minutes; SBE Records & Rules Relating to Community Colleges; Self Study Reports; Presidential Profiles; Faculty Research (Dissertations, if donated); all SPJC Publications; the News-Clippings from which News View is created; Memorabilia from Alumni; Graduation Programs; Photographs; Building Dedication Programs.

1) For each item accepted, excluding photos, type two cards. Each card has the bibliographical citation for the item, if possible, and its location within the Archives Collection.

2) Location is determined by the type of material:
   a. Section 1: State and District Board Level Reports and Statistical Information.
   b. Section 2: Institutional Affairs: Self Study Reports, Budgets, etc.
   c. Section 3: Research and publications.
   d. Section 4: SPJC Publications: Yearbooks, Links, Obelisks.
   e. Section 5: SPJC Publications: Bulletins, Catalogs, Photographs.
   f. Section 6: *The Wooden Horse*.
   g. Section 7: Alumni news, graduation programs, memorabilia.
   h. Section 8: *SPJC Newsview*.

3) No material leaves the room except to be copied. No archival material may be checked out except with the approval of the Librarian-in-Charge.

4) Requests for archive displays must be handled by the Director of Libraries Office. Each request must include the purpose, requested material, date, time and place.

8. WITHDRAWAL OF MATERIALS FROM THE LIBRARY

The withdrawal of materials from the SPJC Library is governed by the procedure listed in the *District Board of Trustees Rules & Procedures Manual*, P6Hx23-5.13, Section VI. "Property Records."

At least annually the libraries shall prepare a list of surplus books and other materials which are determined to be obsolete, or which are uneconomical or inefficient to continue to use, or which serve no useful function. The list shall be submitted to the president and upon his approval, the surplus books and other materials shall be disposed of in accordance with college procedures.

This procedure allows for the periodic review of library books and materials that have become obsolete, physically unusable or are not used. Librarians evaluate the collection periodically for this purpose and consult instructors with expertise in the relevant disciplines for advice concerning retention of the materials.

Various standards from such associations as the American Library Association and the Southern Association of Colleges of Schools state that de-selection or weeding on a regular basis is indispensable to a useful collection and should be done systematically. Not only do obsolete and inappropriate materials occupy expensive space but they also detract from current materials containing important information. These standards suggest that from three to five percent of the collection should be withdrawn and replaced annually.

Books and materials selected for removal must meet at least one of the following conditions before being withdrawn:

1) The books/materials have been infrequently used for an extended period of time. The minimum time for withdrawal due to lack of use is 5 years.
2) There are other books/materials in the collection that better fulfill the same need.
3) The physical condition of the books/materials is such that they cannot be utilized and repair would be impractical.
4) The age of the books/materials is such that they are not useful for either current or historical purposes.
5) Information contained in the books/materials is incorrect or has been superseded.

Books that are listed as sources in heavily used indexes and bibliographies such as *Play Index, 20th Century Short Story Explication, Granger's Index to Poetry*, etc., are retained unless physically unusable and are then replaced, if possible. Book titles that receive heavy use are checked in *Books in Print* before discarding, and are replaced with newer editions if available.

The primary times for removing materials from the collection are during the summer months and immediately after Term I. However, faculty members and librarians are encouraged to evaluate the collection in the areas of their special interests throughout the year.

PROCEDURE

1) Check materials designated for withdrawal in the appropriate indexes as outlined in the policy statement.
2) Put the checkout cards for the designated materials in call number order and check them against the information in the Intelligent Catalog.
3) If there are no other copies of the item listed for the site, pull the card set from the card catalog and place it with the material being withdrawn. Send the checkout card to LPC requesting that the shelf list cards and the intelligent catalog be changed accordingly. Do not remove the card sets if the item is being reordered.
4) If there are other copies of the item listed in the Intelligent Catalog, do not pull the card set from the card catalog. Send the check-out card to LPC requesting that the copy be marked as deleted on the shelf list and the Intelligent Catalog be changed to reflect the deletion.
5) Add the item to the campus list of withdrawn materials. This list indicates the reason for withdrawal, such as obsolete or superseded. Send the updated list to LPC twice annually (August and January).
6) Box the materials being withdrawn and send them to temporary storage.
7) Place materials on shelves in the storage area and made available for review by the site librarians.
8) If an item is to be transferred, pull the item and send it and the transfer information to LPC. LPC updates the shelf list card and the Intelligent Catalog. Transfers are deleted from the appropriate withdrawn list by LPC.
9) LPC consolidates the campus withdrawn lists annually and sends it on or before March 1 to the Director of Libraries who submits the list for approval to the College President, through the Vice-President for Academic and Student Services. Upon approval of the withdrawn list by the President, other academic,

school and public librarians are invited to review and select from the materials for their libraries.

10) LPC stamps "SPJC Surplus Property" on the flyleaf and title page of materials selected by another library. Non-print items are stamped wherever the stamp will be visible. LPC designates that the materials have been withdrawn on the checkout cards and indicates the receiving institution. SPJC Library markings are removed or blanked out.

11) Stamp the materials that are unwanted by community libraries with the surplus property stamp as listed in the previous step and all book card pockets are removed.

12) Box and store materials until the annual college auction.

13) Statistics are kept by LPC for the withdrawn items by title and by volume including purchase cost if available. Shelf list cards are retained and marked withdrawn.

14) If there are no other copies listed for the site, pull the card set from the card catalog and place it with the material being withdrawn. Send the checkout card to LPC requesting that the shelf list cards and the Intelligent Catalog be changed accordingly. Do not remove the card sets if the item is being recorded.

15) If there are other copies of the item listed in the Intelligent Catalog, do not pull the card set from the card catalog. Send the checkout card to LPC requesting that the copy be marked as deleted on the shelf list and the Intelligent Catalog be changed to reflect the deletion.

16) Box up the materials being withdrawn and send them directly to the area designated for temporary storage.

17) The materials will be placed on shelves in the storage area and will be made available for review by the site librarians.

18) If the site librarians find an item that they want transferred to their site, they will pull the item and indicate the desire for transfer to LPC.

19) Once the site librarians have reviewed the materials, local school and public librarians are invited to review them.

20) If a library in the community desires some of the materials, the LPC withdraws the materials by stamping "SPJC Surplus Property" on the flyleaf and title page. Non-print items are stamped wherever the stamp will be visible. LPC will designate that the materials have been withdrawn on the checkout cards and will indicate the receiving institution.

21) Materials that are unwanted are stamped with the surplus property stamp as listed in the previous step and all book card pockets are removed.

22) The materials are boxed and sent to District Office for storage until the annual college auction.

23) The LPC keeps statistics for the withdrawn items by title and by volume. Shelf list cards are also marked.

9. SECONDARY STORAGE OF LIBRARY MATERIALS

To make better use of the space at the library sites, the SPJC Library maintains a secondary storage area for materials that are not in constant demand but remain useful. Annually, faculty and librarians are invited to review the collection in their area of expertise and to indicate materials that could be placed in secondary storage. The final decision whether items are placed in storage is made by the Librarian-in-Charge in cooperation with the Director of Libraries.

PROCEDURE

(1) Pull the checkout cards and mark them with the date and the words "secondary storage." The cards are kept at the circulation or reference desk, arranged by call number or main entry depending upon site policy.

(2) Pack the materials in boxes that are clearly labeled "For secondary storage."

(3) Send the materials to the storage site.

(4) A staff member from the library will arrange the material on shelves in call number order by site.

10. RECONSIDERATION OF MATERIALS

As is stated in the *SPJC Faculty Manual* and in Policy 7 of this section of the procedures manual, the SPJC Library supports the principles stated in the Library Bill of Rights and opposes efforts at censorship in its "maintenance of . . . responsibility to provide public information and enlightenment." This responsibility also entails establishing a formal procedure for reconsideration of materials. Should a library user encounter material he or she feels is objectionable, he/she has the right to complete the

"User's Request for Reconsideration of Library Material," Form LI 407.

Materials that are under reconsideration are brought to the College-wide Library Committee, who study the situation and then make their recommendation for action to the Director of Libraries. The final decision is the sole responsibility of the Director and the Director's designees.

PROCEDURE

The following procedure is a modification of the recommendations for action from the Intellectual Freedom Committee of the Florida Library Association in cases of attempted censorship.

1) When the person complains about the material, try to resolve the complaint informally at the point of initial contact, usually at the circulation or reference desk.

2) Listen to the person's objections in a calm, courteous, reasonable manner, seeking to defuse the situation without committing the library to any specific course of action. (It is estimated that 90 percent of complaints about library materials are resolved informally.)

3) If the person insists on pursuing the complaint, take the complainant to the Librarian-in-Charge.

4) The Librarian-in-Charge will provide the complainant with a copy of the Library Bill of Rights and a copy of the SPJC Library's Collection Development Policy.

5) Again, attempt to reason and explain the Library's position before anything is put in writing.

6) If there is still no resolution, give the complainant a copy of Form LI 407 and ask him/her to fill it out completely.

7) Notify the Director of Libraries about the complaint. The Director may decide to notify the FLA Intellectual Freedom Committee of the incident.

8) When the complainant returns the completed form, inform him/her that his/her complaint will be taken to the College-wide Library Committee for discussion and recommendation, and that he/she will be notified in writing of the action taken.

9) The Director of Libraries presents the request for reconsideration to the Committee and asks for their recommendations.

10) The Director makes the final decision concerning the request for reconsideration and notifies the complainant of the decision in

writing, explaining the procedure and justifying the final decision.
11) The Director notifies all the LINCs about the situation and informs them about its resolution.

11. GIFT ACCEPTANCE

The SPJC Library uses the same criteria as that governing the selection of purchased items in evaluating gift materials chosen for inclusion in the Library's collection. The Library reserves the right to dispose of materials not chosen for inclusion in the collection as it sees fit, operating within the guidelines of the District Board of Trustees' rules regarding surplus library materials.

The library is not responsible for determining a monetary value for gift items, although the Director of Libraries will acknowledge receipt of the number of items accepted. Under certain circumstances, a "gift" may be used as a replacement for lost library materials.

PROCEDURE--DONATIONS

1) Before donations are accepted, donors are advised courteously that the following stipulations may apply:
   a. Materials should have a copyright or publication date within five years of the current date, unless the material has important historical value or is of particular use to an individual site library.
   b. The gift must meet materials selection criteria.
   c. Materials should be in good condition with no evidence of water, insect or mold damage.
   d. The donor will be asked to sign the Gift and Donations Form before materials are accepted at any site.
2) Materials may be delivered to any site library and sent to the library site receiving the gift.
3) The staff member accepting the materials fills out the Gift and Donations Form and has the donor sign and date the form.
4) The receiving staff member gives a copy of the form to the donor.
5) If the material is being sent to another site, a copy of the form is kept, indicating the date sent to the other site and enclosing the form with the materials being sent.

6) At the designated site, the librarians will select the items to be added to the collection.
7) The staff disposes of unwanted items by placing them on a cart marked "Free Materials" and allowing library users to take what they want. If the material is in poor condition, it is thrown out.
8) The Librarian-in-Charge notifies the Director of Libraries of the number of items accepted.
9) The Director of Libraries forwards a thank you letter to the donor for the number of items accepted.

REPLACEMENT OF "LOST" ITEMS

1) At the discretion of the Librarian-in-Charge, library users who have lost library materials may replace them by making a gift of a new copy of the lost item(s).
2) The item is withdrawn at LPC and counted as withdrawn.
3) The new item is processed.

COMPLIMENTARY TEXTBOOK COPIES

1) The library accepts any donations from faculty members of complimentary copies of textbooks with the understanding that only those that are currently in use or that have special value will be added to the collection.
2) Those not added to the collection will be marked as SPJC Surplus Property and made available to the students and public as "Free Materials."

12. LIBRARY BILL OF RIGHTS

The SPJC Library endorses the following document from the American Library Association. The American Library Association affirms that all libraries are forums for information and ideas, and that the following basic policies should guide their services:
1) Books and other Library resources should be provided for the interest, information and enlightenment of all the people of the community the Library serves. Materials should not be excluded because of the origin, background, or view of those contributing to their creation.
2) Libraries should provide materials and information presenting all points of view on current and historical

issues. Materials should not be proscribed or removed from
libraries because of partisan or doctrinal disapproval.

3) Libraries should challenge censorship in the fulfillment of their
   responsibility to provide information and enlightenment.

4) Libraries should cooperate with all persons and groups
   concerned with resisting abridgment of free expression and free
   access to ideas.

5) A person's rights to use a Library should not be denied or
   abridged because of origin, age, background or views.

6) Libraries that make exhibit spaces and meeting rooms available to the public they serve should make such facilities
   available on an equitable basis, regardless of the beliefs or
   affiliations of individuals or groups requesting their use.

13. FREEDOM TO READ

The SPJC Library endorses the following document from the
American Library Association and Association of American
Publishers.

1) It is in the public interest for publishers and librarians to make
   available the widest diversity of views and expressions, including those that are unorthodox or unpopular with the majority.

2) Publishers, librarians and booksellers do not need to endorse
   every idea or presentation contained in the books they make
   available. It would conflict with the public interest for them to
   establish their own political, moral or aesthetic views as a
   standard for determining what books should be published or
   circulated.

3) It is contrary to the public interest for publishers or librarians to
   determine the acceptability of a book on the basis of the
   personal history or political affiliations of the author.

4) There is no place in our society for efforts to coerce the taste of
   others, to confine adults to the reading matter deemed suitable
   for adolescents, or to inhibit the efforts of writers to achieve
   artistic expression.

5) It is not in the public interest to force a reader to accept with any
   book the prejudgment of a label characterizing the book or
   author as subversive or dangerous.

6) It is the responsibility of publishers and librarians, as guardians
   of the people's freedom to read, to contest encroachments upon

that freedom by individuals or groups seeking to impose their
own standards or tastes upon the community at large.

7) It is the responsibility of publishers and librarians to give full
meaning to the freedom to read by providing books that enrich
the quality and diversity of though and expression. By the
exercise of this affirmative responsibility, bookmen can demonstrate that the answer to a bad book is a good one, the answer
to a bad idea is a good one.

14. WEEDING

Weeding of the periodicals collection is performed to eliminate
extraneous copies of periodicals that have been replaced in other
formats, and to dispose of material that is no longer relevant. The
latter is true of subscriptions that have ceased at some time in the
past, are incomplete and have no enduring value as research tools
in a community college library. Ephemeral materials, those titles
whose relevancy is limited and whose research value is minimal,
are generally retained for a limited period (from 1 to 5 years), then
discarded.

PROCEDURE

Weeding of periodicals that have been replaced by microform is
performed after the microform has been check in. Weeding of
ephemera is generally performed once a year during the summer
months when the library is less busy.

1) The Periodicals Committee Chair prepares a list annually each
fall of all withdrawn titles and volumes and send this to the
Director of Libraries.

2) The Director of Libraries sends the list to the President of the
College for approval.

3) Faculty members are contacted to see if any of the discarded
titles might be useful to them in their classrooms.

4) Remaining withdrawn periodicals are offered for sale to
periodical vendors.

5) Pull the periodicals that have been designated for discard,
checking to make sure no other titles are included by accident.

6) Stamp thoroughly with the "SPJC Surplus Property" stamp.
Remove or blank-out all SPJC Library markings.

7) Desensitize all periodicals.

8) Notify the periodicals committee chair and the LPC of changes in backfile format or titles or volumes withdrawn. LPC makes appropriate changes to the database.
9) Unsold withdrawn periodicals are discarded.

15. ALA STATEMENT ON PROFESSIONAL ETHICS

The SPJC Library endorses the following statement from the American Library Association governing professional ethics for librarians.

1) Librarians must provide the highest level of service through appropriate and usefully organized collections, fair and equitable circulation and service policies, and skillful, accurate, unbiased, and courteous responses to all requests for assistance.
2) Librarians must resist all efforts by groups or individuals to censor Library materials.
3) Librarians must protect each user's right to privacy with respect to information sought or received, and materials consulted, borrowed, or acquired.
4) Librarians must adhere to the principles of due process and equality of opportunity in peer relationships and personnel actions.
5) Librarians must distinguish clearly in their actions and statements between their personal philosophies and attitudes and those of an institution or professional body.
6) Librarians must avoid situations in which personal interests might be served or financial benefits gained at the expense of Library users, colleagues, or the employing institution.

16. COPYRIGHT GUIDELINES

The SPJC Library adheres to all provisions of the U. S. Copyright Law (17 U. S. C. section 107). It also promotes compliance by the college community.

Property Accountability—Surplus Library Books and Materials
(See Legal Authority P6Hx23-5.13. Page V-53, 6 of 8; 11/17/92, Revision 20.) Periodically library books and materials should be reviewed by library staff to identify items valued at less than $500

which have become obsolete or the continued use of which would be uneconomical, inefficient, or which would serve no useful function.

These books/materials should be removed from circulation in accordance with established internal procedures following approval of the site librarian.

A. Books and materials selected for removal must meet one of the following tests before they may be purged from the collection.
   1) The books/materials have been infrequently utilized for an extended period of time.
   2) There are other books/materials in the collection which fulfill the same need more adequately.
   3) The physical condition of the books/materials is such that they cannot be utilized and repair would be impractical.
   4) The age of the books/materials is such that they are not useful for either current or historical purposes.
B. In evaluating books/materials under (A), an instructor with expertise in the relevant discipline should be consulted if library staff question whether removal of the item is appropriate.
C. Books/materials approved for disposal shall be canceled and marked as "SPJC Surplus Property" by the site librarian in charge of acquisitions in accordance with established internal procedures.
D. Books/materials withdrawn from the collection shall be recorded in the Cancellation Statistics. Book cards and catalog card sets shall be retained for a period of three (3) years arranged by classification order by year of withdrawal.
E. Books/materials approved for removal from circulation shall be boxed. They will be picked up by Central Services after the department has submitted a Move Request, Form PR 418.
F. After presidential approval has been obtained, the Vice President for Facilities Planning and Institutional Services shall dispose of surplus library books/materials by: sale at the annual college auction; donation to a charitable organization, if of no commercial value; destruction, if of no commercial value.

Property Accountability—Donations
Donations to the college are categorized as follows:

Category 1: Includes items of personal property having no unusual liability and no maintenance cost.

Category 2: Includes items of personal property having either unusual liability or maintenance cost with the annual   cost of maintenance not exceeding $500.

Category 3: Includes items of personal property with liability or unusual maintenance cost with cost of maintenance exceeding $500 annually.

Category 4: Includes all real property (land or buildings).

From time to time members of the college staff will be contacted by an individual or organization that wishes to donate property to the college. When this occurs, the college employee is to refer the matter to the appropriate member of the President's Cabinet. Said cabinet member will determine the exact nature of the donation and present the information concerning the donation to the President's Cabinet. If the cabinet approves the donation, the president will accept the gift in the name of the college on behalf of the District Board of Trustees, and will write a letter of thanks to the donor. The cabinet member will designate an administrator to make the actual acceptance. This administrator will be charged with the responsibility for preparing and forwarding a copy of the gift acceptance form to the Property Management Office. Gifts valued at $500 or more are required to be tagged by the Property Management Office and placed in the inventory.

17. COLLECTION DEVELOPMENT POLICY FOR PERSONS WITH DISABILITIES

Persons with disabilities have equal access to information and sources under the provisions of the American with Disabilities Act (ADA) and Section 504 of the Rehabilitation Act of 1973 to the extent possible within the mission guidelines of the M. M. Bennett Libraries.

PROCEDURE

1) The Collection Development Librarian and/or others appointed by the Librarian-in-Charge at each site will read *The Americans with Disabilities Act and Libraries: Questions and Answers*, prepared by the Libraries Serving Special Populations Section

of the Association of Specialized and Cooperative Library agencies, a division of American Library Association (on file in each site library) and other information about the ADA and Section 504 of the Rehabilitation Act of 1973.

2) Each session will send a list of the disabilities currently represented by the student population at that site to the Librarian-in-Charge.

3) The Collection Development Librarian and/or others appointed by the Librarian-in-Charge at each site will conduct a self-evaluation after notification to identify areas of the materials collection which need to be improved or made more accessible in order to meet the needs of the students and/or staff with disabilities. The self-evaluation must:
   a. contain a list of the interested persons consulted;
   b. include students and/or staff with disabilities who use or are interested in the libraries to determine what kinds of formats your library should make available;
   c. describe the areas examined and identify the problems;
   d. describe the modifications made, such as borrowing special equipment from other sites or agencies, etc.

4) The Collection Development Librarian will develop resources as appropriate, and also will arrange to resource share with other libraries and agencies to meet the needs of the users with disabilities.

5) The Collection Development Librarian will make available to faculty and others involved in selection bibliographies available from the National Library Services for the Blind and Physically Handicapped (The Library of Congress, Washington, D.C. 20542) such as *Reading Materials in Large Type, Reference Books in Special Media, Magazines in Special Media, Building a Library Collection on Blindness and Physical Disabilities;* Basic Materials to use in selecting materials. Other bibliographies on disabilities can be acquired from:
   a. National Captioning Institute; 5203 Leesburg Pike; Falls Church, VA 22041.
   b. National Technical Institute for the Deaf; One Lamb Memorial Drive; P. O. Box 9887; Rochester, NY 14623-0887.
   c. Captioned Films/Videos for the Deaf, Modern Talking Picture Service; 5000 Park Street North; St. Petersburg, FL 33709.

    d. Florida Department of State; Division of Library and Information Service; R. A. Gray Building; Tallahassee, FL 32399-0250.

    e. Florida Department of Education; Division of Blind Services; Bureau of Library Services for the Blind and Physically Handicapped; 420 Platt Street; Daytona Beach, FL 32114.

    f. National Rehabilitation Information Center; 8455 Colesville Road, Suite 935; Silver Springs, MD 20910-3319.

    g. Another useful source for materials selection are special periodicals and newspapers dealing with disabilities. A list of some newsletters and periodicals have been given to the Collection Development Librarian at each site.

    h. R. R. Bowker publishes *The Complete Directory of Large Print Books and Serials* which can be a selection tool.

6) The Collection Development Librarian at each site will make available resources for persons with disabilities, such as:

    a. Special materials dealing with disabilities, including resource directories.

    b. Books in large type, Braille, print/Braille, audio tape, depending on the opinions of the users with vision impairments.

    c. Sign language books.

    d. Closed caption videos.

    e. Collection of special software programs for library users who are sight or hearing impaired to use with computers.

    f. CD-ROM materials with the necessary equipment to scan standard print to turn it into an electronic format for enlargement, printing out in large print or Braille, and converting into speech.

    g. Computers with synthesized speech and large monitor displays and CD-ROM players.

    h. A union list of specialized equipment available on each site.

7) The emphasis in materials selection for those persons with disabilities will be first, to provide materials to support college curricula; second, to provide materials on employment potential and possibilities for persons with disabilities; third, to provide materials creating awareness and attitudes toward acceptance of persons with disabili-

ties. Sign language materials should be comprehensive and up to date.

FAIRBANKS NORTH STAR BOROUGH PUBLIC LIBRARY
Fairbanks, Alaska

CONTENTS

I. INTRODUCTION

The *Collection Development Plan* states the principles upon which the Fairbanks North Star Borough Public Library's collection is being built. These principles derive from the library's mission statement.

The *Collection Development Plan* expands the mission statement by describing user needs that the collection is intended to address and the extent that materials will be purchased in specific areas. The collection development principles are supported by separate statements that describe the rationale and methods used relating to assessment, intellectual freedom, selection, user suggestions, and maintenance.

Annually, the Director of the Fairbanks North Star Borough Public Library will present the plan governing collection development to the Library Commission for review.

II. COLLECTION PURPOSE

The purpose of the Fairbanks North Star Borough Public Library System's collection is to provide materials to assist individuals in pursuit of their personal, educational, recreational, and professional needs and goals. Materials provided correspond to the primary and secondary roles of the library as follows:

A. Reference Library (primary)
1. Materials that provide short answers to specific and/or quantifiable questions.
2. Materials that constitute a standardized subject core collection of resources necessary for a library.

B. Popular Materials Library (primary)
1. Materials that provide entertainment and pleasure.
2. Materials that help individuals pursue their recreational activities and hobbies.

C. Independent Learning Center (secondary)
1. Materials that support self-education pursued apart from a formal on-site program.

2. Materials that improve or enhance careers or jobs or relate to personal understanding or growth.

D. Preschooler's Door to Learning (secondary)
  1. Materials that introduce young children to their written heritage.
  2. Materials that help adults engage a child's curiosity and eagerness to understand.

III. USER NEEDS

The library acknowledges that each person in the community has information needs that are important to that individual. It also recognizes that it has limited financial resources to respond to these needs. While the library's materials collection will not deny any need consistent with its mission, emphasis will be given to materials which support the library's primary and secondary roles in the community. To meet the needs of its clientele, the library strives to maintain at least a minimal level collection of materials in all Library of Congress classification divisions so that a full range of knowledge is provided.

The library supports cooperative collection development between libraries and is establishing agreements with other libraries in the state and locally. [Appendices deleted in this book.] In these agreements, the library will identify and prioritize subject areas for which it will attempt to provide in-depth collections and will likewise identify subject areas for which it will rely on other cooperating libraries to provide in-depth collections. Also, in view of the resources available at the Rasmuson Library, no subject areas will be developed beyond an advanced study level. The library will consider such factors as user surveys, community demographic studies, staff consensus, and the collection assessment, as well as the designated mission and roles when determining these priority subject areas.

All collection development efforts at the Fairbanks North Star Borough Library will be user-driven. Satisfaction of user needs will always be the impetus for the selection and maintenance of the material collection. The library is responsible for regularly evaluating and redirecting resources as necessary so that potential users can achieve their purposes through the library.

IV. COLLECTION ASSESSMENT AND PROFILES

A. Assessment

Precise standards for measuring the quality of library collections do not exist. As a participant in the Alaska Cooperative Collection Development Project, as well as the Pacific Northwest Collection Development Program, the Fairbanks North Star Borough Public Library employs a collection assessment method of evaluating and assigning support levels to subject areas of the collection. This method employs established criteria for appraising subject areas within the collection. The Collection Level Indicators assigned for the categories in the 24 WLN Conspectus Database divisions describe the quality and depth of the collection that is available.

B. Profiles

Profiles have been written for specific areas of the collection to delineate unique collection development criteria and procedures for these areas. Included are Alaskana, media, North Pole Branch, periodicals and newspapers, reference, regional services, youth, antiquarian, and miscellaneous. [Appendix deleted in this book.]

V. INTELLECTUAL FREEDOM

The Fairbanks North Star Borough Public Library subscribes to and supports the American Library Association's Library Bill of Rights and its interpretations and the American Library Association Freedom to Read Statement. [Appendices deleted in this book.]

The library takes no sides on public issues and does not attempt to promote any beliefs or points of view through its collection. The library also does not endorse the opinions expressed in the materials held. The library recognizes its responsibility to provide materials presenting various and diverse points of view.

The standards stated in this policy will apply equally to the materials for children. The library believes that individuals may reject for themselves or their children materials which they find unsuitable. Parents are responsible for the borrowing of library material by their own children. Parents who wish to limit or restrict the use of the library by their children should personally oversee their selections.

VI. SELECTION

Selection of library materials, whether purchased or donated, is based upon the informational, educational, recreational, and professional needs of the community but is limited by factors such as budget, space, agreements with other libraries, and content of existing collections.

Every item must be considered in terms of its own excellence and the audience for whom it is intended. There is no single standard which can be applied in all acquisition decisions. Some materials may be judged primarily in terms of artistic merit, scholarship, or value as human documents; others are selected to satisfy the recreational or informational needs of the community. Materials are judged on total effect rather than specific illustrations, words, passages, or scenes which in themselves may be considered by some to be offensive.

A policy, however thorough, cannot replace the judgement of individual librarians but only provides guidelines to assist them in choosing from the vast array of available materials. In selection, the librarian uses professional judgement and expertise, based on understanding of user needs and a knowledge of authors and publishers. Reviews from professional, specialized, and general periodicals, in addition to standard lists of basic works, are also consulted. At times, the library staff may consult with others more knowledgeable in a specific subject for advice on developing that area.

Expanding areas of knowledge, changing social values, technological advances, and cultural differences require flexibility, open-mindedness, and responsiveness in the evaluation and re-evaluation of all library materials. Material will not be excluded because of the race, nationality, or the political or religious views of the writer. In order to build collections of merit, whether purchased or donated, materials will be considered according to both general and specific criteria as listed below:

A. General Criteria for the Evaluation of Library Materials
 1. Reputation and/or significance of the author, producer, performer, etc.;
 2. Suitability of subject and style for intended audience;
 3. Relation to existing collection and other material on the subject;

4. Suitability of physical format for library use;
5. Present and potential relevance to community needs;
6. Appropriateness and effectiveness of medium to content;
7. Insight into human and social conditions;
8. Importance as a document of the times;
9. Skill, competence, and purpose of author, producer, performer, etc.;
10. Attention of critics, reviewers, and public; and/or
11. Prizes, awards, or honors received.

B. Specific Criteria for the Evaluation of Works of Information and Opinion
1. Authority of author;
2. Comprehensiveness and depth of treatment;
3. Objectivity and integrity;
4. Clarity, accuracy, and logic of presentation;
5. Representation of challenging works, including extreme and/or minority points of view; and/or
6. Contribution to subject balance of the entire collection.

C. Specific Criteria for the Evaluation of Works of Imagination
1. Representation of important movement, genre, trend, or national culture;
2. Vitality and originality;
3. Artistic expression, presentation, and experimentation;
4. Sustained interest; and/or
5. Effective characterization.

VII. USER SUGGESTIONS

A. Recommendations
User recommendations for purchase of materials will be accepted for consideration. Purchase decisions will be made by the Collection Development Librarian in accordance with established selection criteria. [Suggestion form deleted.]

B. Reconsideration
Patrons concerned about material in the collection are welcome to discuss those concerns with a professional staff member. When patrons want the Selection Committee to reconsider items in the

collection, they will be given the Request for Reconsideration form [deleted] and informed of the reconsideration procedure. When the patron returns the completed form, the Collection Development Librarian in the case of adult materials or the Youth Services Librarian in the case of youth materials will report to the Selection Committee. The Committee will re-evaluate the item in terms of the selection criteria, collection assessment data, collection profiles, and the library's mission and roles statements. The Library Director will communicate the Committee's decision to the individual who submitted the Request for Reconsideration.

If the patron wishes to appeal the decision of the Selection Committee, the Library Director will bring the complaint and supporting documentation to the Library Commission at the next regularly scheduled Commission meeting. In accordance with Borough Ordinance 2.32.041, four members of the Commission shall be required for a quorum and four affirmative votes shall be necessary to carry the question. The decision of the Commission shall be final. Further appeal must be referred to a court of competent jurisdiction.

VIII. COLLECTION MANAGEMENT

A. Selection Responsibilities
The initial responsibility for selection lies with the Collection Development Librarian. The library Selection Committee, made up of the professional librarians, assists by reviewing and recommending materials for purchase in assigned subject areas. Ultimate responsibility for materials selection rests with the Library Director.

B. Assessment and Other Duties
In addition to selection responsibilities, staff librarians will participate in the accomplishment of collection development goals of the library through collection assessment and other duties, as needed. The Collection Development Librarian will coordinate the assignment of such tasks as reviewing interlibrary loan requests, inspecting damaged materials, compiling pertinent statistical reports, and sorting donations.

The Selection Committee will hold regularly scheduled meetings in order to discuss issues relevant to collection development, such as evaluating current collections and procedures, establishing development goals, setting priorities, and assigning tasks. These meetings are organized and scheduled by the Collection Development Librarian.

C. Donations/Memorials

Donations of books, magazines, and audiovisual items will be accepted with the provision that they will be subject to the standard selection criteria and procedures of the library. Donated materials not added to the collection will be made available to the public through the book sale. The library will acknowledge receipt of donations if requested, but will not give a monetary valuation for materials received.

Memorials and gift monies will be accepted, and materials purchased for the library collection with these funds are also subject to selection procedures and criteria. The library will acknowledge contributions and provide a memorial book plate when requested.

D. Non-English Language Material

Non-English language material is not emphasized. As a general rule, selection will be limited to dictionaries and instructional materials. A minimal number of popular reading materials will be added. Addition of these reading materials will be based on local demand. The collection currently includes, but is not necessarily limited to, French, Spanish, German, Korean, Vietnamese, Japanese, Russian and Alaskan Native American languages. Non-English materials will be located in the appropriate language.

E. Textbooks/Workbooks

Cooperation with the entire educational community is a basic aspect of public library service. However, extensive duplication to meet mass assignments is not feasible. General use of the library by students is encouraged, and the library will endeavor to provide some supplementary materials for students.

No attempt is made to systematically acquire textbooks or other curriculum-related materials, such as workbooks, teachers' manuals, and flashcards for the public library collection. A few basic textbooks in broad subject areas may be purchased, but textbooks or readers used in area schools will not be collected.

The library does not purchase workbooks that require the reader to complete forms or record answers or data. However, the library does provide study guides for civil service and other national, standardized tests.

F. Duplication of Materials

Librarians selecting for individual agencies have the responsibility for evaluating the demands and needs of their users and are expected to plan for sufficient duplication. More than 5 reserves per copy indicates a need to purchase additional copies.

The branch library may hold titles exclusive of the Noel Wien collection and vice versa. For the most part, materials are not duplicated in the juvenile and adult fiction circulating collections. A reading level is determined and all copies receive uniform classification. A minimum number of exceptions will be made based on the recommendation of the children's services staff. Children's editions of adult classics are shelved with the juvenile collection.

Circulating copies of reference titles may be purchased as needed. Superseded reference titles may be added to the circulating or branch collections or recycled to other libraries as appropriate.

G. Paperback Editions

Paperbacks are purchased when:
1. There is immediate demand for multiple copies;
2. The information is expected to be revised and new editions are available annually or more frequently;
3. There is a high loss or theft rate for the item;
4. The demand is expected to be relatively short-lived;
5. The only edition available is paper; or
6. It is the most appropriate format for the intended user.
The decision to bind or rebind paperback editions depends primarily on the nature of the material and the length of time the title is expected to remain in the collection. Titles to be retained but not particularly subject to loss in popularity should be bound. Trade paperback editions are often as durable as hardcover editions and are less expensive, even if the book must eventually be rebound. This type of edition is especially appropriate where circulation is not expected to be especially high.

H. Discarding

Materials which become useless due to poor physical condition, decreased demand, or obsolete information may be withdrawn. Librarians serving on the Selection Committee are expected to use the selection criteria, their own experience, and good judgement to remove such items from the collection. Discarded material is either offered to other libraries or disposed of according to Borough policy. Any last copies in the system scheduled for discard by any agency will be reviewed by the Collection Development Librarian.

I. Replacements/Rebinding

The library cannot replace all lost, damaged or worn materials. Worn, damaged or missing items are regularly reviewed for purposes of ordering replacements. Factors to be considered are circulation data; continuing demand for the particular title or subject; similar or related material remaining in the collection; and better or more current material available for purchase. Where possible and appropriate, items will be rebound instead of replaced. Out of print titles are not routinely acquired except for Alaskana where demand warrants and cost is reasonable.

J. Nonprint Materials

To help patrons find all the library's holdings on any given topic, nonfiction videos, nonfiction tapes accompanied by manuals or other print matter, and multi-tape cassette sets will be interfiled with the print nonfiction collection. Single nonfiction cassette tapes without accompanying print matter will be housed in cassette cabinets. Music cassettes and compact disks will be available in separate shelving. All nonprint materials will be cataloged according to the Library of Congress system.

K. Comic Books

Because of the ephemeral nature of this material, the library will not buy mass market comic books. However, in recognition of their value in reading motivation and entertainment, the library will acquire a limited number of comic book collections produced either with higher quality paper and binding than the mass market publications, or on microfiche. The print items will be shelved with the Berry Browsing collection, and the microfiche items will be located in the Reference section.

The library will also acquire compilations of popular comic strips and graphic, or illustrated, novels and literature. These items will be located in the appropriate section of the nonfiction and fiction collections.

L. Addition of Formats or Collections
Due to the impact on budget, space, and work, the addition of new formats or collections will be decided only by general consensus of the Selection Committee. All material purchased with funds budgeted in the library materials category will be processed.

M. Collection Maintenance
A Disaster Preparedness and Response Plan will be developed by June, 1994, and included in this Plan as Appendix M. At present, there are no provisions for conservation or preservation of materials aside from normal repair techniques. Should more sophisticated measures become necessary or more readily available, appropriate criteria and procedures will be developed and included in this Plan.

HALTOM CITY PUBLIC LIBRARY
Haltom City, Texas

CRITERIA FOR SELECTION OF BOOKS—GENERAL

A. All materials that are required for the library should meet high standards of quality and content, expression, and format.

B. Books that will serve a purpose in the collection will be selected for their factual, accurate, effective style, the suitability and significance of the subject matter, and their reliability and sincerity of opinion. In addition to these qualities, a suitable book must also have durable and attractive paper, binding and print.

C. The systematic withdrawal of lost, damaged, worn or outdated materials no longer useful is essential to maintaining the purpose and quality of the library collection.

D. Requests from groups or individuals to withdraw any library materials from the library shelves shall be referred to the Library Director or his/her appointed representative. The Library welcomes the opportunity to discuss with the citizens of Haltom City the interpretation and application of these book selection principles. However, censorship of books, urged or practiced by volunteer arbiters of morals or political opinion or by organizations that would establish a coercive concept of Americanism, must be challenged by the Library authorities in maintenance of their responsibility to provide public information and enlightenment through the printed word.

E. Neither the Library Director, staff, nor the Library Board can be expected to read every book purchased. For these reasons the selection of books is made through reliable sources such as professional library magazines, book reviewing services, and book review sections of magazines and newspapers.

MEDIA FOR BOOK SELECTION

The following list of media consulted in selection of current literature is not to be considered an exclusive one. All periodicals containing reviews and lists of current publications are consulted in order to select library materials as objectively as possible. The following publications are listed primarily for their almost exclusive devotion to evaluating current literature and for their immediacy of treatment of new publications.

1. *Booklist* and *Subscription Books Bulletin* (ALA)
2. *Publishers Weekly*
3. *Library Journal*
4. *Saturday Review*
5. *School Library Journal*
6. Standard Catalog Series--Wilson
7. *New York Times Book Review*
8. Other weekly and monthly periodicals that carry book reviews

One or more of the following standards will be applied in selecting the materials best suited to Haltom City Public Library.

1. Authoritativeness. The author must be expert and of considerable repute in the field.
2. Relation to the collection. The subject matter must complement the library's collection.
3. Permanency. The book should be of timeless or permanent value.
4. Interests of the community. The book must offer or fill a need for groups or individuals in the community.
5. Is the title available at another library in Tarrant County? This is particularly apropos of the more technical, specialized and expensive materials.
6. Purpose. The purpose or intent of the materials must be acceptable. The moral and ethical offensiveness, violent, and inflammatory presentation of viewpoints of controversial nature, the pornographic and sensational would be excluded.
7. Reputation and significance of author, illustrator and publisher.
8 Readability and popular appeal.
9. Price.
10. Format of materials.

BOOK SELECTION CRITERIA--ADULT BOOKS

Each title is judged individually according to its intrinsic merit, the subject treated, the reader interest and the need for the book in an organized collection. Each title is judged as a whole and isolated passages in themselves are not used as criteria.

In order that readers may get balanced information, the library attempts to provide books that present both or different points of view, even those points which may be regarded by some as controversial, whether because of political expression, affiliation, or moral implication.

The library feels justly proud of its adult fiction collection and it continues to be a considerable portion of the adult acquisitions. Contemporary novels that reflect human nature, experience and the problems of the human race that are treated in a skillful way are added.

Purely pornographic works and books which trade in sensationalism will not be purchased. However, serious fiction, poetry, drama and other non-fiction works which honestly present society today will not be excluded simply because of coarse language or frankness of treatment.

A. The following points should be considered when selecting adult non-fiction books:
1. The subject matter and scope of the book
2. The treatment of the subject--complete or partial? Scholarly or technical?
3. Publication date
4. Author's qualifications
5. Format--durable binding, good paper, clear type, readability or visual appeal
6. Popular demand
7. Historical value
8. Local interest
9. Price
10. Scarcity of information

B. Many of the questions applied to non-fiction also are suitable to ask of fiction. Certainly, it is important for an author to be qualified to write a novel of social, historical or psychological background. In addition, the selector will wish to test fiction with the following points.
1. Characterization--is there vitality and consistency?
2. True representation of life
3. Originality of plot

BOOK SELECTION CRITERIA--YOUNG ADULT

It is the purpose of the young adult collection to help bridge the gap between children's literature and adult literature. These books are selected with the aim of helping young people find self-realization, live useful, well-adjusted lives in the community, and know and understand the world at large. The collection includes books which will widen the boundaries of the adolescent's thinking, offering recreation as well as enrichment for his or her life. The collection covers a wide range of reading levels and interest from simple, wholesome stories to selected adult materials.

SELECTION CRITERIA--CHILDREN'S BOOKS, PUZZLES, PUPPETS, TOYS, ETC.

The selection of juvenile books is governed by the same general objectives as the other departments; but the actual process presents special problems requiring a slightly different approach. A background knowledge of children's literature is needed, since the collection must be kept well supplied with the basic titles for the growing and constantly changing patrons. Under these circumstances, purchase of new titles has to be selective from the annually increasing number of books pouring from the presses. Only a small percentage of all the new books for children published each year ever achieve review space in the regular channels.

This department places emphasis both on quality in writing and content since these are the books which help to build the child's future taste and reading habits and often prove to have a deep influence on his or her life in other aspects.

The physical format of the book is most important in the case of juveniles. Good type for young eyes and attractive illustrations may make all the difference in the book's reception by a child. And since the wear and tear on them is so great, prebinding, though slightly higher, has proven a great saving in both time and money.

To help the process of learning to read along, it is necessary that we purchase a number of primers and easy readers to help the beginner bridge the gap between listening and reading for himself or herself. Puzzles, puppets, toys, etc., are selected to increase awareness of books; to increase play skills and create interest in coming to the library.

BASIS FOR EXCLUSION

The library reserves the to exclude materials which judges to have been written or produced purely to appeal to a taste for sensationalism and/or pornography. However, a serious work which illuminates some problem or aspect of life will not be excluded because its language or subject matter may be offensive to some readers.

Materials on controversial issues and current problems which are inflammatory, sensational, or prejudiced are not generally purchased. Works by national or world figures, even if prejudiced or violent, may be acquired because they have influenced thinking either in our times or in the past.

CONTROVERSIAL TASKS

The library recognizes that many materials are controversial and that any item may offend some patrons. Selections will not be made on the basis of any anticipated approval or disapproval, but solely on the merits of the work in relation to building the collections and to serving the interests of readers.

If any title in the collection is criticized or questioned by individuals, organizations or librarians, the form "Request for Reconsideration of Library Materials" (Form No. 124) may be filled out. Upon receipt of request, complete written reevaluation will be made. If the reevaluation substantiates the original decision to include the title, it will remain in the collection.

The final decision rests with the Director. Library materials will not be marked or identified to show approval or disapproval of the contents.

Responsibility for the choice of children's reading material rests with their parents and legal guardians. Selection will not be inhibited by the possibility that controversial books may come into the possession of children.

SELECTION CRITERIA--PERIODICALS AND NEWSPAPERS

Periodicals and newspapers will be chosen as follows:
1. To supplement the book collection as an additional source of information, especially current information.
2. To satisfy recreational reading needs.
3. To serve the staff as book selection aids and professional reading.

4. To provide a unique source of local history information.
Selection of titles will follow criteria in terms of scope and depth of
subject coverage, with the following special considerations:
1. Community demand
2. Accessibility of content through *Abridged Readers' Guide to Periodical Literature*
3. Price

SELECTION CRITERIA--VIDEO CASSETTES

A. Neither the Library Director, the library staff, nor the Library Board can be expected to view every video cassette purchased. For these reasons, the selection of video cassettes is made through reliable sources such as professional library magazines, video reviewing sources and video review sections of magazines and newspapers. In addition, the following criteria are used:
1. Popular demand by the community
2. Quality of audio and video presentation
3. Price
4. Availability

B. Basis for exclusion
The library reserves the right to exclude video cassettes which it judges to be produced to a taste for sensationalism and/or pornography. However, the serious subject which illuminates some problem or aspect of life will not be excluded because its language or subject matter may be offensive to some viewers.

C. Controversial productions
The library recognizes that many video cassettes are controversial and that any item may offend some patrons. Selections will not be made on the basis of any anticipated approval or disapproval, but solely on the merits of the production in relation to building the collection and to serving the interests of the viewers.

D. Complaints
If any video cassette in the collection is criticized or questioned by individuals, organizations or librarians, the

form "Citizens Request for Reconsideration of Video Cassettes" (Form No. 125) may be filled out. Upon receipt of this request, a complete reevaluation will be made. If the reevaluation substantiates the original decision to include the title, it will remain in the collection; if not, it will be withdrawn. The final decision rests with the Library Director.

E. Ratings
  1. Video cassettes will be marked according to current rating such as G, PG, PG-13, or R.
  2. Video cassettes will not be marked to show approval or disapproval of the contents.

WEEDING

The practice of systematic discarding of materials is critical for library collection maintenance. The library literature recommends the following consideration be made before discarding any item from the library collection:
  1. Frequency of circulation
  2. Overall condition of title
  3. Title's inclusion in standard catalogs
  4. Potential future use; storage
  5. Dated material
  6. Value to total library collection
  7. Availability of information/copies elsewhere

ADULT COLLECTION DEVELOPMENT GUIDELINES

I. Criteria stated in Section VII of Haltom City Public Library Policies Manual (pp. 14-15) will be followed for all materials whether purchased or donated.
II. Collection density levels:
  A. Minimal level. A subject area which is out of scope for the library's collections, and in which few selections are made beyond very basic reference tools.
  B. Basic level. A highly selective collection which serves to introduce and define the subject and to indicate the varieties of information available elsewhere. It includes major dictionaries and encyclopedias, selected editions of important works, historical surveys, important bibliographies, and a few major periodicals in the field.

C. Study level. A collection which is adequate to support sustained independent study; that is, which is adequate to maintain knowledge of a subject required for limited or generalized purpose, of less than research intensity. It includes a wide range of basic monographs, complete collections of the works of more important writers, selections from the works of secondary writers, a selection of representative journals, and the reference tools and fundamental bibliographic apparatus pertaining to the subject.

III. Guidelines for selection by DDC subject.

000 Generalities

001　Includes materials on artificial intelligence; computers; controversial and mysterious occurrences: select representative general material to give a balance of opinion in the 001.9's--minimal level. Select more material in the 001.54's on general ways of communicating--basic level. In the 001.6's and 001.5's, select general works on hardware, software, applications; purchase guides and dictionaries. Works on popular brands/models of hardware, software, and programming languages are also acquired. Weed every 2-3 years--basic level.

010　General bibliographies: purchase for reference and selection needs. Acquire subject bibliographies only where a high demand exists--minimal level.

020　Library science materials: select for staff development/reference--minimal level.

030　General encyclopedias: update every 4-5 years on a rotating basis. Purchase subject encyclopedias for high demand areas only--basic level.

050　General serials: our periodicals are not classified. Purchase will continue in those general areas primarily in the English language with possibility of some Asian languages--basic level.

060　General organization: purchase if public displays need--minimal level.

070　Journalism, publishing, newspapers: purchase general information as it applies to the business and career aspect--minimal level.

080   General collections: acquire only basic sources in English if public demands--minimal level.

090   Manuscripts and book rarities: not purchased, acquired only if donated and fit into our general collection.

100 Philosophy and related disciplines

110   Metaphysics: purchase representative sources--minimal level.

120   Epistemology, causation, humankind: select representative materials--minimal level.

130   Paranormal phenomena and arts: acquire according to demand--minimal level.

140   Specific philosophical viewpoints: select representative titles of each viewpoint to give a balance of opinion--minimal level.

150   Psychology: acquire self-help material and works on family/business relationships. Replace worn/damaged material--basic level.

160   Logic: select where need arises--minimal level.

170   Ethics (moral philosophy): purchase representative materials on basic doctrines--basic level.

180   Ancient, medieval,. oriental philosophy: acquire representative materials, basic sources--minimal level.

190   Modern western philosophy: select only representative sources for most cultures--minimal level.

[The rest of the guidelines for the 200 - 900's have not been duplicated here due to space limitations.]

IV. Withdrawing and weeding
A. The criteria as described in Section VII (p.26) of the Haltom City Public Library Policies Manual will be considered when withdrawing items and weeding the collections.
B. Procedures for marking for withdrawal:
    1. Examine books on shelves to determine whether they fall into any one of several categories as follows:
       a. Out of date: information is no longer accurate. Be sure to examine for special indices or other special materials unavailable elsewhere.

    b. Inappropriate: material does not fit in with the guidelines of selection in that subject area.

    c. Later editions: there are later editions on the shelf which supersede the material in the earlier edition. Be aware of classics in the field.

    d. Multiple copies: no more than two (three?) copies should be on the shelves except in special circumstances. For example, more than two copies of very popular works an classics may be needed.

    e. Condition: a title may be pulled for either deletion or for repair or binding. Be sure the item is clearly marked for whichever process is being suggested.

2. Mark items for withdrawal with white dots, with yellow dots for replacement/repair. Books can be pulled at a later time for removal. Pull card sets on white dotted books.

V. Revision

These guidelines should be reviewed every other year so that the needs of the community will continually be reflected in the development of the collection.

HOUSTON PUBLIC LIBRARY
Houston, Texas

4.1 Purpose, Goals, and Responsibility

(1) Purpose of Policy

The mission of Houston Public Library is to develop and implement a program of modern library services to contribute to the enrichment of the citizens it serves. The fulfillment of this mission requires a collection of considerable scope and variety.

The vast array of resources available and escalating acquisition and processing costs necessitate that the Library have written selection policies to ensure that the materials obtained are those which best serve the needs of the community. This policy is intended to provide guidance for librarians in their role as selectors and to inform the public about the principles upon which decisions are made.

(2) Selection Goals

Within limitations of budget, space, and availability of materials, the Library attempts to provide a large and stimulating collection of materials responsive to community needs. As a basic community institution, the public library is dedicated to the concept of service to everyone. With full awareness of the pluralistic nature of its community, the Library strives to make available materials reflecting the needs of all citizens--individuals of various cultural, ethnic, religious, and philosophical groups; and of differing educational levels; the disabled; the English-speaking; and the non-English speaking. The Library not only has an obligation to give the best service possible to its regular patrons but to search for materials and methods that will assist those in the community who have not been library users. To do this, the Library must study its neighborhoods and constituencies on an ongoing basis to discern present needs that are unmet and to anticipate future trends.

The primary task of Houston Public Library is the provision of materials which will meet the informational and educational needs of the public. The Library also recognizes a duty to make available materials for entertainment and recreation, many of which are of immediate but more short term interest.

In selecting materials for the collection, the Library does not promote any particular belief or view but offers a forum where individuals can examine different sides of issues and make their own decisions.

(3) Responsibility for Selection
Final responsibility and authority for materials selection rests with the Director of Libraries who operates within the policies of the Library Board.

Budgets for each unit are allocated by the Director in consultation with the Assistant Director, the Chiefs, and the Coordinator of Materials Selection.

The Chief of Central and the Chief of Branch Services identify major service and collecting priorities within their divisions.

The Coordinator of Materials Selection oversees the development and maintenance of the collection including monitoring the budget, recommending on collection policies, and approving materials added. Under the Coordinator's supervision, the Adult Specialist and Juvenile Specialist direct the selection process, provide training for selectors, and consult on collection planning and evaluation. The Office exercises advisory and supervisory functions, depending upon the individual agency's concern and the nature of the question involved.

The unit manager is responsible for the general development of all collections within the unit and for ensuring that orders are kept within allotted funds. Under the Adult Specialist's supervision, the daily development and maintenance of the adult collection will be the responsibility of the adult librarian(s) assigned to collection development. Under the Juvenile Specialist's supervision, the daily development and maintenance of the juvenile collection will be the responsibility of the children's librarian.

Selection processes are, by nature, cooperative. Every librarian on the staff participates in selection through reviewing activities, taking responsibility for specific areas within the collection, and/or making suggestions for purchases. The Library also welcomes suggestions from the community. Final decision on inclusion of titles rests with the Library.

4.2 Central and Branch Collections

(1) Central

The Central Division maintains a general, well-balanced collection on the "study level," as defined by the guidelines of the American Library Association's Collection Development Committee. Materials for more advanced research are collected in a limited number of target areas specified in the Division's collection development plan.

The Central Division functions as the major resource center of the Houston Public Library System. The collection is appropriate for the information needs of a complex metropolitan center and serves as a popular library for the immediate neighborhood. Special attention is paid to the collecting practices of libraries which are members of the Houston Area Library System and the Houston Area Research Library Consortium so that unnecessary duplication is avoided and the range of accessible titles enlarged.

(2) Branches

Branch collections offer general interest materials on a variety of subjects to support the needs of the neighborhoods served. All branches share a common core of titles including popular and classic books, high-demand magazines, and basic reference sources. Beyond this core, collections vary considerably from branch to branch depending on the size of the agency and community needs.

Branches are designated small, medium, large or regional according to size of collection and physical plant, number of staff, and range of services offered. Regional collections consist of a wide variety of circulating books, magazines, and reference sources. Regional libraries not only provide materials to meet the needs of the immediate neighborhood but, whenever possible, serve as a back-up for collections of surrounding branches. Regional managers are expected to maintain open lines of communication with nearby branches to assess more accurately the nature of community demand. Small, medium, and large branches offer a range of circulating books, basic reference sources, and magazines chosen to meet defined neighborhood needs. Small, medium, and large branches differ from each other chiefly in number of holdings rather than in the type of materials collected.

Branches of any size may develop collection strength in particular subjects or languages as specified in the Division's collection development plans.

Branch Services supports a number of specialized outreach agencies such as Books-by-Mail, Institutional Services, Westwood Bookstop, and M.D. Anderson. These agencies maintain circulating collections of popular fiction and non-fiction titles.

4.3 Selection Criteria

(1) General

The evaluation of materials is characterized by flexibility, open-mindedness, and responsiveness to the changing needs of the citizens of Houston. The following are among the most important general criteria:

1. Relevance to community needs.
2. Suitability of subject, style, and reading level for intended audience.
3. Insight into human and social conditions.
4. Reputation and/or significance of author.
5. Demand for the material.
6. Reviews by critics and staff members.
7. Reputation of the publisher or producer.
8. Availability and accessibility of materials in the collection on the same subject.
9. Clarity, accuracy, and logic of presentation.
10. Suitability of format for library use.

An item need not meet all criteria to be added to the collection. Some titles may be judged primarily in terms of artistic merit, scholarship, information content, or value as human documents. Others are chosen chiefly on the basis of patron demand. Although the Library will not purchase sufficient copies of titles for classroom use, the system has a strong commitment to provide a variety of supplemental materials in support of classroom assignments.

(2) The Library will attempt to select materials that represent a range of viewpoints and will do its best to exercise impartiality in selection decisions. The collection will represent as many sides of controversial issues as budget, space, and availability of materials allow. Selection will be based on criteria given throughout this policy. The race, religion, nationality, or political views of an author, the frankness or coarseness of language, the controversial content of an item or the endorsement or approval of an individual or group in the community will not automatically cause an item to be included or excluded.

Materials are evaluated as a whole and not on the basis of a particular passage or illustration.

The Houston Public Library recognizes that some items are controversial and that any given title may offend some patron. Thus, some citizens may seek out a particular title while others may quite legitimately find this same title inappropriate for themselves. The same principle applies in the selection of materials which are read by minors. The Houston Public Library does not have the right or responsibility to serve in loco parentis. It is the parents, and only the parents, who may restrict their children from access to library materials. Responsibility for the reading of minors rests with the parents or legal guardians. Selection of adult materials will not be inhibited by the possibility that materials may inadvertently come into the possession of children.

The Houston Public Library supports intellectual freedom end endorses the concepts embodied in the Freedom to Read statement and Library Bill of Rights issued by the American Library Association.

(3) Gifts

Houston Public Library accepts gifts of books and other materials with the understanding that items added to the collection must meet the same criteria as purchased materials. The Library retains the authority to accept or reject gifts, and to make all decisions as to their use, housing, and final disposition. All gift titles added to the collection must be approved by the Coordinator. Library staff do not appraise gift materials for tax purposes.

4.4 Collection Management

(1) Collection/Community Analysis

Houston Public Library recognizes that its community is continuously evolving. Under the guidance of the appropriate Chief or Assistant Chief, each unit conducts a comprehensive marketing and community analysis once every seven years, or more frequently as required. These studies incorporate data directly pertinent to materials selection including levels of user satisfaction, potential markets for specially tailored collections, and major demographic shifts that have occurred.

This data will be used to develop a plan addressing collection strengths and weaknesses and ways that selection should be adjusted to meet changing needs. The unit manager, in consultation with the Coordinator of Materials Selection and the appropriate Chief or Assistant Chief, is responsible for preparing this plan. The manager will draft annual updates to record progress made in implementation and specific activities planned for the year. These plans will be utilized by the Coordinator and Chiefs in recommending budget allocations.

(2) Management Issues

The collection is regularly reviewed for weeding, transfers, binding, and repairs to ensure that holdings are timely and inviting to users. No item shall be discarded from the collection or transferred from one agency to another without the approval of the Coordinator of Materials Selection.

Houston Public Library houses in closed stack areas materials which are necessary, but which are not needed on a daily basis.

The Coordinator, Adult Specialist, and Juvenile Specialist regularly identify materials for rush processing that should be made available to the public on a priority basis.

The acquisition of approval materials through direct contact between the Houston Public Library and outside agencies is an authorized procedure. In order that such transactions be of a coordinated nature, no such contact should be made without prior approval of the Office of Materials Selection.

4.5 Selection by Levels

(1) Adult Materials

Collections of adult material must fill the informational, educational, and recreational needs of a wide range of users whose reading levels vary greatly. These needs are met by many media and forms of materials in English, Spanish, and other languages.

For the age group from fourteen through seventeen, it is recognized that there is a body of literature that deals frankly, honestly, and realistically with the growth situations confronting the young person. This literature is designed to equip young people with positive personal development skills for situations in contemporary society. These materials will be selected according to the same general criteria as discussed above. The Coordinator of Materials Selection will make the initial decision in referring titles to adult or juvenile selection. Titles intended for the fourteen- to seventeen-year-old must be physically located in the adult collection area and should not be separately cataloged or interfiled with juvenile books.

(2) Juvenile Materials

The juvenile collection includes items for informational, educational, and recreational purposes for children from infancy through age thirteen. The overriding goal in selecting materials for children is to provide the best new materials and copies of older titles of lasting value. Materials are collected in English, Spanish, and other languages as required by the community.

Under the direction of the Juvenile Specialist, the Council of Children's Librarians oversees the review, selection, and placement of juvenile materials. Review copies of books are critically read by a children's librarian before they are purchased.

Materials in this area are selected according to the same criteria as discussed above. However, it is understood that the reading level and maturity of the patrons to be served influence the interpretation of those criteria. Some areas present selection problems not encountered in the adult collection. Special attention must be paid to such factors as quality of illustrations, suitability of format, reading level, and general appeal. All books are evaluated with regard to racism, sexism, ageism, and other stereotypes. Careful consideration is given in deciding which of the available new titles merit inclusion in the collection.

Ordinarily, books containing objectionable words, illustrations, or phrases are not suited to a collection for children but may be accepted if the overall level is of high merit.

Materials for infants and pre-schoolers are chosen to offer a first introduction to words, pictures, and concepts. Emphasis on materials for this age level is made in recognition of the fact that the public library is the only major library resource freely available to them.

Materials are chosen to match the developing reading skills and enlarging interests of children during the years of elementary education and to satisfy the more sophisticated curiosities and tastes of early adolescents. Titles intended for the middle school student (ages eleven through thirteen) may be separately displayed within the juvenile collection but should not be interfiled with material from the adult collection.

4.6 Reconsideration of Library Materials

The Library will review the selection of a specific item upon request of a member of the community. The form "Request for Reconsideration of Library Materials" is available at all service desks. The Library Director, in consultation with the Coordinator of Materials Selection and other appropriate staff, review the request in light of the criteria delineated in this policy. A letter will be sent promptly to the person or organization making the request. If the individual is not satisfied with the action taken, he/she may appeal to the Library Board.

4.7 Review

This policy will be reviewed periodically to ensure that it is responsive to the changing needs of the Library System and of the general community.

MICKEY REILY PUBLIC LIBRARY
Corrigan, Texas

I. Mission Statement

The Mickey Reily Public Library provides materials and services to help community and area residents obtain information meeting their recreational, educational, and professional needs. Special emphasis is placed on supporting students at all academic levels and on stimulating young children's interest in and appreciation for reading and learning.

Fiction and nonfiction, popular materials, reference materials, periodicals, and videos will be the mainstay of the library holdings, but further information requests will be met through interlibrary loan cooperation and reference back-up services made available through membership in the Houston Area Library System. The Mickey Reily Public Library serves as a learning, educational, leisure-reading, and information center for all residents of the community and those who live in outlying areas.

II. Description of Community and Service Area

Corrigan is a small rural community with a population of 1,764 within the city limits. The Mickey Reily Public Library offers services to persons residing both inside and outside the city limits--with a service area population of 7,981.

The economy is largely dependent upon the three wood products mills located in the area. There are also several small family owned businesses. Many people commute to the area to work at the mills or to teach at the local schools. There are also many who commute to other areas to work, or to attend area colleges and universities.

The median age of persons in the area is 30.9, with the largest percentage group being age 25 to 59. The next largest group is those who are under 18 years of age. There is also a large group of citizens who are over the age of 60. The population is made up of 47.50% white, 39.68% black, 0.11% American Indian, 0.34% Asian or Pacific Islander and 12.35% other race.

III. The Library Bill of Rights

The American Library Association affirms that all libraries are forums for information and ideas, and that the following basic policies should guide their services:

1. Books and other library resources should be provided for the interest, information, and enlightenment of all people of the community the library serves. Materials should not be excluded because of the origin, background, or views of those contributing to their creation.
2. Libraries should provide materials and information presenting all points of view on current and historical issues. Materials should not be proscribed or removed because of partisan or doctrinal disapproval.
3. Libraries should challenge censorship in the fulfillment of their responsibility to provide information and enlightenment.
4. Libraries should cooperate with all persons and groups concerned with resisting abridgment of free expression and free access to ideas.
5. A person's right to use a library should not be denied or abridged because of origin, age, background, or views.
6. Libraries which make exhibit spaces and meeting rooms available to the public they serve should make such facilities available on an equitable basis, regardless of the beliefs or affiliations of individuals or groups requesting their use.

IV. General Subject Boundaries

The Library exists to provide materials for all ages, from preschool to adult. The purpose of the adult book collection is to make available books and other materials that will meet educational, informational, cultural, recreational, and leisure-reading interests and needs of the patrons. To this end, the library endeavors to maintain a carefully selected collection of highly recommended, representative books of permanent value and of current interest. Each title is judged individually according to its intrinsic merit--the subject treated, the reader interest, and the need for the book in an organized collection. Likewise, each title is judged as a whole, and isolated passages in themselves are not used as criteria.

The children's collection is selected to provide pleasurable reading for reading's sake and, insofar as possible, to provide information in all fields of knowledge which are of interest to children. The collection is carefully selected for children of all ages and abilities, and emphasis is placed upon books which stimulate imagination, mental growth, and the development of taste for good literature and beautifully made books.

Young people's books are selected with the aim of helping teenagers find self-realization, live useful and well-adjusted lives in the community, and know and understand the world at large. The materials are selected to widen the adolescent's thinking, to enrich his life, and to help him fulfill his recreational and emotional needs.

Mickey Reily Public Library will provide, as far as possible, materials treating all sides of controversial issues--materials that give evidence of a sincere desire to be factual, that are written in a reasonable fashion, and that show results of careful study.

Materials on controversial issues that present only one side of a question and are written in a violent, sensational, and inflammatory manner will ordinarily not be selected. Books of short term value, such as campaign biographies or fiction about which there is great curiosity, will occasionally be acquired by the library; these kinds of materials will be discarded when they have served their purpose of meeting a strong, though temporary, demand.

Since it is possible to make a mistake--even when carefully applying these principles--the librarian stands ready to review individual decisions upon written request. (See attached Request for Reconsideration form). Such requests will be considered by the librarian and/or the board of directors.

V. Gift Policy

The library accepts gifts of books, periodicals, audio-cassettes and the like with the understanding that they will be added to the collection only when needed. The library makes an effort to dispose carefully and thoughtfully of all gift materials which it does not add to its own collection. Upon request, a letter of receipt will be issued for donated items. However, determination of dollar value will be left to the donor.

VI. Weeding

Once materials are deemed no longer useful to library patrons, they will be withdrawn from the collection and discarded at the discretion of the librarian and/or the board of directors. Weeding will be done methodically and on an on-going basis, and according to accepted professional practices as described in the publication, *The Crew Manual*.

This is to ensure that the needs and demands of the library's users and potential users are being met to the best of our ability--by providing current, up-to-date materials that are attractive and appealing to our patrons--and to closely monitor the strengths and weaknesses of the collection.

VII. Conclusion

This document is to serve as a guideline for building and maintaining the collection of Mickey Reily Public Library. This document will be reviewed and revised from time to time, in an attempt to meet the ever-changing needs and demands of our patrons.

Sources Used

1) *The Dynamic Community Library: Creative, Practical, and Inexpensive Ideas for the Director*, by Beth Wheeler Fox.
2) *Intellectual Freedom Handbook*, 4th ed., rev. 1990. Prepared by Intellectual Freedom Committee, Texas Library Association.
3) *TLA Public Library Selection Policy Handbook*.
4) *Evaluating and Weeding Collections in Small and Medium-sized Public Libraries: The CREW Method*, by Joseph P. Segal.
5) *Operation Circuit Rider: Collection Development Planning Handbook*, by Ronnie Storey-Ewoldt.
6) Houston Area Library System, Collection Development Workshop FY 1993: Developing a Written Collection Development Policy Plan. Presented by Jo Amandes, Library Consultant.
7) 1990 Census, U. S. Department of Commerce.

PETERSBURG PUBLIC LIBRARY
Petersburg, Alaska

1.1 MISSION AND CLIENTELE

The primary mission of the Petersburg Public Library is to serve as a reliable source of information for the community by acquiring, organizing, and disseminating information. The library serves recreational needs by providing popular materials; it provides opportunities for independent learning for all people from toddlers to the elderly; and it provides timely, accurate, and useful information to meet the diverse and constantly changing informational needs of those it serves.

The library strives to offer the most complete and balanced collection possible within existing fiscal and physical limitations. Meeting the educational, cultural, informational and recreational needs of people in Petersburg requires both a carefully built collection locally and access to resources beyond the library's own collection.

While Petersburg is a small town (population 3,600 in 1993), the range of interests and demands for information is not small. The high school and grade school each have a library focused on student curriculum support, but because of our geographical isolation, people do not have access to any other libraries. As a result, this library must provide services for the entire range of informational needs, from first board books for babies to specialized materials for people doing doctoral research. Cooperation with other libraries through the interlibrary loan system and reference backup is essential to meet specialized needs.

1.2 COLLECTION RESPONSIBILITY

The City Librarian has the final responsibility for the maintenance and development of the collections of the Petersburg Public Library, operating within the framework of policies determined by the Petersburg Public Library Board.

Purchase suggestions from library users are encouraged. All Interlibrary Loan requests are considered as purchase suggestions. The librarian will review all purchase requests and determine whether they fall within selection criteria. The amount of potential use will be an important factor in deciding whether to purchase suggested titles.

1.3 SELECTION GUIDELINES

Selection of library materials is based on the professional judgment of the library staff, on book reviews, and on other professional tools such as standard catalogs and bibliographies. Major selection tools for the Library include *Booklist*, *Library Journal*, *Horn Book*, and *Wilson's Public Library*, *Fiction*, and *Children's Catalogs*.

No single standard exists which can be applied in all acquisition decisions. Some materials must be judged primarily on their artistic merits, some on their scholarship, some on their value as human documents; others are intended to satisfy recreational and entertainment needs; each needs to be considered in terms of the audience for whom it is intended. Materials are judged on the basis of the work as a whole, not on a part taken out of context.

1.4 GENERAL CRITERIA

Considerations in evaluation and reevaluation of materials for the Petersburg Public Library include the following:

(1) Administrative criteria: suitability of physical form for library use, funds and space.
(2) Substantive criteria: cultural, recreational, informational and/or educational value; usefulness in relation to other materials in the collection; suitability of content and style for intended audience; contribution of work toward balanced collection representing a broad range of perspectives and opinions, including extreme and/or minority points of view; authority, effectiveness, timeliness of presentation; attention of critics, reviewers, and public; reputation and/or significance of author.

Two categories excluded from the collection as clearly not within selection criteria are as follows:

(1) forms of expression that are unprotected by the First Amendment, and
(2) explicit and direct instructions for the manufacture of contraband materials.

1.5 SPECIAL CRITERIA

In addition to the above, the following apply to some segments of the collections:

In selecting books for children, the library's objective is to make available a collection which satisfies their informational, recreational, and cultural reading needs and potentials. Since elementary and high school students already have access to school library service especially developed to meet their academic needs, the public library will not focus its collections on curriculum support.

Young people (grades 7 through 12, approximately) are served from the general collection but also have access to a fiction collection specially selected to meet the recreational and emotional concerns of this age group. The Young Adult collection should be fluid, flexible, current and attractive, containing materials which are (1) in demand, and (2) of special quality which will help young adults understand themselves and others, broaden their viewpoints and knowledge of the world, stimulate their curiosity, and expand both their reading ability and reading enjoyment. Emphasis is on popular browsing materials.

The Alaska Collection includes materials of special interest to Alaska and its wider region. In general the goal will be: (1) as complete coverage as possible of the immediate Petersburg area, (2) broad coverage for Southeast Alaska, and (3) selected coverage for the rest of Alaska, based on expected demand and popular appeal. The Alaska Reference collection will include standard reference titles and out-of-print Alaskana which could not be replaced if lost in circulation.

Duplication. A book in heavy demand should be duplicated if long use is anticipated. However, the library will not duplicate at the expense of the rest of the collection.

Video Selection Policy. Videos for home use will be offered for checkout. Materials in video format are collected, as are materials in all other formats, to meet the informational needs of the general public. Petersburg has several video rental outlets. The Petersburg Public Library concentrates on meeting needs which commercial suppliers do not meet. That is not to say that the library will never overlap any of the offerings of any of the local video retailers.

Rather, the library's primary focus will be on categories of material for which there is little or no commercial availability within Petersburg. Special consideration will be given to subjects most effectively presented in visual form, such as drama and dance, quality features, documentaries, and classic works originally created for the film medium. For children's materials, the library will prefer presentations based on original illustrations and high-quality children's literature. Initial video collection development will focus on titles with special regional interest, such as Alaskana and fisheries; health and safety; and subjects which are most effectively presented in video format. Public Performance Rights will be obtained for subject areas of critical public interest (e.g. AIDS, health and safety, etc.).

Literacy Materials. The library will maintain a small collection of materials specifically designed for beginning adult readers and will cooperate with local efforts to teach literacy skills.

Foreign Language Materials. The library collects dictionaries, grammars, and learning materials in major languages. English-as-a-second-language materials are collected for non-English speakers in Petersburg. A few fiction titles and supplementary materials are collected in languages taught in Petersburg, including German, Spanish, and French. A somewhat larger collection of Norwegian materials is maintained, including historical materials that date from the founding of Petersburg by Norwegian immigrants, titles by distinguished Norwegian authors, and books on crafts and skills of particular interest in Petersburg, such as rosemaling, cooking, and Norwegian costumes.

Large Print and Materials for the Visually Handicapped. The library participates in a large print book circuit with other Southeast libraries to provide a rotating collection of large print materials. Large print titles owned by this library are interfiled with the general collection and may be found through the library catalog. The State Library offers services directly to those unable to read print.

Petersburg Municipal Publications. The Petersburg Public Library will attempt to keep one copy of every publication produced by or for the City of Petersburg. City departments are requested to send two copies of each publication, so that one may be kept and one sent to the Alaska State Historical Library. (Publications are usually bound and are intended for public use. Other materials, such as the municipal budget, which are of public interest will be collected as space allows.) As a general rule, municipal publications do not circulate. However, when the publication is current and on a topic of special public interest, the library will attempt to have additional copies which may be loaned for home use.

Audio Materials. Spoken-word cassette recordings are offered for both children and adults. Phonograph records are no longer collected due to space limitations and the difficulty of maintaining records in usable condition. Some items of AV equipment (projectors, players) are available for short term checkout on a reserve basis.

1.6 INTELLECTUAL FREEDOM
The library does not promote particular beliefs or views, nor is the selection of any book or item equivalent to endorsement of the viewpoint of the author expressed therein. To be a resource where the free individual can examine many points of view and make his or her own decisions is one of the essential purposes of the public library. The library attempts to provide materials representing different sides of controversial issues.

The Petersburg Public Library Board endorses the American Library Association's Library Bill of Rights, the Freedom to Read Statement, and the Intellectual Freedom Statement. These three documents are considered guiding principles for this collection development policy.

Access to library materials will not be restricted beyond what is required to protect materials from theft or damage. Responsibility for the reading of children rests with their parents and legal guardians. Parents who wish to limit or restrict the reading of their own child should personally oversee that child's choice of reading material. Selection of library materials will not be inhibited by the possibility that books may come into the possession of children.

1.7 DISCARDING
Materials which are no longer useful in the light of stated objectives will be systematically weeded from the collection and withdrawn from the library. Prime candidates for deselection are:
(1) items which contain outdated or inaccurate information, unless of historical value,
(2) superseded editions,

(3) worn out or damaged items, and

(4) seldom used materials.

Discards may be offered to other libraries, schools or nonprofit groups, sold, or otherwise disposed of.

1.8 GIFTS

The library accepts donations of materials, or money to purchase them, with the following understanding:

(1) that, to be added to the collection, gift materials must meet established selection criteria, and

(2) that gift materials not retained for the collection may be given to other libraries, or schools or nonprofit groups, sold, or otherwise disposed of, the choice being the library's entirely.

No condition or restriction on gifts can be honored unless agreed upon by the librarian and donor in advance of delivery of the gift. The library cannot legally appraise gifts for tax purposes. Gifts of money, real property, and/or stock will be accepted if any conditions attached to them are acceptable to the Library Board.

1.9 COPYRIGHT

The Petersburg Public Library intends to abide by copyright law. Patrons who are using library materials are responsible for the legal use of those materials.

1.10 FORMAT OF MATERIALS

The library will provide materials in a variety of formats to meet its goals and objectives. Materials may include: books, periodicals, pamphlets, newspapers, pictures, slides, film, video, maps, audio cassettes, and microfilm.

1.11 RECONSIDERATION OF MATERIALS

Because some materials are of necessity acquired without benefit of critical review, reconsideration is an integral part of the collection development process. Reconsideration may be either staff initiated or citizen initiated. The Petersburg Public Library recognizes that within the Petersburg area there are groups and individuals with widely separate and diverse interests, backgrounds, cultural heritages, social values and needs and that any given item may offend some patrons. Selection of materials will not be made on the basis of anticipated approval or disapproval of their contents,

and no library material will be sequestered, except to protect it from injury or theft. Complaints from patrons on library materials will:
1. Be handled in an informal manner by the city librarian. The selection policy will be explained to the patron. Material in question will not be removed or restricted at any point in this process unless an official determination has been made to do so following the procedures in 2-5 below.
2. If the patron is not satisfied with the informal discussion, the city librarian will provide a Materials Selection Inquiry for the patron to fill out and return.
3. Upon receiving the Inquiry the city librarian will make a decision whether to retain the material or remove it.
4. The patron will be notified immediately of the recommendation and given a full explanation of the decision. Information concerning the appeal process will be included as well.
5. If the patron is not satisfied with the recommendation from the city librarian he or she may file a written appeal with the Petersburg Public Library Board. In considering the complaint the board shall:
    (1) Read, view, or listen to the material in its entirety;
    (2) Check general acceptance of the material by reading reviews and consulting recommended lists;
    (3) Judge the material for the strengths and values as a whole and not in part, and apply all appropriate substantive selection criteria to the work. The board shall notify the complainant of its decision in writing. No further appeals will be heard. No other reconsideration of this material will be addressed, unless the grounds for complaint are substantially different from the previous reconsideration.

[Note: The policy adopted by the Petersburg Public Library Board March 14, 1990. Petersburg is a small public library in a fishing town of 3,600 on an island in Southeast Alaska, The library circulates 34,000 items a year, has a collection of 28,000, and a budget of $140,000.]

BRAZOSPORT INDEPENDENT SCHOOL DISTRICT
Freeport, Texas

INSTRUCTIONAL MATERIALS SELECTION POLICY

SELECTION OF LEARNING RESOURCES

The Board, through its professional staff, shall provide a wide range of learning resources at varying levels of difficulty, with diversity of appeal and the presentation of different points of view to meet the needs of students and teachers.

OBJECTIVES

For the purposes of this policy, the term "learning resources" refers to any material (whether acquired or locally produced) with instructional content or function that is used for formal or informal teaching/learning purposes. The primary objective of learning resources is to support, enrich, and help to implement the educational program of the District. The professional staff shall:

1. Provide materials that will enrich and support the curriculum, taking into consideration the varied interests, abilities, learning styles, and maturity levels of the students served.
2. Provide materials that will stimulate growth in factual knowledge, literary appreciation, aesthetic values, and societal standards.
3. Provide materials on various sides of controversial issues so that students may have an opportunity to develop under guidance the practice of critical analysis and make informed judgments in their daily lives.
4. Provide materials representative of the many religious, ethnic, and cultural groups and their contributions to national heritage and the world community.

The Board delegates the responsibility for the selection of learning resources to the professional staff employed by the District and declares that selections made shall be held to have been made by the Board.

CRITERIA
Criteria for selection shall be that learning resources:

1. Support and be consistent with the general educational goals of the state and the District and the aims and objectives of individual schools and specific courses.
2. Be chosen to enrich and support the curriculum and the personal needs of users.
3. Meet high standards of quality in:
   a. Presentation.
   b. Physical format.
   c. Educational significance.
   d. Readability.
   e. Authenticity.
   f. Artistic quality and/or literary style.
   g. Factual content.
4. Be appropriate for the subject area and for the age, emotional development, ability level, learning styles, and social development of the students for whom the materials are selected.
5. Be designed to provide a background of information that will motivate students and staff to examine their own attitudes and behavior, to comprehend their duties, responsibilities, rights and privileges as participating citizens in our society, and to make intelligent judgments in their daily lives.
6. Provide information on opposing sides of controversial issues so that users may develop under guidance the skill of critical analysis.

The selection of learning resources on controversial issues shall be directed toward maintaining a balanced collection representing various views. Learning resources shall clarify historical and contemporary forces by presenting and analyzing intergroup tension and conflict objectively, placing emphasis on recognizing and understanding social and economic problems.

Recommendations for purchase shall involve administrators, teachers, students, District personnel, and community persons, as appropriate. Gift materials shall be judged by the criteria outlined and shall be accepted or rejected by those criteria.

Selection of materials is an ongoing process which shall include the removal of materials no longer appropriate and the replacement of lost and worn materials still of educational value.

CHALLENGED MATERIALS

Any resident or employee of the District may formally challenge learning resources used in the District's educational program on the basis of appropriateness.

REQUEST FOR INFORMAL RECONSIDERATION

The school receiving a complaint regarding a learning resource shall try to resolve the issue informally:

1. The principal or other appropriate staff shall explain to the questioner the school's selection procedure, criteria, and qualifications of those persons selecting the resource.
2. The principal or other appropriate staff shall explain the particular place the questioned resource occupies in the educational program, its intended educational usefulness, and additional information regarding its use, or refer the party to someone who can identify and explain the use of the resource.
3. If the questioner wishes to file a formal challenge, a copy of the District's selection of learning resources policy and a request for reconsideration of learning resources form (see EFA-E) shall be handed or mailed to the concerned party by the principal.

REQUEST FOR FORMAL RECONSIDERATION

The following procedures shall be adhered to when a person requests formal reconsideration of a learning resource:

1. All formal objections to learning resources shall be made on the request for reconsideration of learning resources forms. The form shall be signed by the questioner and filed with the principal or someone so designated by the principal.
2. Upon receipt of a request for formal reconsideration of a learning resource, the principal shall appoint a reconsideration committee.

The reconsideration committee shall review the challenged resource and judge whether it conforms to the principles of selection outlined in the District's policy of learning resource policy.

LIBRARY SYSTEM

The District shall provide and maintain school libraries as integral parts of the District's instructional resources. Materials shall be selected from all forms of media in accordance with EFA (Local), taking into consideration the interests, vocabulary, and maturity and ability levels of all students within the school served.

The Superintendent or designee shall develop rules, regulations, and procedures to ensure the systematic maintenance of libraries as current resources for teachers and students. Principals shall ensure the effective use of the libraries within schools and shall establish library hours and procedures that best serve the needs of the students.

Adequate funding for libraries shall be made through the annual budget. Funds for the purchase of library materials shall be allocated on an equitable basis to the various schools using an expenditure per student formula. Librarians shall consider the cost of rebinding books when projecting and requesting funds for library supplies.

LIBRARY MEDIA CENTER MATERIALS SELECTION POLICY

I. INTRODUCTION

A. The modern school library media center must maintain a comprehensive collection of carefully selected instructional materials, both print and non-print, to support and augment the curriculum. The extent which many Brazosport students of today will be creative, knowledgeable, and intellectually mature will be limited by the boundaries established for the content and services of library media centers within the schools. In providing materials, a major goal must be to develop within students a high degree of independence and self-direction in learning as well as an inner courage and security with which to face an increasingly complex world.

B. The Board of Education has the legal responsibility for providing instructional materials for use in the schools that make up the Brazosport Independent School District. The volume of learning materials currently being produced makes the wise selection of appropriate materials a problem of utmost importance to the

Board. For this reason, the following materials policy has been developed as a summation of the principles which underlie the choice of resource materials for the school library media centers of the Brazosport Independent School District.

C. The purpose of this materials selection policy is:
   1. To provide a statement of philosophy and objectives for the guidance of those involved in the procedure for selection.
   2. To define the role of those who share in the responsibility for the selection of instructional materials.
   3. To set forth criteria for selection and evaluation of materials.
   4. To outline the techniques for the application of the criteria.
   5. To clarify for the community the philosophy and procedure used in evaluating and selecting instructional materials.
   6. To provide a procedure for the consideration of objections to the use of particular materials in the educational progress.

II. PHILOSOPHY AND OBJECTIVES

A. The School Library Bill of Rights for School Library Media Center Programs sets forth a philosophy of materials selection, and this Library Bill of Rights is endorsed by the Brazosport Independent School District: The American Association of School Librarians (AASL) reaffirms its belief in the Library Bill of Rights of the American Library Association. Media personnel are concerned with generating understanding of American freedoms through the development of informed and responsible citizens. To this end the AASL asserts that the responsibility of the school library media center is:

To provide a comprehensive collection of instructional materials selected in compliance with basic written selection principles, and to provide maximum accessibility to these materials.

To provide materials that will support the curriculum, taking into consideration the individual's needs, and the varied interests, abilities, socio-economic backgrounds, and maturity levels of the students served.

To provide materials for teachers and students that will encourage growth in knowledge, and will develop literary, cultural, and aesthetic appreciation, and ethical standards.

To provide materials which reflect the ideas and beliefs of religious, social, political historical, and ethnic groups and their contribution to the American and world heritage and culture, thereby enabling students to develop an intellectual integrity in forming judgements.

To provide a written statement, approved by the local Boards of Education, of the procedures for meeting the challenge of censorship of materials in school library media centers.

To provide qualified professional personnel to serve teachers and students.

B. The school library media center program should foster intellectual curiosity, assist in the development of lifetime reading habits, and instruct in the selective use of all available materials. The library media center should reflect the information students have at their fingertips: past, present, future, and thus provide for their intellectual, physical, social, moral and spiritual development.

C. The program should be designed so that teachers and counselors can:

1. Achieve instructional objectives.
2. Enrich course content.
3. Prepare assignments that provide for the needs and abilities of individual students.
4. Motivate students to use material for curricular and non-curricular purposes.
5. Have the materials needed in counseling students in many aspects of guidance work.
6. Use materials directly with students in the classroom.
7. Teach students to use materials and library media centers.
8. Have materials easily accessible and efficiently organized so the time is not wasted in locating materials for examination and use.
9. Keep abreast with the best ideas and educational practices.
10. Use materials to broaden knowledge and to derive personal enrichment.

III. RESPONSIBILITY FOR SELECTION

The purchase of library materials is legally vested in the Board of Education. The Board delegates to professional librarians, who know the courses of study, the methods of teaching, and the individual needs of the student, the primary responsibility for recommendations to the Board. Librarians are aided by suggestions from administrators, faculty, students, and parents. Wide participation is encouraged, but the individual school librarian is responsible for the primary evaluation and selection for all materials for the library media center. The Board shall always have the final responsibility for choice of library materials.

IV. PRINCIPLES OF EVALUATION AND SELECTION

A. Librarians should be guided in the selection of materials by examination at supply stores, exhibits, and other libraries; by review at area meetings; and by the judicious use of standard reviewing tools and authoritative lists.

B. Materials selected should support all phases of the curriculum, and librarians should base decisions on a knowledge of the curriculum and of the existing collection.

C. Selection should be guided by a knowledge of the abilities, needs, interests, problems, motivations, cultural patterns, and maturity levels of the students, who should be involved directly in the selection process. Materials should represent all levels of understanding and experience. Formal procedure for insuring that the desires of students are processed to the librarians will be developed and communicated to students.

D. Materials should be provided which interpret the contemporary world and present varying opinions on controversial issues and social problems.

E. Two basic factors, truth and art, are to be considered in the selection of media.
   1. Truth includes accuracy, timeliness, authoritativeness, and freedom from bias.

2. Art includes aesthetic values, imagination, creativity, and style appropriate to the material and to the maturity of the student.

F. In selecting controversial materials, the following criteria should be given consideration:
1. Materials on controversial issues should represent contrasting views.
2. The race, nationality, or political views of a writers should not prohibit inclusion of their works.
3. In a literary work of established quality, the use of profanity or the treatment of sex is not an adequate reason for eliminating the material.
4. Materials should be evaluated as a whole; the purpose, style, and theme should overshadow any isolated offensive section. The masking, clipping, or other alteration of an individual work should be avoided.
5. A writer's expression of a certain viewpoint is not to be considered a disparagement when it represents the historical or contemporary views held by some persons or groups.
6. Materials on physiology, physical maturation, or personal hygiene should be accurate and in good taste.
7. Materials should be selected for their strengths rather than rejected for their weaknesses.

G. The library media centers welcome books and other resource material from individuals and organizations but reserve the right of placement. The materials, to be acceptable, must meet the standards and criteria established within this policy.

H. In selecting learning resources, professional personnel will evaluate available resources and curriculum needs and will consult reputable, professionally prepared aids to selection and other appropriate sources. Among sources to be consulted are:

Bibliographies and reviewing tools:
Guide to Reference Books
Senior High School Library Catalog
AASA Science Books and Films

The Book Report
School Library Journal

Other sources will be consulted as deemed appropriate, such as newspapers and magazines.

CENSORSHIP POLICY
LIBRARY MATERIALS CHALLENGED AND RESOLVED

CHALLENGED MATERIALS
It is expected that occasional objections to selections may be made despite the care taken by the professionals charged with the responsibility for selection of materials for library media centers. Any resident or employee of B.I.S.D. may formally challenge learning resources used in the district's educational program on the basis of appropriateness.

PRELIMINARY PROCEDURES
The following procedure should be allowed:

Each school will have and make available a request for a reconsideration form.

The request shall be signed by the questioner and filed with the librarian, principal, and anyone else designated by the principal.

The request for reconsideration shall be referred to a committee for evaluation.

RECONSIDERATION COMMITTEE
Upon receipt of a request for formal reconsideration the principal shall:

Appoint a reconsideration committee: One member of the district staff, one member of the school teaching staff, one or two students from the student body, one or two librarians;

Name a chairperson of the committee, and

Arrange for a reconsideration committee meeting within ten working days.

RESOLUTION
Each committee member shall examine the questioned material and prepare an evaluation. The chairperson shall prepare a written report.

The written report shall be discussed with the questioner. The written report shall be retained by the principal, with copies forwarded to the assistant superintendent for instruction. Written reports, once filed, are confidential and available for examination by trustees and appropriate officials only.

The decision of the reconsideration committee is binding for the individual school.

The questioner shall have the right to appeal any decision of the reconsideration committee to the board of trustees as the final review panel.

CYPRESS-FAIRBANKS INDEPENDENT SCHOOL DISTRICT

Houston, Texas

SELECTION OF LEARNING RESOURCES

The Board, through its professional staff, shall provide a wide range of learning resources at varying levels of difficulty, with diversity of appeal and the presentation of different points of view to meet the needs of students and teachers.

OBJECTIVES

For the purposes of this policy, the term "learning resources" refers to any material (whether acquired or locally produced) with instructional content or function that is used for formal or informal teaching/learning purposes. The primary objective of learning resources is to support, enrich, and help to implement the educational program of the District. The professional staff shall:

1. Provide materials that will enrich and support the curriculum, taking into consideration the varied interests, abilities, learning styles, and maturity levels of the students served.
2. Provide materials that will stimulate growth. In factual knowledge, literary appreciation, aesthetic values, and societal standards.
3. Provide materials on various sides of controversial issues so that students may have an opportunity to develop under guidance the practice of critical analysis and make informed judgments in their daily lives.
4. Provide materials representative of the many religious, ethnic, and cultural groups and their contributions to national heritage and the world community.

The Board delegates the responsibility for the selection of learning resources to the professional staff employed by the District and declares that selections made shall be held to have been made by the Board.

CRITERIA

Criteria for selection shall be that learning resources:

1. Support and be consistent with the general educational goals of the state and the District and the aims and objectives of individual schools and specific courses.
2. Be chosen to enrich and support the curriculum and the personal needs of users.
3. Meet high standards of
   a. Presentation.
   b. Physical format.
   c. Educational significance.
   d. Readability.
   e. Authenticity.
   f. Artistic quality and/or literary style.
   g. Factual content.
4. Be appropriate for the subject area and for the age, emotional development, ability level, learning styles, and social development of the students for whom the materials are selected.
5. Be designed to provide a background of information that will motivate students and staff to examine their own attitudes and behavior, to comprehend their duties, responsibilities, rights and privileges as participating citizens in our society, and to make intelligent judgments in their daily lives.
6. Provide information on opposing sides of controversial issues so that users may develop under guidance the skill of critical analysis.

The selection of learning resources on controversial issues shall be directed toward maintaining a balanced collection representing various views. Learning resources shall clarify historical and contemporary forces by presenting and analyzing intergroup tension and conflict objectively, placing emphasis on recognizing and understanding social and economic problems.

Recommendations for purchases shall involve administrators, teachers, students, District personnel, and community persons, as appropriate. Gift materials shall be judged by the criteria outlined and shall be accepted or rejected by those criteria.

Selection of materials is an ongoing process which shall include the removal of materials no longer appropriate and replacement of lost and worn materials still of educational value.

Collection Development

CHALLENGED MATERIALS

Any resident or employee of the District may formally challenge learning resources used in the District's educational program on the basis of appropriateness.

REQUEST FOR INFORMAL RECONSIDERATION

The school receiving a complaint regarding a learning resource shall try to resolve the issue informally:

1. The principal or other appropriate staff shall explain to the questioner the school's selection procedure, criteria, and qualifications of those persons selecting the resource.
2. The principal or other appropriate staff shall explain the particular place the questioned resource occupies in the educational program, its intended educational usefulness, and additional information regarding its use, or refer the party to someone who can identify and explain the use of the resource.
3. If the questioner wishes to file a formal challenge, a copy of this policy and a Request for Reconsideration of Instructional Materials form (see EFA-E) shall be handed or mailed to the concerned party by the principal.

REQUEST FOR FORMAL RECONSIDERATION

The following procedures shall be adhered to when a person requests formal reconsideration of a learning resource:

1. All formal objections to learning resources shall be made on the Request for Reconsideration of Instructional Materials form. The form shall be signed by the questioner and filed with the principal or someone so designated by the principal.
2. Upon receipt of a request for formal reconsideration of a learning resource, the principal shall appoint a reconsideration committee.

The reconsideration committee shall review the challenged resource and judge whether it conforms to the principles of selection outlined in this policy. The decision of the reconsideration committee is binding for the individual school. Notwithstanding any procedure outlined in this policy, the questioner shall have the right to appeal any decision of the reconsideration committee to the Board as the final review panel.

Employees appealing such decisions shall follow DGBA(L), beginning at Level Two; students shall follow FNG(L), beginning at Level Two; other District residents shall follow GF(L), beginning at Level Two.

If the Central Office Committee upholds the School Committee's decision, the questioner shall have the right to appeal this decision as well. Such appeal should be made to the Superintendent who will review the materials. He may refer the questioned materials back to the Central Office Committee for a re-examination if he disagrees with its decisions. If the Superintendent concurs with the Central Office Committee's decision, he will place the matter on the next regular Board meeting agenda.

The Board, after examining the questioned material and the Citizen's Request for Reconsideration of a Work form, will determine by vote in its regular meeting whether or not the material will be retained or removed from the curriculum or library circulation.

GUIDING PRINCIPLES

The following principles shall guide the Board and staff in responding to challenges of materials:

1. Any resident or employee of the District may raise objection to learning resources used in a school's educational program despite the fact that the individuals selecting such resources were duly qualified to make the selection, followed the proper procedure, and observed the criteria for selecting learning resources.
2. The principal shall review the selection and objection rules with the teaching staff at least annually. The staff shall be reminded that the right to object to learning resources is one granted by policies enacted by the Board.
3. No parent has the right to determine reading, viewing, or listening matter for students other than his or her own children.
4. When learning resources are challenged the principles of the freedom to read/listen/view must be defended as well.
5. Access to challenged material shall not be restricted during the reconsideration process.

6. The major criterion for the final decision is the appropriateness of the material for its intended educational use. No material shall be removed solely because of the ideas expressed.

7. A decision to sustain a challenge shall not necessarily be interpreted as a judgment of irresponsibility on the part of the professional involved in the original selection and/or use of the material.

JENNINGS COUNTY SCHOOLS
Jennings, Indiana

INSTRUCTIONAL MATERIALS AND SERVICES

The Board shall make provisions to provide instructional materials and services according to the recommendations of the office of the Superintendent within applicable regulations and available funds.

INSTRUCTIONAL MEDIA CENTER

The Board shall provide for facilities, services, and equipment so organized and managed as to contribute to the total educational program.

1. Instructional Media Center Materials Selection

   Instructional Media Center materials shall be selected in accordance with the following general statement:

   a. Materials shall be selected for values of interest and enlightenment of the student.

   b. Materials shall not be excluded because of the race, nationality, or religious views of the author or producer.

   c. There shall be the fullest possible provision for materials presenting all points of view on local, national and international problems and the selection of materials of sound factual authority shall be encouraged.

   d. Material selected shall be appropriate to the age and maturity of the user.

   e. Materials selection will be assisted by reading and examination of the materials when possible and/or checking of standard evaluation aids. In addition, careful consideration shall be given to: educational significance; need and value to the collection; reputation and significance of the author or producer; clarity, adequacy and scope of presentation; validity, accuracy, objectivity, up-to-datedness, and appropriateness of the presentation; high degree of comprehensibility and user appeal; high artistic quality and literary style; and value commensurate with cost and/or need.

   f. Materials selected shall reflect both the educational program needs and the personal interests of students.

   g. Gift materials will be accepted from students. faculty, and community with the understanding that any item which does not meet the criteria presented in these general statements will be respectfully declined.

2. Instructional Media Center Equipment
   The Board recognizes that equipment of various kinds is necessary to take full advantage of instructional materials available. To that end, the Board shall allot funds to purchase, repair and replace equipment in Instructional Media Centers according to need and within available funds.
3. Instructional Media Center Resources for Staff
   The Board encourages the acquisition of necessary professional resources for staff use in the operation of the educational programs.

COMPLAINTS REGARDING INSTRUCTIONAL MATERIALS

In the event that complaints are made regarding instructional materials, a written criticism of the materials will be requested and shall be presented to the school principal. The principal shall present the written criticism to a committee appointed by the Superintendent. The committee shall be composed of management personnel, instructional personnel, and community members. Use of the material under question shall be suspended at least until a written decision from the committee is presented to the Superintendent and the plaintiff is notified.

If the plaintiff is not willing to accept the ruling of the committee, s/he may then proceed to take the written complaint to the Superintendent. If the plaintiff does not accept the Superintendent's ruling s/he may then request a hearing with the Board which has final authority in such a matter.

INSTRUCTIONAL EQUIPMENT

The school district shall purchase, repair, and replace instructional equipment that is necessary to the operation of the educational program. The Board directs the office of the Superintendent to schedule an appropriate purchase, repair, and replacement program and to budget same according to available funds.

MEDIA CENTER—CRITERIA AND PROCEDURES FOR SELECTION

The media center of Jennings County High School, in addition to conforming with the American Library Association's Library Bill of Rights, approved by the American Association of School Librarians, needs to reflect the basic philosophy and objectives of the school itself. The criteria for the selection of all materials should be based on the needs of the school's teachers and students.

Media center materials should be chosen through use of the following guidelines:

1. Materials meet the curriculum needs of the school.
2. Materials meet the need of each student and teacher.
3. Materials are authoritative, appealing, and up-to-date.
4. Materials feature good format.
5. Materials provide a wide scope of levels of difficulty and different points of view.

In the process of selecting media, all available resources should be utilized and should include selection aids such as the ALA's *Booklist*, as well as bibliographies and reviews prepared by qualified professional educators, the examination of collections and exhibits, preview copies from publishers and producers, and specialists in different fields of study.

Each type of media has some unusual features and therefore can provide a unique contribution. Each item of media should be selected for the contributions that it can make, and, in the case of audio-visual materials, should be selected for the contribution that its content and method of delivery together can provide. It is important that all materials and equipment be acquired in relation to well-defined purposes for the improvement of instruction.

In evaluating the existing media collection as a basis for selection, the media specialist should count only one copy of a title for a true picture of subject distribution.

RESPONSIBILITY FOR SELECTION

The Jennings County Board of Education is legally responsible for all matters relating to the operation of Jennings County Schools. The coordination of the selection and acquisition of materials and equipment related to media should be the delegated responsibility of the media specialists.

In order to assist the media specialists to determine selections on the basis of school objectives and priority of needs, consideration should be given to forming a committee consisting of the media specialist and teachers representing all subject areas in the school. The total selection process should involve many people: media coordinator, media specialist, teachers, and students.

POLICY RELATION TO SPECIAL CONSIDERATIONS

1. GIFTS should be judged by the same standards as other materials in the collection.
2. DUPLICATES should be added as use indicates need.
3. REFERENCE MATERIALS should be kept up-to-date, with encyclopedias being replaced at regular intervals. Authoritative selection aids should be referred to before purchasing any sets of expensive reference books.
4. NON-BOOK MATERIALS should include filmstrips, recordings, realia, pictures, maps, globes, microfilm, slides, and tapes and should be selected by the same criteria.
5. WEEDING AND DISCARDING should be on a consistent and systematic basis in order that all materials will meet standards as set in the selection policies of the Jennings County School Media Center.
6. REBINDING should be done on a consistent and systematic basis in order that all materials to be rebound will meet the same standards as set in the selection policies of the Jennings County School Media Center.
7. PERIODICALS, PAMPHLETS, NEWSPAPERS–Periodicals will be selected to supplement the curriculum and IMC collection of materials. A factor in selection will be the indexing of the periodicals in standard indexes used in the IMC. When selecting periodicals, the director will use the same criteria as for selecting books. The same criteria will be used for selecting pamphlets for the vertical file. The newspapers will include local, statewide, and nationally circulated papers.
8. COMPLAINTS REGARDING INSTRUCTIONAL MATERIALS--In the event that complaints are made regarding instructional materials, a written criticism of the materials will be requested and shall be presented to the school principal. The principal shall present the written criticism to a committee appointed by the Superintendent. The committee shall be composed of management personnel, instructional personnel, and community members. Use of the material under question shall be suspended at least until a written decision from the committee is presented to the Superintendent and the plaintiff is notified.

   If the plaintiff is not willing to accept the ruling of the committee, he/she may then proceed to take the written complaint to the Superintendent.

If the plaintiff does not accept the Superintendent's ruling he/she may then request a hearing with the Board which has final authority in such a matter.

WEEDING MATERIALS

Systematic weeding of materials is necessary in media operation. Additionally, preventive maintenance and repair to ensure that the media remain useful at all times is a must in an effective media program. Media collections should contain only quality media with recency and should excluded obsolete, badly worn, and inappropriate items.

Materials which have become obsolete or worn out are to be discarded by the media specialist, who should consider the following areas:

1. Materials too worn to be mended or rebound.
2. Materials with worn or missing pages or parts.
3. Materials with fine print which causes difficult reading.
4. Materials beyond comprehension of the readers.
5. Materials with content out-of-date.
6. Textbooks not useful for reference.
7. Mediocre materials, including some series.
8. Sets of materials out-of-date or beyond comprehension.
9. Government documents not valuable.
10. Out-of-date vertical file materials.

The procedure for discarding obsolete, badly worn, and inappropriate material is simple:

1. Discard the item by writing DISCARD on it.
2. Pull all cards for the item from the shelflist and card catalogs. If item(s) are to be replaced, file catalog cards in withdrawal file.
3. Write DISCARD on the shelflist card or in the appropriate column in the accession book. If shelflist method of accessioning is used, hold shelflist card in file marked DISCARDS until after inventory for current school year.

DRAFT EQUIPMENT SELECTION POLICY

The purchase of equipment for use in the instructional media program of Jennings County High School is contingent on meeting the needs of the instructional staff and students.

The amount and condition of equipment on hand is constantly being evaluated to be sure that equipment is available for use when requested by a faculty member, and the amount of repair work that a particular piece of equipment is taking.

These two criteria are measured first. The next item taken into account is the current state of media software and hardware. If new forms of hardware are being requested then an evaluation of their appropriateness for use in the program is taken into account and equipment is purchased if the need is there. In addition, an amount of hardware is purchased to meet the anticipated need whenever a new form of software is added to the media program.

The overall equipment purchase philosophy is to keep equipment on hand that is needed in the instructional program.

Upgrading of present equipment is done based on budget amounts, age of existing equipment, and features that new equipment may have that the existing equipment does not that will make the job of using or creating media easier or, more importantly, better.

Once the decision to purchase a certain type of hardware is made, then reviewing sources such as *Epiegram*, professional literature and guidelines established in Media Equipment, a *Guide and Dictionary*, by Rosenberg and Doskey ,are used for guidance.

When we replace existing equipment we evaluate the models we have in stock and discuss possible new acquisitions with other professionals.

Whenever possible hands-on use of a new type of equipment is done before the decision is made to purchase the equipment.

An attempt is made to keep one manufacture's equipment on hand, because of the ease of training, operation, and repair. However, this does not preclude the purchase of other types when the applications of these guidelines deem appropriate.

ILLINOIS STATE LIBRARY

Springfield, Illinois

INTRODUCTION

The Illinois State Library (ISL) is a specialized library. The collections and services of the ISL are focused on the professional needs and interests of the elected officials and agency staff of state government. When the collections and services designed to meet the needs of state government are of interest and use to the citizens of the state, they are made conveniently available.

The collection management policy of the ISL both describes the materials gathered during the library's 150 year history and serves as a guide to the future development and management of those collections. This policy is intended to inform staff and library patrons of what they may expect to find in the ISL's collections. While the policy reflects current practice, it is also based on the historical perspective provided by the collections, as they exist on the shelves.

The collection management policy is a primary tool to guide the selection of new material for the general and reference collections. It seeks to facilitate annual and long-range fiscal planning and to assist individual subject selectors in setting priorities in their areas of responsibility. It is also an important document in the orientation and training of new staff throughout the library. The collection management policy provides guidelines for the efficient and effective expenditure of materials acquisition funds.

The collection management policy is useful in the effective management of documentary holdings of the ISL. While the selection of federal and state documents may not be under the control of this policy, it is important to identify the interrelationships between the elements of the collection when determining the overall capacity of the information resources to provide services to users. In addition, the strengths of the documentary holdings should be taken into consideration when items are selected for the general collection.

The collection management policy is a general statement and is not a definitive record of the collection's content. It requires periodic revision because the collection is subject to continual development. For this reason, the policy is produced in a looseleaf format, to allow easy updating. While the policy is not an access tool, it may suggest productive avenues for resource sharing and service referral.

Finally, it should be noted that this policy is a collaborative work. The staff have analyzed and evaluated the elements of the collection. They have reviewed and revised the scope and depth information.

MISSION OF THE ILLINOIS STATE LIBRARY

It is the mission of the ISL to provide state government officials and employees with the information they need to make informed decisions as well as to develop and promote libraries in order to enrich the quality of life for the people of Illinois.

SERVICE ROLES OF THE ILLINOIS STATE LIBRARY

Primary Roles:

Government Service Library. The Illinois State Library provides a wide range of general interest and technical information to support the legislative, administrative, regulatory, and routine functions of government. The Library serves all branches of government.

General Information Center. ISL attempts to answer requests for information of general interest to employees of state government and the general public, within the limitation of its collection and resources.

Documents Depository. ISL serves as the regional federal documents depository for Illinois and as the statutory depository for publications produced by the state of Illinois. These collections are for the use of the general public and state government.

Patent & Trademark Depository. ISL serves as a depository for all federal patents and trademarks. These materials are for the use of the public at large.

Secondary Roles:

Network Resource Library. ISL endeavors to serve the citizens of Illinois by accepting information request referrals from ILLINET libraries and regional systems. The collections of the Library are made liberally available for this purpose. Collection materials are not selected or acquired solely to meet the needs f this role.

INTENT AND GOALS OF COLLECTION MANAGEMENT

The collections of the ISL are built and maintained in a focused manner to meet the demonstrable information needs of state government.

The collections of the ISL seek to provide a balanced treatment of subjects and issues.

The collections of the ISL provide timely, accurate information of current or anticipated interest to its primary clientele and such historical context and perspective as are appropriate to the subject.

The collections of the ISL will be acquired and maintained in any format and in such quantity as are appropriate to the subject.

The ISL maintains extensive holdings of state and federal publications and seeks to foster the use and understanding of government documents as an information resource.

The ISL shares its collections to meet statewide information needs and promote library networking.

The ISL enters into mutually beneficial cooperative arrangements to build, preserve, manage, and share collections with other libraries or groups of libraries.

GENERAL POLICIES

Library materials are produced in an ever-increasing variety of forms. These can range from stone tablets to electronic impulses. The ISL's collection consists predominantly of printed and microformatted materials in the English language. The ISL will consider materials in any format. However, the cost and availability of specialized equipment or technology may limit the library's ability to acquire items in a specific form. The primary consideration shall be the content of the resource, rather than its form.

The library's collection comprises primarily adult, nonfiction works in the English language. Several categories of material are generally excluded from the ISL collection. Fiction and other imaginative works are not routinely collected, with the exception of the Illinois Authors Collection described below. Neither fiction nor nonfiction materials intended for children and young adults are collected. Popular or ephemeral works that do not relate directly to the operation of state government or are not useful as ready reference sources are not collected. Works in languages other than English are not collected, although foreign language items received as gifts may be retained.

The following general policies apply to all of the detailed subject policies that follow. These general policies describe the State Library's current ability and intent to collect materials in the forms specified.

Monographs

The bulk of the library's general collection consists of monographs. In addition, monographs comprise a significant segment of the Illinois and federal documents collections. Bound print volumes are collected in preference to mass market paperbacks which are not collected. A variety of the library's monographs, in both the general and documents collections, are held in microformats.

The selection of monographs for the general collection, regardless of format, is to be guided by the scope and depth indicators specified in the appropriate subject policy below.

No attempt will be made to acquire variant imprints of a title. New or substantially revised editions of a work may be considered after a complete reevaluation of the title using appropriate subject policy criteria.

Multiple copies of a work are not generally acquired. However, up to three copies of Illinois documents are maintained in the depository collection.

Replacement copies for lost or damaged books are acquired only after the title has been reevaluated according to the appropriate subject policy.

Illinois and federal document monographs are acquired through depository agreements and statutory mandates. Guidelines for their retention are described in appropriate regulations, agreements, and policies.

Monographic Series

The ISL acquires monographs issued as a series of related publications selectively and in keeping with the scope and depth levels recommended in the appropriate specific subject policies. Individual titles from a series may be acquired separately under the general policy for monographs and according to the levels indicated in the specific subject policies. Standing orders for monographic series are subject to periodic review to ensure that the series conforms to any revisions in the scope or depth of appropriate subject policies.

Serials—Periodicals

The ISL seeks to acquire and maintain a representative collection of current and retrospective journals and periodicals. By definition, a periodical is a serial publication issued at least three times in a calendar year. Periodical titles are acquired in accordance with the scope and depth indicators of the subject policies below.

It is understood that the information contained in most periodicals will, over time, pertain to several subjects specified in the policy. Hence, the guidance of all appropriate subject policies should be sought when making periodical acquisition, retention, and withdrawal decisions. Consideration in the selection and retention of a periodical should be given to the bibliographic access to the contents of the title, and the presence of those access tools at the State Library.

Each periodical title currently received by the ISL shall have a specified period of retention. Microform holdings and backfiles of periodicals previously acquired due to space and budget considerations will be retained but are subject to periodic retention review based on criteria in appropriate subject policies. Additions to the ISL's microform periodical holdings will be based on subject policy criteria and not to conserve space or, solely, to maintain complete runs. Illinois and federal document periodicals are acquired through depository agreements and statutory mandates. They are maintained according to appropriate to the statutes, rules, or agreements in force.

Serials—Continuations

The Illinois State Library acquires a wide range of serial publications in support of its mission and services. A serial is a publication intended to be issued segmentally. Serial publications are usually organized thematically with the content varying with each issue or with volumes superseding previous volumes.

At the Illinois State Library , serial publications issued less than three times per year are considered to be continuations. Continuations are selected at levels indicated in specific subject policies below. Continuation standing orders are subject to periodic review to ensure that specific titles conform to revisions in scope and depth of the collection policy in appropriate subject policies. Each serial continuation is subject to a specific retention schedule established in keeping with the scope and depth of the collection in the appropriate subject area.

Newspapers
The ISL maintains a selective list of newspaper subscriptions. Microform backfiles are for high demand titles. All newspapers are subject to retention review on a regular basis to ensure optimum resource utilization.

Sound Recordings
The Illinois State Library acquires sound recordings in several media on a highly selective basis. Selections are based on the scope and depth indicated in specific subject policies. Additional sound recordings are acquired through deposit, primarily in the Illinois documents collection and are managed according to appropriate statutes and guidelines.

Video Recordings
The ISL maintains a highly selective holding of video recordings in a variety of film and tape formats. Selections are based on the scope and depth indicated in specific subject policies.

Additional video recordings are obtained through deposit, primarily as Illinois documents. Illinois or federal documents in video format are managed according to appropriate statutes and guidelines.

Instructional Materials
The Illinois State Library does not collect textbooks, study guides or other instructional material routinely. Exceptions are made

when such materials are the only or best source of information on a subject. Instructional materials may also be acquired to support specifically focused educational programs of the agency or state government.

Instructional materials and textbooks obtained through deposit in the state or federal documents collections are retained in accordance with appropriate guidelines.

With the exception of state and federal documents, only instructional material of current value will be retained. No historical files will be maintained and no retrospective acquisitions considered.

Braille & Other Media for the Visually Impaired

The Illinois State Library does not collect material in braille, large print or other media intended for the visually impaired. Random items in these forms are received as gifts for the general collection or may be found in the documents collections, where they are retained according to depository guidelines or statutes. The State Library maintains assistive equipment for the use of visually impaired patrons.

Dissertations & Theses

The ISL does not systematically collect doctoral dissertations or master's theses. Individual titles may be acquired in keeping with the scope and depth levels of specific subject policies.

Manuscripts

The ISL does not systematically collect archives or manuscripts. Such collecting is the principal responsibility of the Illinois State Archives and/or the Illinois State Historical Library.

Rare Books

The Illinois State Library does not maintain a separate collection of rare books. Due to cost and exhibit constraints, rare books are not acquired. Gifts of such materials will be considered within the limits of the library's ability to preserve and keep items secure.

In certain cases, rare or expensive materials identified in the existing collection may have their use restricted and/or may be removed to secure, environmentally controlled conditions.

Translations
The ISL will acquire materials translated into English in keeping with the scope and depth indicators in specific subject policies. Primary consideration will be given to the importance of the work in the subject and the quality of the translation.

Machine Readable Files and/or Their Printed Output
The ISL does not collect machine readable files in any magnetic format for its general collection. The printed output of a computer file may be acquired according to the scope and depth in a particular subject policy.

CD-ROM databases and other electronic formats are acquired as part of the Reference Collection to provide bibliographic access to the serial holdings of the library and to support the interlibrary loan function.

Electronic information products received as depository documents will be maintained in the collection according to appropriate guidelines. No special provision will be made to supply equipment or software support to make such resources readily useable by patrons, unless the sources contribute to the established service program of the State Library.

Reprints
The ISL will acquire reprinted materials according to the scope and depth indicators in specific subject policies.

Pamphlets
The ISL does not systematically collect ephemeral pamphlet material in any subject area. The Illinois and/or federal documents depository collections contains some pamphlet items. Such items are managed according to appropriate guidelines.

Art Work
The ISL does not collect art work in any medium for its collection.

Posters
The Illinois State Library does not acquire posters for its general or Illinois documents collection. Posters are in the documents depository collection and are according to appropriate guidelines.

Musical Scores

The ISL does not collect musical scores in manuscript or published form.

Gifts of Library Materials

The ISL gratefully accepts books and other information resources as gifts or memorials from authors, library patrons, and the general public.

Only unconditional gifts of books, periodicals, microforms, electronic media and other physical formats may be accepted. The right to retain, organize, preserve, and house items accepted as gifts is reserved to the staff of the Illinois State Library.

All gifts will be reviewed for inclusion in the collection in accordance with the appropriate subject policies.

The State Library cannot provide appraisals of gifts for income tax or other purposes. All gifts will be acknowledged in writing.

SPECIAL COLLECTIONS

Patent & Trademark Depository

The Patent & Trademark Depository Library (PTDL) exists at the ISL by virtue of the ISL's designation as a depository by the U.S. Patent and Trademark Office. In securing this designation, the ISL entered into a contractual agreement with the Patent and Trademark Office (PTO) to abide by the requirements of the program as outlined in *Notes on Becoming a Patent Depository Library*. One of these requirements is to maintain a collection of classification and research publications and documents which are necessary to the effective utilization of the patent file. In the years since our designation the focus of our responsibilities has been broadened to include trademarks, copyrights, and other forms of intellectual property. The core of this collection is deposited with the ISL by the U.S. Patent and Trademark Office in exchange for payment of the statutory fee. This includes the fulltext of all varieties of U.S. patent documents, a set of all the basic search tools, automated access to patent and trademark information and a wide variety of other information, publications, and searching aids covering all facets of intellectual property.

The second component of the PTDL's base collection are the materials received through our U.S. Government Printing Office

Federal Document Depository status. As a result of a cooperative agreement between the two federal agencies, the PTO does not supply us directly with the documents that are part of the normal GPO distribution. The PTO does, however, supply us with extra copies of high use items such as the Official Gazettes and the basic search tools. The current PTO materials are housed in the PTDL collection with a few exceptions. The GPO depository copy of superseded editions are housed in the stacks with the exception of the *Classification Definitions* on microfiche which are withdrawn when superseded. Materials distributed by other agencies should also be considered for inclusion in the PTDL collection when they deal with intellectual property issues, particularly those documents from the Library of Congress Copyright Office and the Department of Agriculture, Plant Variety Protection Office.

The "desired" goal of the PTDL collection is to complete the backfile in each of the primary documents categories. There are only two areas that have yet to be completed. As soon as space allows, efforts should be made to complete the *Official Gazette* paper collection by acquiring the 1836 - 1911 collection. This can probably by accomplished at no cost or the minimal cost of postage through the PTO, Patent and Trademark Depository Library Program Office. The second area, which is currently in progress, is to complete the annual index collection back to 1790. This is simply a matter of pulling the serial set volumes from our stack collection, having them designated for the PTDL collection and notifying the collection maintenance coordinator and the documents coordinator.

The PTDL general collection takes into consideration a number of factors such as the strong applied science collections at Chicago Public Library and St. Louis Public Library's PTDL; the strong pure science collections at the University of Illinois at Champaign-Urbana and Southern Illinois University School of Medicine; Illinois State Library's strong historical federal documents collection in this area; and the needs of our patrons. These factors have shaped the support collection into one with several focus points which build on ISL's strengths and remain within the scope of the organization's overall collection development policies.

Scientific and Technical. This material should only be collected at the very basic levels sufficient to provide basic information and definitions of terms, fields of research and experts' names such as general scientific and technical encyclopedias and dictionaries.

Historical Access. Materials that assist in giving dates, names or other necessary information to identify a particular intellectual property event should be given consideration for inclusion in this collection. Accessing the historical information available in patents and trademarks has become an important patron driven specialty of this PTDL and is one that is largely ignored by our neighboring PTDLs.

Intellectual Property Law Building on a complete collection, the Illinois State Library completed a backfile of the *Decisions of the Commissioner*, *United States Patent Quarterly* and *Shephard's Citations--Patents*, *Trademarks and Copyrights*. This is an important and rare collection in the national PTDL community. Every effort should be made to keep these two items current. Other legal materials should be acquired at a very moderate level. Our current legal collection, if simply maintained at its current level, is excellent.

Self-Help Materials - Since the majority of our patrons are attempting to proceed through the process without legal assistance we should collect materials to assist them at a moderate level. Caution should be used in selecting these materials to avoid inaccurate sources.

Project XL The Project XL program is a Parent Teacher Organization supported program which encourages the teaching of creative thinking and problem solving skills to children. There are a variety of individual programs available to teachers. The Illinois State Library is beginning to build a collection of materials that promote and assist teachers in this area. The materials selected for inclusion can be geared either toward the teacher or the children and should encompass all grade levels kindergarten through twelve. In addition to making them available to our patrons on an individual basis, the intent is to have the collection "travel" when it reaches sufficient size. The collection would be sent to appropriate sponsors such as systems and/or school district offices so that teachers and librarians in the area could use it as an acquisition tool for their own collections or classrooms. This concept is in keeping with the Illinois State Library's commitment to library development and educational support in the state of Illinois.

Map Collection

Maps, atlases, and related reference tools are basic to any research collection. No type of map or atlas--historical, geologic, nautical--should be automatically excluded. In the past, the ISL has not acquired historical aerial photography, as the University of Illinois had the major collection. Because of the need to access other map collections, developed cooperatively, the appropriate tools for doing so are necessary. No format of cartographic data shall be automatically excluded from the ISL map collection due to technological or financial factors, as more information becomes available only in microform or digital format. Appropriate hardware, therefore, also needs to be acquired.

The map collection consists not only of the sheet maps shelved in horizontal map cases, but of the atlases, gazetteers, reference books and where they are housed, i.e. the county atlases in the Folio Room, the BGN gazetteers or soil surveys in the basement, the current plat books in the Reference Room, the Geokatalog in the Map Reading Room, Illinois Geological Survey circulars on the third floor, etc. Because of this integrated nature, because all reference staff need to be able to answer some map questions, because of the physical environment, and because of staffing, the Map Reference Collection in the Map Reading Room has purposely been left extremely small and the bulk of the Map Reference Collection remains on the second floor, which necessitates communication between the two service staffs. Procedures still need to be classified. Duplication should be kept to an absolute minimum.

As a general rule, the map collection strives for research coverage of Illinois as a whole and locally, if readily available, basic coverage of the other states and the United States, and minimal coverage of the rest of the world. These coverages shall be supported by gift, depository status, and/or purchase. For instance, taking these three geographies in reverse order, Illinois

State Library receives the ONC charts for the world at the scale of 1:1,000,000 on GPO deposit, rather than acquire the 1:50,000 Canadian topographic quads. The University of Illinois owns the Canadian topos, Illinois State Library has the index map and can use it to request the topos on interlibrary loan for Illinois State Library patrons. For the forty-nine states, the Illinois State Library acquires state atlases and gazetteers, selective city street maps from Chambers of Commerce, state highway maps, USGS 7 112 minute topos and other items on GPO deposit. The Illinois State Library shall continue to participate as a regional depository library in the GPO depository program, thereby receiving maps from USGS, DMA, NOS, and other federal agencies. Many categories of deposit maps shall be kept only on a current basis, such as the sectional aeronautical charts, the majority of the states' topo quads (the six states surrounding Illinois are kept indefinitely), the airport obstruction charts, etc.

For Illinois, the Illinois State Document Depository Program provides the basis for the collection. All state agency produced maps should be obtained. Three copies of published maps are added to the collection, two circulating and one archival copy. When state agency maps are not "published" per se, such as the blue line prints of the Department of Revenue's county taxing district maps, or the Geological Survey's county coal mine maps, or ENR's computer plotted school district maps, one copy shall be sufficient. Access to all cartographic data shall be pursued, even if the data cannot be housed at the ISL. Contacts with mapping personnel at state agencies shall be maintained, not only so the ISL receives all current mapping, but also to encourage the agencies to send the ISL their discards to fill in gaps from the past.

Another large percentage of the Illinois collection consists of federal documents acquired from the federal agencies and through the joint USGS/GPO deposit program. The Illinois USGS collection shall be comprehensive, whether acquired by deposit or otherwise. The large scale topo collection shall be a historical collection and two copies acquired and maintained where possible by gift. Nondeposit federal maps on Illinois, such as the FEMA flood maps, or the Census Bureau's ED, block, and tract maps shall be obtained, free if possible, either directly from the federal agency or through a second party. Withdrawals from other libraries fill in the gaps in the ISL's collection or add a second copy, but many vital

sub-collections are available only by purchase. The county atlas!
plat book collection and the microfilmed Sanborn atlases are two
such valuable resources which shall be supported.

Illinois Authors Collection
While the ISL is primarily a special library, with predominant
collection emphasis in the social sciences and areas of technology, the ISL also fulfills an important role as a statewide cultural
and educational institution. The ISL's principal thrust in this element
of its mission is in the promotion of reading, with emphasis on the
literary heritage of Illinois. In order to fulfill its responsibility and
develop worthwhile programs, the ISL has undertaken the
development of a collection of and works by Illinois authors. This
is the only segment of the collection where fiction, poetry, drama,
and imaginative works are systematically acquired.

The goal of the Illinois Authors Collection is to build and
maintain a representative collection of works by individuals who
were born or lived in Illinois. Special consideration will be given to
works that are set in Illinois or where the state plays an important
intellectual or structural role in the work. The intent is not to build a
rare book collection, although gifts of rare books or first editions will
be considered. Neither is the Illinois Authors Collection intended to
be an exhaustive resource. Little effort will be expended to acquire
multiple, variant, or foreign language editions of particular works.
Dissertations, theses, self-published works and family histories are
not collected as part of the Authors Collection. The Authors
Collection is intended to demonstrate the breadth of Illinois letters
and scholarship throughout its history and to highlight the works of
new and emerging authors. The books in the Authors Collection,
with a few exceptions, circulate and are frequently used in displays
and programs.

Within the general goals and guidelines for the inclusion of a
work in the Illinois Authors Collection, there are several aspects
that receive particular attention.

Authors Honored on the Building Frieze: Thirty-five authors have
been memorialized on the frieze of the ISL Building. The Illinois
Authors Collection seeks to include copies of all of the works of
these distinguished authors. Where necessary, rare and out-of-
print sources will be used to build this segment of the collection.

First Editions of First Works: In an effort to include new authors and to represent lesser known authors, the Illinois Authors Collection will make a special effort to obtain copies of the first edition of the first published work of as many contemporary Illinois authors as possible. Rare and out-of-print dealers will be used to build this segment of the collection. In addition, the scholarly and literary communities will be solicited to identify new authors, whose first works can be acquired.

SPECIFIC SUBJECT POLICIES

The Illinois State Library's collections are developed and organized by subject. What follows are descriptions of general subject categories and specific subjects, evaluations of the current strength of the State Library's holdings in these areas, and guidance for selectors in making acquisitions decisions. The subject policies reflect the mission of the library and its current service program.

The acquisition targets and long term collecting goals expressed in the policies will be refined and modified annually through the budget allocation process and as the result of the continuous review of the collection management policy by the staff.

Organization of the Specific Subject Policies

There are thirty-five broad subject categories arranged alphabetically in the collection management policy. Within these categories slightly more than 400 specific subjects are listed. Both the broad categories and specific subjects are taken from the organization of the Illinois Collections Analysis Matrix, which is a version of the RLG Conspectus. This organization is recommended in the *Guide for Written Collection Policy Statements* issued by the American Library Association.

The information provided for each category and subject includes a definition of the category; scope, depth, and format selection guidelines; brief indications of collection strength in the general collection, depository documents, and microforms; detailed conspectus evaluations of specific subjects; general comments; target service audiences; and possible sources for referral.

1. Definition:The brief definitions derive from a variety of general reference sources. They are provided to orient the selectors.

They are not meant to be comprehensive or universal. Specific subjects are not separately defined in the policies.

2. Scope: All subject categories are assigned a scope. A scope is a relative measure of the centrality of a subject category to the service program of the library. It is an expression of an intent to support services with the selection process and the documents depository programs. The scope defines a general range of importance, against which selectors can judge individual title choices. The three scopes used in this policy are core, secondary, and peripheral.

> Core subject categories are of primary value and importance to the services and programs of the State Library. They relate most directly to the functions and interests of state government. Funding decisions will emphasize core areas.

> Secondary subject categories are clearly related to the interests of state government or specific agencies. They tend, however to offer more general support and background or are heavily technical and clinical in nature. Funding will be provided at proportionately lower levels than for core areas. Selectors need to exercise discretion in making individual choices in secondary subject categories.

> Peripheral subject categories are not central to the functions of state government or the service program of the State Library. Selections may be made in peripheral areas when they clearly support a service or program or when they relate directly to the operation of government entities. Limited funding will be available for selections in peripheral subject categories. Depository collections may add substantial collection strength in such areas. Selectors should establish rigorous criteria for making selections in peripheral subject areas.

3. Depth: All subject categories have an assigned depth indicator. These indicators refer to the levels of treatment a

subject category receives in individual works. It represents an assessment of the intellectual or technical level needed in the collection to meet the needs of the library's service program. Selectors should use the depth indicator to discriminate works written at appropriate levels from those that are too general and simplistic or too specialized, technical or esoteric. The State Library is a special library and, as such, does not attempt to represent materials at all depths in any particular subject area. The three depths used in this policy are basic, support, and research.

Basic depth indicates the most general type of collecting. Selections are focused on introducing and defining the fundamental character of a subject category. Some ability to direct the user to more in-depth resources should be available at the basic collecting level. The intent at the basic level is to broadly inform users.

Support depth denotes collecting at a level capable of sustaining the principal information needs of state government. Issues and topics should be defined and all schools of thought should be identified. Important and timely works should be acquired and bibliography and resources should be adequate to access the State Library's holdings and initiate requests for information through referral or resource sharing. Support level collections should be sufficient to meet the needs of the library staff in developing and supplying services and programs to users.

Research depth indicates a collection capable of supporting the independent creation of new knowledge by users. The work of state government is primarily synthetic and applied in nature. Therefore, the State Library collects at research depth in very few areas. Research level collecting entails the acquisition of both major and secondary works. timely information on new issues and findings, reports of research, extensive journal holdings, and substantial bibliographic access to resources held elsewhere.

4. **Format:**   Collecting in particular subject categories or specific subjects may be qualified by format. Any such restrictions will be noted in this field for the convenience of selectors. If there are no qualifiers noted, items in any form may be considered. This does not mean that the State Library will actively build holdings in nonprint forms.

5. **Areas of Strength:**   The comments recorded in these fields provide further explanations and refinements of the general subject category descriptions. They reflect the particular strengths, weaknesses, and characteristics of the holdings of the Illinois State Library. They provide selectors with historical context and current directions upon which they may base decisions.

    General collection comments will include information on historical collecting strengths and current service programs being supported. If there are particular areas within the general category that need explanation or differential treatment, they will be recorded in this field. Weaknesses needing attention will be identified.

    Documents will contain a summary of the documentary holdings relevant to the subject category. Information on both state and federal documents will be included. Reference and access sources for the documents' sources may be noted. Selectors should consider the information in this field when recommending acquisitions. The content of this field will be reviewed by the documents coordinator.

    Microforms will consist of a listing and description of all significant, non-document microform holdings in the subject category. It is provided to give the selector a complete perspective of the available resources. The information will be provided by the coordinator of Collection Management.

6. **Conspectus Evaluations:**   Within each general discipline described in the policies a series of specific subjects have been identified. For each subject an evaluation of the collection has

been conducted by the appropriate staff subject selector. The summary information is coded and may be entered into three columns for each subject. The columns are labeled CL, AC, and GL.

CL stands for "current level" of collection strength. The codes reflect the evaluator's assessment of the potential for all of the library's relevant sources on this subject to provide service and support programs. Documentary holdings and microforms must be considered in the evaluation.

AC stands for "acquisitions" commitment. This is a statement of the library's intent to obtain materials in the subject area. Significant deposits of documents should be considered and reflected, as well as purchased material. Because the State Library has not yet established acquisition fund allocation procedures, the AC column has been left blank.

GL stands for "goal." This is a statement of the desired strength of the collection based on the defined service program of the library.

For each subject an alphanumeric code is recorded in each appropriate column. This is the expression of the capacity of the collection to meet the demands of the library's service program. These codes provide the basic guidance for selectors in making decisions. The information is also essential in designing new service initiatives. The codes are explained in detail on the following pages.

Each code may be modified by a language code. For convenience, if no language modifier is noted, collecting is done solely in English. Explanations of the language codes follow the code descriptions.

0   Out of Scope.
The library does not collect in this subject.

1   Minimal Level.
A subject area in which few selections are made beyond

very basic works. A collection at this level is frequently and systematically reviewed for currency of information. Superseded editions and titles containing outdated information are withdrawn.

la Minimal Level, Uneven Coverage.
Few selections are made, and there is unsystematic representation of subject.

lb Minimal Level, Even Coverage.
Few selections are made, but basic authors, some core works, or a spectrum of ideological views are represented.

2 Basic Information Level.
A selective collection of materials that serves to introduce and define a subject and to indicate the varieties of information available elsewhere. It may include dictionaries, encyclopedias, access to appropriate bibliographic databases, selected editions of important works, historical surveys, bibliographies, handbooks, and a few major periodicals. The collection is frequently and systematically reviewed for currency of information.

2a Basic Information Level, Introductory.
The emphasis at this level is on providing resources that introduce and define a subject. A collection at this level includes basic reference tools and explanatory works, such as textbooks; historical descriptions of the subject's development; general works devoted to major topics and figures in the field; and selective major periodicals. The introductory level of a basic information collection is only sufficient to support patrons attempting to locate general information about a subject or students enrolled in introductory level courses.

2b Basic Information Level, Advanced.
At the advanced level, basic information about a subject is provided on a wider range of topics and with more

depth.   There is a broader selection of basic
explanatory works, historical descriptions, tools, and
periodicals that serve to introduce and define a subject.
An advanced basic information level is sufficient to
support students in basic courses as well as supporting
the basic information needs of patrons in public and
special libraries.

3   Study or Instructional Support Level.
A collection that is adequate to impart and maintain
knowledge about a subject in a systematic way but at a
level of less than research intensity. The collection includes
a wide range of basic works in appropriate formats, a
significant number of classic retrospective materials,
complete collections of the works of more important writers,
selections from the works of secondary writers, a selection
of representative journals, access to appropriate machine-
readable data files, and the reference tools and
fundamental bibliographical apparatus pertaining to the
subject.   At the study or instructional support level, a
collection is adequate to support independent study and
most learning needs of the clientele of public and special
libraries, as well as undergraduate and some graduate
instruction.   The collection is systematically reviewed for
currency of information and to assure that essential and
significant information is retained.

3a Study or Instructional Support Level, Introductory.
This subdivision of a level 3 collection is adequate to
support independent study and most learning needs of
the clientele of public topics of a subject area. The
collection includes a broad range of basic works in
appropriate formats, classic retrospective materials, all
key journals on primary topics, selected journals and
seminar works on secondary topics, access to
appropriate machine-readable data files, and the
reference tools and fundamental bibliographical
apparatus pertaining to the subject.   In academic
libraries the level 3a supports undergraduate courses,
including advanced undergraduate courses.   In public

and special libraries 3a supports most independent study needs of the primary clientele

3b Study or Instructional Support Level, Advanced.
The advanced subdivision of level 3 provides resources adequate for imparting and maintaining knowledge about the primary and secondary topics of a subject area. The collection includes a significant number of seminal works and journals on the primary and secondary topics in the field; a significant number of retrospective materials; a substantial collection of works by secondary figures; works that provide more in-depth discussions of research, techniques, and evaluation; access to appropriate machine-readable data files; and reference tools and fundamental bibliographic apparatus pertaining to the subject. This level supports all courses of undergraduate study and master's degree programs as well as the more advanced independent study needs of the patrons of public and special libraries.

4   Research Level.
A collection that includes the major published source materials required for dissertation and independent research, including materials containing research reporting, new findings, scientific experimental results, and other information useful to researchers. It is intended to include all important reference works and a wide selection of specialized monographs, as well as a very extensive collection of journals and major indexing and abstracting services in the field. Pertinent foreign language materials are included. Older material is usually retained for historical research and actively preserved. A collection at this level supports doctoral and other original research.

5   Comprehensive Level.
A collection in which a library endeavors, so far as it is reasonably possible, to include all significant works of recorded knowledge (publications, manuscripts, other forms in all applicable languages, for a necessarily defined

and limited field). This level of collection intensity is one that maintains a "special collection"; the aim, if not the achievement, is exhaustiveness. Older material is retained for historical research with active preservation efforts.

Language Codes and Definitions
Language codes indicate the language priorities and limitations that govern a library's collecting policies in a given subject. As in the case of the collection level rating, language coverage must be assessed against the universe of resources in the subject. For each collection level assigned, a language code is also assigned.

Code	Label	Definition
E	English	English language material predominates; little or no foreign language material is in the collection.
F	Selected non-English	Selected other language material is included in addition to the English language material.
W	Wide Selection	Wide selection of material in all applicable languages. No programmatic decision is made to restrict materials according to language.
Y	Non-English	Material is primarily in one non-English language. The overall focus is on collecting material in the vernacular of the area.

7. Comments: This field is used to record any specific information that might elaborate or modify the coded information in the conspectus evaluation. Specific holdings of note may be recorded or significant weaknesses noted.

8. Potential Audience: This field is used to record those agencies or units of state government that might be served

well by information in the subjects listed. This information is used in the development of a State Library service liaison network and the development of specific programs. Selectors should consider this information when developing and focusing their acquisition strategies.

9. Suggested Referrals: The State Library is an active participant in resource sharing. As a special library, there are substantial areas in which no collection strength is maintained. This field records options available to patron staff for obtaining information.

[Authors' note: The next section of the ISL policy includes selection guidelines, scope, depth, format, areas of strength, and conspectus analyses by broad subject areas. Only Agriculture and Related Technologies is included in this book due to space limitations.]

AGRICULTURE & RELATED TECHNOLOGIES

Definition
The practice of cultivating the soil, harvesting crops, and raising livestock. The agricultural sciences pertain to food and fiber production. Related technologies include farm production, crop growing and harvesting, animal husbandry, processing of plant and animal products for human consumption or use, agricultural economics, agricultural engineering, and related industries that supply machinery, agrichemicals, buildings and processing services.

Selection Guidelines
    Scope. Secondary
    Depth. Support
    Format. Microform

Areas of Strength:

    Illinois Documents.

    Federal Documents. The depository collections provide ISL with an extensive ag collection, particularly USDA, of material from popular to scientific literature. See class ranges A, EP, E, FCA, FHL, HE, I.

Microforms,

General Collection. Purchased material should concentrate on the relation of agriculture to problems of social issues and public policy, e.g., trends affecting land use, zoning, pollution; economics of agribusiness, environmental law & policy issues, taxation and revenue, social/health/economic statuses of populations involved.

Conspectus Analysis

Agriculture & Related Technologies

Dewey Class	Line Number	Division and Categories	Collection Codes AC	GL
630	AGD010	Agric. & Related Technologies	lb	3a
631	AGD020	Crops & Their Production	lb	3a
632	ADD030	Plant Injuries, Diseases, Pests	lb	3a
633	AGD040	Field Crops	lb	3a
634	AGD050	Orchards, Fruits, Forestry	lb	3a
635	AGD060	Garden Crops, Vegetables	2a	3a
636	AGD070	Animal Husbandry	lb	3a
637	AGD080	Dairy & Related Technologies	lb	3a
638	AGD090	Insect Culture	lb	3a
639	AGD100	Nondomestic. Animals & Plants	1b	3a

Comments

The Agriculture collection's major strength is the Federal Documents portion of the collection. The circulation collection of agricultural material has now become dated. It is supplemented by a very strong collection of federal documents (mainly generated by the U.S. Dept. of Agriculture) and a strong collection of Illinois documents (largely due to the very strong College of Agriculture publications program at the University of Illinois). The Reference Collection has a good percentage of the titles recommended by

Sheehy's *Guide to Reference Sources*. Periodical coverage is only fair in general coverage.

Potential Audience
Dept. of Agriculture; Rural Affairs Council; Dept. of Conservation; Environmental Protection Agency; geological administration services staff; economic, fiscal, and legislative service agencies

Suggested Referrals
University of Illinois of Agriculture as an applied science. Southern Illinois University at Carbondale--College of Agriculture.

[This is a partial list of nearly 500 subject categories. The reader can consult the Illinois State Library for the entire list.]

ILLINOIS COLLECTIONS ANALYSIS MATRIX

The Illinois Collections Analysis Matrix (ICAM) is a cooperative collections analysis project of the Cooperative Collection Management Coordinating Committee. It is intended to build a database of comparative information about library collections in the state. It has evolved to incorporate elements of the conspectus analysis presented in the specific subject policies of this document.

Another element of the ICAM is a computer generated count of collection holdings arranged in the National Shelflist Count subject categories. The ICAM builds these counts off the Illinet Online (10) database tapes. What follows is the Illinois State Library's ICAM collection count as of January 1992. It represents only that portion of the collection with machine-readable records. It can, however, be used in conjunction with conspectus analysis to evaluate collection strengths and measure collection development over time.

1.	Collections	298	0.051%
2.	Encyclopedias	283	0.048%
3.	General Reference Works	0	0.000%
4.	Indexes	0	0.000%
5.	Museums, Collectors & Collecting	159	0.027%
6.	Newspapers (if used by campus)	975	0.167%

7. Periodicals	170	0.029%
8. Societies, Academies	226	0.038%
9. Yearbooks, Almanacs, Directories	0	0.000%
10. History of the Sciences in General, Scholarship, Learning	46	0.007%
11. Philosophy: Periodicals, Societies, Congresses, etc.	898	0.154%
12. Philosophy: History and Systems, Ancient through Renaissance	54	0.009%
13. Philosophy: History and Systems, Post-Renaissance,	471	0.253%
14. Logic	238	0.040%

June 1993
George H. Ryan, Secretary of State and State Librarian and
Bridget L. Lamont, Director, Illinois State Library

This policy was prepared by: Thomas J. Dorst, Associate Director for Library Services; Jane Rishel, Coordinator of Collectionv Management; with the assistance of: Liz Alexander, Documents Coordinator; Laura Frizol ,Coordinator of Collection Access; Alyce Scott, Coordinator of Collection Maintenance; Maria Reed, Coordinator of Public Services; Arlyn Sherwood, Map Librarian; Jeanne Oliver, Patent and Trademark Librarian; and Subject Selectors: Barbara Allen, Kim Bauer, Raymond Collins, Mary Kate Field, Carol Fox, Cheryl Goza-Smith, Margaret Groninger, Christine Henderson, Jane Running.

NEW MEXICO STATE LIBRARY
Santa Fe, New Mexico

INTRODUCTION

The New Mexico State Library is established under New Mexico law, Chapter 18, Article 2, *New Mexico Statutes Annotated 1978*

Vision
The State Library's purpose is to assure that all New Mexicans have the information they need, when they need it.

Mission
Our mission is to enable the development, coordination, and delivery of information in appropriate formats by strengthening and developing libraries statewide or, where necessary, providing direct library services.

Goals
1. To provide library service to citizens without access to local libraries, specifically to remote citizens and those who because of physical disability cannot use regular printed materials.
2. To strengthen library services statewide by assisting libraries to improve collections, facilities, personnel and programs.
3. To strengthen resource sharing among libraries of all types.
4. To assure information services are provided to state government.
5. To provide information to citizens on special subjects such as government, Southwest history and culture, library science, and government publications.

Purpose
The purpose of this collection development policy is to define the collection and provide guidelines for staff responsible for selecting and weeding materials. This collection development policy should be looked upon as a working paper reflecting the current needs of the clientele served, and should be reviewed to reflect changes in these needs and uses.

New Mexico State Library

Clientele Served
The primary groups served by this policy are state agencies, libraries throughout the state, and citizens with information needs related to government.

Funding Considerations
Financing for the collection is included in the State Library's annual budget as determined by the State Legislature. Allocations are established by the State Library according to a formula based on need in the subject area, importance to the mission, and cost for and use of the materials in that subject area.

Responsibility for Selection
The final responsibility for selection of materials, as for all library activities, rests with the State Librarian. The delegated responsibility for the professional supervision of the selection and acquisition of library materials rests with the Administrative Librarian for Information Services. The selection of materials is a responsibility of the subject specialists.

Coordination with Other Libraries
Since New Mexico has an effective Interlibrary Loan service, the State Library's collection development policy takes into account other library resources in the state library system. The State Library tries to avoid duplication of costly materials in specialized collections such as the Supreme Court Law Library, the Legislative Council Service, individual state agency libraries, and the popular materials in public libraries. Whenever possible, we cooperate with area libraries, both agency and public, including the Santa Fe area and Los Alamos.

STANDARDS FOR SELECTING LIBRARY MATERIAL

Selection of materials is determined by: state law, the library's mission statement, the informational needs of the clientele served, the library's acquisition goals as defined in this policy, existing collections in other agencies and institutions available through cooperative efforts, and available funds.

Also taken into account are the following selection criteria: the author's qualifications and other published works, reliability and reputation of the publisher, accuracy of contents, literary excellence of style and readability, originality of work, the inclusion of special features such as indexes, bibliographies, charts, maps, diagrams, photographic material.

The State Library may collect and preserve material in any form, i.e., print, tape, compact discs, maps, microform, film, electronic. Materials in all these formats may include monographs, periodicals, serials intended to result in complete sets, serials intended to recur indefinitely, leased materials, and rights to access information over a fixed time span which function as library materials, even when no material object is added to the physical collection. The decision to provide access to a particular body of knowledge in a particular format is determined by need, cost, and ease of access. Additional formats may be added in the future as appropriate and available.

TYPES OF MATERIAL ACQUIRED

In general, the State Library does not collect adult fiction, textbooks, juvenile works, large print books, rare books and manuscripts, non-English language works and genealogies.

Adult Nonfiction
The library's objective is to develop a collection sufficient in scope and depth to support library service to state government and to fulfill the State Library's role as a reference center to public libraries and to citizens with information needs related to government.

Newspapers
The State Library seeks a comprehensive, historical collection of New Mexico newspapers, The *New York Times* and the *Wall Street Journal* on microfilm. Current subscriptions to hard copy include selective titles from around the state, and at least one national paper.

Serials and Periodicals
The State Library acquires serial services and periodical titles to support and strengthen the subject areas according to the collection levels. In many subject areas, the most timely and important material available is that in periodicals.

Government Publications
The State Library is a regional federal publications depository, the official depository for New Mexico state publications, and the administrative agency for the New Mexico State Documents.

Depository Clearinghouse Program
Materials are acquired to complement these collections, both adding publications which are not depository items and acquiring finding aids and indexes.

Pamphlet/Other Vertical File Materials
Materials such as publications under fifty pages, pamphlets, clippings, printouts from computerized data bases, and other materials not suitable for shelf organization are collected for the following vertical files:

Southwest Historical Vertical File: All subjects related in general to the Southwest and specifically to New Mexico. This file is not weeded and some of the major areas of research interest are preserved on microfilm.

General Vertical File: This file is selected by the Information Services librarians to supplement the general reference collection. It should be weeded periodically.

Library Development Vertical File: Materials maintained by the Development Consultants for statewide library concerns. It should be weeded periodically.

Multiple Copies
More than one copy of a title may sometimes be required to meet special needs. Acquisition of multiple copies may occur in accordance with the collection development policy. A second, circulating copy may be purchased when deemed useful.

Gifts
The State Library accepts gifts in all forms of print and non-print material appropriate to the mission statement. Monetary gifts are also accepted. The library reserves the right to accept or dispose of, through donation to other libraries in New Mexico, any gift offered. Gifts and donations will be evaluated in accordance with the collection development policy. The State

Library will not provide appraisal for gifts received. [Gift form deleted]

Challenges and Censorship

The Library Development Bureau of the State Library serves as the Intellectual Freedom Clearinghouse for the state of New Mexico. The Bureau provides information and guidance to the State Library and other New Mexico libraries and institutions in meeting challenges to library materials. The State Library supports intellectual freedom and endorses the following statements: the Library Bill of Rights and the Intellectual Freedom Statement from the American Library Association, which will be found in Appendix C [not reproduced here in this policy].

The State Library recognizes the right of individuals to question materials in the library's collection. An individual questioning material is free to discuss such material with designated members of the library staff. An individual may state his or her opinion in writing on the Request for Reconsideration of Library Materials (Appendix C [not included in this book]). The request will be forwarded to the Administrative Librarian who supervises the unit in which the questioned material was selected. Questioned materials will be reviewed by the State Library Commission. The State Library Commission will recommend to the State Librarian what action should be taken with regard to the questioned material. The State Librarian will make a final decision on disposition of the questioned material and will reply in writing to the individual who initiated the inquiry.

COLLECTIONS

Level of Selection

The terms used to define selection level of a subject area were adapted from those definitions developed by the American Library Association. They have been modified to meet the needs of this collection and its clientele.

Basic:a collection which aids in the immediate understanding of a subject, and indicates the variety of materials available for further investigation; most selection is for the reference collection.

Support: a collection or subject area intended as a resource to back up governmental and library programs and interests; selection done for both circulating and non-circulating materials

Research: a collection or subject area which includes major secondary source materials for governmental or independent research.

Scope statements for areas which are currently purchased for the circulating Dewey collection follow a general description of current development policies.

Circulating Collections

The intent of the State Library's circulating collections is to support state government programs and interests, to support library development needs statewide, and to provide citizen access to government publications and information. The following collections are maintained:

(1) Dewey Decimal Classification Collection: A support level collection of current materials is maintained for governmental programs of the executive branch and for the development of library programs and personnel throughout the state. Pertinent non-depository federal, state, regional, or local publications are added when appropriate.

As funds permit second copies of titles in the Southwest collection which meet the following criteria will be added to the circulating Dewey collection: useful to state agency programs, on significant state or local issues, or by prominent New Mexico authors.

(2) Superintendent of Documents Classification Collection: The State Library has been a Regional Depository since 1962. Regional depositories of federal documents must receive, retain and provide access to at least one copy of all government publications made available under the Depository Library Program.

Documents distributed through the Federal Depository Library Program are and remain government property. Depository libraries are entrusted with the maintenance of these materials while they are in the custody of the library. The Federal government does not distinguish among formats- all are considered equally important for information access.

Regionals may only discard those depository materials that have been authorized by the Superintendent of Documents. Regionals should treat those discards as "secondary publications"

and offer them to other depository libraries through the Needs and
Offers lists. Regionals should routinely search the lists to fill gaps
in their collections and to obtain needed copies.

(3)   New Mexico State Publications Classification Collection:
The State Library is designated an official depository of all
publications, pamphlets, reports, notices, proclamations and
similar instruments issued by a state agency filed with the New
Mexico Record Center.

The Record Center, in turn, shall deliver three copies of any of
these depository items to the State Library, which shall keep one
copy available for public inspection during office hours. This copy
is housed with the Southwest collection. All other copies may be
circulated.

The State Library also actively seeks to acquire state publications which fall outside the scope of the Record Center. The
collection is both current and historical.

State documents are not generally weeded except for
superseded regulations.

General Reference Collection
The intent of this collection is to be a non-circulating general
reference resource center for government agencies and libraries
throughout New Mexico. The Information Services staff provides
reference and research assistance to government agencies and
direct users and, through a toll free interlibrary reference line, to
librarians throughout the state.

Special Collections Within General Reference:
Foundation Center: The State Library is part of the Foundation
Center's Cooperating Collection Network. A core collection is
provided with the annual membership fee. The State Library
acquires materials which supplement this collection, including
information on private foundations, corporate giving and proposals.

Census Data Center: The State Library as an official Census
Data Center for New Mexico acquires, maintains and makes
available public census information from the U.S. Census Bureau,
University of New Mexico and New Mexico State University. The
State Library agrees to provide space, staff and user support.

Federal Government Information Reference: In order to assist
the Information Services staff in providing timely reference service,

some federal publications will be housed in the reference area. In addition, appropriate commercial funding and indexes in various formats are acquired to ease access to and understanding of federal publications.

Southwest Collection: This special collection provides a reference collection of both current and retrospective research materials, largely from secondary sources, for state agencies, scholars, students, and the general public for the study of New Mexico's past, present, and future. Since the Southwest collection is a retrospective research collection, materials are not weeded.

The Southwest collection consists of: the reference copy of state publications; other relevant regional government publications, including New Mexico environmental impact statements; WIPP materials; a comprehensive collection of New Mexico newspapers, current and retrospective; the Southwest historical vertical file; a comprehensive collection of periodicals and newsletters published in New Mexico whose subjects pertain primarily to New Mexico; material about New Mexico on any subject; material about the Southwest which includes a significant contribution to knowledge about New Mexico; fiction about New Mexico, or primarily about New Mexico.

Current buying focuses on new historical studies and contemporary issues of importance to the state, such as water rights, wildlife, forestry and grazing issues, economic development, land use, health problems and racial and ethnic studies.

Materials by authors living in New Mexico may be bought for the circulating or reference collections but will not be placed in the Southwest collection unless these materials fall within the collection guidelines outlined above.

Other Special Collections

Talking Books Library: The New Mexico Talking Books Library (NMTBL) is a regional library in the National Library Service (NLS) for the Blind and Physically Handicapped. As such, NMTBL is required to collect at least one copy of every book in the basic NLS collection. The NLS books remain federal property assigned to the NMTBL collection.

In addition, NLS encourages regional libraries to collect books beyond those provided by NLS. NMTBL houses two small additional collections:

1. NMTBL accepts occasional gifts and volunteer-recorded books, especially in the areas of New Mexico history and literature; and education, self-development, and independent living for the blind and print handicapped. TBL reserves the right to determine the ultimate disposition of gifts.
2. The Friends of the New Mexico Talking Book Library, Inc., provide some books on long-term loan, especially in New Mexico history and literature. The Library is not responsible for loss or damage.

Film/Video Collection: At present, the State Library buys films and videos in only three areas: library science, management, and Southwest. These circulate only to registered groups or agencies.

Working Tools. The library buys a reasonable number of materials in any necessary format, not for the collections, but as working tools for library staff to better perform work related activities.

Collection Maintenance

Binding: Rebinding, repair or replacement of materials is considered for those items unsuitable for withdrawal from the collection. The following criteria are used: sufficient funds for rebinding, repair or replacement; ability of staff to meet rebinding or repair needs; demand for the particular title or subject; similarity of material in the collection; availability of more up-to-date material; number of copies in the collection.

Weeding: The collection of the State Library receives on-going revision and weeding to maintain the best possible condition for the collection, accurate to the library's mission, and to meet the demand of space limitations in the library's facility. The Collection Development Liaison shall be responsible for coordinating maintenance activities between the selectors and Technical Services. The librarian responsible for selection in a specific subject area or special collection is responsible for weeding that area or collection.

Exceptions to weeding are materials received on a contract depository basis which allows for discard only under specific terms of the contract, or where the State Library is committed by policy to the preservation of all materials in a given field.

Guidelines for weeding will be based on the CREW (Continuous Review, Evaluation, and Weeding) method which is to be found at the end of this policy.

Disposal of Weeded Material : Materials weeded from the State Library collection are offered, upon the recommendation of the selector, to other libraries through the statewide Gifts and Exchange program. Materials not selected by another library or which are in poor physical condition are recycled according to established procedures.

Scope statements

The scope statements which follow only apply to the circulating Dewey collection.

Education

The State Library selects titles in education that will support state agencies in research, planning, and policy making for New Mexico's schools. Educational materials are collected at the support level.

Social Services/Sciences

Materials are selected at the support level in social services/sciences to build a collection which will assist state agencies in effective policy making and public administration in this area. Categories include: social welfare, political, economic, and legal considerations, public housing, problems of and services for the disabled, public safety, criminal justice and the theory and methodology of social sciences.

Business and Management

Materials are selected at the support level for the broad topic of management.   Materials suited to profit, non-profit and government organizations are included.   Topics include the management of systems, offices, human resources, teamwork, records, organizations, finances and time. Some business and management titles fall into the areas of ethics and psychology.

Business materials are currently selected with emphasis on the Department of Economic Development's role in business start-ups and expansions.

Computers and Telecommunications
Current materials relating to computers and telecommunications are selected at the support level to be of use to state agencies and libraries in their work. Topics include how this technology works, how to use software and hardware commonly available in state agencies, workplace safety issues, information for management decisions and the future of information technology.

Environmental Materials
Environmental materials are selected at the support level to provide background information and to supplement the collection on these subjects in reference, Southwest, and government publications for the use of state agencies and local governments.

Library Science
Library science materials are currently selected at the support level. The objective of the library science collection is to provide a selection of timely materials relating to all aspects of library work for the use of librarians, staff members, library science students, and others. The collection should provide a balance between historic and current practice, and among the varied interests of all types of libraries. The particular needs of public, academic, school, and special libraries, as well as the State Library are always considered.

Public Administration, Political Science
Materials are selected at the support level pertaining to the creation of public policy, the administration of public agencies, government operations, and politics with limited foreign coverage.

Public Health
Materials are selected at the support level dealing with public health including, but not limited to, health promotion, health services, health administration and planning, and health education.

The Crew Guidelines for Weeding Your Collection

The formulas given here for the various Dewey classes are rules of thumb based on professional opinions in the literature and practical experience. The formula in each case consists of three parts: 1) The first figure refers to the years since the book's latest copyright date (age of material in the book); 2) the second figure refers to the maximum permissible time without usage (in terms of years since its last recorded circulation); 3) the third refers to the presence of various negative factors, called MUSTY factors. For example, the formula "8/3/MUSTY" could be read: "Consider a book in this class for discard when its latest copyright is more than eight (8) years ago; and/or, when its last circulation was more than three (3) years ago; and/or, when it possesses one or more of the MUSTY factors." Most formulas include a "3" in the usage category and a MUSTY in the negative factors category. The figure in the age category varies considerably from subject to subject. If any one of the three factors is not applicable to a specific subject, the category is filled with an "X."

MUSTY is an easily remembered acronym for five negative factors which frequently ruin a book's usefulness and mark it for weeding:

M = Misleading (and/or factually inaccurate)
U = Ugly (worn and beyond mending or rebinding)
S = Superseded (by a truly *new* edition or by a much better book on the subject)
T = Trivial (of no discernible literary or scientific merit)
Y = Your collection has no use for this book (irrelevant to the needs and interests of your community).

This selection policy is approved as official policy of the New Mexico State Library.

Karen Watkins, State Librarian, 7/10/92

LIBRARY OF CONGRESS
Washington D. C.

The Collection Policy Statements of the Library of Congress implement its responsibilities to serve (1) the Congress as well as the United States Government as a whole, (2) the scholarly community, and (3) the general public. These policies aim at a comprehensive plan for developing the collection and maintaining its existing strengths. They set forth the scope, level of collecting intensity and goals sought by the Library in fulfilling its service missions for particular subjects, special formats of materials, or broad categories of publications (for example, religion, manuscript collections, government documents--foreign and domestic).

The Library has based its Collection Policy Statements on the fundamental principles, or "canons of selection," which succinctly summarize its collections development programs: (1) the Library should possess all books and other library materials necessary to the Congress and the various officers of the Federal government to perform their duties; (2) the Library should possess all books and other materials (whether in original form or copy) which cover the life and achievement of the American people; and (3) the Library should possess, in some useful form, the records of other societies present, and should accumulate, in original or in copy, full and representative collections of the written records of those societies and peoples whose experience is of most immediate concern to the people of the United States.

The Library has always recognized that its preeminent role is to collect at the national level. While striving to develop richly representative collections in all fields except technical agriculture and clinical medicine (where it yields precedence to the National Agricultural Library and the National Library of Medicine respectively), the Library has consciously confined itself to acquiring materials which are of utmost importance to the American record and world culture. This is particularly true of its special collections, such as manuscripts, motion pictures, music, prints and photographs. Unless they are felt to contribute in an especially significant way to needs of researchers who use these national collections, purely local publications and special collections whose content is primarily of local interest have not been collected. The Library has, instead, encouraged local and state repositories to develop strong collections of such materials.

The Library has also encouraged research institutions and libraries which have developed very strong collections in particular subject areas to expand and consolidate these strengths and, correspondingly, has limited both the nature and growth of its own collections in such subjects.

The Library's Collection Policy Statements are not static. Rather, they dynamically undergo continual revision and expansion to meet changing service needs and reflect new technological developments. For instance, the Library has received increasing requests in recent years to document the rapid changes that are occurring in the society and political structure of many areas of the world which are of particular strategic and/or political concern to the United States. In response to this need, the Library has expanded its policy to acquire examples of current political ephemera, a field of publishing traditionally excluded from the collections. This resulted in the publication of the Collections Policy Statement to reflect this change.

In another area of interest, the Library, as a means of sharpening the focus of collecting manuscript materials, reexamined its long-established policy which had included the collecting of organizational records. As a result, the revised Policy Statement for manuscripts severely limits the circumstances under which such files may be acquired. In yet another quarter, the Library is in the continuing process of defining its service needs as well as the budgetary, legal and physical requirements involved in acquiring computer files accessible within the framework of its services to the public. These media, which are undergoing rapid evolution and diversification, will have an increasing impact on the Library's services in the coming years, and will ultimately require a definitive policy statement which is fully responsive to these developments.

In sum, the Library's collections policies must be flexible yet at the same time ensure consistency and continuity with the historical development of our national collections. It is the Library's responsibility, therefore, to keep the policies up-to-date and responsive to its developing service needs.

[The below policies are representative ones of the Library of Congress; others which not included cover topics such as comic books, computer files, microforms, non-library materials, television, and postage stamps.]

PHOTOGRAPHY

I. Documentary photographs

A. The Library endeavors to acquire a wide selection of photographs documenting United States history and culture, and including:
   1. noteworthy individuals;
   2. events of national political, historical, or cultural interest;
   3. certain periods or subjects, such as the Depression, the Civil Rights Movement, etc.;
   4. changing styles in architecture, costume, etc.

B. The Library endeavors to acquire photographs illustrative of the categories listed under A. (above) on a world-wide basis.

C. Materials of strictly local interest are not generally accepted, but are referred to the appropriate regional institutions.

II. Artistic photographs

The Library acquires, on a highly selective basis, photographs which show excellence as works of art, in conception and presentation of image and form, and illustrative of a movement, an aesthetic theory, or a particular period of artistic photography.

III. History of the medium

The Library endeavors to acquire a selection of photographs which illustrate the history and technical advancement of the medium.

IV. Collection of photographs

The Library acquires, on a highly selective basis, collections in any of the above categories which represent a complete, self-contained unit. In most cases, these constitute the work of a single individual or are the product of a single institution. The Library will not acquire pictorial records of Federal agencies, as these are the responsibility of the National Archives.

V. Slides and transparencies

A. The Library endeavors to acquire for its permanent collections only those slides and transparencies which present information of value for reference or research which is not available in the Library in another form.

B. Slides or transparencies which are original photographs will be acquired on a selective basis.

C. Written or recorded texts which are issued with slides or transparencies will be retained with them.

VI. Technical considerations

In determining the acceptability of any photographic materials, consideration should be given to their size, quality, physical condition, and relationship to other materials in the Library. Practical matters such as the organization, housing, and use of collections must also be taken into consideration. A degree of flexibility in applying the following criteria is desirable. If a possible acquisition would fill a significant gap in the Library's holdings, its importance might balance possible negative factors.

A. In acquiring all photographic materials, the highest technical and expressive quality will be sought. Whenever possible, the materials should meet accepted archival standards. American National Standards Institute standards for negatives, prints, and transparencies, both in black-and-white and color, will be followed when they are issued.

B. Photographic materials should be accompanied by identifying data. Collections should be organized and cataloged, with negatives keyed to prints, negatives jacketed and prints in good condition.

C. Before the decision is made to acquire a collection, all problems concerning its physical location, processing if necessary, and plans for preservation should be documented in writing.

D. Questions of legal rights and restrictions should be considered where pertinent, and should be documented in writing before any acquisition is final.

VII. Books and periodicals

The Library of Congress endeavors to acquire monographs, exhibit and oeuvre catalogs, and serials relating to the history, criticism, techniques, and uses of photography. Publications issued in the United States and abroad will be collected at the research level, with special emphasis on materials pertaining to the medium's history, influence, and contemporary expression in the United States. The following guidelines will be followed:

A. Technical manuals and works on the study and teaching of photography will be collected on a highly selective basis.
B. Special emphasis will be placed on acquiring publications needed to support research in the Library's collection of original documentary and artistic photographs.
C. Publications in other subject areas, but illustrated with photographs or photographic reproductions of documentary or aesthetic interest, will be acquired. However, efforts will be made to avoid those photo-illustrated publications that are derivative and offer virtually no new information.

FINE AND APPLIED ARTS–NON-BOOK MATERIALS

I. Fine prints

The Library of Congress will endeavor to acquire selectively woodcuts, engravings, etchings, lithographs, and other types of original prints of the highest quality which relate to and complement the Library's existing fine print collection.

A. Particular emphasis in this area will be on prints of United States origin produced since 1870. In special instances efforts may be made to acquire the complete oeuvre of an American printmaker, as with James McNeill Whistler and Joseph Pennell.
B. In acquiring works by contemporary United States and foreign artists, the Library will seek to include in its collections only major works by those who have had or potentially will have an impact on printmaking in the United States.
C. The Library will collect foreign prints which support the research collections and interests of the Library's various area studies divisions.
D. Existing strengths of the Fine Prints Collections, in such areas as early lithography, chiaroscuro woodcuts and French nineteenth-century printmaking, will be further developed through the acquisition of important examples of work in those areas. Prints which are appropriate to a study collection on the history of printmaking technique will also be acquired.
E. The Library of Congress will generally not acquire fine prints which are represented in other national collections in Washington.

II. Posters

The Library will endeavor, within available resources, to acquire outstanding examples of posters produced throughout the world, with emphasis on:

A. Examples illustrative of political, military, social, economic, industrial and cultural history, including advertising and propaganda, with priority given to documentation of the United States life and history;
B. Examples of the work of major artists, with priority given to work of United States origin;
C. Examples illustrative of the history of the poster as an art form, and as a medium of communication.
Every effort will be made to achieve worldwide coverage.

III. Reproductions of works of art

The Library of Congress will endeavor to acquire selectively reproductions relating directly to the materials and artists represented in the Prints and Photographs Division, but only if comparable high-quality material is not available in book, microform, or other collected form.

IV. Artists' drawings

A. The Library will endeavor to acquire drawings which substantially support or enrich the Library's existing graphic arts collections or which serve as primary research documents for American political, economic and social history, including the following:
   1. Fine, representative examples of preparatory studies, sketches, and finished drawings prepared for illustrations in American books and magazines.
   2. Selected drawings which support and relate to the Library's existing collections of fine and historical prints and posters. These would include drawings by major printmakers represented in the Library's collections and drawings executed in preparation for or closely relating to prints and posters in the collections.
   3. Drawings for American political and social cartoons and caricatures as documents of public opinion and of the history of visual satire and propaganda. Drawings for

foreign political cartoons and caricature drawings of personalities of international prominence will be acquired selectively as documents of the comparative history of visual satire and propaganda.

4. Topographical drawings of a scenographic character and other drawings of documentary value as records of American historical events and American urban and rural buildings, structures, and scenery.

B. The Library will not acquire the following types of materials: drawings for portraits of American public figures, these being considered the responsibility of the National Portrait Gallery. Examples illustrative of the history of the poster as an art form, and as a medium of communication. Every effort will be made to achieve worldwide coverage.

V. Architectural drawings and documentation

A. The Library of Congress will endeavor to acquire architectural drawings, photographs, and related documents of research value that substantially support or enrich the Library's existing architectural collection and will serve as primary research materials for the study of the architecture of the United States, its territories and possessions. Materials to be acquired include:

1. Selected original drawings by significant or potentially significant American architects, designers and planners. The Library will not normally collect detailed engineering drawings, or the entire output of an architect's office. The emphasis will be on buildings other than those erected by the Federal government, since the National Archives and Records Service is responsible for the building records of the majority of these structures.

2. Selected measured drawings, photographs, and other documentation lost and, in some cases, unexecuted buildings; characteristic building types and technologies; historic structures; and the work of notable architects, craftsmen, engineers, landscape architects, urban planners and interior designers active in the United States. These materials include, but are not limited to, the Historic American Buildings Survey/Historic American Engineering Record.

3. Selected drawings, photographs, and other documentation of buildings or sites outside the United States representing particular designers, techniques, building types and styles, technical or design innovations, etc., that have had notable impact on work in the United States or were influenced by work in this country.

4. Materials relating to foreign buildings and sites that substantially strengthen or supplement the existing holdings of the Library, or fill notable gaps in the Library's record of the history of architecture in all countries.

B. For Western architecture before 1800, the library will attempt to coordinate its acquisitions with those of the National Gallery of Art in order to avoid needless duplication. Similarly, the Library will work with the Dumbarton Oaks Library to avoid unwarranted duplication in the field of garden and landscape architecture.

C. In general, the Library will not endeavor to build large collections of original architectural drawings, blueprints and specifications relating to the construction and building trades, as these fall within the scope of the collections of the National Building Museum.

D. The Library, as part of its work towards the Cooperative Preservation of Architectural Records (COPAR), will encourage the placement of archives of limited subject or geographical interest in appropriate regional collections. The Library will collect information about such holdings and, where possible, microform copies of the same.

VI. Engineering drawing and documentation

A. The Library of Congress will endeavor to build a documentary collection of drawings and related documents showing the history, monuments, and achievements of civil engineering in the United States, to complement the Historic American Engineering Record (HAER). The purpose of HAER is to record the accomplishments of engineering in the United States, its territories and possessions, as shown in such installations as bridges, canals, waterworks irrigation systems, transportation systems, dams, tunnels, etc. The types of materials to be acquired include measured drawings from existing structures, photographs, and accompanying historical and technical data. (Subject to review and revision in coordination with the development of the National Building Museum.)

B. The Library will not endeavor, in general, to build large collections of original engineering or technical drawings, blueprints and specifications. The Library will attempt to coordinate its acquisitions in the field of historic engineering with those of the National Museum of American History in order to avoid needless duplication.

VI. Popular and applied graphic art

The Library will endeavor to acquire selectively popular and historical prints which are important documents of American history and the history of graphic art in the United States, or which relate to and complement the Library's existing graphic art study collection.

A. Particular emphasis will be placed on the acquisition of prints which are important pictorial records of the people, history, and culture of the United States and of its present and former territories or possessions. These will include views of American buildings, cities, urban and rural sites, people, and events or personalities of world significance or of special importance to the history of the United States and will be acquired on a selective basis.

B. The Library will endeavor to acquire on a selective basis important examples of the ornamental and functional uses of the graphic arts in the United States. The types of materials include, but are not limited to, illustrated sheet music, advertising labels, and bank-note engravings. Outstanding examples of foreign works in these categories will be acquired if they can be shown to have influenced developments in American illustration and graphic design.

C. The Library will collect foreign prints of historical significance which support the research interests and collections of the Library's various area studies divisions.

D. Works which are of strictly local significance will be considered the province of regional repositories. The Library will attempt to direct such works to the appropriate institutions.

E. Collections will in most cases be confined to individually issued prints or series of prints, as distinct from those originally included in books or periodicals.

F. In acquiring examples of popular and applied graphic arts, the holdings of other institutions in the Washington area will be taken into account so that duplication is generally, though not necessarily, avoided. For example, the Library of Congress will not normally acquire portraits of American statesmen and public figures, as this intrudes upon the collection mission of the National Portrait Gallery.

G. The Library will endeavor to acquire on a comprehensive basis American and foreign political satires, allegories, and caricatures and other types of political prints from the Reformation period to the present.

MANUSCRIPTS

I. Scope
This policy statement pertains to original manuscripts (personal papers, organizational records, single items or small groups), microform copies, and facsimile editions of individual manuscripts and codices. It does not pertain to music manuscripts or to original manuscripts in Oriental languages.

II. General policy
The Library of Congress will endeavor to acquire manuscript source material for the study of the history, law, and civilization of the United States. The Library will not acquire manuscripts merely for their value as autographs, nor will it ordinarily acquire (except by gift) separate manuscripts for which photographic copies, accurate transcriptions, or archival copies are generally available. Practical considerations which necessitate a selective policy within this broad field include the present collections of the Library of Congress, its primary responsibility to Congress, limitations of staff and space, and the collections of other U.S. institutions.

III. Personal papers--United States
A. The Library of Congress will acquire the personal papers of nationally eminent Americans whose activities have significantly influenced the history, law, and culture of the United States or the national policy of the United States government, and whose

papers constitute important source material for the study of the period which they cover, throwing light on major movements, developments, controversies, or events.

B. The Library will also acquire the papers of individuals who are not nationally eminent if these papers constitute source material of substantial importance. Examples of such materials include letters of soldiers and sailors written during the Civil War, and letters and papers of migrants crossing the Western plains during the nineteenth Century.

C. An effort will be made to acquire collections which provide a representative coverage of each period in the history of the United States.

D. Collections of personal papers which qualify under the terms above will be sought and acquired, provided that the integrity of a collection is respected; i.e., the collection has not been divided, with the major part already present in, or committed to, another repository.

IV. Fragmentary groups of personal papers

The Library of Congress will endeavor to acquire fragmentary groups of personal papers that conform to the stipulations of Paragraph III under the following conditions:

A. When the fragmentary group fills a gap in, or is complementary to an existing collection in the Library of Congress;

B. When the fragmentary group appears to be all that has survived (as is often true of collections of the more distant past);

C. When a donor cannot be persuaded of the inadvisability of dividing a collection;

D. When additional fragmentary groups are known to exist at other repositories, no one of which can be considered the main body of the papers in question. (As stated in Paragraph III. D, the Library will not acquire fragmentary groups of personal papers when the body of these papers is known to be in another American repository and the fragmentary papers are sought by that repository);

E. When the fragmentary group forms a part of a special subject collection which embraces other forms of library materials (books, prints, maps, etc.), and the entire collection is desired by the Library.

V. Single items

Single items which conform to the stipulations of Paragraph IV which will be acquired only when:

A. They fill gaps in collections already in the Library, or
B. They are of considerable importance, e.g., diaries, narratives, letters or speeches describing or commenting on a particular historical event, period or personage.

VI. Personal papers—foreign countries

Ordinarily, the Library of Congress will not acquire the personal papers of citizens of foreign countries. In considering individual exceptions to this general policy, the following criteria are used:

A. The importance of the papers as source material for the study of the United States;
B. The presence in the Library of closely related collections which the proposed acquisition would complement;
C. The eminence of the individual as a world figure and the importance of his/her papers as source material for the study of history and culture generally;
D. The prior rights in the papers of the individual's own country;
E. The location and ownership of the collection (in the United States or elsewhere, in institutional or private hands, etc.);
F. Whether the collection is available as a gift or by purchase;
G. The holdings of other American repositories in relation to the collection under consideration;
H. The present safety and security of the papers.

VII. Manuscripts of published works

It is the policy of the Library of Congress not to acquire manuscripts of published works apart from the personal papers of the author. Individual exceptions to this general policy may be made when some or all of the following considerations apply:

A. The author is nationally eminent, the work is intrinsically important, and the manuscript contains materials, such as extensive revisions, which are important for a study of the author's creative methods in general and the individual work in particular;
B. The manuscript would significantly supplement personal papers of the author or of related figures already in the Library;

C. The acceptance of the manuscript would contribute substantially to the acquisition of personal papers desired by the Library.

VIII. Records of organizations—United States

The Library of Congress does not normally acquire the records of organizations. The Library may, however, consider in occasional cases of special importance exceptional acquisitions of: (1) records from organizations with which the Library conducts joint programs to promote Library activities, goals or objectives; (2) records from ad hoc or other transitory organizations that have enduring value in documenting issues and episodes in American politics and culture; and (3) records of organizations of national scope that are assured to have broad interests and enduring scholarly value.

The Library of Congress will receive additions to records of organizations already in the collections, if those records clearly have broad scholarly interest and if they augment collecting areas of pre-eminent strength.

Records of organizations that do not meet these criteria will not be solicited or acquired if offered. Records already part of the Library's holdings which, upon review, are found not to meet these criteria will be considered as candidates for deaccessioning from the Library's collections. Disposal of any records recommended for de-accessioning will be subject to the provisions of LCR 515, *Disposal of materials not needed for the Library of Congress collections*, or to such prior understandings as may have been reached with the originating organization (or legal successors) at the time of acquisition, or execution of any relevant legally binding agreements, such as Instruments of Gifts, etc.

Future records received from organizations must, as a general rule, be processed (prepared for reader use) by the originating organization (or legal successor) before they arrive at the Library. The Library of Congress will be prepared to offer advice and, in some cases, assistance to enable such organizations (or their successors) to process collections on their premises prior to delivery to the Library. Alternatively, they may supply the Library with funds or personnel to process organizational records once they arrive here.

The Library of Congress believes that it is generally in the best interest of organizations to retain their own records and to develop programs to administer and preserve them according to canons of modern archival practice. The Library is prepared to offer advice on these matters to organizations that request it.

IX. Records of organizations--foreign countries

The Library of Congress will not ordinarily acquire the original records of organizations in foreign countries. Individual exceptions to this policy will be made only in the rarest instances and only when, in addition to meeting the conditions specified in Paragraph VI, the foreign organization is considered to have played a role of such enduring national importance in the history and culture of the United States that its records would constitute source material of exceptional importance for the study of American history and culture. All of the specifications and criteria set forth in Paragraph VIII shall apply.

X. Reproductions of manuscripts

Manuscript collections in microform may be acquired by copyright deposit, exchange, gift, or purchase, and shall not be subject to the limitations noted above for original manuscripts. The public offer of a commercially filmed manuscript collection shall be considered publication, and the acquisition policies for other publications shall be followed as far as applicable. When a micropublishing project includes a variety of original formats, any problems concerning assignment of custody and service will be resolved by the Collections Development Office, in consultation with the recommending officers and custodial division concerned. In acquiring microform copies of manuscripts, the provisions of APS 66 (Microforms--Quality) will be adhered to.

XI. Manuscripts: microform copies--United States

The Library will acquire microform copies of selected unpublished manuscript and archival materials when such materials meet the criteria specified above for original manuscript materials. In judging the importance of two or more items, when funds are limited, the following priority order will be followed:
A. Collections in private hands, especially when the integrity or preservation of the collection is imperiled;

B. Collections of Presidential papers;
C. Collections that will complete, supplement or complement existing collections of the Library of Congress;
D. Other available collections of widespread potential research value.

XII. Manuscripts: microform copies–foreign countries

The Library will observe the following policies in acquiring microform copies of unpublished manuscript and archival materials originating in other countries:

A. A special effort will be made to acquire the following:
  1. unpublished materials relating to the history of the United States;
  2. bodies of manuscripts relating to the general history of the Americas.

B. The following will be acquired on a selective basis:
  1. materials from the archives of foreign governments, and other manuscript and archival collections of potential research value in any subject of major concern to the Library, except those mentioned in A. above;
  2. unpublished guides, catalogs, calendars, other means of access to collections abroad;
  3. codices antedating the general use of printing which supplement the library's holdings.

XIII. Legal documents

The Library of Congress will endeavor to acquire records and briefs from the United States Supreme Court and the United States Courts of Appeals in original format or microform. It will not ordinarily acquire transcripts of trials or other legal documents from state or federal lower courts of record or administrative tribunals except to the extent that the item would constitute unique source material not generally available in the collections of other U. S institutions. The Library will endeavor to acquire the appeal papers of the British House of Lords and cases of the Judicial Committee of the Privy Council of Great Britain in microform. It will not ordinarily acquire other foreign court or administrative tribunal records or documents, except to the extent that the item would constitute unique source material of unusual significance.

XIV. Codices and individual manuscripts: facsimile editions

The Library will endeavor to acquire a comprehensive collection of codices in facsimile editions, especially those originating prior to the year 1500 A.D. The Library will acquire facsimile editions of individual manuscripts in accordance with its customary policies governing acquisition of current printed materials. The following criteria will be taken into account:

A. Completeness (all introductory pages, even without text, should be included);
B. Color accuracy;
C. Preservation of original size and format;
D. Margins and binding of facsimile to correspond to original;
E. Uniqueness of work being printed;
F. Meaningful commentary, translation of text.

If Facsimile editions are available in more than one size, the order of preference is:

A. The same size as the original;
B. Smaller than the original;
C. Larger than the original.

MOTION PICTURES

The Library of Congress will endeavor to acquire for its permanent collections all motion pictures (however recorded) of recognized merit, a representative sampling of other motion pictures typical of commercial productions for entertainment purposes, and a comprehensive collection of motion pictures which contribute to the knowledge and understanding of all countries.

Motion pictures will be acquired on the basis of their value as sources for reference and research in all subject fields within the scope of the Library. Particular emphasis will be given to fields such as the following: sociology, customs, history, institutions, human resources, art, education, entertainment, sport and recreation, economic activities, industrial processes, scientific and technological progress with special attention to that of the motion picture industry, geographical features, natural resources, political affairs, governmental operations, the technique of communicating ideas, and the use of the motion picture medium as a fine, or applied, or dramatic art.

I. Definition

The term *motion picture* is intended to include all types of works consisting of a series of images which, when shown in succession, impart an impression of motion, together with any accompanying sounds, whether recorded on film, tape, paper, or any other media that may be devised.

II. Means of acquisition

Motion pictures are acquired through copyright, gift, exchange, transfer, and purchase. Copies are also obtained in exchange for the use of Library films for copying purposes. The Library will not permit copying of any film that is protected by copyright or other restriction, without the permission of the copyright owner or the restrictor.

III. Selection

Selection of motion pictures for addition to the collections may be delegated by the Selection Officer to the Head, Motion Picture Section, Prints and Photographs Division, in consultation with other appropriate Library officers and, whenever necessary, with outside experts.

IV. Forms of copies

When a motion picture is available in more than one edition, the library will seek to acquire the most complete, uncut, and authentic edition available. As to the form of the copies, the Library generally prefers, and will select or try to acquire, the following:

A. Copies reproduced on either 35 mm. or 16mm. film, if available, the preference depending on which gauge represents the form in which copies of the work are most widely distributed for public exhibition. The Library's general preference as to size is not affected by the existence of copies in any larger or smaller size or of copies that have been reproduced by a process requiring special or unconventional forms of projection. Where copies have been issued in the form of video tape, the Library still prefers to receive a film transfer if available.

B. Copies reproduced in color, if readily available in the size preferred by the Library, rather than in monochrome.

C. Copies accompanied by sound, where both sound and silent versions are available; where versions exist in different languages, the Library prefers the original version, but will also attempt to acquire, when needed, the English version.

D. Where copies exist only in the form of video tape, copies reproduced on 2-inch tape, if available.

Exceptions to the above policies will be made under the following conditions:

1. If the motion picture has been produced by a new process or a unique combination of processes, if it exists in a new or unique format, or if the copies require a new or unique method for their showing, the Library prefers to acquire copies reflecting the new or unique process, format, or method. Where the copies in such a case are copyright deposits, the Head of the Motion Picture Section of the Prints and Photographs Division will notify the Head of the Arts Section in the Examining Division, Copyright Office, that an exception should be made.

2. Where the person depositing for copyright registration proposes to submit copies that do not satisfy the general acquisitions policies outlined above, the Copyright Office will consult the Head of the Motion Picture section who may, after weighing the factors, recommend that an exception be made for one or more works.

3. Where the person depositing for copyright registration proposes to submit copies that, although satisfying the general acquisitions policies outlined above, are different in form from the copy of the particular work that the Library wishes to retain for its collections, the Copyright office will consult the Head of the Motion Picture Section. The latter may, after weighing the factors, recommend that the deposit copies be accepted for copyright registration only on condition that the claimant bind himself/herself under a Supplemental Motion Agreement to deliver on demand a copy of a different description.

V. Sources--copyright

A. American news film. The Library will make a comprehensive selection of American news film.

B. American citations. All motion pictures receiving public or critical acclaim of one kind or another (industry, critics, and festival objective critical approval in various publications and other media, box office approval, etc.) are generally selected.

C. **American miscellaneous.** This group represents a cross-section of the industry's output including television programs. It is intended to convey a picture of the motion picture production and consumption pattern over a wide area of interest.

D. **American non-theatricals.** This group consists principally of factual expository material used for teaching, training, and documenting purposes. It includes films and television programs on industry science, non-clinical medicine, education, religion, travel, etc. A large portion of this group is selected for its reference and research value. Because of the large output of this type of material, a sampling technique will of necessity be employed in selection.

E. **Foreign miscellaneous.** A well-balanced representation of foreign productions, selected for the most part on the basis of professional critical opinion or the reference and research needs of the Library, is chosen from this group.

F. **Television commercials.** Outstanding commercials will be selected yearly on the basis of the ratings of winners of national polls or festivals of commercial films.

G. **U.S. government agencies: motion pictures.** (See also Paragraph VI.) Documentary and scientific motion pictures produced by private concerns in cooperation with U .S. Government agencies such as NASA, USOE, the Department of Agriculture, USIA, etc., will be selected, when copyrighted, according to the criteria set down for non-government motion pictures. However, no comprehensive coverage of this type of motion picture will be attempted.

H. **Unpublished motion pictures** registered by means of a deposit of still shots will be requested as gifts when desired for the collections.

VI. Sources--other than copyright

Titles available through sources other than copyright will be selected, where applicable, by applying the criteria listed above.

A. **Gift.** The gifts of a selection of uncopyrighted motion pictures produced by commercial and educational producers will be requested each year. The criteria for this selection are those listed above.

B. **Exchange.** The Exchange and Gift Division arranges, in consultation with and on the recommendation of the Motion Picture Section, exchange and motion picture copies with reputable and reliable film archives, educational organizations, and motion picture collections, as follows:

1. motion picture films which are still protected by copyright in the United States are not exchanged without the permission of the copyright owner;
2. Public Law 87-846 gives the Library the right to exchange divested copyrighted motion pictures;
3. the Library also exchanges duplicate copies from its collections of films which are in the public domain.

C. **Transfer.** Certain motion picture films are produced by or for agencies of the United States government in pursuance of their functions, and copies of them become, in consequence of such production, part of the records of those agencies as defined by law (44 USC 366). An agreement between the National Archives and the Library of Congress relative to motion picture films designates the former as the repository of government film. Under this agreement the Library acquires a limited amount of this type of film for possible exchange and similar purposes and for its own collections, as needed, in accordance with the criteria stated above.

D. **Purchase.** Motion pictures suitable for the Library collections, but not otherwise available, may be purchased as funds permit.

SOUND RECORDINGS

I. **Musical recordings**

The Library of Congress will endeavor to acquire for its permanent collections:

A. All published musical sound recordings produced in the United States.

B. A balanced selection of those published in other countries, reflecting a concentration on serious musical art works, performances not available in the United States, and authentic performances of folk music.

C. A representative sampling of popular music of other countries.

D. A representative sampling of elementary instructional recordings, of both domestic and foreign origin.

II. Non-musical recordings

The Library will endeavor to acquire for its permanent collections:

A. Non-musical recordings of enduring research and cultural value, including literary readings, drama, the utterances of persons important in the arts, sciences, humanities, politics, and government.

B. Documentary recordings of important events, such as selected meetings; radio broadcasts of research value; authentic recordings of non-musical folklore; documentary recordings of audible scientific phenomena, both natural and physical; and recordings documenting the history of broadcasting and recorded sound.

C. Selected recordings of instructional or informative materials above the high school level, which are not readily available in printed form or which are more useful in recorded form.

D. A representative sampling of recordings of humor and juvenile recordings.

III. Recordings generated by the Library of Congress

Recordings produced under the Library's own auspices will give special attention to material appropriate to the Archive of Folk Song, the Archive of Recorded Poetry and Literature, the Archive of Hispanic Literature on Tape, and oral history recordings, as well as the concerts, lectures, poetry readings, and dramatic performances which are produced in the Library.

IV. Definition

The term *sound recording* is intended to include all carriers of sound which may be reproduced, and includes cylinders, discs, piano rolls and other devices intended to activate mechanical musical instruments, film (excluding motion picture sound tracks), magnetic wire and tape, and any other sound carriers which may be devised.

V. Form of copies

When a sound recording is available in more than one edition, the Library will seek to acquire the most complete, uncut, and authentic edition available. As to the form of the copies, the Library will acquire the following media in descending order of preference: vinyl pressing, open reel tape, cartridge, cassette.

VI. Mixed media

In the case of materials in mixed media which include both a visual medium (filmstrips, slides, etc.) and a sound recording, where the visual medium is the most important element, the acquisitions policies for the visual medium will be given first consideration, but with due regard for the quality of the recording.

NATIONAL LIBRARY OF MEDICINE
Bethesda, Maryland

PREFACE

The *Collection Development Manual of the National Library of Medicine*, third edition (1993), supersedes the 1985 edition.[1] It is the most recent in a series of manuals developed to guide staff in the selection of literature for the NLM collection. Because the collection affects many NLM services, the *Manual* also is designed to explain NLM's collecting practices to its users including the staffs of other health sciences and research libraries.

Establishing reasonable borders for the NLM collection is a difficult task complicated by the increasingly interdisciplinary nature of biomedicine; the prominence of political, ethical, economic and social issues in contemporary biomedical practice and research; rapid advances in health care technology and research; and the proliferation of information sources and formats. The Library's goal is to meet the information needs of health science professionals by focusing on the biomedical literature broadly defined.

The *Manual* provides a conceptual and philosophical framework for the selection of biomedical materials. Like its predecessors, it attempts to define the range of subjects to be acquired and the extent of NLM's collecting effort within these subjects. The third edition attempts to clarify and improve selection guidelines in a number of areas and also addresses topics of growing interest to health professionals such as health services research, environ-mental medicine, health care technology and molecular biology. The importance of a variety of literature and format types is recognized in new or expanded sections covering standards and guidelines, electronic publications and technical reports.

Over the past two years a number of individuals made significant contributions to the production of the new *Manual*. Former Collection Development Officer Daniel T. Richards developed the plan for the revision effort and directed much of the work assisted by former Collection Development Librarian Brenda Whittaker Lucas. An Internal NLM Working Group wrote and edited the *Manual*. Members of that group included: Duane Arenales, Chief, Technical Services Division; Margaret Byrnes, Head, Preservation Section; Judith Eannarino, Head, Selection Unit;

National Library of Medicine 315

Margaret Kaiser, librarian, History of Medicine Division; Carol Krueger, Librarian, Serial Records Section; Ms. Lucas and Mr. Richards. The Collection Development Discussion Group, comprised of all NLM selectors, tested the application of the new edition and made many useful suggestions. Minhchau Nguyen provided clerical support.

NLM is indebted to the following consultants and members of the NLM senior staff for their expert advice on the content and format of the *Manual*: Faye Abdellah, Ed.D., Deputy Surgeon General and Chief Nurse Officer, U.S. Public Health Service (retired); Rachael K. Anderson, Director, University of Arizona Health Sciences Center Library, and NLM Board of Regents liaison to the project; Milton April, D.V.M., Director, AIDS Animal Models Program, National Center for Research Resources, NIH; Ross W. Atkinson, Assistant University Librarian, Collection Development and Preservation, Cornell University; Marilyn Bergner, Ph.D., Professor, Health Policy and Management, Johns Hopkins University; Lois Ann Colaianni, Associate Director, Library Operations, NLM; Milton Corn, M.D., Acting Associate Director, Extramural Programs, NLM; Dottie Eakin, Director, Medical Sciences Library, Texas A & M University; Betsy Humphreys, Deputy Associate Director, Library Operations, NLM; Thomas A. Massaro, M.D., Professor of Pediatrics, Biomedical Engineering and Business Administration, Medical School, University of Virginia; Anne M. Pascarelli, Director, Sheppard Library, Massachusetts College of Pharmacy & Allied Health Sciences; John Patruno, Jr., Director, Health Sciences Library, University of Tennessee; Harold M. Schoolman, M.D., Deputy Director for Research and Education, NLM.

NLM is committed to the continuing evaluation of its selection policies and its collection as part of its overall mission to improve the delivery of biomedical information in support of medicine and health care. The production of this edition of the *Collection Development Manual* is a significant accomplishment, but its real value is dependent on how successfully it reflects and anticipates the information needs of health professionals and how effectively its concepts and guidelines are used and interpreted.

Donald A. B. Lindberg, M.D., Director,
National Library of Medicine

INTRODUCTION

The *Collection Development Manual of the National Library of Medicine*[1] (NLM) is intended primarily to guide NLM staff in the selection of biomedical materials appropriate for the Library's permanent collection. The document describes NLM's collections and presents NLM's current collecting policies and selection principles. This *Manual* does not present principles for the selection of materials temporarily retained for the use of on-site users; nor is the intent of the *Manual* to describe the full range of information resources, including databases, to which NLM provides access.

NLM has produced written guidelines to assist library staff in the selection of biomedical literature since 1944. Periodic revisions are made to ensure that the selection process continues to reflect the full scope of the biomedical literature.

The structure and emphasis of the present edition has been strongly influenced by the nature of contemporary biomedicine: interdisciplinary trends in research and health care; the increasing focus on the cellular and molecular basis of medicine; the inter-dependence of research and practice; and the growing influence of social, political and economic issues on medical practice and biomedical research.

The goal of this document is to ensure that today's selection efforts will result in a collection which supports contemporary medical and health care practice and research as well as future scholarship.

COLLECTION DEVELOPMENT POLICY

The National Library of Medicine (NLM) is one of three national libraries in the United States and is the world's largest research library in a single scientific and professional field. NLM's primary mission, as mandated by the Congress, is service to the health professional. To support this mission, the Library comprehensively collects materials in biomedical subjects. NLM holdings include more than 4.9 million items in over 70 languages from virtually every country of the world.

The authority for NLM to determine which materials shall be collected is implicit in the National Library of Medicine Act of 1956, which empowers it to "acquire and preserve books, periodicals, prints, films, recordings and other library materials pertinent to medicine."[2] Building on this mandate, the National Library of Medicine's Board of Regents, an advisory body to the Secretary of Health and Human Services (HHS) on matters affecting the Library, adopted a collecting policy in June 1976. This policy was subsequently updated in 1983 and most recently in October 1992. This *Collection Development Policy* is established for the National Library of Medicine (NLM) pursuant to the authority contained in the National Library of Medicine Act of 1956 (P.L. 84-941).

Since every area of human activity may affect or be affected by the health of the human community, NLM cannot presume to collect all literature that has some relevance, however remote, to health. In its collecting practices, NLM shall concentrate on the biomedical literature without being limited by present perceptions, recognizing that the boundaries of that literature are constantly changing.

The National Library of Medicine has the responsibility for acquiring the biomedical literature in any format deemed appropriate to the fulfillment of its mission.

Coverage of the scholarly biomedical literature shall be comprehensive; coverage of other biomedical literature may be more selective. The intent is to ensure that the collection represents the intellectual content and diversity of the world's biomedical literature. In determining coverage, NLM will take into consideration its role as the national resource for the provision of biomedical literature not otherwise readily available, and as the national bibliographic center for biomedical literature for the health professions.

The healing arts can only be understood in their cultural context; therefore, collection development criteria will be interpreted with flexibility in acquiring literature relating to the history of medicine.

NLM is aware of the acquisitions policies and collection emphases of the Library of Congress and the National Agricultural Library. While a certain amount of duplication of collections among the three national libraries is inevitable, and indeed necessary, NLM recognizes the ultimate interdependence of these libraries, and its collecting policies will reflect this.

Nothing in this policy statement should be construed to require the disposal of any literature previously acquired by NLM that would not be eligible for acquisition under this policy or under any present or future collection development document, nor should this policy statement be construed to limit the acquisition by NLM of literature that may be needed by NLM staff in the fulfillment of their duties, or that may reasonably be provided for the reference convenience of NLM reading room users.

Guidelines for the scope and coverage of acquisitions for the NLM collection shall be detailed for operational purposes in a document to be developed and amended from time to time in a manner to be determined by the Director. A group of senior NLM staff should be designated by the Director for the purpose of meeting regularly to consider the need for changes and to recommend appropriate changes to the Director.

DEFINITIONS

Biomedical pertaining to health care, to the practice of the science and art of medicine broadly conceived, and to those branches of the life sciences which are fundamental to that science and art.

Collect: to acquire for inclusion in the literature holdings of NLM.

Coverage: the extent of NLM's collecting effort within the biomedical subjects.

Health Professions: includes persons engaged in health policy and health services research, the administration of health activities, the provision of health services, or in research, education, or information dissemination concerned with the advancement or history of medicine or with other health related sciences.

Literature: organized information in the form of written, printed, or non-print works, including audiovisual materials, computer files, and other electronic formats.

Scholarly: resulting from professional study or research.

Scope: the range of subjects which NLM collects.

SCOPE OF THE COLLECTION

The Board of Regents statement on scope and coverage directs NLM to concentrate its collecting efforts on the biomedical literature without being limited by present perceptions and recognizing that the boundaries of that literature are constantly changing. As the nation's premier biomedical information resource for the health professions, NLM seeks to assemble a collection which reflects the dynamic field of biomedicine. Describing the field of biomedicine is therefore equivalent to defining the scope of the collection.

COVERAGE OF THE COLLECTION

The National Library of Medicine's coverage of the biomedical literature is defined primarily by its responsibility to collect materials for individuals engaged in the health professions. The collection of the National Library of Medicine is developed to meet the present and future information needs of six broad professional groups primarily concerned with the science and art of medicine:

- Health care providers;
- Administrators and staff of health care services, organizations and institutions;
- Researchers whose goal is the improvement of patient care, the expansion of biomedical knowledge, or the development of biomedical technology;
- Educators in professional health sciences programs and in health care settings, as well as librarians and information professionals in medicine and the health sciences;
- Scholars, historians and writers concerned with the practice of medicine and health related issues;
- Policy makers, health economists, and health care insurers, as well as corporate entities, including commercial enterprises, foundations, societies, government agencies, and others which have as their focus biomedical research or the provision of health care.

In order to fulfill its mandate to its defined user community, The National Library of Medicine attempts to assemble a comprehensive collection of the research and professional biomedical literature, broadly defined. The National Library of Medicine's concept of comprehensive collecting is compatible with the Comprehensive Level defined by the Research Libraries Group (RLG):

Comprehensive Level: A collection in which a library endeavors, so far as reasonably possible, to include all significant works of recorded knowledge (publications, manuscripts, other forms) in all applicable languages, for a necessarily defined and limited field. This level of collecting intensity is one that maintains a "special collection"; the aim, if not the achievement, is exhaustiveness. Older material is retained for historical research.[3]

The scope of the NLM collection, encompassing as it does all of biomedicine, is significantly broader than is generally understood for the "special collection" referred to in the RLG definition.

NLM recognizes that while it is possible to assemble a collection which addresses all topics in biomedicine, it is impossible even for a national library to gather a complete, worldwide collection of all biomedical materials in all formats. The section, "Special Considerations in Selection," presents strategies for identifying and selecting particular types of materials in order to allow NLM to approach, insofar as possible, the ideal of a comprehensive collection in biomedicine.

PRESERVATION POLICY

In order to fulfill the mandate to maintain and preserve the biomedical literature, the National Library of Medicine carries out an extensive preservation program. The decision to select a title for the NLM generally also implies a responsibility to preserve the material. The following Preservation Policy was adopted in February 1986 by the Board of Regents:[4]

PRESERVATION OF THE BIOMEDICAL LITERATURE

In accordance with the terms of the NLM Act and the clearly expressed intent of Congress, the fundamental responsibility of the National Library of Medicine is to preserve permanently the content of books, periodicals, and other library materials pertinent to medicine. The determination of what is pertinent to medicine shall be based on the guidelines for selection of literature for the NLM collection as described in the *Collection Development Manual of the National Library of Medicine*, which is revised periodically to reflect the information needs of the biomedical community. NLM's principal responsibility is to ensure the preservation of the core biomedical literature as defined in that document.

Means of preservation may include: (1) preservation of the original; (2) acquisition of materials in archival formats; and (3) replication of materials in archival formats. NLM staff shall monitor developments in preservation techniques to ensure the use of the most effective methods available and shall participate in research, development, testing and evaluation of preservation technology. Operational guidelines and procedures for selecting items to be preserved and choosing preservation techniques shall be developed, reviewed and if necessary amended, from time to time in a manner to be determined by the Director.

While the preservation of NLM's own collection is a major step toward the preservation of the entire scholarly biomedical record, NLM also has a responsibility to assist the preservation of important biomedical literature held by other U.S. institutions. NLM's preservation efforts are to be coordinated with those of other national libraries, research libraries, and biomedical libraries.

Much of the preservation problem can be stopped at its source if the scholarly record is published on archival media that are not predisposed to rapid deterioration. To lessen the need for preservation treatment of prospective publications, NLM shall actively encourage the publishing industry to use more durable materials in the production of the biomedical literature.

NLM AS A NATIONAL LIBRARY

The three national libraries--the Library of Congress, the National Agricultural Library and NLM--strive to keep collecting duplication to the minimum necessary to serve their diverse user populations. A dialogue is maintained among the national libraries, and joint collecting statements are developed to define areas of mutual collecting interest. Over the past several years, cooperative statements on Veterinary Science, Human Nutrition, Biotechnology, and the AIDS literature have been developed.

The principal areas of mutual collecting interest between the NLM and the Library of Congress (LC) are the political, economic, social, and cultural aspects of health care and health care delivery systems. NLM assumes responsibility for collecting the research and professional literature of the health sciences for the use of the health professional; LC primarily collects health related literature addressed to general audiences and such works as are deemed necessary to support its congressional mission. LC also collects works in non-traditional medicine, public health, and other areas of considerable cultural, social, and economic scholarly interest.[5] As the broadest in scope of the three national libraries, it assumes responsibility for maintaining a comprehensive collection in the physical and natural sciences, the social sciences, and the humanities.[6] The medical literature collecting policy of the Library of Congress appears in the appendix [not included here].

The principal areas of significant overlap between the NLM and the National Agricultural Library (NAL) collections are in Biotechnology, Human Nutrition, Laboratory Animal Science, and Veterinary Medicine. NLM's collecting emphasis in these areas centers on those topics which comparatively, experimentally, theoretically, or directly impact or advance either human health care or biomedical research. NAL, on the other hand, focuses collecting effort on those materials which relate experimentally, theoretically, or directly to the production of agricultural commodities, agronomy, consumer nutrition education, food safety, food science, animal husbandry, animal health, and animal culture.[7]

NLM AND OTHER BIOMEDICAL LIBRARIES
Beyond the three national libraries are important and rich collections in other federal agencies, academic institutions, public libraries, special libraries, museums, archives, and research centers. Although no national inventory has been attempted, it is clear that many of these collections are important in their own right and that they contain unique materials and special collections not held by the national libraries.

The centrality of the NLM collection to the concept of a national collection in biomedicine and the complementary nature of other library collections is well recognized. NLM, in its 1986 Long Range Plan describes a "distributed library of record" for the biomedical sciences and acknowledges that "even within any narrowly identified scope of biomedical materials, there is more than any single library can acquire. Indeed, among the nation's biomedical libraries are many collections of unique materials."

The national collection in any discipline, therefore, is not limited to the holdings of a single national library, nor is it simply the sum of all titles within a given subject. It is a composite of individual titles and important special collections located in many different institutions. NLM seeks to identify existing strengths in other collections and to encourage other libraries to collect unique materials, particularly state and local biomedical literature, manuscripts, and items of strong local interest.

HISTORY OF THE COLLECTION
The National Library of Medicine evolved from a small collection of books and journals in the Office of the Surgeon General in the

Medical Department of the Army. The Library was begun by Joseph Lovell, Surgeon General from 1818 to 1836, and grew slowly at first. The first request for funds--$150 to buy books--appeared in the 1836 estimate of expenses for the Medical Department. In 1840, the first *Catalogue of Books in the Library of the Surgeon General's Office* was prepared. This handwritten list records only 134 titles representing about 200 volumes, considerably smaller than the personal libraries of many mid-nineteenth century physicians and far exceeded by those of established medical schools, medical societies and institutions.

In 1842 Congress, apparently alarmed at the growth of government libraries laid down guidelines for the purchase of books through a provision in the appropriations act. During fiscal year 1842-1843 the Surgeon General had to affirm to the Secretary of War that such works as he ordered were "necessary and proper to carry on the business" [of his office]. The Secretary approved subscriptions to several medical journals and other strictly medical works, but not to Audubon's *Birds of America* . . . .[8]

Although the medical advances and concerns of the Civil War stimulated use of the Library, its collection had grown to only 1800 volumes by 1864. In that year, Surgeon General Joseph K. Barnes published the first printed catalog. It listed books alphabetically by author under nine subject headings: anatomy; physiology; materia medica; pharmacy and therapeutics; general pathology and practice of medicine; surgery; midwifery and diseases of women and children; medical jurisprudence and medical policy; natural philosophy; chemistry, etc. It also listed miscellaneous journals, reviews, reports, encyclopedias, etc.

After Lee's surrender at Appomattox, the Army closed all temporary military hospitals, dismantled their libraries and sent the most valuable of their works to the Army Medical Library in Washington. In addition to medical works, books accessioned during this period covered such diverse subjects as navigation, astronomy, geology and agriculture. In October 1865, John Shaw Billings, then an assistant to the Surgeon General, was given responsibility for building and managing the growing collection of medical books and journals. Under Billings' leadership acquisitions expanded dramatically. By 1870, the Library was among the largest medical libraries in the United States, exceeded only by those of the Pennsylvania Hospital and the College of Physicians in Philadelphia.

Sometime during 1871, discussions between Billings and Surgeon General Barnes led to a decision to broaden the objectives of the Library to include the development of a collection to serve the entire American medical profession, rather than the military exclusively. Their vision was to develop a "National Medical Library" with a collection of medical literature that would contain "every medical book published in this country and every work relating to public health and state medicine."[10]

Billings was indefatigable in his pursuit of this aim. Although he collected all types of medical publications, Billings concentrated on acquiring and maintaining complete files of American medical journals. In a form letter written in 1872, he states, "We are trying to make the files of (American) medical journals in our Library complete, so that there may be one complete collection of that sort to refer to, which at present is not the case."[11] By that time, the collection had grown to include 73,475 books, 39,412 volumes of journals and transactions, and over 200,000 individual pamphlets and theses. During his tenure the Library also made its first significant efforts to acquire rare books, manuscripts, visual records of the history of medicine, and to develop literature exchange programs with domestic and foreign institutions.

Over the course of the twentieth century the collection continued to expand. However, by World War II, the collection's growth rate, which had been the most rapid in the country under Billings, had declined due to low appropriations, low staffing levels and insufficient space until it was the slowest among America's large research libraries.[12] Wartime demand for increased medical information stimulated a survey to suggest ways of improving the Library's operations and management. The resulting report recommended an aggressive acquisition program including an increased book budget and an active gift and exchange program.[13]

After the war, the Library set out to remedy the deficiencies in its collection. The Library initiated programs to acquire U.S. works published during the depression, to secure literature published in enemy countries during the war, and to reestablish relations with book dealers in all areas of the world. As wartime Army hospitals were closed, their books and journals were shipped to the Library in Washington.

In 1949, Library Director Frank Bradway Rogers established the first internal committee on scope and coverage. The aim of the committee was "to define the subjects to be collected and the degree of collecting within each subject."[14] The Committee, chaired by Estelle Brodman, used the Library of Congress classification as an outline to define and establish which medical and non-medical subjects (such as physics, chemistry and technology) the Library should acquire. It also defined four degrees of coverage for all subjects: skeletal, reference, research and exhaustive. Finally, it recommended collecting policies for specialized areas within the Library such as a History of Medicine Division. The Committee's report was in essence a basic guide for materials selection, which has since been refined numerous times to reflect contemporary collecting policy and the growth and specialization of biomedicine.

In 1956, Billings' dream of a true national library was realized when Senators Lister Hill and John F. Kennedy submitted to Congress a bill "to promote the progress of medicine and to advance the national health and welfare by creating a National Library of Medicine."[15] On August 3, 1956, the National Library of Medicine Act was signed into law. The Library is an official part of the National Institutes of Health within the U.S. Department of Health and Human Services.

Since that time, the collections of the Library have grown considerably. Collection expansion in the area of non-print materials has been especially notable. A collection of audiovisual and electronic materials has been established and a program to acquire posters important to the history of medicine begun. In 1976, NLM was officially designated a U.S. Government Partial Depository for biomedical information.

In 1986, the Library established a Preservation Section to oversee and implement the National Plan for the Preservation of the Biomedical Literature. A series of collection assessment projects was initiated in 1989, the goals of which include the identification of lacunae in the collection and the refinement of collection development policy.

OVERVIEW OF THE COLLECTION

The collection of the National Library of Medicine numbered more than 4.8 million items by the end of the 1992 fiscal year. The collection of printed materials totaled approximately 648,000 monographs, over 950,000 bound serial volumes, 172,000 pamphlets and 282,000 dissertations. There were also 57,000 prints and photographs and 2.4 million manuscript pieces in the Library's historical collection. The collection of non-print materials included approximately 54,000 audiovisuals, 600 items in electronic format, and 323,000 microforms.

NLM's extensive collection is intended to serve the present and future information needs of U.S. health science professionals, scholars and researchers. Biomedical materials may be consulted on-site or requested on interlibrary loan through libraries, including the more than 3,600 libraries which constitute the National Network of Libraries of Medicine.

POST-1913 MATERIALS
The majority of post-1913 materials including monographs and serials are held in the general collection. Interactive and electronic materials and audiovisuals produced since 1970 also are housed in the general collection.

HISTORICAL AND SPECIAL MATERIALS
John Shaw Billings' collection of important medical works formed the nucleus of what has grown through judicious and careful selection of materials to be one of the world's finest research collections of rare books, manuscripts, and materials related to the history of medicine in the world.

Selection decisions for an historical collection reflect an understanding of the course of medical history and require a broad interpretation and understanding of medical thought and practice. The selection of the primary source literature of medicine reflects medicine as it has been practiced from antiquity to the present. Through the ages, the literature of humankind's attempts to cure, alleviate and prevent disease covers a wide spectrum of subjects as diverse as meteorology and wine-making. Subjects such as botany, chemistry and meteorology, though distinct from medicine today, were closely related to medicine in the fifteenth through the eighteenth centuries. The inclusion of materials in seemingly unrelated subjects is based on the importance of those subjects to medicine historically, rather than the relation of those subjects to medicine today.

Printed works

The Library's earliest printed works are two volumes dating from 1467. The Library holds over 500 incunabula, almost 6,000 volumes printed in the sixteenth century, and about 67,000 works (including serials and theses) printed in the seventeenth and eighteenth centuries. NLM holds not only many of the great landmark works in medicine such as William Harvey's *De motu cordis*, 1628, but also the many works of lesser authors necessary for historical research and scholarship.

Many factors are taken into account when making selection decisions in rare and historical materials: the presence of other editions of the same work in the collection, comparison with editions already in the collection, availability of the work through other libraries, and price. Although NLM cannot presume to collect comprehensively in all areas of knowledge, the Library casts a wider net in developing the historical collections than for contemporary collecting.

Manuscripts

The Library divides its manuscript collections into early Western (pre-1601) manuscripts, Oriental (especially Arabic and Persian) manuscripts, and modern manuscripts. The library holds 90 early Western manuscripts (before 1600) and microfilm copies of about 600 manuscripts held by European libraries.

The modern manuscript collection comprises over 2,000,000 items in over 900 collections. These range in size from single items to several thousand documents, and were acquired over the past century as part of the general collection of historical materials. These unique handwritten or typed documents, papers and other materials include associated printed, near-print and some non-print pieces having a common source in areas of core scholarship in the history of medicine. The modern manuscript collection is particularly rich in eighteenth and nineteenth century American and British materials and is also quite strong in twentieth century American medicine. Areas of special strength and interest include biochemistry, biotechnology, and molecular biology; surgery; pediatrics and child development; medical information; the history of medicine; military medicine; and the Public Health Service (including the National Institutes of Health and the National Library of Medicine).

The Library seeks personal papers of those individuals who have made significant contributions to contemporary medicine or whose personal papers contribute to an understanding of modern medicine. Particularly noteworthy acquisitions have included the papers of such medical figures as Stanhope Bayne-Jones, Henry Nelson Harkins, Alan Gregg, Chauncey Leake, John Shaw Billings, William S. Middleton and C. Everett Koop.

Oral History
The oral history collection consists of about 200 memoirs of important figures in the health sciences. The collection is comprised of audiotapes and unpublished or restricted transcripts of potential value to scholars. Interviews in other formats (e.g., video recordings) or published personal narratives are housed in the general collection.

NLM Archives
A special collection of materials published by NLM is maintained in an NLM Publications Archive. It may, to some extent, duplicate materials in the other NLM collections.

Prints and Photographs
The print and photograph collection consists of some 57,000 items ranging from fifteenth century woodcuts to twentieth century photographs. The collection includes many individual portraits of physicians, pharmacists, nurses, dentists, and others who have contributed to the health services and professions. Visual sources also represent health care facilities and laboratories, medical procedures and equipment, and other images which document the practice of medicine. The visual formats include fine prints, historical and contemporary photographic processes, posters, and visual ephemera such as patent medicine trade cards. The Library owns over 3,000 fine prints, including several hundred caricatures on medically related subjects. Artists represented in the collection include Daumier, Gillray, Hogarth and Rowlandson.

Audiovisuals
In addition to current audiovisuals, the Library's collection includes approximately 4,000 audiovisual titles ranging in date from circa

1910 through 1969. Post-1969 productions of particular historical importance also are housed with this older material.

On-site use collections

The library maintains two reading room collections and a learning resource center for the use of on-site clientele:

- The main reading room contains a collection of commonly used medical journals, the principal indexes and abstracting resources, a collection of reference works representing all areas of biomedicine, and some general reference works.
- The History of Medicine Division also maintains a reading room for use by health professionals, historians and researchers. This reading room houses a reference collection containing the major bibliographic resources necessary for historical research, as well as standard works in the history of medicine.
- The learning resource center contains a collection of current audiovisuals, computer assisted instruction materials, interactive video programs, and information in other electronic formats.

SELECTION GUIDELINES BY SUBJECT

This section contains guidance for the selection of contemporary materials by subject. Subject descriptions are based on a current understanding of the trends in biomedical research, medical practice, and associated issues. It is organized alphabetically according to subject category and applies to selection of post-1913 materials. Selection decisions for historical materials are based more broadly on the importance of a certain discipline to the historical practice of medicine. Selection guidance for some specific literature types is found in the section entitled "Special Considerations in Selection."

NLM collects all aspects of biomedicine, broadly defined. This section of the *Manual* is not intended to be an exhaustive description of every subject collected. Instead, this section focuses on subjects which represent emerging disciplines, present complex selection challenges, require additional elaboration as to NLM's collecting interest, or constitute an especially large body of literature. No attempt has been made to establish mutually exclusive subject categories.

Most terms are consistent with *Medical Subject Headings* (MeSH®), NLM's controlled vocabulary, which is used in indexing journal articles for *Index Medicus®* and MEDLINE® as well as for subject cataloging. In some instances non-MeSH terms have been included because of their usefulness in the selection process. Additional terms are included in the index.

Each subject category begins with the major term, followed by a definition reflecting NLM's usage in the selection process. Definitions are derived from a variety of authoritative sources including: *Dorland's Illustrated Medical Dictionary*, 27th edition. Philadelphia, Saunders, 1988; National Library of Medicine. *MeSH Scope Notes*. Bethesda, National Library of Medicine, 1991; and standard works in each discipline.

The descriptive matter in each category is intended as a conceptual foundation for selection. Where broad categories, such as Anatomy, are addressed, NLM's collecting focus or emphasis is stated. Categories in the subject section are often described in terms of illustrative subtopics, especially in those subjects that may present selection problems. These are intended as guides rather than lists designed to limit subject scope. If a subtopic is not mentioned, it does not imply that NLM will not collect in that area. Rather, works that fall within the subject category must be judged within the framework of overall collection development guidelines. Only a definition is provided for those subjects which do not appear to require clarification for selection purposes. Notes are used to provide additional information as required. "See also" references direct the reader to other topics which offer additional selection guidance. Following are some additional general principles which apply to many subjects in this section.

Natural Sciences: The natural sciences have historically provided the scientific basis for medical knowledge, observation and inquiry. Today, modern biomedicine has evolved into specialized disciplines distinct from their parent natural science fields; however, techniques, advances and discoveries in natural science disciplines continue to influence the course of modern biomedical specialties.

With this edition, only the biomedical aspects of broad natural science subjects (Chemistry, Physics, Botany, etc.) have been included to reflect NLM's specific interest in collecting biomedical works. For example, while Botany does not appear as a subject classification, Medical Botany is listed as a collecting category. Also, NLM collects many biomedical topics which derive their scientific basis from natural science disciplines; e.g., biophysics, toxicology. Works in the natural sciences which have little or no relationship to biomedicine usually are not collected.

Life Sciences: NLM's collecting emphasis in the life sciences is on works related to humans, other primates, and laboratory animals; works which compare humans to animals; and other works in which the subject is related to biomedical research. NLM places particular importance on research at the cellular and subcellular level because of its comparative potential. Of particular collecting interest are works about physiological and biochemical mechanisms within the cell such as response to drugs, chemical and physical agents, the immune response, metabolic mechanisms, and the genetic regulation of protein synthesis.

Chemistry: The science of chemistry is historically and conceptually fundamental to many disciplines in the physical, biological and medical sciences. Chemistry as a discipline is concerned with the structure and behavior of atoms; the composition and properties of compounds; the reactions that occur between substances; and the laws that govern these phenomena. NLM collects works in the biomedical disciplines such as biochemistry, biotechnology and toxicology which have evolved from chemistry.

Biomedical Research draws on techniques which were developed using principles from analytical chemistry, organic chemistry, and physical chemistry; and chemical principles are useful in virtually every biomedical science. The literature of these non-biomedical disciplines is not collected at NLM, except for historically valuable materials which influenced medicine before the rise of the modern chemically based biomedical sciences.

Religion: NLM's interest in collecting works with religious themes is limited to the contemporary or historical influences of religion on health care policy and practice, or on biomedical research. The Library collects medical works in which religion is an integral topic and also collects materials on aspects of medicine viewed from a religious perspective. A scholarly work entitled *Healing Herbs of the Bible*, for example, would be collected because of NLM's interest in Medical Botany; similarly, a book on religious factors in psychiatric practice would be appropriate because of its focus on Psychiatry. The collecting policy for such materials is found under those specific medical topics, especially Biomedical Ethics, History of Medicine, Medical Anthropology, Medical Sociology, Psychology, and Therapeutics.

Social Sciences: Social science and behavioral science disciplines such as sociology, psychology, anthropology, political science, and economics have long influenced the medical philosophy and the practice of medicine. Principles and techniques from the social sciences often guide the observations and investigations which expand humankind's knowledge of the biomedical sciences.

Today, the influence of social science research on medicine and health related subjects is particularly strong. Interdisciplinary fields such as Health Services Research, which combine knowledge and techniques of the social sciences with those from the health sciences, are increasingly important in determining the future of health services, medical practice, and biomedical research.

With this edition, broad social sciences such as Political Science/Law, Economics, Sociology, etc. have been omitted. Core biomedical aspects of these disciplines will be found under such new categories as Health Policy, Health Economics, and Medical Sociology.

Addiction Medicine: The branch of medicine concerned with the study, prevention and treatment of addictive diseases; the physiological and psychological disorders associated with substance dependence.

Includes: Alcoholism, Drug addiction, Fetal, neonatal, infant or child health disorders associated with maternal substance dependence, Smoking.

See Also: Medical Sociology, Psychology, Physical Medicine and Rehabilitation, Public Health

Aerospace Medicine: The field of medicine concerned with the health effects of air and space flight.

Includes: Biomedical research in space.

See also: Environmental Health

AIDS (Acquired Immunodeficiency Syndrome): An acquired defect of cellular immunity typically associated with infection by the human immunodeficiency virus (HIV) and increased susceptibility to opportunistic infections and malignant neoplasms.

Includes: pharmaceutical, diagnosis, treatment, and epidemiology of AIDS and AIDS related disorders, as well as the psychological aspects of AIDS/HIV

Note: Though NLM's interest in AIDS/HIV literature centers on works concerned with research, health care, and health policy, other substantive AIDS-related literature which chronicles health-related developments or trends associated with the AIDS/HIV crisis is also broadly collected.

See also Public Health

[The above are the first three of over eighty examples from various fields or branches of medicine.]

SPECIAL CONSIDERATIONS IN SELECTION: FORMATS AND LITERATURE TYPES

The National Library of Medicine concentrates its collecting effort on assembling a comprehensive collection in the professional and research literature of biomedicine, maintaining an international focus; however, NLM recognizes the impossibility and impracticality of achieving comprehensiveness in all formats and literature types. When exhaustive collecting is not feasible or desirable, NLM collects certain categories of biomedical materials selectively. The Library's goal is to assemble a collection which contains those works most essential for present and future medical practice, research and scholarship. This section contains guidance for the consideration of these selectively acquired materials.

The universe of scholarly biomedical literature includes a wide variety of formats and literature types such as manuscripts, pamphlets and annual reports. In considering these materials, NLM concentrates on selecting a range of important and unique works which will be most useful to the biomedical professional or scholar.

In some categories, the Library's collecting emphasis is on materials which characterize or influence U.S. health care thought, practice, research and policy.

NLM's selective collecting strategy implies the inclusion of those materials which best represent major or influential sources, typify or characterize the whole, or illustrate a unique aspect or approach. These works may include both important and minor items. Selective collecting may also be done to achieve balance within a format or literature type based on such criteria as geography or language, or to insure that the collection contains materials which illustrate a variety of philosophical, cultural, or political perspectives on medical topics. In some cases, NLM collects representative examples of materials in order to provide a balanced literature complement to the scholarly biomedical record.

Special collecting effort is directed at those materials that present information not found elsewhere in the scholarly literature. In building its collection, NLM seeks to avoid unnecessary duplication and redundancy. The decision to acquire materials in one format as opposed to another is an internal decision which may be based on practical considerations such as access, preservation or bibliographic control.

The formats and literature types addressed in the following section may present special problems for the selector. In making selection decisions, NLM takes into consideration the chara cteristics of each category and its relative importance to the completeness of the biomedical record. Since source of publication may have a direct bearing on an item's importance to the collection, certain major publication source categories such as association and government publications, are also discussed in this section. In collecting materials in any literature type or format, NLM generally emphasizes the publications of leading institutions which significantly influence U.S. health care and research. Categories are arranged in alphabetical order. Some categories cannot be considered in isolation. In these cases "see also" references have been provided to identify other format and literature type categories which may offer the selector guidance.

Abstracts, Indexes and Bibliographies
Biomedical abstracts, indexes and bibliographies are an integral part of the scholarly record. NLM collects those bibliographic

works which are essential to provide access to the biomedical literature. Selection decisions are made based on their comprehensiveness, uniqueness, and usefulness for research and scholarship. To avoid redundant collecting, subsets or abridgements of a single work are not collected; however, bibliographic resources which combine information from a number of other works may be collected.

NLM also collects and maintains general bibliographic resources sufficient to provide access to the world's biomedical literature. These resources include national bibliographies, as well as general indexes and abstracts, which provide access to core literature which is not available through biomedical bibliographic resources.

See also Translations

Academic Dissertations

Academic dissertations, including theses and post-doctoral dissertations, played an important role in communicating results of original biomedical research before the rise of commercial scientific publishing. NLM therefore collects historical biomedical dissertations. The dissertation literature remains an important source of original research in some fields, such as the history of medicine and paleopathology. In most cases, original disse-rtation research subsequently is reported elsewhere in the scientific literature. Other biomedical dissertations provide secondary review and analysis of research literature, but little primary research. NLM generally does not collect modern biomedical dissertations unless they contain significant primary research not likely to be reported in other literature held at the Library.

Alumni and Student Publications

Alumni and student publications provide information concerning developments in medical education, trace the development of a school, chronicle its history, and report the accomplishments of its alumni, students and staff. NLM collects selected publications directed toward the students and alumni of U.S. health related institutions. Collecting emphasis is on the publications of influential institutions, though publications of unique or distinctive institutions may also be selected. NLM selects those publications which contain signed original articles, biographical information, or other material of potential historical value.

See also Catalogs, Directories, Newsletters and Newspapers.

Annual Reports

Health related government agencies, professional societies, institutions, corporations and foundations issue annual reports which may provide valuable information concerning their purposes and activities. NLM collects selected annual reports with an emphasis on those of influential U.S. national organizations. Reports of international and foreign organizations which significantly influence U.S. health care thought and practice, and reports of lesser known but unique organizations may also be selected. NLM selects materials published by U.S. state and local governments and agencies when they are especially important to the U.S. scholarly biomedical record. NLM also collects a diverse sample of the annual reports of U.S. health care institutions.

Association Publications

NLM collects biomedical literature issued by a wide variety of health related associations. Collecting emphasis is on the publications of major national and international associations which influence health policy, medical practice, and professional education. Official specialty journals, standards and guidelines, conference proceedings, and monographs of these associations are collected comprehensively. Other materials, such as membership directories, annual reports, and pamphlets are also selected.

Publications of less influential organizations (e.g., regional, state and local associations, and international and national groups of less prominence) are collected selectively. Collecting emphasis is on publications which are of broad interest to U.S. health professionals, which represent alternative viewpoints, or which characterize health issues in a unique context.

See also individual format or literature type categories

Audiovisual Materials

NLM collects audiovisual materials less broadly than print formats. Materials are considered for selection if the information is considerably enhanced by audiovisual presentation. NLM's collecting interest is in audiovisuals produced for use by health professionals or those that are of potential interest to historians. Especially important to the NLM collection are works which document innovations, procedures, attitudes, issues or policies concerning or affecting health care and biomedical science as well as those which document significant events or the life and work of individuals important in biomedicine. Audiovisuals of historical interest may include those on health related topics produced for a broad audience. Contemporary examples of authoritative audiovisuals intended for professional use in continuing medical education, patient instruction, patient treatment, or health education are also selected. Materials intended for independent patient use usually are not selected, except for historical purposes. Audiovisuals in standard U.S. formats are collected for the general collection, though other formats may be selected if necessary for the historical collection. Audiovisuals in foreign languages, including those produced in the U.S., and audiovisuals produced outside the U.S., even in English, are collected only when they contain unique information and are of special historical importance.

See also Health Education and Patient Instruction Materials, Instructional Materials for the Health Professions

Biographical Works
Biographical works include biographies, autobiographies, personal narratives, memoirs, and published oral history transcripts. They generally are written for a broad audience and are important chronicles of the course of biomedicine. Firsthand accounts, such as autobiographies and personal narratives, may be especially valuable as primary source materials.

NLM collects medical histories of famous persons and biographical works about individuals who have contributed significantly to biomedicine. NLM selects other biographical works about prominent or lesser known individuals if they characterize the health care environment, practice or attitudes of a given time or place; influence public perceptions about health; document medical innovations; or contain significant biomedical information. Personal accounts of an illness generally are not collected, except for historical interest.

See also *Manuscripts*

Catalogs

Sales and trade catalogs present descriptions, prices, and intended uses of medical equipment, drugs, preparations and devices. NLM collects examples of these catalogs for historical purposes.

Catalogs of academic health science institutions provide a record of the development of those institutions, and changes in health science curricula. NLM collects representative examples of catalogs from influential academic health science institutions as well as those of some lesser known but unique institutions. NLM collects catalogs of biomedical exhibits which provide valuable illustrative and descriptive material.

Collected Works

NLM acquires collected works, including anthologies, when the original works are not in the collection, when the compilation contains additional information or commentary, or when presentation of the material as a unit is useful.

See also Reprints and Facsimiles, Textbooks

Conference Publications

NLM collects comprehensively the proceedings of national and international biomedical conferences, congresses and symposia. Conference programs containing abstracts may also be collected if the abstracts do not appear in the journal literature or if publication of complete conference proceedings is not anticipated. If neither complete proceedings nor abstracts are available, conference programs may be collected if they are of historical interest or when they document important biomedical research activity not represented in the scholarly literature. NLM collects very selectively the proceedings of other meetings as well as single papers and lectures not issued as part of proceedings. Collecting emphasis is on those of historical importance or of widespread topical interest to health professionals. Recordings of significant conference proceedings may be acquired if a print version is not available or when the recording itself is historically important.

Dictionaries

NLM collects dictionaries of biomedical terms, names, subjects, phrases, abbreviations, acronyms and symbols which are useful to health professionals and scholars. Biomedical dictionaries in any language may be selected in order to meet scholarly or research needs. Bilingual dictionaries are collected more selectively, with collecting emphasis on works which contain English or other languages important to U.S. health professionals and scholars.

Directories

Directories of professional health organizations may provide information regarding the association's history, purpose, activities, and influence on biomedicine. They may also contain biographical information. NLM's collecting emphasis is on directories of U.S. national professional organizations, particularly those which issue standards, have authority to certify, or assume responsibility for professional education. Directories of health facilities, products and services, health related institutions, corporations, research laboratories, educational programs and facilities may contain useful specific information. NLM collects representative examples of such directories with an emphasis on national sources widely used in the U.S. Foreign and multinational directories containing information important to the U.S. health professional also are selected.

Electronic Formats

The variety of biomedical literature offered in electronic format is rapidly expanding. Electronic materials may appear as distinct units such as data files, computer files, interactive video programs, or as transmitted information which may be accessed online, captured, and stored on another medium. Examples of the transmitted electronic literature include electronic journals and conferences.

NLM collects materials in electronic format selectively, taking into account their availability in other media. NLM also considers the utility of an electronic work and its implications for NLM's existing collection. Electronic materials produced for access in the U.S., using standard, widely available equipment and protocols, are selected. Selection preference is given to materials in the format most practical to retain, preserve and make available to the U.S. biomedical community.

An electronic work is considered for selection if the content is original or is significantly enhanced by electronic presentation. The item should also be accompanied by adequate documen-tation, present authoritative information, and be of good technical quality. Selection preference is given to electronic literature issued by major U.S. professional associations. Collecting emphasis is on those materials which are of particular topical interest to U.S. health professionals, are appropriate as library materials, and are important to the U.S. scholarly biomedical record.

NLM selects contemporary examples of instructional materials in interactive video and computer file format very selectively. Collecting emphasis is on those which are particularly effective in demonstrating contemporary techniques in medical education through simulations, decision making models, or computer graphics.

Electronic indexes and bibliographies normally are selected for the general collection only if they contain information which is not available in other media or if they are deemed of historical interest. Some health instruction materials are intentionally designed to be altered by the user. Other electronic materials are systems or databases containing raw information useful only in a health science setting or with additional equipment, programs and documentation. NLM does not collect these materials.

See also Examination Review Guides, Instructional Materials for the Health Professions

Encyclopedias
Medical encyclopedias present a review of biomedical thought and practice in summary form. NLM collects medical encyclopedias in any language to support biomedical research and scholarship. In order to document the status of health information disseminated to the public, NLM also collects selected examples of widely used medical encyclopedias written for a general audience. Collecting emphasis is on those that are written by leading experts or endorsed by major professional organizations, and appropriate for a U.S. audience.

Ephemera
Materials designed for short term use are considered ephemera. They vary greatly in size (from broadsides to patent medicine

cards), sophistication (from fine art prints to comic book illustrations), and format (from pamphlets to matchbooks). Ephemeral materials provide a glimpse into the everyday life of a certain time period. By capturing information not available in the formal written record, ephemera allow the scholar to reconstruct the past with a precision of detail not otherwise possible. Medical ephemera may deal with orthodox medicine or alternative medicine. Examples of both are desirable in the collection.

NLM collects selected examples of ephemera of particular interest such as posters, pamphlets and fact sheets. Other types of ephemera are collected more selectively based on their relevance to health care and historical value. For additional explanation, see the entries for particular types of ephemera, such as fact sheets, pamphlets and posters.

Examination Review Guides

Examination review guides in the health sciences which are published as aids in preparing for entrance, board certification or recertification examinations, provide both contemporary and historical information concerning the generally recognized standards, requirements and prerequisites for formal education and licensure in the health professions.

NLM collects examination review guides selectively with an emphasis on materials produced by major commercial publishers or recognized professional organizations. Selection is generally limited to works widely used to prepare for U.S. professional health examinations.

Fact Sheets

Health related agencies and professional associations produce fact sheets and leaflets in order to disseminate health information to the general public in an economical, easily distributed form. Their value to historians is in providing, in capsule form, authoritative information concerning current health topics.

The National Library of Medicine collects selected fact sheets for historical purposes. Collecting emphasis is on those published by the U.S. Public Health Service agencies, particularly the National Institutes of Health, and other authoritative or widely influential sources.

See also Ephemera

Government Publications

Governments influence the course of biomedicine and health care practice by establishing and enforcing health related standards, laws and regulations; and by funding health research, health care programs and services. NLM collects U.S. federal agency documents and reports issued by the executive branch pertaining to health care and health issues. Of particular collecting importance are federal health agency policies, practice guidelines, studies of health care issues, regulations, and health and vital statistics. Collecting emphasis is on the publications of the health agencies of the Department of Health and Human Services. NLM also collects representative examples of health education materials, fact sheets, pamphlets and posters issued by U.S. federal health agencies. For additional explanation, see entries for those categories.

The Library of Congress assumes national collecting responsibility for U.S. congressional documents. NLM may select health related congressional publications; including committee reports, hearings, and final legislation; with emphasis on those of importance to the scholarly biomedical record. In collecting these materials, NLM takes into account their availability and accessibility in various formats.

International quasi-governmental health agencies, such as the World Health Organization and the Pan American Health Organization, exert major influence on health care and biomedicine throughout the world. Their publications are of particular collecting interest. The National Library of Medicine selects materials published by foreign national, U.S. state and local governments and agencies when they are of broad interest to U.S. health professionals and scholars.

See also Statistical Works, Technical Reports.

Health Education and Patient Instruction Materials

The distribution of health education materials is an important strategy in the practice of health and preventive medicine. NLM collects selected examples of these materials in order to chronicle preventive medicine and public health outreach efforts. Collecting emphasis is on unique, influential or authoritative works which address major health issues.

Instructional materials produced for the patient are often used by health providers as a technique in direct patient care. NLM collects materials for patient instruction very selectively. Collecting emphasis is on authoritative materials widely used in U.S. health care.

See also Audiovisual Materials, Pamphlets

Humorous and Satirical Works
Humorous and satirical works, including caricatures, provide unique insight into controversies and opinions in health care, depict health care professionals as seen through the eyes of their contemporaries, and illuminate the political and social setting of health care and the health professions.

NLM collects these works selectively with emphasis on those which deal with historically important issues, events and personalities, or which address topics of current concern to U.S. health professionals.

Instructional Materials for the Health Professions
Instructional materials provide evidence of the intellectual content, instructional techniques, and educational philosophies found in formal education for the health professions. These materials generally contain information collected from other sources and reorganized into forms more suitable for a didactic purpose. NLM collects representative examples of such materials used in the U.S. to provide insight into educational trends in the health sciences.

Continuing education materials which describe new concepts, demonstrate new techniques, or document contemporary concerns of the U.S. health professional are of particular collecting interest. Supplemental instructional aids typically intended for classroom use such as instructor's manuals, student laboratory manuals, syllabi, course outlines, student workbooks, charts, and regalia generally are not collected unless they provide essential insight into important trends in professional health science education.

See also Audiovisual Materials, Electronic Format Materials, Examination Review Guides, Textbooks

Interim Reports
Interim reports generally are issued for studies conducted over a considerable period of time. Such reports show the development

of data, concepts or consensus, and present timely information about the status of projects and other work in progress.

Published interim reports on topics of major concern to U.S. health professionals are collected with an emphasis on publications of the U.S. Department of Health and Human Services and the World Health Organization.

Laboratory Manuals

Laboratory manuals contain descriptions of standard laboratory procedures, current techniques and safety measures, as well as formulae and other technical information. NLM collects representative examples of laboratory manuals written for the biomedical professional. Selection is limited to authoritative manuals widely used in U.S. clinical and biomedical research laboratories.

Limited Distribution Materials

NLM collects publications intended for limited distribution and proprietary use when they are available to NLM without restrictions on access.

Looseleaf Service Publications

Looseleaf subscription services are generally designed to be updated by means of interfiled or replacement pages. They typically provide information compiled from other sources. NLM collects looseleaf services very selectively. Collecting emphasis is on those which compile information not readily accessible or available in other formats.

Manuscripts

Manuscripts are important to the scholarly biomedical record as primary source materials. NLM divides its manuscript collections into early Western (pre-1601) manuscripts, Oriental (primarily Arabic and Persian) manuscripts, and modern manuscripts. Early Western and Oriental manuscripts are collected selectively, taking into account their historical significance, their value for scholarship, and the price of the work. Modern manuscripts are collected selectively with an emphasis on twentieth century U.S. medicine. Priority is given to manuscripts and collections of papers written by or about individuals who have contributed significantly to the health sciences, and those which contain other information important to the history of medicine. Materials selected for the modern manuscript collection include unique handwritten or typed documents and papers, associated printed or near print materials, and oral history transcripts and tapes. Areas of special collecting interest include: biochemistry, biotechnology and molecular biology, surgery, pediatrics and child development, medical information, the history of medicine, military medicine, and the U.S. Public Health Service, including the National Institutes of Health.

See also Biographical Works

Market Surveys

Biomedical market surveys are specialized reports describing specific commercial opportunities and produced exclusively for managers in health related industries. These surveys assess the specific need for a product in a particular environment, describe potential commercial gain, and recommend marketing strategies. NLM collects market surveys very selectively as resources for the future study of health economics rather than to provide current information. Selection is limited to those which illustrate important developments or trends in the health marketplace relating to equipment, products or services. Reports which describe specific markets for name brand items or specialized consulting services generally are not collected.

Newsletters and Newspapers

Newsletters and newspapers may represent a unique historical chronicle of health related issues. They often contain the most current information on health topics, research and policy. Newsletters may focus on emerging areas of research or health care before such fields are adequately represented in the primary journal literature.

NLM collects selected newsletters with an emphasis on those issued by major U.S. and international professional health organizations. Of particular collecting interest are those which focus on contemporary health issues and concerns, represent emerging health areas, or document health outreach efforts to populations at risk. NLM collects newsletters with original content or commentary rather than those which contain digests of articles reprinted or abridged from other publications. Newsletters which represent non-traditional treatment philosophies or specific health issues of topical interest to scholars or U.S. health professionals are collected selectively.

Foreign newsletters are collected very selectively with an emphasis on those published by major organizations on topics of particular concern to U.S. health professionals.

Medical newspapers written for a national audience are collected if they contain substantive health related information that is probably not duplicated elsewhere or are published in a country for which little medical information is available. In collecting newsletters and newspapers, NLM takes into account the availability of comparable information in the journal literature.

Pamphlets

Pamphlets are short, unbound, printed works which generally deal with subjects of current interest. They are an efficient means for the distribution of health care standards, guidelines, and capsule summaries of a biomedical topic. Pamphlets are also an effective medium for public health outreach, patient instruction, consumer health information, and commercial advertising literature.

NLM collects representative examples of the pamphlet literature to provide a balanced collection of typical, influential, authoritative and unique items dealing with health issues of particular interest. Collecting emphasis is on publications of U.S. national health organizations, health agencies, and authoritative or widely influential institutions. Examples of pamphlets produced by influential international health organizations and those which present unique health care strategies and concerns also are selected. Other items which present health outreach efforts, conflicting opinion, and alternative practice are also of collecting interest.

See also Ephemera, Standards and Guidelines.

Pharmacopoeias and Formularies

Pharmacopoeias and formularies are authoritative treatises on drug standards and preparation. They may contain descriptions of pharmaceutical products, tests for determining their identity or purity, preparation formulas, or dispensing and dosage information. These works provide an historical record of pharmacy practice, drug use, and drug availability.

NLM collects selected pharmacopoeias and formularies which are widely used or which present unique information. Collecting emphasis is on national formularies and pharmacopoeias.

Posters

Posters are designed to be displayed publicly to communicate a message or to advertise a product or service. Posters provide historically valuable visual evidence of developments in health care, public health outreach campaigns, and official responses to health crises.

The National Library of Medicine collects representative examples of historical and contemporary posters. Of particular collecting interest are posters concerning the spread of infectious diseases (e.g., tuberculosis, AIDS, measles), smoking, substance abuse, preventive medicine, and maternal and child health. Posters of any origin and language are selected. Collecting emphasis is on posters issued by professional health associations, and medical or public health organizations.

Practice Management Materials

Practice management materials include a wide variety of practical business aids and systems intended to assist health care providers and administrators with accounting, billing, contracts, file management, marketing, etc. These materials are considered supplementary to the general professional practice management literature and are often issued in looseleaf, unbound, electronic, or audiovisual format. The majority of these aids and systems are only useful when integrated into a hospital or office setting, and are not appropriate for library collections.

The National Library of Medicine selects practice management resources (such as a compendium of medical form letters or a litigation manual) only if they are of general interest to United .States health professionals and contain information not captured elsewhere in the literature. Selection emphasis is on resources issued by major U.S. professional associations.

Prints and Photographs
Prints and photographs document visually the history and development of medicine from early times to recent decades. NLM's collection includes fine prints, historical and contemporary photographic processes, posters, and ephemera such as patent medicine trade cards. Collecting emphasis is on portraits of health professionals and biomedical scientists who have contributed to the development of medicine, images of health institutions such as hospitals and medical schools, fine prints with medically related themes, and public health posters. Images reproduced from existing works are also added to the prints and photographs collection.

Reprints and Facsimiles
Reprints and facsimiles are collected when they provide useful information such as a commentary or bibliography which did not appear in previous printings. They are also selected when NLM lacks the original, when NLM's copy is in poor condition, or when they are historically significant single items.
See also Collected Works

Standards and Guidelines
Institutions, associations, and government agencies issue health related standards and guidelines which are widely used and recognized in the U.S. Standards are authoritative statements which articulate minimal, acceptable or excellent levels of performance or which describe expected outcomes in health care delivery, biomedical research and development, health care technology, or professional health care. Guidelines are statements of principles or procedures which assist professionals in ensuring quality in such areas as clinical practice, biomedical research, and health services. Practice guidelines assist the health care practitioner with patient care decisions about appropriate diagnostic, therapeutic, or other clinical procedures for specific clinical circumstances.
NLM collects comprehensively the following types of standards and guidelines: Practice guidelines; Official U.S. national

standards in health care technology, biomedical research and development, and health care; Standards of conduct and professional competence for U.S. health care professionals; Standards and guidelines issued by the World Health Organization; Other influential or widely recognized standards and guidelines also are collected.

Statistical Works

Statistical works are important resources in biomedical research, health care practice, and health policy making. NLM collects selected statistical works in biomedicine. Of particular interest are works which report vital statistics, disease incidence, health status indicators (e.g., smoking or nutrition), population variables which influence health expectations (e.g., fertility, age, sex, ethnic groups), factors which have direct impact on health care research (e.g., government funding for health care), and health outcomes (e.g., disabilities). Non-medical statistical works (e.g., accidents, demographic characteristics) are considered for the collection when they relate to the cause or effect of a disease or disorder.

NLM's collecting emphasis is on cumulated works which are national or international in scope, and on those which describe populations of special epidemiological interest. Compendia of U.S. state health and vital statistics are also collected. In addition, NLM selectively acquires compilations of health related statistics issued by other jurisdictions of particular interest. Other U.S. state and local statistical works are collected when they provide data or data analysis on important topics. Statistics in the form of raw data files, whether in electronic format or in print, are not collected.

Technical Reports

Technical reports are valuable sources of research based information on specific scientific, technical, management, or policy problems in biomedicine. In selecting technical reports, NLM's focus is on those which provide unique information in emerging fields of biomedical research and other areas of widespread interest among U.S. health professionals (e.g., health services research, environmental health, biotechnology, health care technology assessment, and risk management). NLM's collecting emphasis is on health related reports published by U.S. federal agencies and eminent research organizations.

See also Interim Reports

Tests

Specific tests are used as instruments to measure, diagnose, or evaluate psychological conditions and mental processes, or to assess physical status. The National Library of Medicine selects examples of those published tests and assessments which are widely used in the United .States. to enhance its existing collection of works on diagnostic and evaluative procedures.

Textbooks

A textbook, although primarily intended for student instruction, may also be of interest to the biomedical professional and historian as a reference source, an historical record of medical education, a chronicle of societal attitudes toward health and disease, or a synthesis of knowledge in a subject.

NLM collects textbooks intended for the education of U.S. health professionals. Other textbooks also may be selected. These include U.S. texts in pre-clinical subjects such as biochemistry, cytology, or abnormal psychology; U.S. college level texts on health issues; and foreign texts. Collecting emphasis is on advanced textbooks notable for their comprehensiveness, authority, or presentation; and on texts which contain unique information or have historical value.

See also Instructional Materials for the Health Professions

Translations

NLM collects foreign biomedical works in their original language. When available, an English translation is also acquired. If a work is published in a language not widely understood in the U.S. and no English language translation is available, the work may also be acquired in a language more likely to be familiar to a U.S. audience.

Translations from English to a foreign language generally are not collected. When works are issued simultaneously in several languages, NLM generally collects the English version only. Excepted in both cases are works of specific historical interest, those with significant added material, and those which characterize the dissemination of health information to populations whose primary language is not English.

See also Manuscripts

[Authors' note: as a federal government publication, the *Collection Development Manual of the National Library of Medicine* is not protected against copying within the United States. It may be ordered through NTIS; the order number is PB93-177046/GBB. Alternately, it is available electronically through the TECHSERV directory in NLM's anonymous ftp publications service on Internet. Only portions of it have been reproduced here.]

ENDNOTES

1. National Library of Medicine (U. S.) Technical Services Division. *Collection Development Manual of the National Library of Medicine*. Bethesda, MD: U. S. Department of Health and Human Services, Public Health Service, National Institutes of Health, 1985.

2. National Library of Medicine Act of 1956. 84th Congress. PL 84-941.

3. *RLG Collection Development Manual*, Stanford, CA: Research Libraries Group, 1981, p. 18.

4. *Preservation of the Biomedical Literature*. Revision to the Preservation Policy. Approved, Board of Regents February 6-7,1986.

5. *Library of Congress Acquisition Policy Statement No. 22-b: Medicine*. Adopted March 4, 1982.

6. *Library of Congress Acquisition Policy Statement No.3: Scholarly Publications*. Approved April 19, 1956.

7. National Agricultural Library. United States Department of Agriculture. Collection Development Policy of the National

Agricultural Library. Beltville, MD: National Agricultural Library, 1988.

8. National Library of Medicine (U. S.) *Long Range Plan. Report of Panel 1. Building and Organizing the Library's Collection.* Bethesda, MD: The Library, 1986, p. 28.

9. Wyndham D. Miles. *A History of the National Library of Medicine, the Nation's Treasury of Medical Knowledge.* Washington, D.C.: Government Printing Office, 1982, p.5.

10. Ibid., p.36. Letter, Surg. Gen. Barnes to Rep. J.A. Garfield, Jan. 6,1872; also letter, Barnes to Sen. L.M. Morrill, Feb. 9,1872.

11. Ibid, p. 42. Quote from a Billings letter to "Dear Doctor," Jan. 23, 1872; MS/C/81.

12. Miles, p. 293.

13. *The National Medical Library: Report of a Survey of the Army Medical Library.* Chicago: American Library Association, 1944.

14. *Report of [the] Committee on Scope and Coverage.* Army Medical Library. Presented to [the] Association of Honorary Consultants to [the] Army Medical Library, 20 October 1950. Appendix 1, authorization for Committee.

15. 84th Congress. 2d. sess. bill S. 3430. 1956.

16. Library of Congress, op.cit.

HIRSCH LIBRARY
MUSEUM OF FINE ARTS
Houston, Texas

I. Mission
The Hirsch Library's main purpose is to meet the research needs of the professional staff of The Museum of Fine Arts, Houston, as well as its docents and members; secondarily, the library serves researchers, university art and art history professors, their students, and the general public.

II. Scope of Collection
The scope of the Library's collection encompasses European, American, Asian, African and Oceanic art in all media from antiquity to the present. Decorative art, photography, costume, prints and drawings, painting and sculpture are included. Emphasis is on areas where the Museum's collection is strong, and in areas of curatorial expertise.

III. General Guidelines for Selection
The library collects background information on areas in which the Museum collects, and collects in anticipation of future acquisitions and exhibitions. Curators will be consulted for advice on acquisitions to determine relevance and quality, especially for out-of-print material, and items for which reviews have not been found.

IV. Types of Materials
The library will attempt to acquire works in hard copy when available, but will also consider titles in microform or electronic format. The types of materials sought will include: monographs, catalogues raisonnes, surveys of art history, conference proceedings, specialized bibliographies, dictionaries, directories, catalogs of library collections, periodical sets and continuations, indexes and abstracts, exhibition catalogs, handbooks and catalogs of museum and private collections, auction and sale catalogs, generally limited to areas of the Museum's collections.

Publication date: While emphasis is given the acquisition of current titles, out-of-print material is purchased to fill in gaps in the collection.

V. Subject Areas

In terms of acquisitions, the subject areas below are placed in groups of their current relative importance. Subjects are not prioritized within each group and may occasionally vary in importance to reflect changes in Museum acquisition policy.

Primary interest areas:
    African, Oceanic, Pre-Columbian art
    American Indian art
    Asian art
    Decorative arts, European and American
    Painting, European and American
    Photography
    Prints & drawings
    Sculpture

Secondary interest areas:
    Aesthetics and criticism
    Architecture
    Conservation
    Costume and fashion
    Film
    Iconography
    Material culture
    Textiles

Tertiary interest areas:
    Anthropology
    Art education
    Artists' books
    Book arts
    Collecting
    Facsimiles
    Gardening
    History
    Information science
    Museology
    Performance art
    Rare books
    Travel

VI. Coordination with Other Libraries

Recorded information that meets the informational and research needs of the Library's constituents is appropriate for inclusion, regardless of format or language, but practical limitations are also considered. The universe of published information has become too extensive for even the largest and richest libraries to accumulate; cooperative resource sharing at the local, regional and national levels is therefore essential.

Specific areas of coordination with libraries at the University of Houston and Rice University are:

1. Architecture
2. Archaeology
3. American history
4. Related arts, such as music, dance and theater
5. Interdisciplinary studies

With the Menil Collection, areas of coordination include:

1. Contemporary art, especially major reference works
2. Ancient art
3. Byzantine and Medieval art

VII. Gifts

Gifts are accepted only if no restrictions are attached. They are integrated into the collection and the librarian reserves the right to select and dispose as seems appropriate. Acknowledgments of gifts are sent, but no appraisals are made for IRS purposes.

FIRST BAPTIST CHURCH
Huntsville, Texas

The following policy guides the library staff in selecting materials for the library so that all materials are of the highest quality and of the greatest benefit to the church leaders and members.

1. All materials for the library will be approved by the librarian, associate librarian, or a staff member.
2. All materials will be as accurate as possible in facts, scriptural interpretation, and doctrine.
3. All materials will be constructive in influence and morally sound.
4. All materials will reflect Christian standards of conduct and will be free of racial and religious prejudice, political bias, social injustice, and other evidences of unchristian attitudes and actions.
5. All materials will be of high literary or technical quality.
6. All materials will include and reflect sound educational methods and will aid in teaching and learning.
7. Gifts to the media library are encouraged. It is suggested that gifts of money be made. The librarian will determine the specific item to be given, taking into consideration any suggestions from the giver.
8. All gifts to the library must meet the same standards as purchased items.
9. The following selection aids will be used: *Media Magazine*, *Children's Catalog*, *Elementary School Library Collection*, *Baptist Standard*, denominational journals and literature.

Submitted by
Bonnie Thorne, Librarian
Barbara Lewis, Associate Librarian

HUNTSMAN CHEMICAL CORPORATION
Chesapeake, Virginia

HISTORY
The Library began its existence as a collection of the books and journals acquired over the years by the Research and Development department of the polystyrene division. For this reason, and because its physical location is in the R&D building in Chesapeake, its core collection of materials is focused on the research and development and analysis of polystyrene and, now, polypropylene, and on the technology involved in processing those resins into finished products.

However, as the organization of the corporation has grown, so have the informational responsibilities of the Library. The Library staff now routinely answers questions on a large variety of subjects for all departments of the corporation, particularly the sales divisions and corporate headquarters. The Library staff also compiles and distributes newsletters to departments and individuals to keep them up-to-date on current developments which concern them.

PRIMARY GOALS
These three primary responsibilities: research, analysis, and technology; corporate-wide reference; and current event newsletters form the basis for decisions about the development of the Library's collection. Because the Library is part of the Research and Development Department, the materials collected within the Library itself will remain primarily those devoted to plastics research and technology. The core collection is well-grounded in these subjects. Care should be taken to consistently build on these strong points by adding relevant new material as it becomes available. Areas which should be strengthened may be identified by noting those questions from the R&D staff which cannot be adequately answered from the existing collection, and by consulting the standard lists (see Appendix I).

Since the cost of maintaining comprehensive up-to-date general and business reference collections would be prohibitive, the Library will rely on the wide range of information sources available through online services for answering these types of reference questions from all departments of the corporation. Therefore, online services, which are not physically collected within the Library, must nevertheless be considered an important part of the collection development policy. Current awareness publications from the Library will continue to be compiled primarily from articles retrieved through online searching.

SELECTION RESPONSIBILITY

The Librarian has the primary authority for determining which materials to add to the Library's collection. The Librarian will order materials to maintain the collection based on current literature in the field and on recommendations from the staff.

"Desk copies" of standard reference works needed by the R&D staff may be purchased by the Library, cataloged and circulated. "Desk copies" of materials for staff in other departments may be ordered through the Library so as to take advantage of the Library's book jobber, but they will be charged to those departmental accounts. Materials ordered in this way will be thus considered property of those departments and will not be added to the Library collection.

Materials requested by the R&D staff which do not fit within the scope of the Library's collection development policies, or which are beyond the normal budgetary limitations of the Library, may still be purchased by and for the Library if approved by the Vice President for Research and Development.

COOPERATIVE PROGRAMS

The Library uses the OCLC Interlibrary Loan Subsystem to augment our holdings. ILL is available to all members of the corporation for research. Because the Library is privately funded and intended for the sole use of the corporation's staff, monographs in the collection will not circulate on interlibrary loan. However, the Library recognizes its responsibility to share the information in its journals collection, which is unique in this area of the state. Accordingly, the Library's journals holdings have been added to the OCLC database through the Virginia Group Access project.

We provide photocopies to other libraries in our group at no charge. This is also an important link to the general public, which may be important for purposes of our being considered an "accessible" library under the terms outlined in the copyright law (Title 17, sections 107 and 108, of the U.S. Code).

GENERAL COLLECTION GUIDELINES

Languages: The primary language of the collection is English, but materials in other languages are acquired selectively. Translations into English are preferred whenever available.

Chronological Guidelines: Emphasis is on current developments in polymers research and technology, but historical materials may be maintained in the collection.

Geographical Guidelines: Not applicable.

Treatment of Subject: Emphasis is on research and on the latest in technology, including additives, modifiers, molding techniques, and parts design. Thus, current editions of the research level and of a fairly advanced technological nature are preferred. Proceedings of professional organizations such as the Society of Plastics Engineers, the Society of the Plastics Industry, and the Flame Retardant Chemicals Association are also collected.

Non-print Media: Microfiche has proven to be an unsatisfactory medium and will not be collected. Computer-based formats, both downloadable databases and CD-ROM, may be considered.

Date of Publication: Current works are preferred, but "classics" (such as *Styrene: Its Polymers and Copolymers* by Ray Boundy) are acquired as needed.

Other General Considerations: Core journals and books are identified in the standard lists (see Appendix I). These may be used as a guide for retrospective augmentation of the collection as staff, time and budgeting allow. However, since polymer science is constantly developing, emphasis in collecting must be placed on the most recent works.

STANDARDS AND PATENTS

The Library will maintain holdings of various U.S. and foreign industrial and military specifications and of U.S. and foreign patents. Most of these are acquired as requested by staff members as a result of citations retrieved through our CAS current awareness profiles, our U.S. patents alert profile, or through online patents searching.

Some standards must be maintained in their most current editions by the Library. These include:

- *The Annual Book of ASTM Standards* [volumes for Plastics, and other selected volumes]
- *The Department of Defense Industrial Standards and Specifications* published by the USGPO
- Selected numbers of *Underwriters' Laboratory* standards and guidelines

REFERENCE

The Reference Collection consists of books and materials frequently consulted by members of the R&D department. These materials will be for Library use only. "Desk copies" may be ordered for an individual's office use, if the cost is not prohibitive. Certain works in the Reference Collection *must* be kept up-to-date because their information is crucial to the corporation. A list of those materials so identified is in Appendix II.

TECHNICAL REPORTS

One copy of all Research and Development technical reports will be maintained in the Library. These will be cataloged in the ProCite database on the R&D computer network.

JOURNALS

The Library will maintain subscriptions to the core polymer science, analytical chemistry, chemical business and plastics technology journals. These journals will be bound and maintained in the Library, since they represent a collection unique in the local area. Those polymer science and analytical chemistry journals which are prohibitively expensive or are of peripheral use will be followed either in the profile maintained by the Institute for Scientific Information for our *Research Alert*, in *Polymer Contents*, or in CAS profiles.

The Library will maintain subscriptions for a limited number of Library journals, which will be bound and housed in the Library. The Library will maintain subscriptions to a limited number of general business journals. These will be routed throughout the Chesapeake site. They will be retained for a year and then discarded, since they duplicate the holdings of numerous local libraries.

OTHER TYPES OF MATERIALS
Encyclopedias, treatises, compendia, papers, proceedings, trans-actions of professional congresses, conferences, and symposia are sought for inclusion.

GOVERNMENT PUBLICATIONS
These are not specifically sought for the collection, but are purchased on demand if they fall within the subject areas being collected by the Library.

MONOGRAPHS
Guidelines for the acquisition of monographs are given for the Library of Congress classes which comprise the core of the Library's collection. Monographs in other subject classifications may be added at the discretion of the Librarian.

QA: MATHEMATICS: Some instructional level manuals in computer software use; a limited number of research level monographs in statistics, probability, and analysis.

QD: CHEMISTRY: Research level monographs in analytical, organic, and physical and theoretical chemistry, particularly those related to polymer chemistry. The managers of the Analysis and Testing groups should be sent information about new publications in this field so they can help keep the Library's collection current.

TA: ENGINEERING: The collection concentrates on the "400-500" series in this classification, "Materials of Engineering and Construction." Monographs dealing with the physical properties and the testing of polymers and plastics should be sought out through publisher's catalogs and book review sources. This is an area which should be strengthened.

TD: ENVIRONMENTAL TECHNOLOGY: Some popular works are included in the collection to provide the "public's perception" of the state of plastics' contribution to environmental conservation/destruction. Research level works concerning recycling/reuse of plastics which have positive book reviews or which are recommended by the staff should be added as they are published.

TH: BUILDING CONSTRUCTION: The "9446" section contains many important works relating to the flammability of plastics. Research and professional materials of this nature should be considered for acquisition.

TP: CHEMICAL   TECHNOLOGY: "155-156,"   "Chemical Engineering" and "200-248," "Chemicals--Manufacture, Use, Etc." are essential to the operation of any chemical manufacturing concern. Research and professional level works should be added as needed.
       The "1101-1185" sections of this classification, "Plastics and Plastics Manufacture," and the "980's," which contain works on some resins and elastomers, are, of course, the heart of the Library's collection. Monographs at the research level and professional series published in this area should be seriously considered for inclusion.

ONLINE SERVICES
The Library will utilize online services for reference queries, for current awareness services, and for interlibrary loans.

Reference: The Library will maintain membership in DIALOG and STN and use these services to access the information needed for answering reference questions which are beyond the scope of the Library's physical collection. These questions may range from simple requests for physical data on a competitor's product to a request for a major research project on a resin or a company. The Library staff should also identify sources in the Internet community which can be of service in this area.

Current Awareness: The Library will maintain current awareness profiles in various online databases on topics in polymer science and the plastics business, and will circulate the results from those profiles to the interested individuals. Copyright fees are negotiated with each database supplier.

Present (March, 1993) current awareness profiles are listed in the appendix as a guideline.

Interlibrary Loans: Using the OCLC ILL subsystem is the most efficient and economical way of obtaining materials from other libraries.

GIFTS
Gift materials which fit within the Library's scope of development will be accepted for inclusion.

REPLACEMENTS
Books which are lost or damaged will be replaced only if they are of current importance or of significant historical value.

EVALUATION AND DESELECTION
Although some older materials may be of continuing value, either as "classics" of the polymer literature, or because of historical interest, many chemistry and polymer science works become so outdated as to be of little significance to the research effort. From time to time, books which do not appear in the standard book lists (Appendix I) should be gathered by the Librarian, placed on a book truck, and carefully examined by the chemists and chemical engineers to determine whether or not to keep these materials.

REVISIONS
This document should be reviewed by the Librarian and the Vice President for Research and Development annually, and the policy guidelines revised as necessary to reflect the latest developments in the Library's information services.

Jan Mitchell, Librarian

APPENDIX I
Standard Book Lists
These lists must be used with caution, since polymer science and plastics technology are constantly changing. These may be used as a guide to evaluate materials which might be weeded from the collection and as an aid to "filling in" areas which need to be strengthened.

Encyclopedia of Polymer Science and Engineering (New York: Wiley, 1987). "Literature of Polymers" by Julia T. Lee

George Patterson. *Plastics Book List* (Westport, Conn.: Technomic, 1975).

APPENDIX II:
Crucial Reference Works
Care must be taken to ensure that the latest edition of the following works are available in the Library's Reference collection:

Dangerous Properties of Industrial Materials by Sax
Polymer Handbook by Brandrup
Perry's Chemical Engineer's Handbook
The Encyclopedia of Polymer Science and Engineering
Plastics Engineering Handbook of the Society of the Plastics Industry
Handbook of Plastic Materials and Technology by Rubin
U.S. Pharmacopeia National Formulary
Facts and Figures of the U.S. Plastics Industry
DeWitt Polystyrene Book
OMAl Polystyrene Book
CMAl Polyolefins Book

A book listing the latest in plastics additives.

Books detailing the latest in extrusion, injection, and blow molding.

The Librarian must depend upon publishers' catalogs, *Science Books & Films*, and other pertinent journals, and information from other members of the R&D department to keep up-to date on the last two items.

MARINE SCIENCE LIBRARY
University of Texas
Port Aransas, Texas

I. PURPOSE
The Library supports both original and applied research programs in marine science. It must meet the needs of the teaching program for the Department of Marine Science (a multi-disciplinary program with emphasis in the fields of botany, biochemistry, marine chemistry, geochemistry, geology, mari-culture, physiology, oceanography, and zoology) through the Ph.D. level. The library will collect both published and unpublished Gulf of Mexico literature, including its estuarine and brackish water ecosystems.

II. GENERAL COLLECTION GUIDELINES
A. *Languages:* English is the preferred (primary) language in the collection. Publications in languages other than Chinese, French, German, Italian, Japanese, Portuguese, Russian, and Spanish will require English translations. Textbooks and popular works are acquired in English only.
B. *Chronological Guidelines:* Emphasis is primarily on the twentieth century and current scholarship.
C. *Geographical Guidelines:* Generally worldwide with emphasis on Gulf of Mexico and its estuarine communities.
D. *Treatment of Subject:* Textbooks are purchased selectively. Monographic publications must reflect current research programs and graduate student emphasis. Publications from primary societies (e.g. American Fisheries Society, etc.) are actively selected.
E. *Types of Materials:* The collection includes selected publications of conferences, symposia, workshops, congresses, and atlases. Technical reports, government documents, theses and dissertations are generally included. Emphasis is on current journal literature. Non-print media include microforms, videos, and specimens.
F. *Date of Publication:* Primarily the last ten years, although some earlier works may be acquired.
G. *Other General Considerations:* General marine science reference tools and general science methods relevant to marine science (e.g. standard methods) will be collected.

The library committee, senior scientists and faculty will keep the bibliographer informed about their changing research and teaching needs.

III. QUALIFICATIONS BY SUBJECT AND LC CLASSIFICATION

Within each classification there will be some general and specific marine science publications. These titles will selectively be collected [by the Marine Science Bibliographer.]

Subject	LC Class
Academic & learned societies, international associations, congresses, conferences, etc.	AS
Geography (general)	G 1-9980
Mathematical geography	GA
Physical geography	GB 1-2998
Language (dictionaries, directories)	P, PA-PZ
Science (general)	Q
Mathematics	QA 76, 273-939
Astronomy as applied to marine science, tides, etc.	QB 1-991
Physics	QC 1-999
Chemistry	QD 1-999
Geology	QE 1-996
Natural history	QH 1-671
Botany	QK 1-938
Zoology	QL 1-991
Physiology	QP 1-981
Microbiology	R 1-484
Toxicology public aspects of medicine	RA 1190-1270
Pathology	RB
Therapeutics, pharmacology	RM 1-862
Agriculture (general)	S
Plant culture	SB
Animal culture	SF
Aquaculture, fisheries, angling	SH
Technology (limited to marine applications)	T-TZ
Bibliography	Z 1001-8999

SHELL OIL COMPANY
Information and Library Services, Central Library
Houston, Texas

TABLE OF CONTENTS

I. INTRODUCTION

A. Objective of ILS-Central Library Collection
    The collection of material housed in the Information and Library
    Services-Central Library (hereafter referred to as ILS-Library
    or Library) is intended to answer the requests and needs of
    Head Office personnel, as well as those requests from any field
    locations not served by their own information group. In addition,

the collection is intended to fill the professional needs of the Library staff.

B. Purpose of Policy

The purpose of the ILS - Library collection development policy is to define and support the specific subject needs of its users. The policy addresses how the subject areas of emphasis are determined and defines the procedures the Library follows in constructing a responsive collection.

C. Types of Materials Included and Purchased

1. Form

The subject selection priorities contained within this policy apply primarily to books and journals.

a. Books

The Library generally orders one copy of a new book. New additions to the collection are announced in a monthly publication called the New Acquisition List. If there have been ten or more requests for a title, it is reviewed by an Analyst to determine if additional copies should be ordered.

Replacement copies are ordered on the basis of the book's popularity, subject, and age. An exempt staff member approves all requests for replacement copies.

b. Journals

The Library subscribes to journals or periodicals for two purposes. The first is to have current information for use in searching. The second is to have circulating periodicals that are routed to downtown Shell employees and then returned to the Library.

Employees are added to a routing list by submitting in writing their name, location, the periodicals desired, and a monetary approval signature. When there are a large number of readers for one title, the Library may obtain additional subscriptions if warranted by frequency, timeliness of content, and cost.

The Library may also have a reserve copy subscription of titles that are needed in the Library at all times for use in searching, photocopying, or browsing by users. Reserve copies are not routinely circulated or checked out.

    c. <u>Maps</u>
Maps are limited to road atlases and other geographic atlases necessary for reference questions and searching. Geologic and topographic maps will be primarily purchased by the Woodcreek Library.

    d. <u>Multi-Media</u>
At present, slides, audio recordings, and video cassettes will be considered on the merits of the individual item.

2. <u>Language</u>
The primary language of the collection is English. Foreign language material is considered on the merits of the individual item.

3. <u>Age</u>
The Library emphasizes adding new or current materials to the collection. Older materials will be purchased for two categories: replacement copies and archival materials.

D. **Relation of the ILS-Central Library Collection to Other Shell Libraries**
As the ILS-Central Library focuses on selected subjects, several of the other libraries in the Shell system also have a specific subject emphasis. The following is a list of some of the libraries with their subject emphases.

-Woodcreek--Exploration and Production
-Westhollow Research--Chemistry, Engineering, Refining, Mathematics, Physics, Petrochemicals, and Corrosion
-Bellaire Research--Exploration and Production
-Information Center--Data Processing
-Patents and Licensing--Patents
-Health, Safety and Environment--Toxicology, Environment, and Occupational Safety and Health
-Legal--Law
-Public Affairs Research Service--Petroleum Industry Issues, Public Relations, Government Activities
-Business Information Center--Chemical and Oil Products
-Business, Market Research

The Library purchases reference and core materials to provide a basic collection in these areas, while it supplements its holdings through interlibrary loan with the other Shell libraries. If more information is needed on the activities of the libraries within the Shell system, please consult the Shell Information Centers.

E. Interlibrary Loan

1. Impact on Collection Development

The Library is able to provide materials for low frequency requests in nonemphasized subject areas by borrowing materials from other libraries through interlibrary loan (ILL). This cooperation allows the Library to focus on topics of major importance to ILS users and to be free from the need to purchase all materials on all subjects. The ILL book requests are reviewed by exempt staff members, and if an increased number of requests is made in a subject area, that area will be incorporated into the emphasized subjects.

2. Copyright Review

The Library uses interlibrary loan to obtain photocopies of journal articles from titles not in the collection. A designated Library staff member is responsible for keeping photocopy statistics for articles published in the last five years and initiating a copyright review when more than five photocopies from an individual title are requested within one year.

For the copyright review, a photocopy review form is routed to Library staff to supply the required information (see Appendix A [not included here]). An exempt staff member, after reviewing the collected information, decides what action is necessary for copyright compliance, including adding the title to the collection, recommending that another Shell library subscribe, or paying the royalty fees. In an effort to comply with the copyright laws, the Library occasionally subscribes to a journal covering a subject that is not emphasized in the collection.

F. Gifts

The Library's procedure for handling materials donated to the collection is in Appendix B.

II. COMPANY INFORMATION

A. Company Activities

Shell Oil Company is engaged, principally in the United States, in the exploration for and the development, production, purchase, transportation, and marketing of crude oil and natural gas, and the purchase, manufacture, transportation and marketing of oil and chemical products. In addition, Shell participates with other parties in the exploration for crude oil and natural gas outside the United States. Also, Shell produces and markets coal and is in the process of developing other coal and geothermal steam reserves, and is investigating other energy sources such as tar sands and solar energy. Shell has also entered into a research agreement with the Cetus Corporation of Berkeley, California, to study processes for making interferon by recombinant DNA techniques. Shell Chemical Company and Shell Pipe Line Corporation are wholly owned subsidiaries whose activities are also supported by the Library.

A list of the exploration and production areas, refineries, oil and chemical products, and other energy sources under development can be found in the current annual report. Since the chemical plants do not regularly appear in the annual report, the following is, as of this writing, a listing of the locations: Denver, Co.; El Paso, Tx.; Geismar, La.; Marietta, Oh.; Mobile, Al.; Taft, La.; and Woodbury, N.J.

B. User Groups

The Company's activities are the result of the efforts of Shell employees. These employees comprise the Library's user population with some groups being primarily served by other libraries. The following are major user groupings plus a partial list of component activities.

EMPLOYEE RELATIONS
    Salary & Succession Planning
    Overseas Services
    Employment & Training
    Organization Effectiveness
    Recruitment
    Industrial Relations
    Policy and Benefits
    Employment & Equal Opportunity
    Employment & Support Staff Development
EXECUTIVE OFFICE

FINANCIAL--HEAD OFFICE
    Auditing--Corporate
    Auditing--Other Locations, Offices & Products
    Service Accounts
INFORMATION CENTER
    Information & Computer Services
    Systems Operations
    Computer Technology
    Data Evaluation
    Technical Operations
    (Primarily served by Information Center library)
TULSA CREDIT CARD CENTER
EXPLORATION & PRODUCTION
    Head Office E&P
        Civil Engineering
        Economics
    Eastern E&P Operations
    International E&P
    Western E&P Operations
    (All except Head Office primarily served by Woodcreek library)
HEALTH, SAFETY AND ENVIRONMENT
    Environmental Affairs
    Corporate Medical
    Safety & Industrial Hygiene
    Product Safety & Compliance
    (Primarily served by Health, Safety, and Environment library)
LEGAL
    Natural Resources
    Chemical Products & Energy Controls
    Oil Products Trade Regulations & Intellectual Property
    Corporate Security
    Litigation
    Environment/Labor
    (Primarily served by Legal library)
MINING
    Exploration
    Land
    Planning and Economics
    Uranium

Mining Engineering
Coal Marketing
Safety & Environmental Conservation
(Primarily served by Woodcreek library)
SHELL DEVELOPMENT
Patents & Licensing
Research and Development:
    Modes Biological Sciences Research Center
    Bellaire Research Center
    Westhollow Research Center
(Primarily served by libraries at their facilities)
OPERATIONS
Financial Performance Analysis
Financial Support Transportation and Distribution
Financial Support Manufacturing
Financial Support Supplies
Environmental Conservation
Fuel Logistics
Loss Control
Chemical Logistics
Quality Assurance
International Raw Materials Supply
Domestic Raw Materials Supply
Industry Analysis and Government Regulations
Marine Services
MANUFACTURING FACILITIES
(Some facilities are primarily served by libraries at their locations)
CORPORATE PLANNING
Strategic Planning
Energy Economics
Plans Coordination
PUBLIC AFFAIRS
Community Affairs
Editorial & Graphics
Communications
Issues Analysis
Governmental Affairs
Opinion Research
Plans & Integration

Media Relations
Advertising
(Primarily served by the Public Affairs Research Service)
PURCHASING AND GENERAL SERVICES
Purchasing
Office Systems Development
General Services
Travel Services
Corporate Real Estate
Building Services
TAX
International Tax
Federal Income Tax
State Income Taxes
Compensation and Benefit Taxes
Tax Counsel
Property and Excise Tax
CHEMICAL PRODUCTS
Plastics Business Center
Resins Business Center
Elastomers Business Center
Agribusiness Sales
Detergents Products Business Center
Solvents & Aromatics Business Center
PRODUCTS FINANCE
Products Accounting
Consolidated Accounting
Regulatory Reporting
Regulatory Compliance
OIL PRODUCTS
Distillates/Residuals Products Business Center
Gasoline Business Center
Lubricants Business Center
Government Energy Regulations Analysis
Customer Relations
Product Sales
Plant & Environmental Engineering
PRODUCTS ECONOMICS
Chemical Strategic Studies
Chemical Products Planning & Economics

Business Research
PRODUCTS--OTHER
    Emerging Businesses
    Biological Business Development
    Solar Energy Business Development
    Synfuels Business Development
TECHNICAL
    Technical Finance
    Construction Relations & Engineering Standards
    Plans & Analysis
    Engineering Products
    Site Development & General Facilities
    Engineering
    Research and Development--Oil/Synfuels
    Research and Development--Chemical Products
OTHER SHELL COMPANIES
    Pecten Chemicals, Inc.
    Saudi Petrochemical Company
    Shell Pipe Line Corporation
    Shell Communications, Inc.
    Shell Provident Fund & Pension Trust
    Shell Companies Foundation Incorporated
    Kernridge Oil Company Houston

III. REVIEW OF REFERENCE/SEARCH REQUESTS

An analysis of reference/search requests was completed for 1980 (see Appendix C [not included here]).

A. Requests Common to All Groups
    An analysis of requests indicated four general categories that were common to all groups serviced by the Library. They are: Biographies; Author Searches/Bibliographies; Addresses; Information on Various Businesses/Companies.

B. Subject Aspects by Groups
    [The numbers below in parentheses refer to company department codes which are not included in this policy.]
    In addition, reference/search requests focused on various aspects of two broad subjects: Energy, Business/Economics.

The exploration/production groups (25-28) focused on aspects of energy production, particularly oil and gas. Included were requests for information on exploration and production costs, drilling and well logging, recovery techniques, and other exploration/production procedures.

The operating departments (41-46) focused on methods of transportation and distribution, prices and costs, and government action in the areas of entitlement, windfall profits, and reserves.

The chemical products groups and business centers (63-69) directed their questions to specific products, such as epoxy resins, rubbers, lubricating oils, olefins, and others which Shell manufactures. In addition, requests were also made for prices and manufacturing processes.

The oil products groups (72-78) were primarily concerned with market, product, and sales information for gasoline and other fuels. Market research required statistics on automobile registrations, population, and competitors.

The technical groups (85-88) concentrated on manufacturing processes of plants, process systems for petroleum and chemicals, capacity, and consumption.

The administrative support groups tended to focus on the business aspects of the petroleum and chemical industries. Employee Relations (10) requested information on compensation plans, productivity, and wage and salary information.

The Financial Department (20) and the Information Center (21) emphasized a need for current information on accounting and auditing procedures, cash management techniques, and investment procedures.

The Corporate Planning Department (50) directed requests for information on the economy, oil industry forecasts, and capital formation.

Public Affairs (55) reflected a wide variety of topics in its requests. Subjects included were consumption and price statistics, coal gasification, government activities, and a large amount of biographical information.

The Purchasing and General Services departments (56-61) requested information on corporate land investments, office systems, van pools, work stations, and cost information for plants, equipment, and inventory.

IV. SUBJECT EMPHASIS OF COLLECTION

A. Introduction and Definitions of Levels of Emphasis

Based on the evaluations of Shell Oil's major activities (Section II.A.), the user groups (Section II.B.), the individual department reference/search requests (Appendix C), and the review of the New Acquisition List Library requests (Appendix D), each schedule of the Library of Congress Classification System (the method by which books are physically arranged) was examined and evaluated. Each schedule was assigned a level of development: primary, secondary, tertiary, or not applicable. The following are definitions of these levels:

Primary--of major importance; a majority of the subject emphasis is applicable on all levels (from basic to highly technical materials) and over an indefinite period of time.

Secondary--not as in-depth, extensive coverage as primary; the subjects of interest are those that support the primary emphasis.

Tertiary--area less relevant to the Library information needs; only small aspects of the total schedule are applicable.

Not applicable--the subject, overall, is not relative to Shell's information needs; some general reference works may be needed.

The following is an overall listing of the Library of Congress Classification System with the established level of emphasis:

A	General Works	Tertiary
B-BJ	Philosophy	Not applicable
BL-BX	Religion	Not applicable
C	Auxiliary Sciences of History	Not applicable
D	General and Old World History	Tertiary
E	America, United States	
F	United States Local History, British America, Dutch America, French America, Latin America, Spanish America	Not applicable Tertiary
G	Geography	Secondary
H	Social Sciences	Primary
J	Political Science	Tertiary

KD	Law of the United Kingdom and Ireland	Not applicable
KF	Law of the United States	Tertiary
L	Education	Not applicable
M	Music and Books on Music	Not applicable
N	Fine arts	Not applicable
P-PA	Philology, Linguistics	Not applicable
P-PH	Modern European Languages	Not applicable
PG	Russian Literature	Not applicable
PJ-PM	Asian, African Languages	Not applicable
PN-PZ	English, American, French, Spanish, German, Scandinavian Literatures	Not applicable
Q	Science	Secondary
R	Medicine	Not applicable
S	Agriculture	Not applicable
T	Technology	Primary
U	Military Science	Not applicable
V	Naval Science	Tertiary
Z	Bibliography & Library Science	Secondary

B. New Interest Areas

One of Shell's long-term objectives is to develop new business areas related to our current businesses. Part of the development process is the researching of potential areas to determine which will be of continuing importance to the company.

The Library has the advantage of being at the ground floor of new business areas due to its research function. The Library has a corresponding responsibility to provide the needed information on these topics even though they may not appear within the emphasized subject areas. Therefore, the collection development policy is not intended to be an unchangeable law or a hindrance in the Library's research function. The Library must reserve the ability to respond to requests in areas not specified in the policy as part of its efforts to fulfill its research responsibilities. Those topics which prove to be of continuing interest to the company will then be incorporated into the emphasized subject areas.

C. Selected Library of Congress Classification Schedules

The objective of the Library is not to purchase every book and magazine on the emphasized subjects but instead to have a substantial working collection. The schedules are intended to serve as guidelines to the staff members when ordering materials. When the Analysts consider an individual item, they usually do not know how the title will be cataloged. As a result, the Analysts order by the subject matter of the material rather than by an exact classification number. The Analysts make professional decisions when they determine that the subject(s) of the material correspond to the emphasized schedules and that the title is appropriate for addition to the collection.

Each primary, secondary, and tertiary section will now be shown in detail.

1. SCHEDULE A: GENERAL WORKS
   LEVEL OF COLLECTION DEVELOPMENT: TERTIARY
   SUBJECT EMPHASIS:
   The Library will be updating editions of general works which are included in Schedule A. Materials consist primarily of directories and almanacs that are not specific to any single subject or discipline. The sections of Schedule A which must be supported are:

   AE   Encyclopedias
   AS   Academies and Learned Societies (Information on Associations, Funds, Foundations, and Other Institutions)
   AY   Yearbooks, Almanacs, Directories (U.S. Almanacs, State of Texas Almanacs)

2. SCHEDULE D: GENERAL AND OLD WORLD HISTORY
   LEVEL OF COLLECTION DEVELOPMENT: TERTIARY
   SUBJECT EMPHASIS:
   The Library will be updating and maintaining a core collection of books on the countries in which Shell Oil has business interests. Also to be included are significant works on the political history and foreign relations of the countries. The developing business efforts of Shell may require information on countries in addition to those cited in this schedule.

   The following are the sections of Schedule D which have significance for the Library collection:

DS   Asia
DT   Africa
DU   Oceania

The following is a more detailed listing of these sections:

DS   Asia--Southwestern Asia. Ancient Orient. Near
            East.
DS 41-44.9 Iraq--General.
DS 67-70.8 Iraq--History. Antiquities, Description/Travel, etc.
DS 70.82-96 Iraq--Political History. Foreign Relations.
DS 79-79.8 Iraq--History. 1919 -
[Note: Listings for Syria, Saudi Arabia, Iran, etc.,and Schedules
F, G, etc. are omitted from this policy due to space limitations.]

V. SELECTION TOOLS

A. Periodicals
   1. Periodicals Recommended for Collection Development
      Review
      The following is an alphabetical listing of periodicals that
      contain book reviews of titles in areas of interest to the
      Library. The majority of periodicals review more than one
      book title per issue and give a basic amount of information
      concerning the content of the books.
             The emphasized Library of Congress Classification
      Schedules have been divided into four blocks for selection
      purposes. (See Section VI.)
             Each periodical has been assigned to a block(s) on the
      basis of its subject(s).
             The Roman numeral in parentheses after each periodical
      refers to its assignment block(s).
      -*American Libraries* (Monthly) (I, II, III, IV)
      -*American Petroleum Institute. Library Newsletter* (Monthly;
      lists recent additions to the API Library; covers books,
      reports, periodicals, microfiche, API publications, Senate
      and Congressional publications, recent SEC corporate
      filings, and annual reports; no reviews) (I, II, III, IV)
      -*ANSI Reporter* (Biweekly) (II)
      -*Best of Business Quarterly* (Quarterly) (III, IV)

-*Business Horizons* (Bimonthly, several titles reviewed each issue; vary in appropriateness; focus: business, economics, management, with an emphasis on controversial issues) (III, IV)

-*Business Information Alert* (Ten times/year) (I)

-*Business Library Newsletter* (Monthly) (I, II, III, IV)

-*Business Week* (Weekly; generally reviews only one title per issue; title listed on contents page for scanning; vary in appropriateness; focus: broad definition of business) (IV)

-*Chapter News* (Quarterly) (I)

-*Chemical Engineering* (Biweekly; amount and length vary; sometimes one title with a long review or several with short reviews; focus: broad topic range--pollution, reference works, optical fibers, carcinogens, and handbooks on processes) (I)

-*Chemical Engineering Progress* (Monthly; reviews do not appear in every issue; section mainly a listing of titles with critical comments on a few; focus: broad topic range--technical, computer equipment, management, and reference works) (I, II)

-*Chilton's I&CS* (Monthly; a few titles with short reviews; focus: equipment and control systems--computers, manufacturing management, measurements and control) (I, II)

-*Computer* (Monthly) (IV)

-*Database Programming and Design* (Monthly) (III, IV)

-*DBMS* (Monthly; 1-2 very extensive reviews and 2-4 one-paragraph reviews; focus: from as specific as using a commercial software package to as broad as office automation technologies and issues (III, IV)

-*EIA Publications. New Releases* (Biweekly; a three to four page listing of titles with a one sentence abstract; focus: energy supply; reserves; prices of oil, gas, and coal; electric, nuclear, and hydroelectric power) (I, II, III, IV)

-*Engineering Education* (Monthly) (II)

-*Fortune* (Biweekly; one title with long review; focus: broad view of business and economics--inside the new right, ethnic groups, economics, biographies of business greats) (III, IV)

-*Futurist* (Bimonthly) (I)

-*Harvard Business Review* (Bimonthly; many titles with short reviews; focus: broad view of business and management, human resources management, state owned enterprises, work design) (III, IV)

-*HR Magazine* (Monthly; one to three reviews per issue; focus: various aspects of human resource management) (I, II, IV)

-*High Technology* (Bimonthly; one to two lengthy reviews; focus: energy, engineering, interface between biology and technology, technology) (II)

-*IEEE Computer Society* (Bimonthly) (IV)

-*Industrial Engineering* (I)

-*Information Report* (Bimonthly; short profiles of recent government and related publications of interest to researchers and information groups) (I, II, III, IV)

-*Information Retrieval and Library Automation* (Monthly; lists new publications; no reviews; focus: information retrieval and library automation) (IV)

-*Information Technology and Libraries* (Quarterly; two to five book reviews) (IV)

-*Internal Auditor* (Monthly; 2-3 reviews per issue; focus: those topics of interest to internal auditing staff--white collar crime, management of audits, etc.) (III)

-*Journal for Quality and Participation* (Six times/Year) (I)

-*Journal of Canadian Petroleum Technology* (Bimonthly) (I, II)

-*Journal of Coatings Technology* (Monthly; most issues do not contain reviews; usually one title with long review; focus: all types of coatings) (I)

-*Journal of Energy and Development* (Semiannual; several titles with long reviews; focus: broad topics--international and national energy situation, political histories of oil countries, energy economics, energy future) (I, II, IV)

-*Journal of Loss Prevention in the Process Industries* (Quarterly) (I)

-*Journal of Systems Management* (Monthly; one page of reviews with two or three titles; focus: management of systems, computer languages, office automation) (III)

-*Librarians Newsletter* (Quarterly) (I, II, III, IV)

-*Library Currents* (Monthly) (IV)

-*Library Hi Tech News* (11 times/year) (III)

-*Library Journal* (Semimonthly; primarily a reviewing

journal with books arranged by subject areas) (I, II, III, and IV)

-*Library Software Review* (Semiannually; eight long reviews; focus: languages, handbooks, dictionaries, office automation, computer literacy)

-*Majors New Technical Book List* (Monthly; listing of new titles available from Majors Scientific Books, Inc.; focus: engineering, business, management, computers, chemistry, etc.) (I, II, III, IV)

-*Manageent Review* (Monthly; reviews vary--generally one long and many short reviews; focus: broad manage-ment topics--handbooks, manuals, problem solving, security, long-range planning, productivity, unions, whistle blowing, biographies of industry greats) (III, IV)

-*Marketing Library Services: MLS* (Eight times/year) (IV)

-*Mechanical Engineering* (Monthly; several titles; reviews vary in length; focus: broad topics--ocean engineering, handbooks, computer systems, pressure vessels, thermal energy, robotics) (I)

-*MEED* (Weekly; reviews appear in only one issue per month--usually the third or fourth week; reviews vary in length and number; focus: broad topics--current and historical political relations, overviews of countries, business and economic activities) (IV)

-*Motor Ship* (Monthly; several titles; reviews vary in length; focus: shipping industry--containers, vessel types, machinery and engines, service, reference works, fire safety) (III)

-*National Productivity* Review (I)

-*New and Forthcoming Books and Journals* (Monthly) (I, II, III, IV)

-*New Books* (Bimonthly; listing of many titles; arranged by subject) (I, II, III, IV)

-*New Technical Books* (Monthly; a descriptive list of recent titles acquired by the Science and Technology Research Center of the New York Public Library; focus: pure and applied physical sciences, mathematics, engineering, industrial technology, and related topics) (I, II, III, IV)

-*Newsweek* (Weekly) (III, IV)

-*Office* (Monthly; many short reviews; focus: business

[genera], equipment and management--programming, security, bond and money markets, future economic issues, running conferences and meetings) (III, IV)

-*Office Administration and Automation* (Monthly; 3-5 one-paragraph reviews; focus: management, office automation issues and technologies) (III, IV)

-*On-line Review* (Bimonthly; two to four book reviews and publication notices; focus: on-line information systems.) (IV)

-*On Q* (I)

-*PC: The Independent Guide to IBM Personal Computers* (Bimonthly) (III, IV)

-*PC Computing*

-*PC World* (Monthly) (III)

-*Personnel Journal* (Monthly; reviews not in every issue; many short reviews; focus: human resource management--job evaluation, management styles and techniques, productivity, running meetings, occupational stress, career planning, salary management) (III, IV)

-*Petroleum Economist* (Monthly; number varies; generally one or two sentence description of contents; focus: general international petroleum industry and economic aspects) (II, IV)

-*Petroleum Review* (Monthly; reviews not in every issue; many short reviews; focus: international petroleum industry--reference tools, handbooks, hydraulic and pneumatic equipment, disposal techniques for oil spills, pipeline, drilling equipment, energy availability, pollution and hazards, oil and gas) (II)

-*Pipeline and Gas Journal* (Monthly except semimonthly in April and June; reviews do not appear in every issue; several short reviews; focus: international energy topics--reference works, conference proceedings, examination preparation, data communications, heavy construction costs, energy future, fluid movers, equipment leasing, plant design, cranes and derricks) (I)

-*Planning Review* (Bimonthly) (III, IV)

-*Plastics World* (Monthly; inclusion means recommendation; many short reviews; titles can be repeated in several issues; focus: manufacture of plastic products, types of plastic products, processes) (I)

-*Productivity* (Monthly; one or two lengthy reviews; book reviews not in every issue; focus: productivity, burnout, worker participation) (III)

-*Quality Digest* (Monthly) (I)

-*Quality for Continuous Quality Improvement* (I)

-*Quality Progress* (Monthly) (III)

-*Recent Additions to the Baker Library* (Monthly; listing of many titles; no critical statements or abstracts; arranged by subject--accounting, business, energy resources, management, etc.; focus: subjects of interest to a graduate business school--broad view of business and economics) (I, II, III, IV)

-*RSR: Reference Services Review* (Quarterly) (I)

-*Rubber World* (Monthly; a few long reviews; focus: chemical industry--reference works, handbooks, proceedings, processes, carcinogens, composites) (I)

-*Science* (Weekly; a few long reviews; vary in appropriateness; focus: broad view of science--coming of the iron age, anthropology, sediments, interferon, women workers, health risks, animal behavior, biographies, weather) (II)

-*Sci-Tech News* (Quarterly; each issue contains a list of 10-20 new engineering journals, with bibliographic information only; a "new publications" list covering five to ten publications with annotations usually appears in each issue) (I, II)

-*Selected Acquisitions* (Monthly) (I, II, III, IV)

-*Shell UK Administrative Services. Central Information* (Weekly; 2 or 3 page listing of new books added to the Library; no abstracts or critical statements; no publisher information given; focus: business and energy--need to order selectively since the majority are British publications which would have to be ordered from overseas) (I, II, III, IV)

-*Soundview Summaries* (Thirty times/year; four to eight page summaries of new books; focus: business and management) (III, IV)

-*Special Libraries* (Quarterly; three to five reviews of professional library-related literature plus an annotated list of 8 to 15 recent publications in library/information field) (IV)

-*TAPPI* (Monthly; several reviews with varied lengths; vary in appropriateness; focus: pulp and paper industry--biomass conversion, directories, anodic protection, contaminants, surfactants, test methods) (I)

-*Tapping the Network Journal* (I)

-*Technology Review* (Eight times/year; can scan titles in table of contents; a few long reviews; vary in appropriateness; focus: broad view of technology--ecological basis of revolutionary change, mathematics catastrophe theory, societal risk assessment, physics, solar energy) (I, II)

-*Time* (Weekly) (III, IV)

-*Total Employment Involvement* (I)

-*Training* (Monthly) (IV)

-*Training and Development Journal* (Monthly; 5-7 book reviews per issue, each a paragraph in length; focus: all aspects of human resource management, including supervision, performance assessments, career planning) (I II, IV)

-*Trends in Analytical Chemistry* (10 times/year) (I)

-*U.S. Government Books* (Quarterly) (I, II, III, IV)

2. Determination of Additional Recommended Periodicals
As new periodical subscriptions are added, the titles will be examined to see if they contain book reviews and, if so, to see if the titles should be routed to an Analyst for collection development purposes. (See Section VIII.A. for procedure.)

B. Publishers' Catalogs And Flyers
Catalogs and flyers are the best source for announcements of newly published materials. Since a book review generally appears after the title has been available for several months to a year, the reviewing journals vary in coverage of recently published materials. Consequently, the Analysts rely on those catalogs and flyers to keep them aware of the newest titles from which they can select those of interest to Shell.

The Library receives a large number of unsolicited catalogs and flyers. Initially, a User Assistant sorts the catalogs and discards those which announce materials already in the collection. Then, each week a different Analyst will be responsible for reviewing that week's incoming catalogs and flyers regardless of subject matter, and can route any of the material, if necessary, to other Analysts.

C. Recommendations by Users
Library users frequently submit book and magazine titles for

purchase considerations. Each request is reviewed by an exempt staff member and the user is then notified of the resulting decision. The material is ordered when it is considered useful to the Library and/or to other departments within Shell.

VI. SELECTION PROCESS

A. Budget
The Library has a portion of the budget annually designated for materials acquisition. The responsibility of the collection development staff will be to follow the selection procedure and to stay within budgetary limits. Each month, a statement concerning the budget status will be routed to the staff to assist them in complying with the budget.

B. Selection Procedure--Overview
The exempt staff of the Information Retrieval (IR) group share the responsibility for ordering new materials and submit all orders to the Library Supervisor for approval. The selected Library of Congress Classification Schedules--designated primary, secondary, or tertiary (see Section IV)--are assigned to staff members on a rotating basis for six months at a time. The selection tools of recommended periodicals, publisher catalogs, and flyers (see Section V) are divided by subject and are routed to those staff members assigned the corresponding schedules. The staff members assigned the corresponding schedules. The staff then use the Schedules as guidelines in choosing appropriate books and magazines from the selection tools. The objectives of the procedure are to have an equal division of workload as well as to have a system that minimizes the effect of personal bias on collection development.

C. Assignment Blocks
1. Library of Congress Schedules
The following are the four assignment blocks of the Library of Congress Schedules:

Block I(A):
Schedule T: Technology (Primary) Sections:
TD   Environmental Technology. Sanitary Engineering
TH   Building Construction

      TJ   Mechanical Engineering and Machinery
      TP   Chemical Technology
      TS   Manufactures
      Schedule Q: Science (Secondary)

Block II (B):
      Schedule T: Technology (Primary) Sections:
      T   Technology--General
      TA   Engineering--General. Civil Engineering--General
      TC   Hydraulic Engineering
      TK   Electrical Engineering. Electronics.
      TL   Motor Vehicles. Aeronautics. Astronautics
      TN   Mining Engineering. Metallurgy
      Schedule G: Geography (Tertiary)
      Schedule J: Political Science (Tertiary)
      Schedule KF: Law of the United States (Tertiary)

Block III (C):
      Schedule H: Social Sciences (Primary) Sections:
      HE   Transportation and Communication
      HF   Commerce
      HG   Finance
      HJ   Public Finance
      Schedule V: Naval Science (Tertiary)

Block IV(D):
      Schedule H: Social Sciences (Primary) Sections:
      HA   Statistics
      HB   Economic Theory
      HC   National Production
      HD   Production. Land. Agriculture. Industry
      Schedule D: General and Old World History (Tertiary)
      Schedule Z: Bibliography and Library Science
      (Secondary)
      Schedule F: American History (Tertiary)
      Schedule A: General Works (Tertiary)

2. Periodicals
    The following are the recommended periodicals matched
    with the Schedule Assignment blocks:

Block I:
- *American Libraries* (M)
- *Business Library Newsletter* (M)
- *Chapter News* (Q)
- *Chemical Engineering* (BW)
- *Chemical Engineering Progress* (M)
- *Chilton's I&CS* (M)
- *Industrial Engineering* (M)
- *Journal for Quality and Participation* (6/year)
- *Journal of Canadian Petroleum Technology* (BM)
- *Journal of Coatings Technology* (M)
- *Journal of Energy and Development* (SA)
- *Journal of Loss Prevention in the Process Industries* (Q)
- *Mechanical Engineering* (M)
- *National Productivity Review* (Q)
- *On Q* (M)
- *Quality Digest* (M)
- *Quality for Continuous Quality Improvement* (Q)
- *Plastics World* (M)
- *RSR: Reference Services Review* (Q)
- *Rubber World* (M)
- *Sci-tech News* (Q)
- *TAPPI* (M)
- *Tapping the Network Journal* (Q)
- *Technology Review* (8/year)
- *The Futurist see Futurist* (BM)
- *Total Employee Involvement* (10/year)
- *Trends in Analytical Chemistry* (10/year)
- *U.S. Government Books* (Q)

Block II:
- *American Libraries* (M)
- *ANSI Reporter* (BW)
- *Business Library Newsletter* (M)
- *Chemical Engineering Progress* (M)
- *Chilton's I&CS* (M)
- *Electrical World* (M)
- *Engineering Education* (M)
- *High Technology* (BM)
- *Journal of Canadian Petroleum Technology* (BM)

Journal of Energy and Development (SA)
Materials Performance (M)
Petroleum Economist (M)
Petroleum Review (M)
Pipeline and Gas Journal (M)
Research Management (M)
Science (W)
Sci-tech News (Q)
Technology Review (8/year)
U.S. Government Books (Q)
Welding Journal (M)

Block III:
A. I. Expert (M)
American Libraries (M)
Best of Business Quarterly (Q)
Business Horizons (BM)
Business Library Newsletter (M)
Database Programming and Design (M)
DBMS (M)
Fortune (BW)
Harvard Business Review (BM)
HR Magazine (M)
Internal Auditor (BM)
Journal of Systems Management (M)
Library Hi Tech News (M)
Management Review (M)
Motor Ship (M)
Newsweek (W)
Office (M)
Office Administration and Automation (M)
PC: The Independent Guide to IBM Personal
Computers   (BM)
PC World (M)
Personnel Journal (M)
Planning Review (BM)
Productivity (M)
Quality Progress (M)
Soundview Summaries (30/year)
Time (W)

Training and Development Journal (M)
U.S. Government Books (Q)

Block IV:
American Libraries (M)
Best of Business (SA)
Business Horizons (BM)
Business Library Newsletter (M)
Business Week (W)
Computer (M)
Database Programming and Design (M)
DBMS (M)
Fortune (BW)
Harvard Business Review (BM)
HR Magazine (M)
IEEE Software (BM)
Information Retrieval and Library Automation (M)
Information Technology and Libraries (Q)
Journal of Energy and Development (SA)
Journal of Information and Image Management (M)
Library Currents (M)
Library Software Review (SA)
Management Review (M)
Marketing Library Services: MLS (8/year)
MEED (W)
Newsweek (W)
Office (M)
Office Administration and Automation (M)
On-line Review (SM)
PC: The Independent Guide to IBM Personal
Computers   (BM)
Personnel Journal (M)
Petroleum Economist (M)
Planning Review (BM)
Soundview Summaries (30/year)
Special Libraries (Q)
Time (W)
Training (M)
Training and Development Journal (M)
U.S. Government Books (Q)

3. Collection Development Periodicals

Most of the following titles are subscribed to solely for the purpose of collection development. Due to their multidisciplinary nature, all collection development staff will be on the routing for each title.

American Book Publishing Record (M)
American Libraries (M)
American Petroleum Institute Library Newsletter (M)
Business Library Newsletter (M)
EIA Publications. New Releases (M)
Information Report (BM)
Librarians Newsletter (Q)
Library Journal (SM)
Majors New Technical Book List (M)
New and Forthcoming Books and Journals (M)
New Technical Books (M)
Recent Additions to Baker Library (M)
Selected Acquisitions (M)
Shell UK Administrative Services. Central Information (Weekly)
U. S. Government Books (Q)
U .S. Government Printing Office. New Books (BM)

D. Deacquisitions

1. Books

It is recommended that the book collection be evaluated every five years. The mechanism used will depend on the type of data available or useable at the time. Analysts will be responsible for deacquisition decisions. Books purchased within the last three years will automatically be retained when the collection is evaluated.

Past circumstances have caused portions of the collection to be evaluated. Due to the Library joining RLIN (Research Libraries Information Network) in 1978, the book collection was evaluated and only the titles that remained in the collection were entered into the data base.

The establishment of the Woodcreek Library in 1981 resulted in the Vertical File material being separated and weeded. The book collection was also separated by subject and a portion of the collection was transferred to the Woodcreek Library.

Since the collection has been reviewed in various segments as outlined above, it is recommended that the book collection be weeded again in its entirety in 1985-86 and, thereafter, every five years.

A retention procedure has been established for the Reference Collection. All titles that have regularly appearing editions now have retentions set and disposition determined for the copies of earlier editions.

The following are the criteria to be used in evaluating the collection:

1. Frequency of use.
2. Subject (i.e., is the subject still relevant to the needs and interests of the Library's clientele?).
3. Alternative availability (i.e., is the item available elsewhere locally or regionally?).
4. Special features (i.e., is there something peculiar to the item which makes it worth retaining? E.g., photographs, tables?).
5. Status in history of the subject (i.e., is it a classic, landmark, monument in development of the field?).
6. Date (i.e., is the information still considered valid? Has the Library anything more current? Is the item of historical interest?).
7. Physical state of the item.
8. Language (foreign languages are collected sparingly).
9. Is it a reprint of something already in the collection?

2. Magazines

Magazine retention is set by an Analyst when a new periodical subscription is received. As issues exceed the set retention dates for an individual title, they are removed from the collection and discarded. The Consolidated Periodicals Holdings List is an alphabetical list of titles received by all the Houston Shell libraries and contains the retentions set for the Central Library's journals.

Retention for an individual title can be changed if requests indicate a need for reevaluation.

VII. QUANTITATIVE MEASUREMENT

A. Number of New Items by Call Number

To ensure that the purchasing pattern is following the subject emphasis as described by this policy, a correlation should be made between the number of books ordered and the call numbers assigned to the books using the Library of Congress Classification Schedules. The measurement should be done every five years for books ordered during that period. (The first review should be four years after policy is implemented to mesh with other reviews. The current plans are for implementation in 1982; therefore, first review should be during 1986.)

The new books will be tabulated by the first two letters of the Library of Congress call number. For example, all the HA's, JB's, etc., will be given an individual total: HA's, HB-20; maintain conformity with the non-applicable area definition. (See Section IV.A.) A total will also be calculated for each schedule overall: H-120; Z-25; etc. These overall schedule totals will then be converted to percentages to determine if the schedules designated as primary actually have the largest percentages and if the secondary and tertiary schedules have correspondingly smaller percentages.

Percentages that reflect the schedule designations of primary, secondary, and tertiary will confirm that the collection development selections follow the guidelines established in this policy.

If the results do not totally reflect the schedule designations, the schedules involved will be examined to determine if the Library's needs have changed and require a different subject emphasis. If that is the case, the policy will be revised to reflect the new subject emphasis.

An additional reason for a discrepancy between the percentages and the designated schedules could be the Library's research function as part of Shell's efforts to develop new business areas (see Section IV.B.). Satisfying research requests on these potential areas may require expenditures for materials in non-emphasized subjects. Upon completion of the research phase, the subject then may or may not be of continuing interest to Shell. If the topic is of continuing importance, it will be incorporated into the emphasized subject areas and the policy will be revised accordingly.

If the above circumstances do not explain why the percentages do not reflect the schedule designations, the collection development staff will be instructed to alter their selections to conform with the policy.

B. Cost of New Items by Call Number

An additional quantitative measurement, correlating cost of new books to call numbers assigned to the books, is desirable but not feasible at this time. It is planned that the future acquisition module of ACCIS (Acquisition, Cataloging, Circulation, INQUIRE System) will be written to provide the capability to generate this data. The data would be compared to the policy as in the preceding measurement, ensuring that expenditure amounts and percentages conform to the policy. The correlation procedure will be added to the policy upon completion of the acquisition module.

VIII. PROCEDURES FOR REVISION OF THE COLLECTION DEVELOPMENT POLICY

In an effort to keep the policy viable and reflective of the information needs of the Library, the policy will need to periodically be reviewed.

A. Periodicals Review

Policy corrections may be necessary due to changes in the recommended periodicals.

1. Canceled/Ceased/Changes

If a periodical is canceled or ceases publication, a "Periodical Canceled" or "Periodical Ceased" form (Appendix E or F) is completed and routed to the Library staff. If a periodical title changes, a "Periodical Changes" form (Appendix G) is completed and routed. A designated User Assistant, upon receiving one of the above forms, checks the listing of recommended titles to see if any are affected. If so, the User Assistant is responsible for updating the policy in all appropriate sections (V.A.T., VI.C.2) and having the changes made by the Corporate Correspondence Center.

2. New Periodical Subscriptions

Each new periodical subscription has a "New Periodical Form" (Attachment H) completed by various Library staff members. In the Analyst portion of the form, an Analyst will check yes or no by "Book reviews" to indicate the presence or absence of book reviews. If present, an Analyst will examine the periodical and its book reviews. If the periodical covers a subject of primary, secondary, or tertiary importance to the collection and if the reviews are determined to be useful for selection purposes, the title is assigned to the Analyst(s) who have responsibility for ordering in that subject area.

A User Assistant is responsible for updating the policy in all appropriate sections (V.A.T., VI.C.2) and having the changes made by the Corporate Correspondence Center.

B. Requests Review

It was originally intended that every five years, a compilation should be made of the search requests of the previous year to determine if areas of emphasis should be changed. Instead of above review, a collection development review procedure was developed in 1986 in which a searcher evaluates each search request and determines if material to fill the request should be added to the collection. If a specific item is identified, an order is placed for the item after review by the Section Supervisor. If no specific material is identified, the request is reviewed by the Section Supervisor and is further handled in one of two ways. If the request was completed by a User Assistant, the request is forwarded to the Analyst responsible for the appropriate collection development subject block. If the request was handled by an Analyst, it is returned to that Analyst. In both situations, the Analyst reviews junk mail and collection development journals for appropriate materials. A file of these requests will be kept by the Section Supervisor. A review of these requests will be included as part of regular policy review since information from the search requests used in conjunction with the section on Shell activities would determine if a subject should be deemphasized or if it has increased in importance in collection development.

C Policy Review

The policy should be examined totally every five years to

determine if major changes need to be made in the portions dealing with Shell activities, the Library of Congress Classification Schedules (reviewing for deletions and additions), the selection procedures, the quantitative measure procedures, and the revision procedures. An exempt staff member should coordinate the activity. The first policy review should be conducted during late 1986 or early 1987.

APPENDIX A
Photocopy Review Form--Omitted

APPENDIX B
GIFT POLICY

Gifts are unordered publications given to ILS by Shell employees. (Unordered publications from sources outside Shell are handled by procedures for Unidentified Material.) Gifts usually arrive in the mail and often the sender is unidentified. The material is removed from envelopes and boxes by the mail person, sorted to remove periodicals and items belonging to ILS Reports or other information groups, and placed on the shelf marked "Gifts to Be Reviewed."

An Analyst reviews the gifts on a regular basis, preferably weekly. The gifts are sorted into three groups according to their value: Keep; Place on Giveaway Shelf; or Discard Immediately. Items which meet criteria outlined in Shell's Collection Development Policy should be kept if they are less than two years old. Older items which meet the criteria should be kept only if they have historical value or will be used to answer search requests, since they will not be put on the New Acquisition List and made available for routine circulation.

The Analyst gives items which are to be added to ILS' collection to the Cataloging Assistant. The titles are searched in ACCIS, RLIN and pending binders to see if the material is already owned or on order. If the title is found in any of these places, the Circulation Clerk checks the shelves and System 6 to see if it is needed as a second copy. If not needed, the publication is placed on the "Gifts Reviewed--Discard" shelf. If needed, the publication is returned to the Cataloging Section with a note to make it Copy 2.

Items not wanted in ILS' collection but of possible interest to other Shell employees are placed by the Analyst on the shelf marked "Gifts Reviewed--Discard." These are picked up weekly by the VOE, stamped on the title page with the note "Removed from ILS Collection" and dated. They are then placed on the shelf marked "Giveaways--Help Yourself" to be taken by anyone who wants them. Items which have not been taken in a month should be removed from the shelf and discarded.

Items which the Analyst does not want in ILS' collection and which appear to be of little value to others due to age or content are discarded immediately by placing in the trash can. (Generally, the majority of gifts fall in this category.) The senders are not notified when gifts are discarded unless they have attached a note asking to be called if the items are not wanted.

APPENDIX C
1980 Reference/Search Requests--Omitted

APPENDIX D
REVIEW OF NEW ACQUISITION LIST LIBRARY REQUESTS

Period: July 1979 - October 1980
New Acquisition Lists #78-89
Number of Titles Reviewed--816

The usage statistics for items appearing on New Acquisition Lists No. 78-89 were examined to discern patterns of usage by subject category and by department. In Part I items were ranked by number of requests: Highly Requested (10 or more requests), Moderately Requested (3-9), and Rarely Requested (0-2).

In Part II departments were identified that rarely requested items from New Acquisition Lists. Other activities (search requests, user assistance requests, and photocopy requests) for those departments were examined to determine if their information needs were met by other sources.

When trends appeared in either section, conclusions have been noted and recommendations regarding collection development and promotional activities were made.

I. REVIEW BY SUBJECT AREA

A. GENERAL CONCLUSIONS--ALL SUBJECT AREAS

1. Books for the non-specialist have high usage. These include introductions to technical subjects as well as overviews of petroleum energy subjects. They are excellent for Shell newcomers and nontechnical persons, such as auditors who will audit certain departments and need background.
2. Topics applicable to the individual are also among the most popular, from life planning to a writing guide for engineers.
3. The source of a publication can affect usage. A Kiplinger study (a forecast for the 1980's) had 82 requests. A Harvard Business School study had the largest readership in "Energy and Resources" while a map of pipelines by *Oil and Gas Journal* was among the most popular of the "Transportation" category. Certain publishers, corporate sources, and authors will always be requested.
4. The economic aspects of most subjects, technical or otherwise, are highly requested. This may include planning, forecasting, or efficiency.
5. While there are exceptions, technical books are not generally requested from the list. (Analysts do, however, use them for search requests and thus while they may not be used for current awareness or general reading, this does not mean they are not being used.)
6. Conference proceedings are rarely requested. (However, it is useful to have these in the collection since citations for them are often retrieved online, especially in engineering.)

B. SUBJECT AREA--BUSINESS AND ECONOMICS
Number of Titles Reviewed--241

Highly Requested Topics
1. Management
   a. People aspect--interrelationships, motivation, productivity, team building, communication, and behaviorism.
   b. Theory--how to succeed as a manager, how to make organizations work.
   c. Handling change--how jobs can be redesigned.

2. Planning and forecasting--sources of information and techniques for strategic planning, e.g., *Corporate Planning: Techniques and Applications* (14), *Industrial Products Forecaster* (11).
3. Mathematics, statistical analysis, and economic analysis as related to management (however, programming and computers were not popular).
4. Personal success--managing time, strategy for success, handling stress.
5. Some aspects of economic theories--why economies fail, money market, real estate market.
6. Finance was both very high, e.g., *The Guide to Understanding Financial Statements* (22) and *How to Interpret Financial Reports* (37), and very low, e.g., *The Financial System* (2).
7. Risk management--especially stock and bond returns.
8. Management consulting--only one book had 11 requests.

Moderately Requested Topics
1. Accounting--had an average range of four to six requests per title. Most lists contained some titles.
2. Marketing--had a range of five to seven/title. Very few appeared on lists.
3. Regional discussions of various types of industries in other countries were variable: Canadian Manufacturing (1), Saudi Arabian Oil (7).
4. Sources of business statistics, variable: World Trade in Steel (0), Area Wage Surveys (7).

Rarely Requested Topics
1. Computers/systems applications to business (0-3 range).
2. International issues, including international trade, global interdependence, international business strategy and especially multinational companies: Multinationals in Contention (1), Human Resources Management in the Multinational Company (2).
3. Foreign financial topics--Foreign Exchanges (0), Foreign Investments and Political Risks (1).
4. Labor--Labor Outlook '30 (1), Unionized Construction Workers Are More Productive (1).

5. Management was not automatically requeste--Management of Production Technology (0).

Conclusions/Recommendations

1. Management books stressing communication/relationships will continue to be popular.
2. The different aspects of productivity (measuring, predicting) should continue to be ordered--more than just the human angle, but the cost angle and the construction/design angle.
3. Titles dealing with the future on both the corporate scale and the national scale are consistently requested (although not the international scale). Books on planning/predicting in both business and the economy are always relevant.
4. Since management is multi disciplinary in nature, it makes sense to continue purchasing different types of topics addressed to the manager--math for, economic analysis for, etc.
5. Accounting books are being ordered regularly--perhaps fewer should be purchased since they are not highly requested.
6. Very few marketing books appear--perhaps more titles in that area should be ordered.
7. Conference proceedings, symposiums, etc., are very rarely requested. Purchasing of them as well as business statistics books is probably justified but listing them on the NAL should be evaluated.
8. Since practical books on interpreting financial reports had high readership, perhaps more should be added in that area.

[APPENDIX E (Periodicals Canceled Form), APPENDIX F (Periodical Ceased Form), APPENDIX G (Periodical Changes Form), APPENDIX H (New Periodicals Form), and all ATTACHMENTS are omitted in this book due to space limitations.]

TARLTON LAW LIBRARY
SCHOOL OF LAW
THE UNIVERSITY OF TEXAS AT AUSTIN
Austin, Texas

PART 1--INTRODUCTION

The primary responsibility of the Tarlton Law Library is to develop a collection to support and anticipate the curricular and research needs of the faculty and students of the University of Texas School of Law. As one of the major academic law libraries in the country, the Tarlton Law Library maintains a research collection of primary and secondary United States legal materials and a rapidly growing collection of foreign and international legal materials. Recognizing that law has become increasingly interdisciplinary in the past several decades, the Library has a substantial collection of basic reference and research materials in fields as diverse as economics, history, political science, philosophy, ethics, human rights, and biotechnology. As an aid in acquiring materials, the Library maintains faculty profiles which help keep it apprised of faculty teaching and research interests.

As computer-based information becomes more pervasive and more accessible, the Library has begun to develop programs to coordinate its traditional collection development activities to take into account the increasingly important role that electronic format materials will play in the coming decade. The Library collects, as the opportunities present themselves, law-related rare books of a unique or otherwise historically significant nature. Selection decisions for rare books are made on a title-by-title basis.

PART 2-- GENERAL POLICIES

I. MATERIALS SELECTION
Final responsibility for the development and maintenance of the Library collection rests with the Director of Research in consultation with the law faculty, Library staff, law students, and other Library user groups.

Selection of new acquisitions is determined by the Director of Research, the Associate Director and professional members of the public services staff. Materials concern international and comparative law, foreign jurisdictions, religious law and historic legal systems are selected by the Foreign and International Law Librarian.

A variety of sources is consulted in the selection process. Publishers' brochures and catalogues, trade publications such as *Publishers Weekly* and *Choice*, book reviews and slip services provided by Midwest Library Service and W.H. Everett are screened for titles of possible interest. A monthly compilation of titles requested through interlibrary loan is also reviewed for selection purposes.

II. SELECTION GUIDELINES
Factors considered in selecting materials for purchase include:
1. Relevance to the law school's program of study;
2. Comprehensiveness of holdings with comparable subject matter;
3. Reputation of the author and publisher/producer;
4. Currency, accuracy, and comprehensiveness of the work;
5. Access via remote indexing and bibliographical databases;
6. Availability of alternate formats (microform, online, etc.);
7. Initial purchase price and maintenance costs;
8. Maintenance requirements (shelving space, filing requirements, bibliographic control).

III. FORMATS AND SPECIAL COLLECTIONS
A. Microforms and audio-visual materials
Selection of microforms is based on the value of providing duplication of heavily used print materials and the cost and availability of corresponding print format.

Emphasis is placed on acquiring reproductions of archival and government document collections, newspapers, bar journals, and federal and state statutory and judicial materials. Silver halide microfiche is the preferred format. The sole exception applies to newspapers, acquired in 35mm positive vesicular format.

The Library's collection of video cassettes is comprised of two components. Recordings of significant events and broadcasts related to the judiciary and legal education videos at both the student and practitioner level form a core collection. In addition, feature films depicting trial scenes, featuring characters portraying members of the legal profession, or containing themes germane to the public perception of the law are collected. Because cinematic lawyers have shaped the way Americans think about the legal profession--and even influenced the behavior of lawyers themselves--the Library attempts to thoroughly document the cinematic portrayal of law. Only video cassettes available in ½ inch VHS format are acquired. Audio cassette recordings of CLE programs and AALS and AALL seminars and workshops are selectively collected.

B. Electronic format
The Library subscribes to the online services from both West Publishing Company and Mead Data Central. This duplication provides students training on two different search software programs. The Library also maintains subscriptions to Dialog and DataTimes.

Databases in CD-ROM format form a growing component of the collection. The Library subscribes to Legal Trac, Academic Index, Martindale-Hubbel, and the Matthew Bender Tax Service on CD-ROM. The West Publishing CD-ROM Libraries are available for use in the Computer Assisted Legal Research Lab.

Selection of titles in electronic format is based upon several determinations, including cost, access, and ease-of-use. In some cases, the Library may need to acquire materials in other electronic and print formats.

Cost. Online versions of non-legal indexes and newspapers may be cheaper than hard copy where the anticipated charges for searching are less than the hard copy subscription cost. Publications available on LEXIS/NEXIS or WESTLAW are essentially cost-free since the subscription price to these databases has already been justified. CD-ROM products usually cost more than hard copy versions because CD-ROM is for unlimited use. The costs for CD-ROMs such as Legal Trac and Martindale-Hubbel can be justified on the basis that these products provide enhanced search capabilities over their hard copy counterparts.

Access. Because only law students and faculty have access to the Library's WESTLAW and LEXIS/NEXIS terminals, the Library duplicates materials in hard copy and electronic format when such duplication is the only way to provide access to needed information to public patrons. For example, the Library maintains a core collection of print Shepard's for public use even though Shepard's is available on WESTLAW and LEXIS.

Ease-of-use. Electronic media in the Library are almost exclusively for end-user searching. Difficult searching software, the need to change disks, the inability to down-load searches, etc., are reasons to decide against electronic format even where the access and price criteria have been met.

C. Rare books
Rare books are selectively acquired on a title by title basis when funding permits. Selection decisions are based on a review of antiquarian book dealer lists and notifications. Emphasis is placed on materials concerning Texas and Anglo-American law.

D. Litigated Literature
The Library maintains a unique collection of materials that have been subject to libel actions, to private or governmental censorship, or other types of litigation (e.g., copyright). Located in the Library's Rare Books Room, the "Litigated Literature" collection includes materials as diverse as the Bible and *Lady Chatterly's Lover*. Because the materials in the collection include historical as well as contemporary materials, scholars can use the collection to trace the changing environment and climate of censorship in all of its forms. The Library continues to collect materials that may be of value to scholars and researchers in this area.

The Library limits access to this non-circulating collection to faculty, scholars, attorneys, and students researching first-amendment matters. Because the materials are located in the Rare Books Room, they are not available to or accessible by the casual Library patron.

E. Fiction
Fiction titles are collected along the thematic guidelines established for feature film selection and also include books written by lawyers and judges. The coverage is broader than the traditional "law and literature" concern with the treatment of legal themes by legal writers. The Library's fiction collection attempts to systematically represent the role of law and lawyers in popular culture; an

important genre collected for this purpose is the "legal mystery."
Humorous works dealing with the law are also acquired.

IV. DUPLICATION
A minimum of three copies of all components of the National
Reporter System are acquired. Multiple sets of federal and Texas
statutory compilations and administrative regulations are also
maintained. Duplicates of other materials are collected in accordance with guidelines established under the AALS Bylaw Sec. 8.5.

V. RETENTION GUIDELINES
In general, superseded volumes, pocket parts and pamphlet
supplementation are not retained. Superseded sources of primary
law, especially Texas and federal statutes, are permanently
retained for historical research.

VI. ACQUISITIONS ARRANGEMENTS
The Library maintains a variety of non-title-specific arrangements
to facilitate the acquisitions process and insure the comprehensiveness of holdings for selected imprints. Standing orders with
recognized publishers provide for the automatic shipment of new
titles without purchase order generation. Package plans are
arranged in conjunction with the publishers' guidelines for selected
publication categories. When feasible, arrangements are negotiated to permit full return privileges and maximum discounting.

Institutional and personal memberships in the name of the
Director of Research allow for the acquisition of materials otherwise
unavailable to the Library. Organizations concerned with legal
education, human rights, international law, and library and
information science are emphasized.

The Library is a selective depository of the United States GPO
and a full depository of the European Communities. Six of the
seventeen categories of United Nations publications are selected.
Overall standing orders for all Council of Europe and Organization
of American States English-language publications are maintained.

VII. GIFTS AND EXCHANGES
Gifts from donors outside the law school are accepted at the
discretion of the Head of Reference Services and reviewed for
possible accession to the collection. An extensive collection of

duplicate materials is maintained to provide for replacement copies and for possible sale.

Most publication exchanges involve foreign law schools and bar associations. Exchange offers are evaluated by the Foreign and International Law Librarian and forwarded to the Acquisitions Librarian for formalization and maintenance. Agreements are arranged based on the reputation of the initiating institution, the equal value of exchanged publications, and the cost and availability of offered publications through commercial channels.

PART 3–DETAILED COLLECTION DEVELOPMENT POLICY

I. INTRODUCTION

For the purpose of this Collection Development Policy, the Library's collection activities can be analyzed by jurisdiction and subject area. This part of the Library's Collection Development Policy is organized along the following juris-dictional and subject divisions.

United States
Other common law jurisdictions
Germany, France, Belgium, Spain, Italy, Switzerland
Other countries in Western Europe
Eastern Europe and the Soviet Union
Mexico, Central and South America
Asia, Africa, and the Middle East
Ancient law
Religious law
Public international law
International business transactions

The Library does not collect with equal intensity in all areas. To help describe the Library's current level of collection intensity, this Policy uses the descriptors formulated by the Research Libraries Group to characterize collection activity. The descriptors are:

0   Out of scope: The Library does not collect in this area.

1   Minimal level: A jurisdiction or subject in which few selections are made beyond basic works.

2   Basic information level: A collection or service capability of up-
to-date general materials which will aid readers' immediate
understanding of a subject and will serve to introduce readers
to the subject and to other sources of available information.
Such a collection might include a dictionary, encyclopedia,
handbook or texts, or a combination of these, in the minimum
number which will serve the purpose. A basic information
collection is not sufficiently intensive to support instruction in
any course in the subject area involved.

3   Instructional support level: A collection or service capability
which is adequate to support instruction in law and research at
the J.D. level. It usually consists of a selection of reference tools,
an extensive collection of primary legal materials and documents, the most important monographs, and a selection of the
outstanding journals in the field. The reference tools and
fundamental bibliographic apparatus of legal research are
included. One or more indexing and abstracting services may
be included. Historical material need not be retained. The
emphasis is on building current and representative collections
adequate to maintain knowledge of a subject for limited or
generalized purposes but less than scholarly research.
Furthermore, such a collection will support the daily research needs of most practicing attorneys.

4   Research level: A collection or service capability which
includes all materials and information required for faculty and
graduate law student instruction and research, including
dissertations, graduate papers, and independent research. It
allows for an expansion of the faculty and advanced student
research programs in any way these may develop in the future.
It includes the major published source materials required for
independent research, all basic reference works, and a wide
selection of monographs, as well as a very extensive collection
of journals and major indexing and abstracting services in the
field. Older material is retained for historical research.

5   Comprehensive level: A collection which in a library endeavors, so far as is reasonably possible, to include all significant   works   of   recorded   knowledge   (publications,

manuscripts, other forms), in all applicable languages, for a necessarily defined and limited field. This level of collecting intensity is one that maintains a "special collection"; the aim, if not the achievement, is exhaustiveness. Older materials are retained for historical research. In describing the Library's collecting intensity the following language indicators are used as appropriate to describe the materials collected:

E = English language primarily;
F = Selected foreign language material;
W = Wide selection of languages;
Y = One foreign language predominates

II. UNITED STATES
A. Primary sources
1. Federal

The Library has a comprehensive level (4E) collection of primary federal materials, including legislative, judicial, and executive materials. The collection consists of commercially published materials as well as materials available to the Library through the United States Depository program.

a. Legislative materials

The Library acquires and retains all federal session laws, official and unofficial statutory codifications, congressional hearings, reports, and prints. The Library also collects commercially compiled legislative histories of major legislation. The Library provides access to the legislative materials through numerous indexes including various CIS indexes and the Monthly Catalog.

b. Judicial materials

The Library acquires all official and unofficial reports available for each of the various federal courts with the exception of those of the Supreme Court, the Library does not acquire slip opinions. The Library acquires, both in hard copy and microform, the Records and Briefs of the Supreme Court and the transcribed oral arguments before the Supreme Court in microfiche.

c. Administrative and executive materials

The Library acquires administrative materials available through the GPO depository program, including the Federal Register and the Code of Federal Regulations, as well as opinions, reports, rulings, and annual reports of various federal agencies. For many agencies, the Library acquires commercially published looseleaf services reporting the current activities of the agency. The Library receives executive documents through the depository program.

2. State materials

The Library has a research level (4E) collection of primary materials for each of the 50 states and the District of Columbia available in print, microform, and electronic format. The Library's collection of primary Texas legal materials approaches the comprehensive level (5E).

a. Legislative materials

The Library subscribes to the official and many of the unofficial codes of each of the states and territories; these subscriptions are kept current through legislative session services. Until 1982 the Library acquired all state session laws in print format; after that date the Library began to acquire state session laws on microfiche. The Library subscribes to the Texas session law in print format as well as microfiche.

b. Judicial materials

The Library acquires all available official state reporters alone with the National Reporter System region reporters. The Library acquires the slip opinions of the Texas Supreme Court, the Texas Court of Criminal Appeals, and the Texas Courts of Appeals and the Records and Briefs of cases argued before the Texas Supreme Court.

c. Administrative and executive materials

Until the mid-1980s, the Library acquired the administrative codes from each state. The Library currently subscribes only to the administrative code and register for Texas. State administrative codes are now being added to the WESTLAW and LEXIS databases. Currently, the codes of California, Florida,

Kansas, Minnesota, Ohio, and Pennsylvania are available, and eventually, all administrative codes will be available.

B. Secondary materials
1. Periodicals
The Library subscribes to all journals published by ABA-accredited law schools as well as significant journals from commercial publishers, professional organizations, and learned societies. The Library also subscribes to various legal newspapers and state bar publications.

The Library subscribes to to *Legal Periodical Index* and the *Current Law Index* (print, CD-ROM, and online versions) as well as various other indexes, including PAIS.

2. Subject texts, treatises, and looseleaf services
a. Hornbooks, nutshells, and casebooks
The Library endeavors to collect all hornbooks and nutshells, and casebooks used in Law School courses. The Library will add casebooks not used in Law School courses only when it receives them as gifts.

b. Treatises and looseleafs
Subject to budgetary constraints, the Library endeavors to acquire subject-specific treatises and looseleaf services that are deemed necessary to support the curricular and research needs of the faculty and students. As a general policy, the Library does not acquire treatises and looseleaf services that are likely to be of interest primarily to practitioners.

SUBJECT AREAS

While the Library collects in all law and law-related fields, it does not do so with uniform intensity. The following list provides a quantitative description of the Library's current collecting intensity by subject.

Subject	Collecting Intensity
Administrative law	3
Admiralty	2
Agency and partnership	3

Agricultural law	2
Alternative dispute resolution	5
American Indian law	3
Antitrust & trade regulation	3
Aviation law	3
Banking law	3
Bankrupt	3
Biotechnology and the law	5
Civil procedure (federal)	3
Civil rights	4
Commercial law	3
Communications law	4
Computer law	4
Conflict of laws	4
Constitutional law (federal)	4
Consumer law	3
Contracts	3
Copyright and trademark	3
Corporations	4
Criminal law and procedure	3
Education law	3
Employment discrimination	3
Entertainment law	4
Environmental law	3
Estates and trusts	5
Evidence	3
Family law	4
Federal courts	4
Food, drug & cosmetics law	1
Government contract law	0
Health care law	3
Immigration law	3
Insurance law	3
Judicial administration	4
Jurisprudence	4
Labor law	3
Land use	4
Law & economics	3
Law & psychiatry	4
Law and science/technology	5

Law office management	3
Legal education	4
Legal history	4
Legal profession	3
Legal research	5
Legal writing	4
Legislation	3
Local government	2
Military justice	3
Natural resources	3
Oil & gas law	4
Patents	3
Poverty law	4
Products liability	3
Property	3
Public utilities law	3
Securities relation	3
Sociology of law	3
Torts	4
Trademarks	3
Transportation law	3
Trial and appellate advocacy	4
Workers compensation	3

The methodology used in assessing collecting intensity involved the following procedures:

1. Verifying correct Library of Congress subject headings for each area;
2. Performing a subject search on the RLIN database in both the Book and Serials file for each subject heading;
3. Qualifying search results in each file to retrieve only clusters published after 1984, thereby establishing a universe for each subject area;
4. Qualifying search results a second time to retrieve only records with a Tarlton Law Library (DCUL) identifier.

Data for steps 3 and 4 were tabulated into percentages (i.e., percent of clusters with a TUUL record within a given universe) and the results for the Books and Serials files averaged. Based on a manual review of search results of four subject areas selected at random, tabulations for each subject area were adjusted to account for multiple clusters for single bibliographic entities and for entries for USGPO publications (the Library does not enter cataloging records on RLIN for depository titles). Each of the five RLG collection intensity descriptors was assigned a percentage range and final results were based on a comparison of adjusted results or each subject area against the range assigned to each descriptor.

III. OTHER COMMON LAW JURISDICTIONS
A. General policy
The Library has built important collections in the law of the major common-law jurisdictions. These collections support the active research interests of several members of the faculty, in particular. However, it is generally recognized that a substantial collection of English law is an integral part of any academic law library, and that it is desirable to collect the law of other major common-law jurisdictions, as well.

B. United Kingdom (England, Scotland, Northern Ireland), Ireland, Canada, Australia, New Zealand, and South Africa
1. Primary sources
    The Library maintains research level (4E) collections. The collection of English law is very strong (approaching the comprehensive level, with the exception of government documents), and the Library continues this commitment. The collections of primary materials for the other jurisdictions noted above are almost equally complete. For Canada and Australia, this includes the provincial and state primary materials, respectively, as well as those of the national governments. It should be noted that the Library's collection of South African law reflects only the comparative interest South African holds as an example of a mixed civil- and common-law jurisdiction, and does not reflect any political support of the apartheid regime.

2. Secondary sources
    a. Periodicals
    The collection of law reviews and other legal periodicals for these jurisdictions is almost comprehensive. It includes all United Kingdom periodicals indexed in the U.S. law review indexes, as well as a substantial number of those covered

by the *Legal Journals Index* (U.K.) and the *Index to Canadian Legal Literature*. Both academic and the leading practitioners' journals are collected.

b. Treaties, textbooks, and looseleaf services
The Library collects a wide range of monographs and treatises from the major common-law jurisdictions. The subject coverage includes all areas of public and private law. The result is research level collections of treatises for these jurisdictions. In some cases, only every other edition of expensive treatises is acquired. Looseleaf services, which are often intended mainly for practitioner use, are acquired somewhat more selectively.

c. Other present and former members of the British Commonwealth, and the Philippines
These jurisdictions include India, Pakistan, Singapore, Hong Kong, Malaysia, the Commonwealth Caribbean, Commonwealth Puerto Rico, etc. The Library maintains basic information (2E) or instructional support (3E) level collections. When these jurisdictions publish compiled editions of their legislation, they are acquired. In addition, the Library acquires a selection of textbooks and journals on the law of these countries. The collections for India, Singapore and the Philippines are somewhat stronger in this respect than other jurisdictions in this category. For India, the Library participates with the General Libraries in the modified PL-480 program. However, it will be necessary to update some elements of the Philippines collection in the future.

IV. FOREIGN LAW
A. Western Europe: Germany, France, Belgium, Spain, Italy, Switzerland
The Library's general approach to Western Europe is that these are increasingly important foreign jurisdictions, and that, despite the language barrier, the Library should collect legal materials from these countries. The strength of the collections has varied from country to country. For those mentioned above, the Library maintains research level (3W) collections. The collection of German law is one of the strongest in the United States, and the Library is committed to maintaining it.

B. Other countries in Western Europe

The Library collects at the basic information (2W) or the instructional support level (3W) for the other countries of Western Europe. Recently, the collections for these countries were reviewed. Significant additions were made for Austria, the Netherlands, and Portugal. The Library will continue selectively to strengthen the collections for other countries.

C. Eastern Europe and the Soviet Union

In general, the Library collects at the basic information level (2E). The exception was East Germany, for which, in view of faculty research interest, the Library built a substantial collection. In light of recent political changes, East Germany obviously will no longer be an area of concentration. Regarding the Soviet Union, the Library maintains a substantial collection of English-language materials. Given the changes in the region, the Library will review its collecting policies for Eastern Europe.

D. Mexico, Central and South America

Generally, these collections for have been strong, although collection strength and collecting intensity vary greatly from country to country. The Library's collection of Mexican legal materials is one of the strongest in the United States. It will be maintained at the research level (4Y). For Argentina, Brazil and Chile, the Library has strong collections at the instructional support level (3Y). For the other countries of South and Central America, the collections fall in a range between basic information level (2Y) and instructional support level (3Y). The Library regularly reviews these collections, to update and strengthen them selectively.

E. Asia, Africa, and the Middle East

The Library's general policy is to collect at the minimal level (1E) or at the basic informational level (2E) for most of the jurisdictions in these regions. There are some exceptions. The geographic area known as the Pacific Basin recently has gained importance. Leading jurisdictions in this region (e.g., Japan, Hong Kong, Korea, Singapore, and Taiwan) receive added attention. In the Middle East, the Library maintains a substantial collection of Israeli law at the instructional support level (3E/F), in both English and Hebrew. A gift to the Library brought in a large collection of law books in

Arabic, dealing with the law of several countries in the Middle East, particularly Egypt.

These have in large part been cataloged and added to the collection. However, in light of the language difficulty, the Library currently is not collecting materials in Arabic.

V. OTHER AREAS OF FOREIGN OR COMPARATIVE LAW
A. Ancient law
1. Roman law
   The Library has built a substantial collection of Roman Law at the instructional support level (3E/F). The policy is to continue acquiring materials selectively at this level.
2. Greek Law
   A course in Ancient Greek law was taught in the Law School during 1989-90, and there is a good possibility that it will be offered again from time to time. In response, the Library built up the collection to the instructional support level (3E/Y).
3. Other ancient legal systems
   Collecting is at the basic information level (2E/F).

B. Religious law
This category includes Hindu law, Jewish law, Islamic law, and Canon law. The Library maintains a collection of standard sources and treatises at the basic information level (2E).

VI. PUBLIC INTERNATIONAL LAW
A. General public international law
The Library maintains a research level collection (4E/F) in all subject areas falling within the broad field of public international law. The collection includes all types of documents: treaty collections, collections of judicial and arbitral decisions, yearbooks, journals, treatises and monographs, etc.

B. International organizations
1. United Nations
   The Library has a selective standing order for United Nations documents, concentrating on the Official Records, the documents of the International Court of Justice, and other UN documents dealing with international law and relations. This

collection is at the instructional support level (3E). (Perry-Castaneda Library is a UN depository library. The Library relies on it for other kinds of UN documentation.)

2. European Community

This is a research level collection (4E/F) that approaches the comprehensive level (SE/F). The Library is one of 46 university depository libraries for European Community documents in the United States. This means that the Library receives all the documentation that the EC issues in its depository program, including the *Official Journal* and the Commission *(COM)* documents. These materials are cataloged and added to the general collection. In addition, the Library collects a significant amount of commercial publications dealing with EC law.

3. Organization of American States

The Library has a substantial collection of OAS official records, by means of a standing order for English language documents. The collection is at the instructional support level (3E). The collection of OAS documents should be reviewed for a determination as to its completeness and the possibility of improving the standing order arrangement and the organization of materials in the collection.

4. Council of Europe

Through a selective standing order, the Library maintains a research level collection (4E) for all the publications of the Council of Europe dealing with law in general, and specifically human rights including the documents of both the European Court of Human Rights and the European Commission of Human Rights.

5. General Agreement on Tariffs and Trade (GATT)

By means of a standing order, the Library has a collection at the instructional support level (3E) of GATT documents.

6. Other international organizations

The Library selectively acquires documents by and about other international organizations. This includes such UNspecialized agencies as ILO, IMO, ITU, and UNESCO.

VII. INTERNATIONAL BUSINESS TRANSACTIONS

This is an umbrella phrase covering a large and disparate set of topics in the international aspects of private transactions and dispute settlement. Examples of topics covered are international aspects of antitrust, banking, bankruptcy, intellectual property, payment systems, sales, securities regulation, shipping, and trade regulation. Other important areas include the international aspects of litigation and dispute resolution, including international commercial arbitration. The Library maintains research level collections (4E/F) in these areas.

Appendix A:
ACQUISITIONS ARRANGEMENTS

I. MEMBERSHIPS

Academy of Political Science
American Arbitration Association
American Association of Law Libraries
American Association of University Professors
American Bar Association
American Civil Liberties Union
American Judicature Society
American Law Institute
American Library Association
American Political Science Association
American Professors for Peace in the Middle East
American Society for Information Science
American Society for Legal Historians
American Society of Law and Medicine
American Society of Trial Consultants
Amnesty International of the U.S.A.
Association of College and Research Libraries
Association of the Bar of the City of New York
Association of Trial Lawyers of America
Austin Law Librarians
Bar Association of the Fifth Federal Circuit
British and Irish Association of Law Libraries
Canadian Association of Law Libraries
Canadian Tax Foundation
Canon Law Society of America
Center for Computer-Assisted Legal Instruction
Computer Law Association

Conference on Critical Legal Studies
Dallas Association of Law Librarians
Environmental Defense Fund
Federal Bar Association
Federal Circuit Bar Association
Foreign Tax Law Publishers, Inc.
HALT
Hastings Center
Industrial Relations Research Association
Institute for Criminal Justice Ethics
Institute for Theological Encounters with Science and Technology
International Association of Jewish Lawyers and Jurists
International Association of Law Librarians
Japanese-American Society for Legal Studies
Jewish Law Association
Josephson Institute for the Advancement of Ethics
Law and Humanities Institute
Law and Society Association
Lawyers' Alliance for Nuclear Arms Control
National Association of Criminal Defense Lawyers
National Bar Association
National Committee on Pay Equity
National Criminal Justice Association
National District Attorneys Association
National Hemlock Society
National Institute of Municipal Law Officers
National Tax Association-Tax Institute of America
New York State Bar Association
On-line Audiovisual Catalogers, Inc.
Organization of American Historians
Osgoode Society
Population Reference Bureau
Public Affairs Information Service
Public Affairs Video Archives
Rocky Mountain Mineral Law Foundation
Scribes: The American Society of Writers on Legal Subjects
Selden Society
Society for Computers and Law
Society of American Archivists
Society of American Law Teachers

Society of Public Teachers of Law
Southwestern Association of Law Libraries
Special Libraries Association
Stair Society
Statute Law Society
Supreme Court Historical Society
Texas Council of State University Librarians
Texas Library Association
Travis County Bar Association
United States Trademark Association
Urban Land Institute

II. STANDING ORDERS, PACKAGE PLANS

ALI-ABA Committee on Continuing Legal Education
American Bar Association
American Law Institute
Americas Watch
Asia Watch
Association of American Law Schools
Cambridge University Press
Committee for Economic Development
Congressional Quarterly, Inc.
Council of Europe
Foundation Press
General Agreement on Tariffs and Trade
Gower Federal Service
Helsinki Watch
Illinois State Bar Association
International Commission of Jurists
JUSTICE (British Section of the International Commission of Jurists)
Lawyers' Committee for Human Rights
National Academy Press
National Center for State Courts
National Council for Civil Liberties
National Organization on the Legal Problems of Education
NOLO Press
Oceana Publications, Inc.
Organization of American States
Oxford University Press

The RAND Corporation. Institute for Civil Justice
Fred B. Rothman and Co.
State Bar of Texas
United Nations
West Publishing Co.

III. DEPOSITORY ARRANGEMENTS

Office of Official Publications of the European Community
Texas State Publications Clearinghouse
United States Government Printing Office

IV. EXCHANGE AGREEMENTS

DOMESTIC:
Association of the Bar of the City of New York
Brigham Young University Law Library
Detroit College of Law
Drake University Law Library
Fordham Law Review
Franklin Pierce Center
Institute of Judicial Administration
Judge Advocate General School
Loyola University Law Library (New Orleans)
Maine State Law Library
New York Law School Library
Ohio Legal Center Institute
St. Jolin's University Law Library
U.S. Court of Appeals for the Federal Circuit
U.S. Court of Judiciary Appeals
Universidad Interamericana, Facultad de Derecho
Universidad de Puerto Rico, Escuela de Derecho
University of Florida Legal Information Center
University of Iowa Law Library
University of Kentucky Law Library
University of Louisville Law Library
University of Maine Law Library
University of Minnesota Law Library
University of Nebraska Law Library
University of Oklahoma Law Library

University of Pittsburgh Law Library
University of Washington Law Library
Vermont Law School Library
Wake Forest Law Library

APPENDIX A
MATERIALS SELECTION
AND ACCESSIBILITY POLICY
Montgomery County Library System
Conroe, Texas

I. PRINCIPLES

The materials selection and accessibility policy of the Montgomery County Library System is based on the following principles:

1. The freedom to read, along with the freedom to hear and to view, is protected by the First Amendment to the Constitution. This freedom is held to be essential to our democracy and will be upheld, supported, and defended in the selection and the provision for accessibility of all library materials.

2. Freedom of choice in selecting materials is a necessary safeguard to the freedom to read, to hear, and to view.

3. It is the essence of democracy that citizens shall have the right of free inquiry and equally important right of forming their own opinions. In a society, each individual is free to determine for himself or herself what he or she wishes to read, to hear, or to view, and each group is free to determine what it wishes to recommend to its freely associated members.

4. Selection of materials does not constitute or imply agreement with or approval of the content, viewpoint, implications, or means of expression of the materials.

5. The library and its associated authorities do not serve *in loco parentis*. It is the parents, and only parents, who may restrict their children, and only their own children, from access to library materials. Responsibility for the reading of children rests with their parents and/or legal guardians. Selection will not be inhibited by the possibility that materials may inadvertently come into the possession of children.

6. The library will attempt to provide materials for all members of the community the library serves, without exclusion.

7. A person's right to access to and use of library materials will not be denied or abridged because of origin, age, background, or views.

8. The library is not a judicial body. Laws governing obscenity, subversive materials, and other questionable matters

are subject to interpretation by the courts. Consequently, no challenged material will be removed from the library for complaints of obscenity, pornography, subversiveness, or any other category covered by law until after an independent determination by a judicial officer in a court of competent jurisdiction, following an adversary hearing and in accordance with well established principles of law, shall have ruled against the material. Conversely, no materials will knowingly be selected which have previously been adjudicated to be in noncompliance with the law.

9. The library will attempt to select materials which (within the framework of preserving the freedom to read, hear, and view) will provide for the interest, information, enlightenment, entertainment, pleasure, education, development, appreciation, stimulation, enrichment, and/or self-improvement of library patrons of all ages, walks of life, value and interest patterns, education, opinion, and persuasion to the degree possible within budgetary constraints, material availability and degree of understanding of the above needs and desires.

10. The library will uphold the principles of the American Library Association's Library Bill of Rights, Freedom to Read, Statement on Labeling, and Free Access to Libraries for Minors as well as to the Texas Library Association's Intellectual Freedom Statement, the full text of which are hereby subsumed by reference.

II. Policy

In accordance with the above principles, the following policies will apply in regard to materials selection and accessibility:

1. Selection

    As budgetary constraints limit the procurement of material to a small portion of what is available, the selections made will be made in furtherance of the above principles while attempting tomaintain diversity, quality and responsiveness to interest patterns.

    a. Diversity will be pursued by attempting to meet the purposes for the use of materials (listed in principle #9) for all ages and educational levels, by providing as many subject fields as possible, by providing alternative and/or opposing viewpoints, by providing unpopular as well as popular materials, and by providing diversity of materials reflective of the diversity existing in our culture and society.

b. Quality will be pursued by the application of the professional discretion and standards established by the library profession and through the use of appropriate selection aids. The pursuit of quality will not be carried out contrary to the above principles.

c. Responsiveness to interest patterns will be pursued by careful consideration of requests for purchases, patterns of utilization of existing materials, patterns of purchases of similar materials from retailers, and any other source of information indicative of community interest patterns. An attempt will be made to meet, to the degree possible, the interests of all in the community without exclusion, while acknowledging and recognizing that this is an ideal to be pursued rather than an achievable goal. Responsiveness to the interest of one individual or group will not be restricted on the basis of the dislike or disinterest of another individual or group.

d. Selections may be made on the basis of any one, several, or all of the above considerations.

e. Undue duplication will not occur in the selection of materials. This will generally exclude religious materials that are not of general interest, professional works, textbooks, and others available elsewhere to special interest groups. Materials may also not be selected if the field is already covered by existing collection.

f. Materials will usually be excluded which do not conform to or lend themselves to library use or format, i.e., spiral binding, game books, over- or undersized, etc.

g. Selections will be made within budgetary constraints and with regard to the overall pattern of the existing compliance with all policies and principles.

h. Gifts and unsolicited materials will be evaluated in light of the above policies and principles as per any other selection. (see Gifts, Memorials, and Other Donations Policy).

    i. Patron requests for the purchases of material will be evaluated in light of the above policies and principles as per any other selection. Reporting on requested materials that are not purchased by the library will be made by reference to the Material Selection and Accessibility Policy statement.

2. Accessibility to all library materials will not be restricted or prejudiced

    a. Restriction will be avoided by allowing all patrons access to all materials and by allowing all library card holders to check out any library materials (subject to library card restrictions) regardless of origin, race, age, sex, back-ground, or views.

    b. Prejudice will be avoided by not labeling materials other than by providing classification (Dewey Decimal System), directional aides, and major categorization of interest patterns. The distinction between the children and youth versus the adult section will be made only on the assumed differential interest patterns, respectively. Appropriateness of the materials for minors is the sole responsibility of the parent(s).

3. Complaints

    a. The library recognizes that many books and other materials may be considered controversial or may contain ideas, words, and/or pictures offensive to some people. Selection will not be influenced by any anticipated disapproval. Selection will be based on the merits of the work itself and whether it meets the selection criteria mentioned above.

    b. Any citizen may question whether a title owned by the library is appropriate to the collection. When this occurs, the person will be provided with a copy of this selection policy and a complaint form.
[See the reproduced form below.].

    c. When a completed complaint form is received by the library, an ad hoc committee will be formed by the Director to evaluate the title in question and recommend whether the title should be retained or removed from the collection.

III. RESPONSIBILITY AND AUTHORITY

Final responsibility and authority for materials selection rests with the Director of the Library System who will operate in a framework of policies and principles adopted by the Montgomery County Commissioners Court. The staff of the library will operate under the Director's delegated authority.

Adopted by the Library Board _____

Approved by the Commissioners Court _____

FORMS

Request for Reconsideration of a Book or Other Library Material

To the person requesting reconsideration: Library policy requires that complaints be made on this form for discussion in detail. The materials selection policy will be made available to you. Thank you for taking the time to provide needed information. Please use the back of this form if more space is needed.

Author:
Title:
Request initiated by:
Telephone:
Address:
City: Zip Code:

Requester represents: individual   _____
                       organization_____
                       other group _____

Check one: Book ___   Paperback ___   Magazine _____
Pamphlet _____   Picture ___   Film ___ Other _____

Specifically, to what do you object? (Cite pages, instances, etc.) What do you feel might be the result of reading, hearing or seeing this material?

Is there anything good about this material?

Did you read the entire book or examine the entire item? What parts?

Are you aware of the judgment of this material by professional critics?

What would you like to have your library do about this material?

Date: Signature of complainant:

GENERIC LETTER REPLY TO A MATERIALS COMPLAINT

Date:

[Patron's Name, Address, City, State, Zip]

Dear XXX:
    Your complaint regarding the book XXXXX by XXXXX has been reviewed by several staff librarians including the County Library Director. For the reasons listed below, it has been decided to retain the book in the Library's collection.
    This book received several favorable reviews at the time it was published. It was on the bases of these reviews that the book was purchased by the Library. Copies of these reviews are attached to this letter for your information.
        [INSERT A PARAGRAPH ABOUT QUALITY OR VALUE OF THE BOOK AND/OR ITS AUTHOR. LIST AWARDS THE BOOK OR AUTHOR HAS RECEIVED.]
    Public libraries were originally established in America because people realized that the strength of a democracy depends upon its citizens being well informed. Thus the guiding principle of public libraries is to provide information on all aspects of any subject; to be as inclusive as possible. Since no library can afford to buy everything on every subject, we buy books based on the quality and accuracy of the writing. We do not exclude a book simply because it might offend someone's moral, political, religious, or other views.

It must be the responsibility of the parents or guardians, not the Library, to disallow minors in their care from reading library books of which they disapprove. Obviously, if the Library removed every book to which someone objected, soon the Library would have no books. Someone can find something objectionable about any book.

I have attached to this letter a copy of the Library Bill of Rights and the Freedom to Read statement which are fundamental documents of the American Library Association and all American libraries. These statements should further explain why we must decline your request to remove the book in question. Nevertheless, we do respect your opinions and appreciate your interest and concern.

Sincerely yours,

[Insert staff name, title, attachments, etc.]

APPENDIX B
AMERICAN LIBRARY ASSOCIATION POLICIES

Library Bill of Rights

The American Library Association affirms that all libraries are forums for information and ideas, and that the following basic policies should guide their services.

1. Books and other library resources should be provided for the interest, information, and enlightenment of all people of the community the library serves. Materials should not be excluded because of the origin, background, or views of those contributing to their creation.
2. Libraries should provide materials and information presenting all points of view on current and historical issues. Materials should not be proscribed or removed because of partisan or doctrinal disapproval.
3. Libraries should challenge censorship in the fulfillment of their responsibility to provide information and enlightenment.
4. Libraries should cooperate with all persons and groups concerned with resisting abridgment of free expression and free access to ideas.
5. A person's right to use a library should not be denied or abridged because of origin, age, background, or views.
6. Libraries which make exhibit spaces and meeting rooms available to the public they serve should make such facilities available on an equitable basis, regardless of the beliefs or affiliations of individuals or groups requesting their use.

[Adopted June 18, 1948. Amended February 2, 1961, June 27, 1967, and January 23, 1980 by the ALA Council. Reprinted by permission of the American Library Association.]

The Freedom to Read

The freedom to read is essential to our democracy. It is continuously under attack. Private groups and public authorities in various parts of the country are working to remove books from sale, to censor textbooks, to label "controversial" books, to distribute lists of "objectionable" books or authors, and to purge libraries. These actions apparently rise from a view that our national tradition of free expression is no longer valid: that censorship and suppression are needed to avoid the subversion of politics and the corruption of morals. We, as citizens devoted to the use of books and as librarians and publishers responsible for disseminating them, wish to assert the public interest in the preservation of the freedom to read.

We are deeply concerned about these attempts at suppression. Most such attempts rest on a denial of the fundamental premise of democracy: that the ordinary citizen, by exercising critical judgment, will accept the good and reject the bad. The censors, public and private, assume that they should determine what is good and what is bad for their fellow citizens.

We trust Americans to recognize propaganda and to reject it. We do not believe they need the help of censors to assist them in this task. We do not believe they are prepared to sacrifice their heritage of a free press in order to be "protected" against what others think may be bad for them. We believe they still favor free enterprise in ideas and expression.

We are aware, of course, that books are not alone in being subjected to efforts at suppression. We are aware that these efforts are related to a larger pattern of pressures being brought against education, the press, films radio, and television. The problem is not only one of actual censorship. The shadow of fear cast by these pressures leads, we suspect, to an even larger voluntary curtailment of expression by those who seek to avoid controversy.

Such pressure toward conformity is perhaps natural to a time of uneasy change and pervading fear. Especially when so many of our apprehensions are directed against an ideology, the expression of a dissident idea becomes a thing feared in itself, and we tend to move against it as against a hostile deed, with suppression.

And yet suppression is never more dangerous than in such a time of social tension. Freedom has given the United States the elasticity to endure strain. Freedom keeps open the path of novel and creative solutions, and enables change to come by choice. Every silencing of a heresy, every enforcement of an orthodoxy, diminishes the toughness and resilience of our society and leaves it less able to deal with stress.

Now as always in our history, books are among our greatest instruments of freedom. They are almost the only means for making generally available ideas or manners of expression that can initially command only a small audience. They are the natural medium for the new idea and the untried voice from which come the original contributions to social growth. They are essential to the extended discussion which serious thought requires, and to the accumulation of knowledge and ideas into organized collections.

We believe that free communication is essential to the preservation of a free society and a creative culture. We believe that these pressures towards conformity present the danger of limiting the range and variety of inquiry and expression on which our democracy and our culture depend. We believe that every American community must jealously guard the freedom to publish and to circulate, in order to preserve its own freedom to read. We believe that publishers and librarians have a profound responsibility to give validity to that freedom to read by making it possible for the readers to choose freely from a variety of offerings.

The freedom to read is guaranteed by the Constitution. Those with faith in free people will stand firm on these constitutional guarantees of essential rights and will exercise the responsibilities that accompany these rights.

We therefore affirm these propositions:

1. *It is in the public interest for publishers and librarians to make available the widest diversity of views and expressions, including those which are unorthodox or unpopular with the majority.*

Creative thought is by definition new, and what is new is different. The bearer of every new thought is a rebel until that idea is refined and tested. Totalitarian systems attempt to maintain themselves in power by the ruthless suppression of any concept which challenges the established orthodoxy. The power of a democratic system to adapt to change is vastly strengthened by freedom of its citizens to choose widely from among conflicting opinions offered freely to them. To stifle every nonconformist idea at birth would mark the end of the democratic process. Furthermore, only through the constant activity of weighing and selecting can the democratic mind attain the strength demanded by times like these. We need to know not only what we believe but why we believe it.

2. *Publishers, librarians and booksellers do not need to endorse every idea or presentation contained in the books they make available. It would conflict with the public interest for them to establish their own political, moral or aesthetic views as a*

standard for determining what books should be published or circulated.

Publishers and librarians serve the educational process by helping to make available knowledge and ideas required for the growth of the mind and the increase of learning. They do not foster education by imposing as mentors the patterns of their own thought. The people should have the freedom to read and consider a broader range of ideas than those that may be held by any single librarian or publisher or government or church. It is wrong that what one can read should be confined to what another thinks proper.

3. *It is contrary to the public interest for publisher or librarians to determine the acceptability of a book on the basis of the personal history or political affiliations of the author.*

A book should be judged as a book. No art or literature can flourish if it is to be measured by the political views or private lives of its creators. No society of free people can flourish which draws up lists of writers to whom it will not listen, whatever they may have to say.

4. *There is no place in our society for efforts to coerce the taste of others, to confine adults to the reading matter deemed suitable for adolescents, or to inhibit the efforts of writers to achieve artistic expression.*

To some, much of modern literature is shocking. But is not much of life itself shocking? We cut off literature at the source if we prevent writers from dealing with the stuff of life. Parents and teachers have a responsibility to prepare the young to meet the diversity of experiences in life to which they will be exposed, as they have a responsibility to help them learn to think critically for themselves. These are affirmative responsibilities, not to be discharged simply by preventing them from reading works for which they are not yet prepared. In these matters taste differs, and taste cannot be legislated; nor can machinery be devised which will suit the demands of one group without limiting the freedom of others.

5. *It is not in the public interest to force a reader to accept with any book the prejudgment of a label characterizing the book or author as subversive or dangerous.*

The idea of labeling presupposes the existence of individuals or groups with wisdom to determine by authority what is good or bad for the citizen. It presupposes that individuals must be directed in

making up their minds about the ideas they examine.   But
Americans do not need others to do their thinking for them.

6. *It is the responsibility of publishers and librarians, as
guardians of the people's freedom   to read, to contest
encroachments upon that freedom by individuals or groups
seeking to impose their own standards or tastes upon the
community at large.*

It is inevitable in the give and take of the democratic process
that the political, the moral, or the aesthetic concepts of an
individual or group will occasionally collide with those of another
individual or group.   In a free society individuals are free to
determine for themselves what they wish to read, and each group
is free to determine what it will recommend to its freely associated
members.   But no group has the right to take the law into its own
hands, and to impose its own concept of politics or morality upon
other members of a democratic society.   Freedom is no freedom if
it is accorded only to the accepted and the inoffensive.

7. *It is the responsibility of publishers and librarians to give full
meaning to the freedom to read by providing books that enrich the
quality and diversity of thought and expression. By the exercise of
this affirmative responsibility, they can demonstrate that the
answer to a bad book is a good one, the answer to a bad idea is a
good one.*

The freedom to read is of little consequence when expended on
the trivial; it is frustrated when the reader cannot obtain matter fit for
that reader's purpose. What is needed is not only the absence of
restraint, but the positive provision of opportunity for the people to
read the best that has been thought and said. Books are the
major channel by which the intellectual inheritance is handed
down, and the principal means of its testing and growth. The
defense of their freedom and integrity, and the enlargement of their
service to society, requires of all publishers and librarians the
utmost of their faculties, and deserves of all citizens the fullest of
their support.

We state these propositions neither lightly nor as easy general-
izations. We here stake out a lofty claim for the value of books. We
do so because we believe that they are good, possessed of
enormous variety and usefulness, worthy of cherishing and keeping
free. We realize that the application of these propositions may
mean the dissemination of ideas and manners of expression that

are repugnant to many persons. We do not state these propositions in the comfortable belief that what people read is unimportant. We believe rather that what people read is deeply important; that ideas can be dangerous; but that the suppression of ideas is fatal to a democratic society. Freedom itself is a dangerous way of life, but it is ours.

[This statement was originally issued in May of 1953 by the Westchester Conference of the American Library Association and the American Book Publishers Council, which in 1970 consolidated with the American Educational Publishers Institute to become the Association of American Publishers. Adopted June 25, 1953. Revised January 28, 1972, January 16, 1991, by the ALA Council and the AAP Freedom to Read Committee. A Joint Statement by: American Library Association & Association of American Publishers. Subsequently Endorsed by: American Booksellers Association, American Booksellers Foundation for Free Expression,American Civil Liberties Union, American Federation of Teachers AFL-CIO, Anti-Defamation League of B'nai B'rith Association of American University Presses, Children's Book Council, Freedom to Read Foundation, International Reading Association, Thomas Jefferson Center for the Protection of Free Expression, National Assciation of College Stores, National Council of Teachers of English, P.E.N.-American Center, People for the American Way, Periodical and Book Association of America, Sex Information and Education Council of the U.S., Society of Professional Journalists, Women's National Book Association, YWCA of the U.S.A. Reprinted by permission of the American Library Association.]

The Freedom to View

The freedom to view, along with the freedom to speak, to hear, and to read, is protected by the First Amendment to the Constitution of the United States. In a free society, there is no place for censorship of any medium of expression. Therefore these principles are affirmed:

1. To provide the broadest possible access to film, video, and other audiovisual material because they are a means for the communication of ideas. Liberty of circulation is essential to insure the constitutional guarantee of freedom of expression.

2. To protect the confidentiality of all individuals and institutions using film, video, and other audiovisual materials.

3. To provide film, video, and other audiovisual materials which represent a diversity of views and expression. Selection of a work does not constitute or imply agreement with or approval of the content.

4. To provide a diversity of viewpoints without the constraint of labeling or prejudging film, video and other audiovisual materials on the basis of the moral, religious, or political beliefs of the producer or filmmaker or on the basis of controversial content.

5. To contest vigorously, by all lawful means, every encroachment upon the public's freedom to view.

[This statement was originally drafted by the Freedom to View Committee of the American Film and Video Association (formerly the Educational Film Library Association) and was adopted by the AFVA Board of Directors in February 1979. This statement was updated and approved by the AFVA Board of Directors in 1989.]

Statement on Labeling

Labeling is the practice of describing or designating materials by affixing a prejudicial label and/or segregating them by a prejudicial system. The American Library Association opposes these means of predisposing people's attitudes towards library materials for the following reasons:

1. Labeling is an attempt to prejudice attitudes and as such, it is a censor's tool.

2. Some find it easy and even proper, according to their ethics, to establish criteria for judging publications as objectionable. However, injustice and ignorance rather than justice and enlightenment result from such practices, and the American Library Association opposes the establishment of such criteria.

3. Libraries do not advocate the ideas found in their collections. The presence of books and other resources in a library does not indicate endorsement of their contents by the library.

A variety of private organizations promulgate rating systems and/or review materials as a means of advising either their members or the general public concerning their opinions of the contents and suitability or appropriate age for use of certain books, films, recordings or other materials. For the library to adopt or enforce any of these private systems, to attach such ratings to library materials, to include them in bibliographic records, library catalogs, or other finding aids, or otherwise to endorse them would violate the LIBRARY BILL OF RIGHTS.

While some attempts have been made to adopt these systems into law, the constitutionality of such measures is extremely questionable. If such legislation is passed which applies within a library's jurisdiction, the library should seek competent legal advice concerning its applicability to library operations.

Publishers, industry groups, and distributors sometimes add ratings to material or include them as part of their packaging. Librarians should not endorse such practices. However, removing or obliterating such ratings--if placed there by or with permission of the copyright holder--could constitute expurgations, which is also unacceptable.

The American Library Association opposes efforts which aim at closing any path to knowledge. This statement, however, does not exclude the adoption of organizational schemes designed as directional aids or to facilitate access to materials.

[Adopted July 13, 1951. Amended June 25, 1971, July 1, 1981, June 26, 1990, by the ALA Council. Reprinted by permission of the American Library Association.]

APPENDIX C
SURVEY OF COLLECTION DEVELOPMENT POLICY COMPONENTS

The following list of components was developed by Frank Hoffmann based on the collection development policies in Elizabeth Futas' book, *Library Acquisition Policies and Procedures*, Second Edition. Phoenix, AZ: Oryx, 1984. It lists policy components on the left and the names of the libraries (see abbreviations at end of the appendix) on the right. Some categories are noted briefly under different headings.

- Allocation of Funds: EIU, GC, UD
- Appendices/Forms (usually relate to above categories): UW-S, UD, CSC, SSCC, NYSL, LCL, C-GLS, MPL
- Approval Plans: SDSU
- Archives and Special Collections: EIU, UW-S, UD, CSC, WPC, NYSL, BPL See also: Local History.
- Authorization Section; Signature Page: LCL, OPL, FML
- Background (library history): FML
- Best Sellers: UD
- Bibliography: NYSL
- Books--Adult Circulating Collection: EPL, C-GLS, MPL
- Braille and Other Special Media for the Blind: NYSL
- Branch Libraries: EPL
- Central Library Selection Policy: LCL
- Collection Development Methodologies: TA&M, CSC
- Collection Development Responsibilities: EIU, GC, TA&M, UW-S, UD, CSC, SSCC, NIACC, VSL, FVRL, VBPL, BPL, LCL, C-GLS, MPL, FML
- Continuations/Series: SDSU, WPC See also: Periodicals.
- Copyright: GC
- Data Base Search Service; Computerized Databases: SDSU, UD, NYSL
- Defined User Groups; Eligible Users; Community Background: VSL, CLP, BPL, SJPL
- Definitions: GC, CCPL
- Dissertations and Theses: SDSU, EIU, UW-S, WPC, NYSL
- Duplicate Copies; Bibliographic Variants: SDSU, UD, NYSL, MPL

- Ephemeral Materials: CLP
- Extension Services: EPL
- Faculty Publications: SDSU
- Feedback (from patrons)/Requests: UD
- Fiction: CLP
- Film Selection Policy; Films and Video; Films and Filmstrips: SSCC , NYSL, SJPL
- Foreign Languages and Translations: SDSU, EIU, WPC
- Framed Art; Pictures: VBPL, SJPL
- General Guidelines; Goals and Objectives; Mission Statements: SDSU, TA&M, GC, UW-S, UD, CSC, WPC, SSCC, CCPL, VSL, CLP, NYSL, VBPL, BPL, LCL, OPL, C-GLS, SJPL, MPL, FML
- General Selection/Rejection Guidelines; Evaluative Criteria: TA&M, GC, UD, CSC, WPC, NIACC, CCPL, VSL, CLP, FVRL,VBPL, BPL, LCL, OPL, C-GLS, SJPL, MPL, FML
- Gifts of Commercially Sponsored Materials: SDSU, EIU, GC, UW-S, UD, CSC, WPC, SSCC, VSL, CLP, NYSL, VBPL, LCL, OPL, C-GLS, SJPL, FML
- Government Publications: SDSU, EIU, UD, WPC, VSL, NYSL, VBPL, LCL, C-GLS, SJPL
- Ground Rules for Selection: UW-S
- Index: SDSU
- Integrated Shelving of Resources: UW-S
- Intellectual Freedom (Philosophy): GC, UD, CSC, NIACC, FVRL, BPL, LCL, OPL, C-GLS, MPL, FML
- Intellectual Freedom (Procedures for Handling Complaints): CSC, NIACC, FVRL, VBPL, C-GLS, SJPL, MPL
- Interlibrary Loan: SDSU, UD
- Introduction (background re compilation): UW-S See also: Purpose Statement.
- Inventory/Survey of Holdings: UD, CCPL
- Juvenile Collection; Young Adult and Children's Materials: EIU, UD, CCPL, CLP, VBPL, LCL, EPL, C-GLS, MPL
- Large Print Books (Role of): NYSL, C-GLS
- Legal Responsibilities (acquisition): VSL
- Levels of Collection Intensity: EIU, UD, VSL, NYSL
- Library Networks and Consortia; Cooperative Collection Development; Relationship to Other Libraries: TA&M, EIU, UD, VSL, CLP, NYSL, BPL, OPL, MPL
- Liaison Program: UD

- Library Science Collection: VSL
- Limited Loan Service: SDSU
- Local History; Local Authors: VBPL, C-GLS
- Looseleaf Services: NYSL
- Manuscripts: NYSL, LCL, SJPL
- Maps: SDSU, EIU, UW-S, UD, NYSL, LCL, C-GLS, SJPL
- Materials Selected for Library Collection (with format breakdowns): GC, CSC, NYSL, VBPL, SJPL
- Media (Non-Print or AV) Materials: SDSU, EIU, GC, UW-S, UD, WPC, SSCC, VSL, CLP, LCL, EPL, C-GLS, MPL See also: Recorded Sound.
- Microforms: SDSU, EIU, GC, UW-S, WPC, CLP, VBPL, C-GLS, SJPL
- Monographs: UD, WPC
- Music Scores; Sheet Music: EIU, LCL, SJPL
- Newspapers: SDSU, EIU, GC, UW-S, VSL, NYSL, VBPL, LCL, C-GLS, SJPL
- Organization Chart: EPL
- Out-of-Print Materials: UD, WPC
- Pamphlet Materials or Clippings; Vertical Files: SDSU, GC, UW-S,WPC, CLP, NYSL, VBPL, LCL, C-GLS, SJPL
- Paperbacks; Rotating Collections: UW-S, UD, LCL, SJPL
- Patents: NYSL
- Pattern Collection: LCL
- Periodicals; Serials: SDSU, EIU, GC, UW-S, UD, WPC, SSCC, VSL, NYSL, VBPL, LCL, SJPL
- Physical Facilities: OPL
- Preview Policy: UW-S
- Problem Areas: GC
- Public Relations: OPL
- Purpose/Philosophy Statement (role of collection development policy): SDSU, TA&M, EIU, GC, UD, CSC, WPC, NIACC, VSL, NYSL, LCL, EPL, SJPL, MPL
- Rare Books: EIU, UD, VSL, NYSL See also: Manuscripts.
- Recorded Sound; Records and Cassettes: NYSL, VBPL, SJPL
- Reference Collection: EIU, UD, WPC, VSL, NYSL, EPL, C-GLS, MPL
- Renting or Leasing Materials; McNaughton Plan: WPC, CLP, C-GLS
- Replacements: UD

- Reprints: UW-S
- Research Materials: EIU
- Reserve: UD
- Revision of Policy: VSL, NYSL, VBPL, EPL, SJPL
- Right to Privacy (e.g., circulation records): FVRL, OPL
- Selection Area: EPL
- Selection Guidelines and Selection Tools: SSCC, LCL, C-GLS
  See also: Selection Area.
- Service and Programs: FML
- Slides: SJPL
- Special Service Areas (for handicapped patrons): LCL
- Subject Specialties of the Regionals: CCPL
  See also: General Guidelines
- Table of Contents: EIU, UW-S, UD, CSC, WPC, CCPL, NYSL, EPL
- Table of Selection Levels by Subject or Subject Areas for Collection Development Levels; Policies by Subject: UW-S, VSL, NYSL, SJPL
- Technical Services: EPL
- Textbooks and Readings/Curriculum Materials; Instructional Materials; Workbooks: SDSU, EIU, UW-S, UD, WPC, VBPL, LCL, C-GLS, SJPL
- Translations: NYSL
- Weeding; Collection Maintenance; Collection Review (includes: Discarding, Storage, Replacement, Rebinding): SDSU, EIU, GC, UW-S, UD, CSC, WPC, SSCC, VSL, CLP, FVRL, VBPL, LCL, OPL, C-GLS, MPL

Institution Abbreviation Code

BPL	Boise Public Library
CLP	Carnegie Library of Pittsburgh
C-GLS	Charlotte-Glades Library System
CCPL	Cuyahoga County Public Library
CSC	College of St. Catherine
EIU	Eastern Illinois University
EPL	Elkhart Public Library
FML	Flint Memorial Library
FVRL	Fort Vancouver Regional Library
GC	Gallaudet College

LCL   Lancaster Public Library
MPL   Middleton Public Library
NYSL New York State Library
NIACC North Iowa Area Community College
OPL   Oceanside Public Library
SJPL Saint Joseph Public Library
SDSU San Diego State University
SSCC South Seattle Community College
TA&M Texas A&M University
UD   University of Detroit
UW-S University of Wisconsin--Stout
VBPL Virginia Beach Department of Public Libraries
VSL   Virginia State Library
WPC   William Paterson College

BIBLIOGRAPHY

A. COLLECTION DEVELOPMENT POLICIES

1. GENERAL

American Library Association. Ad Hoc Subcommittee on Guidelines for Collection Development. *Guide for Written Collection Policy Statements*, edited by Bonita Bryant. 2nd ed. Chicago, IL: American Library Association, 1989.

American Library Association. Collection Development Committee. *Guidelines forCollection Development*, edited by David L. Perkins. Chicago, IL: American Library Association, 1979.

Association of Research Libraries Systems and Procedures Exchange Center. *Collection Development Policies* (SPEC Kit 38). Washington, D.C.: The Association, 1977.

Before and After the Censor: A Resource Manual on Intellectual Freedom. Lansing, MI: Michigan Association for Media Studies and Michigan Library Association, Intellectual Freedom Committees, 1987.

Biblarz, Dora. "The Conspectus as a Blueprint for Creating Collection Development Policy Statements," In: *Collection Assessment: A Look at the RLG Conspectus*, edited by Richard J. Wood and Katina Strauch. Binghamton, NY: Haworth, 1992. pp. 169-176.

Boyer, Calvin J., and Nancy L. Eaton, eds. *Book Selection Policies in American Libraries: An Anthology of Policies from College, Public and School Libraries*. Austin, TX: Armadillo, 1971.

Buis, E. "Collection Development Policies: Coordinating Teaching Faculty and Library Staff Interests at Southeast Missouri State University," *Collection Management*. . 13:3 (1990) 11-26.

Bullard, S.R. "Read My Lips: The Politics of Collection Development," *Library Acquisitions*. 13:3 (1989) 251-253.

Cagle, K. R. "The Best of Times, the Worst of Times; the Politics of the Library Collection," North Carolina Libraries. 50 (Summer 1992)

Cargill, Jennifer S. "Collection Development Policies: An Alternative Viewpoint," *Library Acquisitions: Practice and Theory*. 8:1 (1984) 47-49.

Carpenter, Eric J. "Collection Development Policies: The Case For," *Library Acquisitions: Practice and Theory*. 8:1 (1984) 43-45.

Cassell, Kay Ann and Elizabeth Futas. "Collection Development Policies," *Collection Buiilding.* 11:2 (1991) 26-29.

Cline, Hugh F. and Loraine T. Sinnott. *Building Library Collections: Policies and Practices in Academic Libraries.* Lexington, MA: Lexington Books, 1982.

Coleman, Kathleen and Pauline Dickinson. "Drafting a Reference Collection Policy," *College and Research Libraries.* 38:3 (1977) 227-233.

Collins, J., and R. Finer. *National Acquisition Policies and Systems.* London: British Library, 1982.

Crush, Marion. "Policy for Deselection," *Wilson Library Bulletin.* 45 (October 1970) 180-181.

Curley, Arthur and Dorothy Broderick. *Building Library Collections.* 6th ed. Metuchen, NJ: Scarecrow, 1985.

Dienes, F. "Collection Development Policies--Are They a Good Thing or a Necessary Evil?" *New Zealand Libraries.* 45 (June 1989) 5-7ff.

Donahue, Mary K., et al. "Collection Development Policy Making," *Collection Building.* 6:3 (1984) 18-21.

Dowd, Sheila T. "The Formulation of a Collection Development Policy Statement," In: *Collection Development in Libraries: A Treatise, Part A,* edited by Robert D. Stueart and George B. Miller, Jr. (Foundations in Library and Information Science, Volume 10) Greenwich, CT: JAI, 1980. pp. 67-87.

Evans, Robert W. "Collection Development Policy Statements: The Documentation Process," *Collection Management..* 7:1 (1985) 63-73.

Feng, Y.T. "The Necessity for a Collection Development Policy Statement," *Library Resources and Technical Services.* 23:1 (1979) 39-44.

Ferguson, Anthony W., et al. "The RLG Conspectus: Its Uses and Benefits," *College and Research Libraries.* 49 (May 1988) 197-206.

Ferguson, Anthony W., Joan Grant and Joel Rutstein. "Internal Uses of the RLG Conspectus," *Journal of Library Administration.* 8:2 (1987) 35-40.

Fergusson, David G. "You Can't Tell the Players without a Program (policy)," *North Carolina Libraries.* 41 (1983) 80-83.

Forcier, Peggy. "Building Collections Together: The Pacific Northwest Conspectus," *Library Journal.* 113 (April 15,1988) 43-45.

Futas, Elizabeth "Issues in Collection Building: Why Collection Development Policies?" *Collection Building*. 3:1 (1981) 58-60.

Futas, Elizabeth, ed. *Library Acquisition Policies and Procedures*. 2nd ed. Phoenix, AZ: Oryx, 1984.

Futas, Elizabeth. *Library Forms Illustrated Handbook*. New York, NY: Neal-Schuman, 1984.

Giblon, Della L. "Materials Selection Policies and Changing Adult Needs," *Catholic Library World*. 53 (1982) 288-289.

"Guidelines for the Formulation of Collection Development Policies," *Library Resources and Technical Services*. 21 (Winter 1977) 40-7.

Guidelines for the Formulation of Collection Development Policies, Preliminary Edition. Chicago, IL: American Library Association, Resources and Technical Services Division, Resources Section, Collection Development Committee, 1976.

Guyatt, Joy. *Towards a Collection Development Policy: A First Essay*. St. Lucia: University of Queensland, Tertiary Education Institute, 1987.

Hazen, Dan C. "Modelling Collection Development Behavior: A Preliminary Statement," *Collection Management*. 4:1/2 (1982) 1-14.

Johnston, Dick. "Book Selection Policies," *Michigan Librarian*. 28 (1962) 12-13.

Katz, William A. *Collection Development: The Selection of Materials for Libraries*. New York: Holt, Rinehart & Winston, 1980.

Lake, Albert C. "Pursuing a Policy," *Library Journal*. 90 (1965) 2481-2494.

Lane, Alfred H. *Gifts and Exchange Manual*. Westport, CT: Greenwood, 1980.

Magrill, Rose Mary and J.B. Corbin. "Collection Development Policies," In: *Acquisitions Management and Collection Development in Libraries*. 2nd ed. Chicago, IL: American Library Association, 1989. pp. 29-40.

McGraw, Howard F. "Policies and Practices in Discarding," *Library Trends*. 4 (January 1956) 269-282.

McLachlan, Jo. "The Future of Collection Development Policies in Australia," In: *Collection Management in AcademicLibraries: Papers Delivered at a National Seminar, Surfers Paradise, Queensland, 16th-17th February 1984*, edited by Cathryn Crowe, Philip Kent and Barbara Paton. Sydney: Library

Association of Australia, University and College Libraries Section, 1984. pp. 19-30.

Merritt, LeRoy C. *Book Selection and Intellectual Freedom.* New York, NY: Wilson, 1970.

Michigan Association for Media in Education. Intellectual Freedom Committee. *Selection Policies: A Guide to Updating and Writing.* Ann Arbor, MI: The Association, 1977.

Monroe, Margaret. "The Library's Collection in a Time of Crisis," *Wilson Library Bulletin.* 36:5 (1962) 372-374.

Nicholls, P. "CD-ROM Collection Development Policies," *Idaho Librarian.* 44 (January 1992) 18-19.

Oberg, Larry R. "Evaluating the Conspectus Approach for Smaller Library Collections," *College and Research Libraries.* 49 (May 1988) 187-196.

Osburn, Charles B. "Some Practical Observations on the Writing, Implementation and Revision of Collection Policy," *Library Resources and Technical Services.* 23:1 (1979) 7-15.

Perkins, David L. "Writing the Collection Development Manual," *Collection Management.* 4 (Fall 1982) 37-47.

Research Libraries Group. *RLG Collection Development Manual.* 2nd ed. Chicago, IL: Research Libraries Group, 1981.

Stueart, Robert D. "Weeding of Library Materials--Politics and Policies," *Collection Management.* 7:2 (1985) 47-58.

Van Orden, Phyllis and Edith Phillips, eds. *Background Readings in Building Library Collections.* 2nd ed. Metuchen, NJ: Scarecrow, 1979. Includes the following sections within Chapter 3: "Policy Statements," by the Berrien County Library League; "Writing a Selection Policy," by LeRoy Charles Merritt; "Development of a Materials Selection Program," from the *Intellectual Freedom Manual*; "Introduction to Selection Policies in American Libraries"*, by Calvin Boyer; "The Trustee and Intellectual Freedom," by Jane Cameron; "Collection Building and Maintenance (Excerpts)," by Ruth Gregory and Lester Stoffel; "Collection Policy in College and University Libraries," by K. Linda Ward.

2. ACADEMIC

Boyarski, Jennie S. and Kate Hickey, eds. *Collection Management in the Electronic Age: A Manual for Creating Community*

College Collection Development Policy Statements. CJCLS Guide #1. Chicago, IL: American Library Association, 1994.

Bryant, Bonita. "Collection Development Policies in Medium-Sized Academic Libraries," *Collection Building.* 2:3 (1980) 6-26.

Buzzard, Marion L. "Writing a Collection Development Policy for an Academic Library," *Collection Development.* 2 (Winter 1978) 217-228.

Cargill, Jennifer S. "Bridging the Gap Between Acquisitions and Public Services," *Library Acquisitions: Practice and Theory.* 3:1 (1979) 29-31.

Farrell, D. " North American Collections Inventory Project (NCIP), In: *Coordinating Cooperative Collection Development,* edited by W. Luquire. New York: Haworth, 1986. pp. 37-48.

Govdahl, E. "In Search of the Ultimate Video Collection: Development Policies for Florida Academic Libraries," *Florida Libraries.* 36 (May 1993) 86ff.

Gwinn, N.E. and P. H. Mosher. "Coordinating Collection Development, RLG Conspectus." *College and Research Libraries.* 44:2 (March 1980) 128-140.

Hamilton, P. and H. Feiss. "A Model of Cooperative Collection Development Policies for Academic Libraries," *Technicalities.* 9 (August 1989) 9-11.

Hellenga, Robert R. "Departmental Acquisitions Policies for Small College Libraries," *Library Acquisitions: Practice and Theory.* 3 (1979) 81-84.

Horacek, John. "Collection Development Policies," In: *Collection Management in Academic Libraries: Papers Delivered at a National Seminar, Surfers Paradise, Queensland, 16th-17th February 1984,* edited by Cathryn Crowe, Philip Kent and Barbara Paton. Sydney: Library Association of Australia, University and College Libraries Section, 1984. pp. 11-18.

Koenig, Dorothy A. "Rushmore at Berkeley: The Dynamics of Developing a Written Collection Development Policy Statement," *Journal of Academic Librarianship.* 7: 6 (1982) 344-350.

Meyer, Betty J. and John T. Demos. "Acquisition Policy for University Libraries: Selection or Collection," *Library Resources and Technical Services.* 14:3 (1970) 395-399.

Osburn, Charles B. "Planning for a University Library Policy on Collection Development," *International Library Review.* 9:2 (1977) 209-224.

Palais, Elliot S. "Use of Course Analysis in Compiling a Development Policy Statement for a University Library," *Journal of Academic Librarianship*. 13:1 (1987) 8-13.

Reed-Scott, Jutta. *NCIP Manual*. rev. ed. Washington, D.C.: Association of Research Libraries, Office of Management Studies, 1988.

RLG Collection Development Manual. 2nd ed. Stanford, CA: The Research Libraries Group, 1980.

Terwilliger, G. and others. "The Public Services Librarian and Collection Development," In: *Community College Reference Services*, edited by Bill Katz. Metuchen, NJ: Scarecrow, 1992. pp. 326-343.

Wood, Richard J. and Katina Strauch, eds. *Collection Assessment: A Look at the RLG Conspectus*. Binghamton, NY: Haworth, 1992.

3. PUBLIC LIBRARIES

Bartle, F.R. and W.L. Brown. "Book Selection Policies for Public Libraries," *Australian Library Journal*. 32:3 (1983) 5-13.

Capital Planning Information. *Trends in Public Library Policies*. (British National Bibliography Research Fund Reports, No. 29) London: British Library, 1987.

Fergusson, D.G. "You Can't Tell the Players Without a Program," *North Carolina Libraries*. 41 (Summer 1983) 80-83.

Giblon, D.L. "Materials Selection Policies and Changing Adult Needs," *Catholic Library World*. 53 (Fall 1982) 288-289.

Jacob, Merle. "Get It In Writing: A Collection Development Plan for the Skokie Public Library," *Library Journal*. (September 1, 1990) 166-169.

Library Board of Western Australia. *Book Provision and Book Selection Policy and Practice*. Perth: Library Board of Western Australia, 1982.

Little, Paul. "Collection Development for Bookmobiles," In: *The Book Stops Here*, edited by Catherine Suyak Alloway. Metuchen, NJ: Scarecrow, 1990. pp. 59-73.

Moore, Carolyn. "Core Collection Development in a Medium-Sized Public Library," *Library Resources and Technical Services*. 24 (January/March 1982) 37-46.

Norman, Ronald V. "A Method of Book Selection for a Small Public Library," *RQ.* 7 (Winter 1977) 143-145.

Root, N.J. "Decision Making for Collection Management," *Collection Management.* 7 (Spring 1985) 93-101.

Segal, Joseph P. *Evaluating and Weeding Collections in Small and Medium-Sized Public Libraries: The CREW Method.* Chicago, IL: American Library Association, 1980.

"Trends in Public Library Selection Policies," *Library Association Record.* 90 (1988) 31.

4. SCHOOL LIBRARIES

Adams, Helen R. "Media Policy Formulation and Adoption in a Small School District," *Wisconsin Library Bulletin.* 7 (1981) 11-13.

Adams, Helen R. *School Media Policy Development: A Practical Process for Small Districts.* Littleton, CO: Libraries Unlimited, 1986.

American Association of School Librarians. *Policies and Procedures for Selection of School Library Materials.* Chicago, IL: The American Library Association, 1961.

Amey, L.J. "In Defense of Intellectual Freedom: What to Include in a School Library Collection Policy," *Emergency Librarian.* 15 (1988) 9-13.

Bayly, Cynthia. "A Withdrawals Policy," *School Library Bulletin.* 14 (1982) 88-89.

Callison, D. "The Evolution of School Library Collection Development Policies, 1975-1995," *School Library Media Quarterly.* 19 (Fall 1990) 27-34.

Hardesty, V.H. "Selection Protection," *Indiana Media Journal* 7 (Summer 1985) 5-9.

Hunter, D. "Accessibility to Media in the School Library," *Catholic Library World.* 53 (Fall 1982) 378-379.

Taylor, Mary M., ed. *School Library and Media Center Acquisitions Policies and Procedures.* Phoenix, AZ: Oryx, 1981.

5. SPECIAL LIBRARIES

Bedsole, Danny T. "Formulating a Weeding Policy for Books in a Special Library," *Special Libraries.* 49:5 (1958) 205-209.

Collins, J. and R. Finer. "National Acquisition Policies and Systems," *Interlending Review.* 10 (October 1982) 111-118.

Gorman, Gary.E. "Principles and Procedures for Collection Develop-ment with Special Reference to Theological Libraries," *Australian College Libraries.* 5:2/3 (1987) 63-73.

MacAllister, J. "Selection Policies of State Libraries," *Australian Academic and Research Libraries.* 14:1 (1983) 8-14.

Mulliner, B.K. "Library of Congress Acquisitions Policies," *Library Acquisitions: Practice and Theory.* 6:2 (1982) 103-106.

"National Libraries Issue Joint Policy for Collection Development," *Library of Congress Information Bulletin.* 48 (December 11, 1989) 434ff.

Okpokwasili, N.P. and M.L. Bundy. "Study of Selection/ Acquisition Policies of Agricultural Libraries in the U.S.," *Libri.* 39 (December 1989) 319-330.

Tees, M.H. "Special Libraries in the 1980s," *Show-Me Libraries.* 33 (October 1981) 33-36.

Thomas, V.C. "Formulating a Federal Depository Collection Development Statement: Guidelines for Academic Law Library Survival," *Legal Reference Services Quarterly.* 11:1/2 (1991) 111-126.

6. INDIVIDUAL LIBRARY POLICIES

Brigham Young University, Harold B. Lee Library. *Collection Development Policy Statement.* Provo, UT: Brigham Young University, Harold B. Lee Library, 1985.

Metz, P. and B. Obenhaus. "Virginia Tech Sets Policy on Controversial Materials," *College and Research Libraries News.* 7 (July/August 1990) 386-388.

Jacob, M. "Get It In Writing: A Collection Development Plan for the Skokie Public Library," *Library Journal.* 115 (September 1, 1990) 166-169.

"LC, National Library of Medicine Issue AIDS/HIV Collection Policy," *Library of Congress Information Bulletin.* 52 (May 3, 1993) 191.

St. Joseph Public Library. *Materials Selection and Collection Review Policy.* St. Joseph, MO: St. Joseph Public Library, n.d.

Sexton, M. "The Selection Policy of the National Library of Australia," *Australian Academic and Research Libraries.* 14:1 (1983) 1-7.

Singerman, R. "Charting the Course: The University of Florida's Collection Management Policy for Jewish Studies," *Judaica Librarianship*. 6 (Spring 1991-Winter 1992) 115-119.

Stanford University. *The Libraries of Stanford University Collection Development Policy Statement*, edited by Paul H. Mosher. Stanford, CA: Stanford University Libraries, 1980.

State Library of New South Wales. *Draft Collection Development Policy*. Sydney: State Library of New South Wales, 1988.

State Library of Victoria. *State Library of Victoria Selection Policy*. Melbourne: Library Council of Victoria, 1986.

University of California, Berkeley. *Collection Development Policy Statement*. Preliminary ed. Berkeley, CA: University of California Library, 1980.

University of Melbourne. *The University of Melbourne Library Collection Development Policy*. Parkville: University of Melbourne Library, 1983.

University of Texas at Austin. General Libraries. *Collection Development Policy*. 2nd ed. Austin, TX: University of Texas at Austin, General Libraries, 1980.

William Paterson State College of New Jersey. Sarah Byrd Askew Library. *Collection Development Policy*. Wayne, NJ: William Paterson State College of New Jersey, 1982.

Wood, D.N. "Local Acquisition and Discarding Policies in the Light of National Library Resources and Services," *Aslib Proceedings*. 29:1 (1977) 24-34.

B. COLLECTION DEVELOPMENT–SUPPLEMENTARY READINGS

1. GENERAL

Cline, Hugh F. and Loraine T. Sinnott. *Building Library Collections: Policies and Practices in Academic Libraries*. Lexington, MA: Lexington Books, 1982.

Clinton, Alan. *Printed Ephemera: Collection, Organization and Access*. London: Clive Bingley, 1981.

Jaramillo, George R. "Computer Technology and Its Impact on Collection Development," *Collection Management*. 10:1/2 (1988) 1-14.

Kennedy, Gail A. "The Relationship Between Acquisitions and

Collection Development," *Library Acquisitions: Practice and Theory*. 7:3 (1983) 225-232.

Kohl, David F. *Acquisitions, Collection Development and Collection Use: A Handbook for Library Management*. Santa Barbara, CA: ABC-Clio, 1985.

Lee, Sul H., ed. *Serials Collection Development: Choices and Strategies*. (Library Management Series, No. 5) Ann Arbor, MI: Pierian, 1981.

Lynden, Frederick C. "Financial Planning for Collection Management," *Journal of Library Administration*. 3:3/4 (1982) 109-120.

Magrill, Rose Mary and Doralyn J. Hickey. *Acquisitions Management and Collection Development in Libraries*. Chicago, IL: American Library Association, 1984.

Serebnick, Judith, ed. *Collection Management in Public Libraries*. Chicago, IL: American Library Association, 1986.

Van Orden, Phyllis J. *The Collection Program in Schools: Concepts, Practices and Information Sources*. Englewood,CO: Libraries Unlimited, 1988.

White, Brenda H., ed. *Collection Management for School Library Media Centers*. New York: Haworth, 1986.

2. ACQUISITIONS

Collins, Judith and Ruth Finer. *National Acquisition Policies and Systems: A Comparative Study of Existing Systems and Possible Models*. Wetherby, West Yorkshire, England. IFLA International Office for UAP, 1982.

Dole, Wanda V. "Gifts and Block Purchases: Are They Profitable?" *Library Acquisitions: Practice and Theory*. 7:3 (1983) 247-254.

Lane, Alfred H. *Gifts and Exchange Manual*. Westport, CT: Greenwood, 1980.

Reidelbach, John H. and Gary M. Shirk. "Selecting an Approval Plan Vendor: A Step-by-Step Process," *Library Acquisitions: Practice and Theory*. 7:2 (1983) 115-122.

Scudder, Mary C. "Using Choice in an Allocation Formula in a Small Academic Library," *Choice*. 24:10 (1987) 1506-1511.

Werking, Richard J. "Allocating the Academic Library's Book Budget: Historical Perspectives and Current Reflections," *Journal of Academic Librarianship*. 14:3 (1988) 140-144.

3. COMMUNITY ANALYSIS AND USER STUDIES

Aguilar, William. "The Application of Relative Use and Interlibrary Demand in Collection Development," *Collection Management.* 8:1 (1986) 15-24.

Govan, James F. "Community Analysis in an Academic Environment," *Library Trends.* 24:3 (1976) 541-556.

Kim, Choong Han and Robert D. Little. *Public Library Users and Uses: A Market Research Handbook.* Metuchen, NJ: Scarecrow, 1987.

Zweizig, Douglas. "Community Analysis," In: *Local Public Library Administration,* edited by Ellen Altman. 2nd ed. Chicago, IL: American Library Association, 1980. pp. 38-46.

4. CENSORSHIP AND INTELLECTUAL FREEDOM

Asheim, Lester E. "Selection and Censorship: A Reappraisal," *Wilson Library Bulletin.* 58:3 (1983) 180-184.

Before and After the Censor: A Resource Manual on Intellectual Freedom. Lansing, MI: Michigan Association for Media Studies and Michigan Library Association, Intellectual Freedom Committees, 1987.

Bosmajian, Haig A. *Censorship, Libraries and the Law.* New York: Neal-Schuman, 1983.

Burress, Lee and Edward B. Jenkinson. *The Students' Right to Know.* Urbana, IL: National Council of Teachers of English, 1982.

Clark, Elyse. "A Slow, Subtle Exercise in Censorship," *School Library Journal.* 32:7 (1986) 93-96.

Jones, Frances. *Defusing Censorship: The Librarians' Guide to Handling Censorship Conflicts.* Phoenix, AZ: Oryx, 1983.

Office for Intellectual Freedom. American Library Association. *Intellectual Freedom Manual.* 3rd ed. Chicago, IL: American Library Association, 1989. Includes: "Development of a Materials Selection Program," pp. 171-178.

Poppel, Norman and Edwin M. Ashley. "Toward an Understanding of the Censor," *Library Journal.* 111:12 (1986) 39-43.

Robotham, John S. and Gerald Shields. *Freedom of Access to Library Materials.* New York: Neal-Schuman, 1982.

Serebnick, Judith. "Book Reviews and the Selection of Potentially Controversial Books in Public Libraries," *Library Quarterly.* 51:4 (1981) 390-409.

Watson, Jerry J. and Bill C. Snider. "Educating the Potential Self-Censor," *School Media Quarterly.* 9 (1981) 272-276.

White, Howard D. "Majorities for Censorship," *Library Journal.* 111:12 (1986) 31-38.

5. COLLECTION DEVELOPERS

Ryland, John. "Collection Development and Selection: Who Should Do It?" *Library Acquisitions: Practice and Theory* 6:1 (1982) 13-17.

Sandler, Mark. "Organizing Effective Faculty Participation in Collection Development," *Collection Management.* 6:3/4 (1984) 63-72.

Vidor, David L. and Elizabeth W. Futas. "Effective Collection Developers: Librarians or Faculty?" *Library Resources and Technical Services.* 32:2 (1988) 127-136.

6. EVALUATIVE CRITERIA/COLLECTION ASSESSMENT

Broadus, Robert N. *Selecting Materials for Libraries.* 2nd ed. New York: H.W. Wilson, 1981.

Hall, Blaine H. *Collection Assessment Manual for College and University Libraries.* Phoenix, AZ: Oryx, 1985.

Johnson, M.A. "The Value of Evaluation," *Technicalities.* 12 (October 1992) 4-7.

Katz, William A. *Collection Development: The Selection of Materials for Libraries.* New York: Holt, Rinehart and Winston, 1980.

Lee, Sul H., ed. *Collection Assessment and Acquisitions Budgets.* Binghamton, NY: Haworth, 1992.

Loertscher, David V. "Collection Mapping: An Evaluation Strategy for Collection Development," *Drexel Library Quarterly.* 21 (1985) 9-21.

Magrill, Rose Mary. "Evaluation by Type of Library," *Library Trends.* 33:3 (1985) 267-295.

McClung, Patricia A., ed. *Selection of Library Materials in the Humanities, Social Sciences, and Sciences.* Chicago, IL: American Library Association, 1985.

Mosher, Paul H. "Quality and Library Collections: New Directions in Research and Practice in Collection Evaluation," *Advances in Librarianship*, edited by Wesley Simonton. Volume 13. Orlando, FL: Academic, 1984. pp. 211-238.

Nisonger, T.E. *Collection Evaluation in Academic Libraries; A Literature Guide and Annotated Bibliography.* Englewood, CO: Libraries Unlimited, 1992.

Rice, Barbara A. "Evaluation of Online Databases and Their Uses in Collections," *Library Trends.* 33:3 (1985) 297-325.

Rutledge, John and Luke Swindler. "The Selection Decision: Defining Criteria and Establishing Priorities," *College and Research Libraries.* 48:2 (1987) 123-131.

Spiller, David. *Book Selection: An Introduction to Principles and Practice.* 4th ed. London: Clive Bingley, 1986.

Vandergrift, Kay E. "Selection: Reexamination and Reassessment," *School Media Quarterly.* 6:2 (1978) 103-111.

Whitehead, Robert J. *A Guide to Selecting Books for Children.* Metuchen, NJ: Scarecrow, 1984.

7. FORMATS AND RESOURCES WITHIN LIBRARY COLLECTIONS

Binder, M.B. *Videotext and Teletext: New Online Resources for Libraries.* Greenwich, CT: JAI, 1985.

Johnson, J.M. "Government Publications and Collection Development Policies: Implications of a Pilot Study," *Illinois Libraries.* 71 (November 1989) 477-479.

Koepp, D.P. "Map Collections in Public Libraries: A Brighter Future," *Wilson Library Bulletin.* 60 (October 1985) 28-32.

Lettner, L.L. "Videocassettes in Libraries." *Library Journal.* 110 (November 15, 1985) 35-37.

Lewis, S. "Nonprint Materials in the Small Library," *Library Resources and Technical Services.* 29 (April/June 1985) 146-150.

Schurk, William L. "Uncovering the Mysteries of Popular Recording Collection Development," In: *Popular Culture and Acquisitions,* edited by Allen Ellis. Binghamton, NY: Haworth, 1993. pp. 91-98.

Sive, Mary R. *Media Selection Handbook.* Littleton, CO: Libraries Unlimited, 1983.

Smith, D.E. "Media Resources in College Libraries," In: *College Librarianship,* edited by W. Miller and D.S. Rockwood. Metuchen, NJ: Scarecrow, 1981. pp. 205-213.

Spreitzer, Francis F., ed. *Microforms in Libraries: A Manual for Evaluation and Management.* Chicago, IL: American Library Association, 1985.

Weihs, J., S. Lewis and J. Macdonald. *Nonbook Materials: The Organization of Integrated Collections.* 2nd ed. Chicago, IL: American Library Association, 1980.

Wiener, P.B. "A Library Is as Great as Its Film Collection," *Catholic Library World.* 57 (March/April 1986) 233-234.

8. COOPERATIVE COLLECTION DEVELOPMENT

Ballard, Thomas H. *Failure of Resource Sharing in Public Libraries and Alternative Strategies for Service.* Chicago, IL: American Library Association, 1986.

Holickey, B. H. "Collection Development Vs. Resource Sharing," *Journal of Academic Librarianship.* 10 (July 1984) 146-147.

Jaffe, Lawrence L. "Collection Development and Resource Sharing in the Combined School/Public Library," *Collection Management.* 7:3/4 (1985) 205-215.

Kaiser, John R. "Resource Sharing in Collection Development," In: *Collection Development in Libraries: A Treatise, Part A,* edited by Robert D. Stueart and George B. Miller, Jr. Greenwich, CT: JAI, 1980. pp. 139-157.

Luquire, William, ed. *Coordinating Cooperative Collection Development: A National Perspective.* New York: Haworth, 1986.

Mosher, Paul H. and Marcia Pankake. "A Guide to Coordinated and Cooperative Collection Development," *Library Resources and Technical Services.* 27:4 (1983) 417-431.

Sohn, Jeanne. "Cooperative Collection Development: A Brief Overview," *Collection Management.* 8:2 (1986) 1-9.

Stam, David H. "Collaborative Collection Development: Progress, Problems and Potential," *Collection Building.* 7:3 (1986) 3-8.

Stam, David H. "Think Globally--Act Locally: Collection Development and Resource Sharing," *Collection Building.* 5 (1983) 18-21.

9. SELECTION AIDS

Bennion, Bruce C. "The Use of Standard Selection Sources in Undergraduate Library Collection Development," *Collection Management.* 2:2 (1978) 141-152.

D'Aniello, C. "Bibliography and the Beginning Bibliographer," *Collection Building.* 6 (Summer 1984) 11-19.

Furnham, A. "Book Reviews as a Selection Tool for Librarians: Comments from a Psychologist," *Collection Management.* 8:1 (Spring 1986) 33-43.

Walford, A.J., ed. *Reviews and Reviewing: A Guide.* London: Mansell Publishing, 1986.

10. WEEDING

Association of Research Libraries. Office of Management Studies. Systems and Procedures Exchange Center. *Remote Storage.* SPEC Kit 39. Washington, D.C.: Association of Research Libraries, 1977.

Bayly, Cynthia. "A Withdrawals Policy," *School Library Bulletin.* 14 (1982) 88-89.

Bostic, Mary J. "Serials Deselection," *Serials Librarian.* 9:3 (1985) 85-101.

Broadus, Robert N. "A Proposed Method for Eliminating Titles from Periodical Subscription Lists," *College and Research Libraries.* 46:1 (1985) 31-35.

Cerny, R. "When Less Is More: Issues in Collection Development," *School Library Journal.* 37 (March 1991) 130-131.

Doyen, Sally E. "Guidelines for Selective Weeding of a Multi-media Collection," *Ohio Media Spectrum.* 22:2 (1980) 45-49.

Gordon, Anitra. "Weeding--Keeping Up with the Information Explosion," *School Library Journal.* 30 (1983) 45-46.

Hayden, Ron. "If It Circulates, Keep It," *Library Journal.* 112:10 (1987) 80-82.

Lancaster, F. Wilfred. "Obsolescence, Weeding and the Utilization of Space," *Wilson Library Bulletin.* 62:9 (1988) 47-49.

Mahoney, Kay. "Weeding the Small Library Collection," *Connecticut Libraries.* 24 (1982) 45-47.

Reed-Scott, Jutta. "Implementation and Evaluation of a Weeding Program," *Collection Management.* 7:2 (1985) 59-67.

Segal, Joseph P. *Evaluating and Weeding Collections in Small and Medium-Sized Public Libraries: The CREW Method.* Chicago, IL: American Library Association, 1980.

Slote, Stanley J. *Weeding Library Collections--II.* 2nd rev. ed. Littleton, CO: Libraries Unlimited, 1982.

INDEX

Specific topics included in the library collection development policies of this book are not generally indexed here. To locate specific topics within policies, readers should consult the Table of Contents, Part Two, at the front of this book.

ABOUT THE AUTHORS

Dr. Richard J. Wood has served as the Director of Library Services, Sam Houston State University in Huntsville, Texas since August 1990. From 1986 to then Dr. Wood was Director of Library Services at The Citadel, the Military College of South Carolina, in Charleston. He was Head of Circulation (1971-1986) and Coordinator of User Services (1979-1986) at Slippery Rock University of Pennsylvania. Previously, he was the Millcreek Branch librarian of the Erie County Public Library in Erie, Pennsylvania. He has authored numerous articles and, with Katina Strauch, edited *Collection Assessment: A Look at the RLG Conspectus* (Haworth, 1992). He is currently a contributing editor to Meckler's *Library Software Review*. Dr. Wood was awarded the MLS (1969) and PhD (1979) from the University of Pittsburgh.

Dr. Frank W. Hoffmann is a Professor, Department of Library Science, Sam Houston State University in Huntsville, Texas. Dr. Hoffmann teaches courses relating to reference, collection development, popular culture, and library administration to name a few. He was awarded the MLS (1972) and PhD (1977) in Library Science from the University of Pittsburgh. Dr. Hoffmann is best known for publications in the area of popular culture. With William Bailey, he has co-authored *The Encyclopedia of Fads: Arts and Entertainment* (Haworth, 1990), *Sports and Recreation* (1991), *Mind and Society* (1992), *Fashion and Merchandising* (1993) in both hardcover and paper editions. Scarecrow Press has published a number of Dr, Hoffmann's indexes of popular music charts, including *The Cash Box Singles Charts, 1950-1981*, The Cash Box Black Contemporary Singles Charts, 1960-1984 (with George Albert, 1986), and The Cash Box Album Charts, 1975-1985 (with George Alberts, 1987). Numerous articles of his appear in the *Encyclopedia of Recorded Sound, Magazines for Libraries, International Music Journals, Cash Box, Popular Music*, and *Popular Culture in Libraries*, of which he is editor.